Sports Illustrated KIDS
YEAR IN SPORTS 2009

from the Editors of
SPORTS ILLUSTRATED KIDS

SCHOLASTIC

COVER PHOTOGRAPHY CREDITS
LeBron James: John Biever
Eli Manning: Bob Rosato
Sidney Crosby: Lou Capozzola
Candace Parker: Lou Capozzola
Prince Fielder: Mike Ehrmann

BACK COVER PHOTOGRAPHY CREDITS
Michael Phelps: Heinz Kluetmeier
Tim Tebow: Bob Rosato
Torah Bright: Ken Levine/WireImage.com

SPORTS ILLUSTRATED KIDS YEAR IN SPORTS 2009 is a production of SPORTS ILLUSTRATED KIDS and SPORTS ILLUSTRATED KIDS Books: Bob Der, Managing Editor; Michael Northrop, Andrea Woo, Project Editors; Edward Duarte, Cover Design; Gina Houseman, Photo Researcher; Tommy Craggs, Editor; Luke O'Brien, Jim Weber, Writers; Jen Funk Weber, Games and Puzzles; Raul Rodriguez, Rebecca Tachna, Designers; Rebecca Shore, Reporter; Mary Kate Brennan, Alan Garcia, Jason Plautz, Delena Turman, Editorial Interns

Scholastic Staff: Brenda Murray, Editor; Trevor Ingerson, Editorial Intern; Karyn Browne, Managing Editor; Stephanie Anderson, Production Editor; Daniel Letchworth, Production Intern; Becky Terhune, Art Director; Jess White, Manufacturing Coordinator

ISBN-13: 978-0-545-08212-9
ISBN-10: 0-545-08212-9

10 9 8 7 6 5 4 3 2 1   08 09 10 11 12

Printed in the U.S.A.   23
First printing, December 2008

Due to the publication date, records and statistics are current as of July 2008.

CONTENTS

The Underdog Wins It All

On a frigid December night, the New York Giants' late-season collapse looked complete. New York was on the wrong side of an embarrassing 22–10 loss to Washington. The team was 8–6, with the seemingly unbeatable New England Patriots looming on the schedule. One year after losing seven of their final nine games, the Giants faced the very real possibility that they might miss the playoffs.

But a week later, after falling behind 14–0 in Buffalo, something clicked. The Giants fought back. Outscoring the Bills 38–7 over the final three quarters, New York clinched a playoff spot. And with a narrow 38–35 loss to the Patriots in Week 17, the Giants entered the postseason believing they could beat anyone.

If it was going to happen, it would be this season. In the NFL, 2007 was a year of amazing accomplishments. The Patriots set a record for points scored (589) on their way to a 16–0 record. In his eighth game as a pro, the Minnesota Vikings' Adrian Peterson established the NFL single-game rushing record (296 yards). Quarterback Tom Brady (50 passing TDs) and wideout Randy Moss (21 receiving TDs) both set NFL single-season records. And then there was 38-year-old QB Brett Favre, who turned back the clock to lead the Packers to a 13-3 season.

In Super Bowl XLII, no one gave the Giants a chance. In fact, some even suggested New York was the worst team to ever contend for an NFL championship.

The game was billed as the Patriots' record-breaking offense against the Giants' revamped defense. Everyone knew the Giants' game plan: Get pressure on Brady. Led by an imposing defensive front of Michael Strahan, Osi Umenyiora, and Justin Tuck, the G-Men pestered the 2007 NFL Most Valuable Player all game long. Hit nine times and sacked five, Brady finished with just 266 yards passing and one touchdown toss.

Still, trailing 14–10, the Giants needed one last miracle. With a minute remaining, Giants quarterback Eli Manning barely sidestepped a sack and flung the ball 32 yards to receiver David Tyree, who was tightly defended. Tyree leaped, pinned the ball against his helmet, and came down with one of the greatest catches in history.

It's now known as the "Hail Manning." Four plays later, Manning found Plaxico Burress in the end zone for the game-winning TD.

After starting 0–2 and nearly taking a nosedive for the second straight year, the Giants were Super Bowl champs. Manning was the game's MVP. And New York's defense proved to be better, at least for one game, than the greatest offense in NFL history.

Patriots coach Bill Belichick led the most prolific offense in NFL history.

JOHN IACONO

Giants QB Eli Manning threw two touchdowns in Super Bowl XLII and was the game's MVP.

Best Cornerbacks

1 **Champ Bailey, Denver Broncos**
After the 2007 season, the nine-year veteran was named to his eighth Pro Bowl.

2 **Asante Samuel, Philadelphia Eagles**
After picking off 16 passes in his final two years in New England, Samuel signed a big contract with the Eagles.

3 **Antonio Cromartie, San Diego Chargers**
He led the NFL with 10 interceptions in 2007 and scored on a 109-yard FG return.

4 **Marcus Trufant, Seattle Seahawks**
His seven interceptions in 2007 ranked second among CBs.

5 **Nate Clements, San Francisco 49ers**
The 49ers made him the highest-paid defender ever in 2007.

6 **Al Harris, Green Bay Packers**
After being named an alternate three years in a row, Harris was selected to the 2008 Pro Bowl.

7 **Nnamdi Asomugha, Oakland Raiders**
After eight picks in 2006, teams stopped throwing in his direction.

8 **DeAngelo Hall, Oakland Raiders**
Hall was welcomed with open arms by the Silver and Black.

9 **Rashean Mathis, Jacksonville Jaguars**
Mathis leads one of NFL's best defenses.

10 **Terence Newman, Dallas Cowboys**
Newman has turned into a lockdown defender.

Antonio Cromartie

BOB ROSATO

AFC TEAMS

Buffalo Bills
Miami Dolphins
New England Patriots
New York Jets
Baltimore Ravens
Cincinnati Bengals
Cleveland Browns
Pittsburgh Steelers
Houston Texans
Indianapolis Colts
Jacksonville Jaguars
Tennessee Titans
Denver Broncos
Kansas City Chiefs
Oakland Raiders
San Diego Chargers

NFC TEAMS

Dallas Cowboys
New York Giants
Philadelphia Eagles
Washington Redskins
Chicago Bears
Detroit Lions
Green Bay Packers
Minnesota Vikings
Atlanta Falcons
Carolina Panthers
New Orleans Saints
Tampa Bay Buccaneers
Arizona Cardinals
St. Louis Rams
San Francisco 49ers
Seattle Seahawks

DID YOU KNOW?

On September 30, 2007, Brett Favre threw his 421st career touchdown, an all-time record. With his completion to Greg Jennings, Favre passed Dan Marino on the list.

Super Bowl Sudoku

How many NFL teams have played in four or more Super Bowls?

Solve the sudoku puzzle to find out. Use the letters E, G, H, I, L, N, S, T, and V.

Put the 9 letters into the boxes such that each letter appears once in each column, row, and 3x3 box. If you place the letters correctly, the highlighted letters will spell, in order from top to bottom and left to right, the answer.

I	V				E	T		
			G	V			S	I
T		S					V	
L	S	I		T				
		G		I		S		
			N			H	I	G
	L					I		S
V	H			L	I			
		E	T				L	V

ANSWERS ON PAGE 190

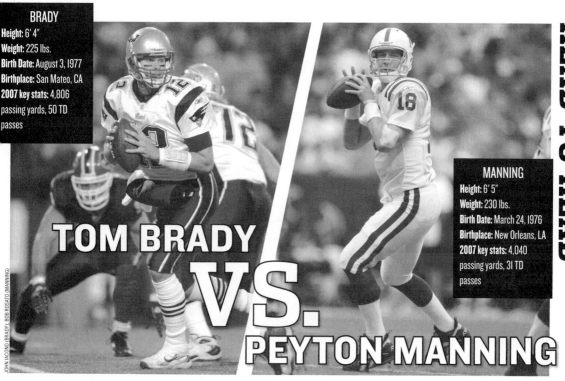

JOHN IACONO (BRADY); BOB ROSATO (MANNING)

BRADY
Height: 6' 4"
Weight: 225 lbs.
Birth Date: August 3, 1977
Birthplace: San Mateo, CA
2007 key stats: 4,806 passing yards, 50 TD passes

MANNING
Height: 6' 5"
Weight: 230 lbs.
Birth Date: March 24, 1976
Birthplace: New Orleans, LA
2007 key stats: 4,040 passing yards, 31 TD passes

TOM BRADY VS. PEYTON MANNING

Two strong-armed quarterbacks face off

New England Patriots, Quarterback	**Team/Position**	Indianapolis Colts, Quarterback
Sixth round (199th overall), New England Patriots, 2000	**Drafted**	First overall, Indianapolis Colts, 1998
Ninth season: 63.0 completion percentage, 26,370 passing yards, 197 TD passes, 86 INT	**Career Stats***	11th season: 64.2 completion percentage, 41,626 passing yards, 306 TD passes, 153 INT
Super Bowl MVP (2002, 2004); four-time Pro Bowler; NFL MVP (2007); most TD passes in a single season (50 in 2007)	**Awards and Accomplishments**	Super Bowl MVP (2007); eight-time Pro Bowler; NFL MVP (2003, 2004); top 10 in NFL history in career completions, passing yards, and TD passes
The "Golden Boy" has been compared to Joe Montana after winning three Super Bowls in his first eight seasons. In 2007, he had one of the greatest years in NFL history but came up just short in the Super Bowl.	**Scouting Report**	If you want a 6' 5", 230-pound quarterback with a rocket arm, he's your guy. His statistics are mind-boggling and he shows no signs of slowing down.
Nothing. The 2007 MVP already has three rings.	**Something to Prove**	After winning The Big One against the Bears, the Colts reverted to old habits in last year's playoffs and were shocked by the Chargers.
"[He has] poise, patience," says teammate Randy Moss. "They give you a fourth-and-24, and Tom's still ready to [get] you."	**What Others Say About Him**	"He is a tremendous player, a great leader. He does everything you can to win ball games," says Colts coach Tony Dungy.
...ly. The Colts won a Super Bowl more recently, but there's no ...ou would rather have under center in a pressure situation.	**Who's Better**	

...ugh 2007 season

Steve Largent

JOHN BIEVER

■ **Steve Largent**, *wide receiver, b. September 28, 1954, Tulsa, Oklahoma.* A 5'11", 187-pound wide receiver from Tulsa, Largent was considered too small and too slow for the NFL. He was traded from the Houston Oilers to the Seattle Seahawks in 1976 for an eighth-round draft pick in one of the all-time biggest trade blunders. Largent had 54 receptions as a rookie, and by his third season, he led the NFL in receptions. A seven-time Pro Bowler, Largent was a true Iron Man; he missed just four games due to injury in his first 13 seasons. When he retired in 1989, he was the NFL's all-time leader in receptions, receiving yards, and touchdown catches. Just five years later, he was elected to the U.S. House of Representatives from his home state of Oklahoma, where he served until 2002.

■ **Red Grange**, *running back/defensive back, b. June 13, 1903, Forksville, Pennsylvania, d. January 28, 1991, Lakes Wales, Florida.* Considered by many to be the greatest college football player ever, the "Galloping Ghost" was the superstar that Chicago Bears owner George Halas craved to heighten the popularity of the National Football League. Grange played for the Bears in 1925 and went on a barnstorming tour that showcased him to the whole country. Grange drew huge crowds, but he left the Bears for the New York Yankees football team of the American Football League. After a devastating knee injury in 1927, Grange lost some of his speed. The Ghost returned to the Bears in 1929 as a star defensive back. Chicago won the 1933 NFL Championship Game, and Grange was inducted to the Hall of Fame in 1963.

Super Bowl: Results

SUPER BOWL	DATE	WINNER	LOSER	SCORE	SITE	ATTENDANCE
XLII	2-3-08	Giants	Patriots	17–14	Glendale, AZ	71,101
XLI	2-4-07	Colts	Bears	29–17	Miami, FL	74,512
XL	2-5-06	Steelers	Seahawks	21–10	Detroit, MI	68,206
XXXIX	2-6-05	Patriots	Eagles	24–21	Jacksonville, FL	78,125
XXXVIII	2-1-04	Patriots	Panthers	32–29	Houston, TX	71,525
XXXVII	1-26-03	Buccaneers	Raiders	48–21	San Diego, CA	67,603
XXXVI	2-3-02	Patriots	Rams	20–17	New Orleans, LA	72,922
XXXV	1-28-01	Ravens	Giants	34–7	Tampa, FL	71,921
XXXIV	1-30-00	Rams	Titans	23–16	Atlanta, GA	72,625
XXXIII	1-31-99	Broncos	Falcons	34–19	Miami, FL	74,803
XXXII	1-25-98	Broncos	Packers	31–24	San Diego, CA	68,912
XXXI	1-26-97	Packers	Patriots	35–21	New Orleans, LA	72,301

Super Bowl: Results (cont.)

SUPER BOWL	DATE	WINNER	LOSER	SCORE	SITE	ATTENDANCE
XXX	1-28-96	Cowboys	Steelers	27–17	Tempe, AZ	76,347
XXIX	1-29-95	49ers	Chargers	49–26	Miami, FL	74,107
XXVIII	1-30-94	Cowboys	Bills	30–13	Atlanta, GA	72,817
XXVII	1-31-93	Cowboys	Bills	52–17	Pasadena, CA	98,374
XXVI	1-26-92	Redskins	Bills	37–24	Minneapolis, MN	63,130
XXV	1-27-91	Giants	Bills	20–19	Tampa, FL	73,813
XXIV	1-28-90	49ers	Broncos	55–10	New Orleans, LA	72,919
XXIII	1-22-89	49ers	Bengals	20–16	Miami, FL	75,129
XXII	1-31-88	Redskins	Broncos	42–10	San Diego, CA	73,302
XXI	1-25-87	Giants	Broncos	39–20	Pasadena, CA	101,063
XX	1-26-86	Bears	Patriots	46–10	New Orleans, LA	73,818
XIX	1-20-85	49ers	Dolphins	38–16	Stanford, CA	84,059
XVIII	1-22-84	Raiders	Redskins	38–9	Tampa, FL	72,920
XVII	1-30-83	Redskins	Dolphins	27–17	Pasadena, CA	103,667
XVI	1-24-82	49ers	Bengals	26–21	Pontiac, MI	81,270
XV	1-25-81	Raiders	Eagles	27–10	New Orleans, LA	76,135
XIV	1-20-80	Steelers	Rams	31–19	Pasadena, CA	103,985
XIII	1-21-79	Steelers	Cowboys	35–31	Miami, FL	79,484
XII	1-15-78	Cowboys	Broncos	27–10	New Orleans, LA	76,400
XI	1-9-77	Raiders	Vikings	32–14	Pasadena, CA	103,438
X	1-18-76	Steelers	Cowboys	21–17	Miami, FL	80,187
IX	1-12-75	Steelers	Vikings	16–6	New Orleans, LA	80,997
VIII	1-13-74	Dolphins	Vikings	24–7	Houston, TX	71,882
VII	1-14-73	Dolphins	Redskins	14–7	Los Angeles, CA	90,182
VI	1-16-72	Cowboys	Dolphins	24–3	New Orleans, LA	81,023
V	1-17-71	Colts	Cowboys	16–13	Miami, FL	79,204
IV	1-11-70	Chiefs	Vikings	23–7	New Orleans, LA	80,562
III	1-12-69	Jets	Colts	16–7	Miami, FL	75,389
II	1-14-68	Packers	Raiders	33–14	Miami, FL	75,546
I	1-15-67	Packers	Chiefs	35–10	Los Angeles, CA	61,946

Super Bowl: Most Valuable Players

SUPER BOWL	PLAYER, TEAM	POSITION	SUPER BOWL	PLAYER, TEAM	POSITION
XLII	Eli Manning, Giants	QB	XX	Richard Dent, Bears	DE
XLI	Peyton Manning, Colts	QB	XIX	Joe Montana, 49ers	QB
XL	Hines Ward, Steelers	WR	XVIII	Marcus Allen, Raiders	RB
XXXIX	Deion Branch, Patriots	WR	XVII	John Riggins, Redskins	RB
XXXVIII	Tom Brady, Patriots	QB	XVI	Joe Montana, 49ers	QB
XXXVII	Dexter Jackson, Buccaneers	S	XV	Jim Plunkett, Raiders	QB
XXXVI	Tom Brady, Patriots	QB	XIV	Terry Bradshaw, Steelers	QB
XXXV	Ray Lewis, Ravens	LB	XIII	Terry Bradshaw, Steelers	QB
XXXIV	Kurt Warner, Rams	QB	XII	Randy White, Cowboys	DT
XXXIII	John Elway, Broncos	QB		Harvey Martin, Cowboys	DE
XXXII	Terrell Davis, Broncos	RB	XI	Fred Biletnikoff, Raiders	WR
XXXI	Desmond Howard, Packers	KR	X	Lynn Swann, Steelers	WR
XXX	Larry Brown, Cowboys	DB	IX	Franco Harris, Steelers	RB
XXIX	Steve Young, 49ers	QB	VIII	Larry Csonka, Dolphins	RB
XXVIII	Emmitt Smith, Cowboys	RB	VII	Jake Scott, Dolphins	S
XXVII	Troy Aikman, Cowboys	QB	VI	Roger Staubach, Cowboys	QB
XXVI	Mark Rypien, Redskins	QB	V	Chuck Howley, Cowboys	LB
XXV	Ottis Anderson, Giants	RB	IV	Len Dawson, Chiefs	QB
XXIV	Joe Montana, 49ers	QB	III	Joe Namath, Jets	QB
XXIII	Jerry Rice, 49ers	WR	II	Bart Starr, Packers	QB
XXII	Doug Williams, Redskins	QB	I	Bart Starr, Packers	QB
XXI	Phil Simms, Giants	QB			

Peyton Manning

KEY: QB=quarterback; WR=wide receiver; S=safety; LB=linebacker; RB=running back; KR=kick returner; DB=defensive back; DE=defensive end; DT=defensive tackle

Super Bowl: Composite Standings

FRANCHISE	W	L	POINTS SCORED	OPPONENTS' POINTS
San Francisco 49ers	5	0	188	89
Baltimore Ravens	1	0	34	7
New York Jets	1	0	16	7
Tampa Bay Buccaneers	1	0	48	21
Pittsburgh Steelers	5	1	141	110
Green Bay Packers	3	1	127	76
Indy./Balt. Colts	2	1	52	46
New York Giants	2	1	66	73
Dallas Cowboys	5	3	221	132
New England Patriots	3	2	107	148
Oakland/LA Raiders	3	2	132	114
Washington Redskins	3	2	122	103
Chicago Bears	1	1	63	39
Kansas City Chiefs	1	1	33	42
Miami Dolphins	2	3	74	103
Denver Broncos	2	4	115	206
St. Louis/LA Rams	1	2	59	67
Atlanta Falcons	0	1	19	34
Carolina Panthers	0	1	29	32
San Diego Chargers	0	1	26	49
Seattle Seahawks	0	1	10	21
Tennessee Titans	0	1	16	23
Cincinnati Bengals	0	2	37	46
Philadelphia Eagles	0	2	31	51
Buffalo Bills	0	4	73	139
Minnesota Vikings	0	4	34	95

Franco Harris

HEINZ KLUETMEIER

Super Bowl: Career Leaders

PASSING									
PLAYER, TEAM	GP	ATT	COMP	PCT	YDS	AVG	TD	INT	LG
Joe Montana, SF	4	122	83	68.0	1,142	9.36	11	0	44
John Elway, Den	5	152	76	50.0	1,128	7.42	3	8	t80
Tom Brady, NE	4	156	100	64.1	1,001	6.42	7	1	52
Terry Bradshaw, Pitt	4	84	49	58.3	932	11.10	9	4	t75
Jim Kelly, Buf	4	145	81	55.9	829	5.72	2	7	61
Kurt Warner, StL	2	89	52	58.4	779	8.75	3	2	t73
Roger Staubach, Dal	4	98	61	62.2	734	7.49	8	4	t45
Troy Aikman, Dal	3	80	56	70.0	689	8.61	5	1	47
Brett Favre, GB	2	69	39	56.5	502	7.28	5	1	t81
Fran Tarkenton, Minn	3	89	46	51.7	489	5.49	1	6	30

RUSHING						
PLAYER, TEAM	GP	YDS	ATT	AVG	LG	TD
Franco Harris, Pitt	4	354	101	3.5	25	4
Larry Csonka, Mia	3	297	57	5.2	49	2
Emmitt Smith, Dal	3	289	70	4.1	38	5
Terrell Davis, Den	2	259	75	4.1	27	3
John Riggins, Wash	2	230	64	3.6	t43	2
Timmy Smith, Wash	1	204	22	9.3	t58	2
Thurman Thomas, Buf	4	204	52	3.9	t31	4
Roger Craig, SF	3	198	52	3.8	18	2
Marcus Allen, Oak	1	191	20	9.6	t74	2
Antowain Smith, NE	2	175	44	4	17	1

RECEIVING						
PLAYER, TEAM	GP	REC	YDS	AVG	LG	TD
Jerry Rice, SF, Oak	4	33	589	17.8	t48	8
Lynn Swann, Pitt	4	16	364	22.8	t64	3
Andre Reed, Buf	4	27	323	12.0	40	0
Deion Branch, NE	2	21	276	13.1	52	1
John Stallworth, Pitt	4	11	268	24.4	t75	3
Michael Irvin, Dal	3	16	256	16.0	25	2
Ricky Sanders, Wash	2	10	234	23.4	t80	2
Antonio Freeman, GB	2	12	231	19.3	t81	3
Issac Bruce, StL	2	11	218	19.8	t73	1
Roger Craig, SF	3	20	212	10.6	40	2

KEY: GP=games played; ATT=attempts; COMP=completions; PCT=completion percentage; YDS=yards, AVG=average; TD=touchdowns; INT=passes intercepted; LG=longest; REC=receptions

■ **Adrian Peterson,** *running back, b. March 21, 1985, Palestine, Texas.* A standout at Oklahoma, Peterson was taken seventh overall in the 2007 draft by the Minnesota Vikings. Peterson flashed his potential in Week 1 with a 60-yard touchdown catch, then made national headlines a month later by rushing for 224 yards and three touchdowns against the Chicago Bears. Peterson was just hitting his stride. Three weeks later he broke the NFL record for rushing yards in a single game with 296 against San Diego. Peterson finished the season with more than 1,300 rushing yards and 12 touchdowns. He was named the NFL Offensive Rookie of the Year and went to his first Pro Bowl.

■ **Braylon Edwards,** *wide receiver, b. February 21, 1983, Detroit, Michigan.* Michigan's all-time leading receiver was taken third overall by the Cleveland Browns in the 2005 draft, but he endured a frustrating rookie season. Edwards caught just 32 balls in 10 games before going down with a torn ACL. He was much more productive in 2006 with 61 receptions, but the Browns' offense still floundered. Sparked by Derek Anderson's emergence in 2007, Edwards exploded for the new high-flying Browns' offense. Edwards finished with 80 catches, nearly 1,300 receiving yards, and 16 TD receptions, second only to Randy Moss. Complemented by Kellen Winslow Jr. and Donte Stallworth, the 2008 Browns should have one of the NFL's top passing offenses.

Adrian Peterson

POWER RANKINGS

Best Defensive Ends

1 Jared Allen, Minnesota Vikings
Wild man led the NFL with 15.5 sacks in 2007 and credits his strong play to his mullet.

2 Osi Umenyiora, New York Giants
This former Troy State star put massive pressure on Tom Brady in the Giants' Super Bowl XLII victory.

3 Patrick Kerney, Seattle Seahawks
A workout freak, he just keeps piling up sacks.

4 Aaron Kampman, Green Bay Packers
Came out of nowhere in 2006 to record 15.5 sacks and followed that up with 12 more the following season.

5 Aaron Schobel, Buffalo Bills
This bull never stops charging, with at least 6.5 sacks in all seven of his NFL seasons.

6 Jason Taylor, Washington Redskins
The 2006 NFL Player of the Year showed he also has a great first step on the dance floor on *Dancing with the Stars.*

7 Mario Williams, Houston Texans
The first overall pick in 2006 exploded for 14 sacks in 2007, half of which came in a three-game stretch.

8 Kyle Vanden Bosch, Tennessee Titans
Rejuvenated his career with the Titans by recording 31 sacks in three seasons.

9 Trent Cole, Philadelphia Eagles
Former fifth-round draft pick replaced Patrick Kearney in the 2008 Pro Bowl.

10 Elvis Dumervil, Denver Broncos
Considered undersized out of college, he made GMs look silly with 21 sacks over his first two seasons.

Mario Williams

NFL: Regular Season Career Leaders

SCORING

PLAYER	YRS	TD	FG	PAT	PTS
Morten Andersen*	25	0	565	849	2,544
Gary Anderson	23	0	538	820	2,434
George Blanda	26	9	335	942	2,002
Matt Stover*	18	0	435	517	1,822
John Carney*	18	0	425	537	1,812
Jason Elam*	15	0	395	601	1,786
Norm Johnson	18	0	366	638	1,736
Nick Lowery	18	0	383	562	1,711
Jan Stenerud	19	0	373	580	1,699
Jason Hanson*	16	0	385	504	1,659
Lou Groza	21	1	264	810	1,608
Eddie Murray	19	0	352	538	1,594
Al Del Greco	17	0	347	543	1,584
John Kasay*	17	0	358	430	1,504
Steve Christie	15	6	336	468	1,476
Pat Leahy	18	0	304	558	1,470
Jim Turner	16	1	304	521	1,439
Matt Bahr	17	0	300	522	1,422
Jeff Wilkins*	14	0	307	495	1,416
Adam Vinatieri*	12	0	311	454	1,389

RUSHING

PLAYER	YRS	ATT	YDS	AVG	LG	TD
Emmitt Smith	15	4,409	18,355	4.2	75	164
Walter Payton	13	3,838	16,726	4.4	76	110
Barry Sanders	10	3,062	15,269	5.0	85	99
Curtis Martin	11	3,518	14,101	4.0	70	90
Jerome Bettis	13	3,479	13,662	3.9	71	91
Eric Dickerson	11	2,996	13,259	4.4	85	90
Tony Dorsett	12	2,936	12,739	4.3	99	77
Jim Brown	9	2,359	12,312	5.2	80	106
Marshall Faulk	12	2,836	12,279	4.3	71	100
Marcus Allen	16	3,022	12,243	4.1	61	123
Franco Harris	13	2,949	12,120	4.1	75	91
Thurman Thomas	13	2,877	12,074	4.2	80	65
Edgerrin James*	9	2,849	11,607	4.1	72	77
John Riggins	14	2,916	11,352	3.9	66	104
Corey Dillon*	10	2,618	11,241	4.3	96	82
O.J. Simpson	11	2,404	11,236	4.7	94	61
Fred Taylor*	10	2,285	10,715	4.7	80	61
LaDainian Tomlinson*	7	2,365	10,650	4.5	85	115
Ricky Watters	10	2,622	10,643	4.1	57	78
Tiki Barber	10	2,216	10,448	4.7	95	55

TOUCHDOWNS

PLAYER	YRS	RUSH	REC	RET	TD
Jerry Rice	20	10	197	0	208
Emmitt Smith	15	164	11	0	175
Marcus Allen	16	123	21	1	145
Marshall Faulk	13	100	36	0	136
Cris Carter	16	0	130	1	131
Terrell Owens*	12	2	129	0	131
LaDainian Tomlinson*	7	115	14	0	129
Jim Brown	9	106	20	0	126
Walter Payton	13	110	15	0	125
Randy Moss*	10	0	124	1	125
Marvin Harrison*	12	0	123	0	123
John Riggins	14	104	12	0	116
Lenny Moore	12	63	48	2	113
Shaun Alexander*	8	100	12	0	112
Barry Sanders	10	99	10	0	109
Tim Brown	17	1	100	4	105
Don Hutson	11	3	99	3	105
Steve Largent	14	1	100	0	101
Franco Harris	13	91	9	0	100
Curtis Martin	11	90	10	0	100

Wide receiver Jerry Rice has the most career TD catches.

PASSING EFFICIENCY**

PLAYER	YRS	ATT	COMP	PCT	YDS	YDS/ATT	TD	INT	RATING
Steve Young	15	4,149	2,667	64.3	33,124	7.98	232	107	96.8
Peyton Manning*	10	5,405	3,468	64.2	41,626	7.70	306	153	94.7
Kurt Warner*	10	2,959	1,926	65.1	24,008	8.11	152	100	93.2
Tom Brady*	8	3,642	2,294	63.0	26,370	7.24	197	86	92.2
Ben Roethlisberger*	4	1,436	908	63.2	11,673	8.12	84	54	92.5
Joe Montana	15	5,391	3,409	63.2	40,551	7.52	273	139	92.3
Carson Palmer*	5	2,036	1,305	64.1	14,899	7.32	104	63	90.1
Daunte Culpepper*	9	2,927	1,867	63.8	22,422	7.66	142	94	88.9
Chad Pennington*	8	1,919	1,259	65.6	13,738	7.16	82	55	88.9
Marc Bulger	7	2,484	1,578	63.5	18,625	7.50	106	74	88.1

* Active in 2007

** 1,500 or more attempts. The passer ratings are based on performance standards established for completion percentage, interception percentage, touchdown percentage, and average gain. Passers are allocated points according to how their marks compare with those standards.

KEY: YRS=years; TD=touchdowns; FG=field goals; PAT=extra points; PTS=points; ATT=attempts; YDS=yards; AVG=average; LG=longest; RUSH=rushing; REC=receiving; RET=returns; COMP=completions; PCT=completion percentage; YDS/ATT=yards per attempt; INT=intercepted passes

NFL: Regular Season Career Leaders (cont.)

PASSING YARDS					
PLAYER	YRS	ATT	COMP	PCT	YDS
Brett Favre*	17	8,758	5,377	61.4	61,655
Dan Marino	17	8,358	4,967	59.4	61,361
John Elway	16	7,250	4,123	56.9	51,475
Warren Moon	17	6,823	3,988	58.4	49,325
Fran Tarkenton	18	6,467	3,686	57.0	47,003
Vinny Testaverde*	21	6,701	3,787	56.5	46,233
Drew Bledsoe	14	6,717	3,839	57.2	44,611
Dan Fouts	15	5,604	3,297	58.8	43,040
Peyton Manning*	10	5,405	3,468	64.2	41,626
Joe Montana	15	5,391	3,409	63.2	40,551
Johnny Unitas	18	5,186	2,830	54.6	40,239
Dave Krieg	19	5,311	3,105	58.5	38,147

PASSING TOUCHDOWNS	
PLAYER	TD
Brett Favre*	442
Dan Marino	420
Fran Tarkenton	342
Peyton Manning*	306
John Elway	300
Warren Moon	291
Johnny Unitas	290
Vinny Testaverde*	275
Joe Montana	273
Dave Krieg	261
Sonny Jurgensen	255
Dan Fouts	254
Drew Bledsoe*	251
Boomer Esiason	247
John Hadl	244
Y.A. Tittle	242
Len Dawson	239

SACKS	
PLAYER	SACKS
Bruce Smith	200.0
Reggie White	198.0
Kevin Greene	160.0
Chris Doleman	150.5
Michael Strahan*	141.5

Note: Stat officially compiled since 1982.

RECEIVING YARDS	
PLAYER	YDS
Jerry Rice	22,895
Tim Brown	14,934
Isaac Bruce*	14,109
James Lofton	14,004
Marvin Harrison*	13,697
Cris Carter	13,899
Henry Ellard	13,777
Andre Reed	13,198
Steve Largent	13,089
Terrell Owens*	13,070
Irving Fryar	12,785

Hall of Fame QB Dan Marino ranks second in career passing yards.

RECEPTIONS						
PLAYER	YRS	REC	YDS	AVG	LG	TD
Jerry Rice	20	1,549	22,895	14.8	96	197
Cris Carter	16	1,101	13,899	12.6	80	130
Tim Brown	17	1,094	14,934	13.7	80	100
Marvin Harrison*	12	1,042	13,944	13.4	80	123
Andre Reed	16	951	13,198	13.9	83	87
Isaac Bruce*	14	942	14,109	15.0	80	84
Art Monk	16	940	12,721	13.5	79	68
Keenan McCardell*	16	883	11,373	12.9	76	63
Terrell Owens*	12	882	13,070	14.8	91	129
Jimmy Smith	12	862	12,287	14.3	75	67
Irving Fryar	17	851	12,785	15.0	80	84
Rod Smith*	12	849	11,389	13.4	85	68
Larry Centers	14	827	6,797	8.2	54	28
Steve Largent	14	819	13,089	16.0	74	100

INTERCEPTIONS						
PLAYER	YRS	NO.	YDS	AVG	LG	TD
Paul Krause	16	81	1,185	14.6	81	3
Emlen Tunnell	14	79	1,282	16.2	55	4
Rod Woodson	17	71	1,483	20.9	98	12
Dick "Night Train" Lane	14	68	1,207	17.8	80	5
Ken Riley	15	65	596	9.2	66	5

? DID YOU KNOW?

Chicago Bears running back Walter Payton held the single-game rushing record for 23 years before it was broken by Corey Dillon in 2000. That mark has since been broken twice, most recently by Adrian Peterson of the Minnesota Vikings.

NFL: Single-Season Leaders

SCORING – POINTS

PLAYER, TEAM	YEAR	TD	PAT	FG	PTS
LaDainian Tomlinson, SD	2006	31	0	0	186
Paul Hornung, GB	1960	15	41	15	176
Shaun Alexander, SD	2005	28	0	0	168
Gary Anderson, Minn	1998	0	59	35	164
Jeff Wilkins, StL	2003	0	46	39	163
Priest Holmes, KC	2003	27	0	0	162
Mark Moseley, Wash	1983	0	62	33	161
Marshall Faulk, StL	2000	26	0	0	160
Gino Cappelletti*, NE	1964	7	36	25	155
Emmitt Smith, Dal	1995	25	0	0	150
Chip Lohmiller, Wash	1991	0	56	31	149

* Cappelletti's 1964 total includes a 2-point conversion.

TOUCHDOWNS

PLAYER, TEAM	YEAR	RUSH	REC	RET	TOTAL
LaDainian Tomlinson, SD	2006	28	3	0	31
Shaun Alexander, Sea	2005	27	1	0	28
Priest Holmes, KC	2003	27	0	0	27
Marshall Faulk, StL	2000	18	8	0	26
Emmitt Smith, Dal	1995	25	0	0	25
John Riggins, Wash	1983	24	0	0	24
Priest Holmes, KC	2002	21	3	0	24
O.J. Simpson, Buf	1975	16	7	0	23
Jerry Rice, SF	1987	1	22	0	23

FIELD GOALS

PLAYER, TEAM	YEAR	ATT	NO.
Neil Rackers, Ari	2005	42	40
Jeff Wilkins, StL	2003	42	39
Olindo Mare, Mia	1999	46	39
John Kasay, Car	1996	45	37
Mike Vanderjagt, Ind	2003	37	37
Cary Blanchard, Ind	1996	40	36

RUSHING YARDS GAINED

PLAYER, TEAM	YEAR	ATT	YDS	AVG
Eric Dickerson, StL	1984	379	2,105	5.6
Jamal Lewis, Bal	2003	387	2,066	5.3
Barry Sanders, Det	1997	335	2,053	6.1
Terrell Davis, Den	1998	392	2,008	5.1
O.J. Simpson, Buf	1973	332	2,003	6.0
Earl Campbell, Hou	1980	373	1,934	5.2
Barry Sanders, Det	1994	331	1,883	5.7
Ahman Green, GB	2003	355	1,883	5.3
Shaun Alexander, Sea	2005	370	1,880	5.1
Jim Brown, CLE	1963	291	1,863	6.4
Tiki Barber, NY Giants	2005	357	1,860	5.1

RUSHING – AVERAGE GAIN

PLAYER, TEAM	YEAR	AVG
Michael Vick, Atl	2006	8.45
Beattie Feathers, Chi	1934	8.44
Michael Vick, Atl	2004	7.50
Michael Vick, Atl	2002	6.88
Bobby Douglass, Chi	1972	6.87

Minimum 100 attempts.

RUSHING TOUCHDOWNS

PLAYER, TEAM	YEAR	NO.
LaDainian Tomlinson, SD	2006	28
Shaun Alexander, Sea	2005	27
Priest Holmes, KC	2003	27
Emmitt Smith, Dal	1995	25
John Riggins, Wash	1983	24

PASSING – YARDS GAINED

PLAYER, TEAM	YEAR	ATT	COMP	PCT	YDS
Dan Marino, Mia	1984	564	362	64.2	5,084
Kurt Warner, StL	2001	546	375	68.7	4,830
Tom Brady, NE	2007	578	398	68.9	4,806
Dan Fouts, SD	1981	609	360	59.1	4,802
Dan Marino, Mia	1986	623	378	60.7	4,746
Daunte Culpepper, Minn	2004	548	379	69.2	4,717
Dan Fouts, SD	1980	589	348	59.1	4,715
Warren Moon, Hou	1991	655	404	61.7	4,690
Warren Moon, Hou	1990	584	362	62.0	4,689
Rich Gannon, Oak	2002	618	418	67.6	4,689
Neil Lomax, Ari	1984	560	345	61.6	4,614

PASSER RATING

PLAYER, TEAM	YEAR	RATING
Peyton Manning, Ind	2004	121.1
Tom Brady, NE	2007	117.2
Steve Young, SF	1994	112.8
Joe Montana, SF	1989	112.4
Daunte Culpepper, Minn	2004	110.9
Milt Plum, Cle	1960	110.4
Sammy Baugh, Wash	1945	109.9

PASSING TOUCHDOWNS

PLAYER, TEAM	YEAR	NO.
Tom Brady, NE	2007	50
Peyton Manning, Ind	2004	49
Dan Marino, Mia	1984	48
Dan Marino, Mia	1986	44
Kurt Warner, StL	1999	41
Brett Favre, GB	1996	39
Daunte Culpepper, Minn	2004	39

RECEPTIONS

PLAYER , TEAM	YEAR	NO.	YDS
Marvin Harrison, Ind	2002	143	1,722
Herman Moore, Det	1995	123	1,686
Cris Carter, Minn	1994	122	1,256
Jerry Rice, SF	1995	122	1,848
Cris Carter, Minn	1995	122	1,371
Isaac Bruce, StL	1995	119	1,781
Torry Holt, StL	2003	117	1,696
Jimmy Smith, Jac	1999	116	1,636
Marvin Harrison, Ind	1999	115	1,663
Rod Smith, Den	2001	113	1,343

RECEIVING – YARDS GAINED

PLAYER, TEAM	YEAR	YDS
Jerry Rice, SF	1995	1,848
Isaac Bruce, StL	1995	1,781
Charley Hennigan, Hou	1961	1,746
Marvin Harrison, Ind	2002	1,722
Torry Holt, Det	2003	1,696
Herman Moore, Det	1995	1,686

RECEIVING TOUCHDOWNS

PLAYER, TEAM	YEAR	NO.
Randy Moss, NE	2007	23
Jerry Rice, SF	1987	22
Mark Clayton, Mia	1984	18
Sterling Sharpe, GB	1994	18

NFL: Single-Season Leaders (cont.)

INTERCEPTIONS				SACKS		
PLAYER, TEAM	**YEAR**	**NO.**		**PLAYER, TEAM**	**YEAR**	**NO.**
Dick "Night Train" Lane, StL	1952	14		Michael Strahan, NY Giants	2001	22.5
Dan Sandifer, Wash	1948	13		Mark Gastineau, NY Jets	1984	22.0
Spec Sanders, NY Yankees	1950	13		Reggie White, Phil	1987	21.0
Lester Hayes, Oak	1980	13		Chris Doleman, Minn	1989	21.0
				Lawrence Taylor, NY Giants	1986	20.5

Pro Bowl Results

DATE	RESULT	DATE	RESULT	DATE	RESULT
2-10-08	NFC 42, AFC 30	1-31-82	AFC 16, NFC 13	1-13-63	NFL East 30, West 20
2-10-07	AFC 31, NFC 28	2-1-81	NFC 21, AFC 7	1-13-63	AFL West 21, East 14
2-12-06	NFC 23, AFC 17	1-27-80	NFC 37, AFC 27	1-14-62	NFL West 31, East 30
2-13-05	AFC 38, NFC 27	1-29-79	NFC 13, AFC 7	1-7-62	AFL West 47, East 27
2-8-04	NFC 55, AFC 52	1-23-78	NFC 14, AFC 13	1-15-61	West 35, East 31
2-2-03	AFC 45, NFC 20	1-17-77	AFC 24, NFC 14	1-17-60	West 38, East 21
2-9-02	AFC 38, NFC 30	1-26-76	NFC 23, AFC 20	1-11-59	East 28, West 21
2-4-01	AFC 38, NFC 17	1-20-75	NFC 17, AFC 10	1-12-58	West 26, East 7
2-6-00	NFC 51, AFC 31	1-20-74	AFC 15, NFC 13	1-13-57	West 19, East 10
2-7-99	AFC 23, NFC 10	1-21-73	AFC 33, NFC 28	1-15-56	East 31, West 30
2-1-98	AFC 29, NFC 24	1-23-72	AFC 26, NFC 13	1-16-55	West 26, East 19
2-2-97	AFC 26, NFC 23	1-24-71	NFC 27, AFC 6	1-17-54	East 20, West 9
2-4-96	NFC 20, AFC 13	1-18-70	NFL West 16, East 13	1-10-53	N. Conf. 27, A. Conf. 7
2-5-95	AFC 41, NFC 13	1-17-70	AFL West 26, East 3	1-12-52	N. Conf. 30, A. Conf. 13
2-6-94	NFC 17, AFC 3	1-19-69	NFL West 10, East 7	1-14-51	A. Conf. 28, N. Conf. 27
2-7-93	AFC 23, NFC 20	1-19-69	AFL West 38, East 25	12-27-42	NFL All-Stars 17, Washington 14
2-2-92	NFC 21, AFC 15	1-21-68	NFL West 38, East 20		
2-3-91	AFC 23, NFC 21	1-21-68	AFL East 25, West 24	1-4-42	Chicago Bears 35, NFL All-Stars 24
2-4-90	NFC 27, AFC 21	1-22-67	NFL East 20, West 10		
1-29-89	NFC 34, AFC 3	1-21-67	AFL East 30, West 23	12-29-40	Chicago Bears 28, NFL All-Stars 14
2-7-88	AFC 15, NFC 6	1-15-66	NFL East 36, West 7		
2-1-87	AFC 10, NFC 6	1-15-66	AFL All-Stars 30, Buffalo 19	1-14-40	Green Bay 16, NFL All-Stars 7
2-2-86	NFC 28, AFC 24	1-16-65	AFL West 38, East 14		
1-27-85	AFC 22, NFC 14	1-10-65	NFL West 34, East 14	1-15-39	NY Giants 13, Pro All-Stars 10
1-29-84	NFC 45, AFC 3	1-19-64	AFL West 27, East 24		
2-6-83	NFC 20, AFC 19	1-12-64	NFL West 31, East 17		

Note: The Pro Bowl was canceled in 1943 because of World War II. The game was brought back after the 1950 season.

⬆ RANKINGS POWER

Best Kickers

1 **Rob Bironas, Tennessee Titans**
Bironas led the NFL with 35 field goals made in 2007, including a league-record eight made against Houston.

2 **Jason Elam, Atlanta Falcons**
Elam hit four game-winners for Denver in 2007.

3 **Adam Vinatieri, Indianapolis Colts**
Still the greatest clutch kicker in NFL history.

4 **Shayne Graham, Cincinnati Bengals**
The second-most accurate kicker in NFL history, converting 85.5 percent of his attempts.

5 **Matt Stover, Baltimore Ravens**
He has not made less than 80 percent of his field goals since 1998.

6 **Robbie Gould, Chicago Bears**
A rock, Gould has connected on 63 field goals over the past two seasons.

7 **Nate Kaeding, San Diego Chargers**
He has missed just 9 of his 80 attempts over the last three seasons.

8 **Mason Crosby, Green Bay Packers**
In 2007, he hit 31 field goals and missed just one under 40 yards.

9 **Phil Dawson, Clevland Browns**
Hit 26 of 30 field goals in 2007, including a 51-yarder for the ages against Baltimore.

10 **Matt Bryant, Tampa Bay Buccaneers**
In 2006, he hit the third-longest field goal in NFL history (62 yards).

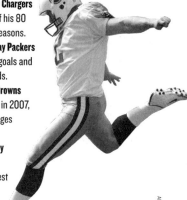

Rob Bironas

2 for 1

Tom Brady and Randy Moss killed two single-season records with one play in their last game of the regular season, 2007. What records did they beat?

Randy Moss

To find out, cross out the letters on the top half of the grid that have incorrect mirror images in the bottom half. Separate the remaining letters into words (they are in the correct order) to reveal one of the records that was set.

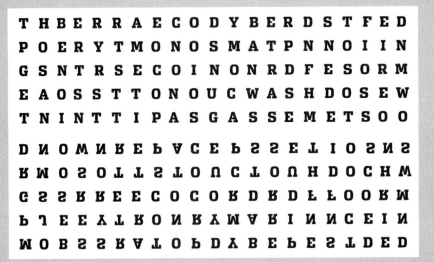

To find the second record that was set, cross out the letters in the bottom half of the grid that have correct mirror images in the top half. The remaining letters spell the answer. It will be easier to read if you hold the page upside down in front of a mirror and read the reflected words.

ANSWERS ON PAGE 190

BOB ROSATO

NFL: Number One Draft Choices

YEAR	PLAYER	POSITION	SCHOOL	TEAM
2008	Jake Long	Offensive Tackle	Michigan	Miami Dolphins
2007	JaMarcus Russell	Quarterback	LSU	Oakland Raiders
2006	Mario Williams	Defensive End	N. Carolina State	Houston Texans
2005	Alex Smith	Quarterback	Utah	San Francisco 49ers
2004	Eli Manning	Quarterback	Mississippi	San Diego Chargers
2003	Carson Palmer	Quarterback	Southern Cal.	Cincinnati Bengals
2002	David Carr	Quarterback	Fresno State	Houston Texans
2001	Michael Vick	Quarterback	Virginia Tech	Atlanta Falcons
2000	Courtney Brown	Defensive End	Penn State	Cleveland Browns
1999	Tim Couch	Quarterback	Kentucky	Cleveland Browns
1998	Peyton Manning	Quarterback	Tennessee	Indianapolis Colts
1997	Orlando Pace	Offensive Tackle	Ohio State	St. Louis Rams
1996	Keyshawn Johnson	Wide Receiver	Southern Cal.	New York Jets
1995	Ki-Jana Carter	Running Back	Penn State	Cincinnati Bengals
1994	Dan Wilkinson	Defensive Tackle	Ohio State	Cincinnati Bengals
1993	Drew Bledsoe	Quarterback	Washington State	New England Patriots

NFL: Number One Draft Choices (cont.)

YEAR	PLAYER	POSITION	SCHOOL	TEAM
1992	Steve Emtman	Defensive Tackle	Washington	Indianapolis Colts
1991	Russell Maryland	Defensive Tackle	Miami (Florida)	Dallas Cowboys
1990	Jeff George	Quarterback	Illinois	Indianapolis Colts
1989	Troy Aikman	Quarterback	UCLA	Dallas Cowboys
1988	Aundray Bruce	Linebacker	Auburn	Atlanta Falcons
1987	Vinny Testaverde	Quarterback	Miami (Florida)	Tampa Bay Buccaneers
1986	Bo Jackson	Running Back	Auburn	Tampa Bay Buccaneers
1985	Bruce Smith	Defensive End	Virginia Tech	Buffalo Bills
1984	Irving Fryar	Wide Receiver	Nebraska	New England Patriots
1983	John Elway	Quarterback	Stanford	Baltimore Colts
1982	Kenneth Sims	Defensive Tackle	Texas	New England Patriots
1981	George Rogers	Running Back	South Carolina	New Orleans Saints
1980	Bill Sims	Running Back	Oklahoma	Detroit Lions
1979	Tom Cousineau	Linebacker	Ohio State	Buffalo Bills
1978	Earl Campbell	Running Back	Texas	Houston Oilers
1977	Ricky Bell	Running Back	Southern Cal.	Tampa Bay Buccaneers
1976	Lee Roy Selmon	Defensive End	Oklahoma	Tampa Bay Buccaneers
1975	Steve Bartkowski	Quarterback	California	Atlanta Falcons
1974	Ed "Too Tall" Jones	Defensive End	Tennessee State	Dallas Cowboys
1973	John Matuszak	Defensive End	Tampa	Houston Oilers
1972	Walt Patulski	Defensive Tackle	Notre Dame	Buffalo Bills
1971	Jim Plunkett	Quarterback	Stanford	New England Patriots
1970	Terry Bradshaw	Quarterback	Louisiana Tech	Pittsburgh Steelers
1969	O.J. Simpson	Running Back	Southern Cal.	Buffalo Bills
1968	Ron Yary	Offensive Tackle	Southern Cal.	Minnesota Vikings
1967	Bubba Smith	Defensive End	Michigan State	Baltimore Colts
1966	Jim Grabowski*	Running Back	Illinois	Miami Dolphins
1966	Tommy Nobis	Linebacker	Texas	Atlanta Falcons
1965	Lawrence Elkins*	Wide Receiver	Baylor	Houston Oilers
1965	Tucker Frederickson	Running Back	Auburn	New York Giants
1964	Jack Concannon*	Quarterback	Boston College	Boston Patriots
1964	Dave Parks	Wide Receiver	Texas Tech	San Francisco 49ers
1963	Buck Buchanan*	Defensive Tackle	Grambling	Kansas City Chiefs
1963	Terry Baker	Quarterback	Oregon State	Los Angeles Rams
1962	Roman Gabriel*	Quarterback	North Carolina State	Oakland Raiders
1962	Ernie Davis	Running Back	Syracuse	Washington Redskins
1961	Ken Rice*	Guard	Auburn	Buffalo Bills
1961	Tommy Mason	Running Back	Tulane	Minnesota Vikings
1960	Billy Cannon	Running Back	Louisiana State	Los Angeles Rams
1959	Randy Duncan	Quarterback	Iowa	Green Bay Packers
1958	King Hill	Quarterback	Rice	Chicago Cardinals
1957	Paul Hornung	Half Back	Notre Dame	Green Bay Packers
1956	Gary Glick	Defensive Back	Colorado A&M	Pittsburgh Steelers
1955	George Shaw	Quarterback	Oregon	Baltimore Colts
1954	Bobby Garrett	Quarterback	Stanford	Cleveland Browns
1953	Harry Babcock	End	Georgia	San Francisco 49ers
1952	Bill Wade	Quarterback	Vanderbilt	Los Angeles Rams
1951	Kyle Rote	Half Back	SMU	New York Giants
1950	Leon Hart	End	Notre Dame	Detroit Lions
1949	Chuck Bednarik	Center/Linebacker	Pennsylvania	Philadelphia Eagles
1948	Harry Gilmer	Quarterback	Alabama	Washington Redskins
1947	Bob Fenimore	Half Back	Oklahoma State	Chicago Bears
1946	Frank Dancewicz	Quarterback	Notre Dame	Boston Yanks
1945	Charley Trippi	Half Back	Georgia	Chicago Cardinals
1944	Angelo Bertelli	Quarterback	Notre Dame	Boston Yanks
1943	Frank Sinkwich	Half Back	Georgia	Detroit Lions
1942	Bill Dudley	Half Back	Virginia	Pittsburgh Steelers
1941	Tom Harmon	Half Back	Michigan	Chicago Bears
1940	George Cafego	Half Back	Tennessee	Chicago Cardinals
1939	Ki Aldrich	Center	Texas Christian	Chicago Cardinals
1938	Corbett Davis	Fullback	Indiana	Cleveland Rams
1937	Sam Francis	Fullback	Nebraska	Philadelphia Eagles
1936	Jay Berwanger	Fullback	Chicago	Philadelphia Eagles

* Selected by the AFL

■ **Calvin Johnson,** *wide receiver, b. September 25, 1985, Tyrone, Georgia.* The second overall pick in the 2007 Draft, Johnson has an unbelievable combination of size, speed, and strength. At 6'5", 235 pounds, he runs a 4.4 40-yard dash and has a 45-inch vertical leap. At Georgia Tech, he set school records for receiving yards (2,927) and touchdowns (28) in just three seasons and won the Biletnikoff Award, given to the nation's top wideout, in 2006. Johnson had a solid 2007 season with 48 catches for over 750 yards as a rookie. And there were moments he left Lions fans in awe, like his 32-yard touchdown run on a reverse in Week 7. With Johnson paired with Roy Williams, the Lions have a great young receiving corps that will fill highlight reels for years to come.

Calvin Johnson

■ **Antonio Cromartie,** *defensive back, b. April 15, 1984, Tallahassee, Florida.* Cromartie was seen as a huge gamble when the San Diego Chargers selected him 19th overall in the 2006 NFL Draft. He'd started only one game at Florida State during his career and missed the entire 2005 season with a knee injury. But the Chargers hit the jackpot. In his second year, Cromartie became one of the most exciting players in the league. He led the NFL in interceptions with 10 and even picked off Peyton Manning three times in one game. And that wasn't even the highlight of his year. Cromartie returned a missed Vikings field goal 109 yards for a touchdown, setting an NFL record. Cromartie was selected to the Pro Bowl for his role in helping the Chargers reach the AFC Championship Game.

Derek Anderson

■ **Derek Anderson,** *quarterback, b. June 15, 1983, Portland, Oregon.* Anderson began the 2007 season as an afterthought. Entering his third season, Anderson lost the starting job to Charlie Frye in training camp. Meanwhile, the Cleveland Browns were grooming their quarterback of the future, Brady Quinn. But after a disastrous 34–7 loss to Pittsburgh in the opener, everything changed. Frye was traded to Seattle and Anderson was thrust into the starting role. His response? More than 300 yards passing and five touchdowns in a 51–45 victory over Cincinnati the next week. Suddenly, Anderson was the toast of the town. He nearly led the Browns to a playoff spot and had a Pro Bowl season in the process, throwing for 3,787 yards and 29 TDs, one short of a team record. While Anderson still has to cut down on his mistakes (19 interceptions), the Browns rewarded him with a three-year, $24 million contract in the offseason.

1 Often called a "pigskin," NFL footballs are actually made from what material?
A. Snakeskin
B. Plastic
C. Leather

2 What franchise is known as "America's Team"?
A. Dallas
B. Washington
C. New York Giants

3 The Super Bowl trophy is named after which legendary coach?
A. Bill Walsh
B. Tom Landry
C. Vince Lombardi

4 Which is the only NFL team with a logo on just one side of its helmet?
A. Tennessee
B. Oakland
C. Pittsburgh

5 What team originally drafted quarterback Brett Favre in 1991?
A. New Orleans
B. Atlanta
C. San Francisco

6 Which team switched from the AFC to the NFC in 2002?
A. Arizona
B. Carolina
C. Seattle

7 The Rams moved to St. Louis in 1995. What city did they move from?
A. San Diego
B. Oakland
C. Los Angeles

8 Baltimore's team name, the Ravens, is a tribute to which poet who lived in that city?
A. Ralph Waldo Emerson
B. Edgar Allen Poe
C. Henry Wadsworth Longfellow

9 Which of the following was NOT an expansion franchise in 1995?
A. Tennessee
B. Jacksonville
C. Carolina

10 Three franchises have won five Super Bowls, the most of any NFL team. Which is one of them?
A. San Francisco
B. New England
C. Denver

11 What is the nickname given to the last player taken in the NFL Draft every year?
A. Captain Zero
B. Mister Irrelevant
C. Sir No-Name

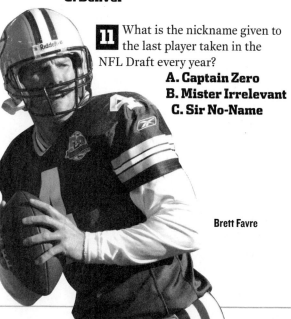

Brett Favre

1.C, 2.A, 3.C, 4.C, 5.B, 6.C, 7.C, 8.B, 9.A, 10.A, 11.B

A Season of Surprises

Anyone trying to predict baseball has been out of luck lately. The past year included more twists and turns than the sport has ever seen before.

Fans might have been a little surprised to see the Boston Red Sox, a franchise that had recently suffered through an 86-year World Series drought, win a second title in the past four seasons. An offense led by David Ortiz and Manny Ramirez and a pitching staff featuring postseason hero Josh Beckett and super-closer Jonathan Papelbon had a bumpy ride overcoming the Cleveland Indians in the AL Championship series. The Sox stormed back from a 3–1 series deficit, then carried that momentum to a World Series sweep of the Colorado Rockies.

It was an amazing accomplishment for the Rockies just to make it to the World Series. Colorado was in fourth place in the NL West as of mid-September. But behind the bats of Matt Holliday, Garrett Atkins, and Todd Helton, they won 14 of their final 15 regular season games, including an extra-innings victory over the San Diego Padres in a tiebreaker game for the Wild Card.

The Rockies then swept the Philadelphia Phillies in the NL Divisional Series and the Arizona Diamondbacks in the NL Championship Series before running into the red-hot Red Sox.

While the Rockies finished hot, the New York Mets finished just as cold. The Mets led the Phillies by seven games in the NL East with only 17 left to play in the regular season. But they lost 12 of those final 17 games, allowing the Phillies to pass them. However, the Mets made one big move to prevent another late-season collapse: They acquired Johan Santana, baseball's best pitcher, from the Minnesota Twins after the season.

The Phillies made it two straight MVPs when shortstop Jimmy Rollins won the award in a season that included 38 doubles, 20 triples, and 30 home runs. In the AL, Alex Rodriguez won his third MVP award with yet another monster season, leading the majors with 54 homers, 156 RBIs, and 143 runs.

Away from the field, baseball's steroid problem continued. Major League Baseball released the findings of its Mitchell Report, an investigation into steroid use among baseball players. The report included the names of 89 current and former players. The biggest name was pitcher Roger Clemens, who denied that he used drugs.

While the Mitchell Report was a major black mark for baseball, it also served a positive purpose. It was a big step forward as baseball moves past the steroid era, allowing fans to focus on the game once again.

Boston Red Sox pitcher Josh Beckett had a 1.20 ERA in the 2007 postseason.

DAMIAN STROHMEYER

Milwaukee Brewers first baseman Prince Fielder led the NL with 50 home runs in 2007.

POWER RANKINGS

Best Left-Handed Pitchers

1 **Johan Santana, New York Mets**
Arguably the best pitcher in baseball, Santana was the unanimous AL Cy Young Award winner in 2004 and 2006.

2 **C.C. Sabathia, Milwaukee Brewers**
The 2007 AL Cy Young Award winner, Sabathia was the youngest pitcher to reach 100 career wins (at 27 years, 69 days old) since Greg Maddux in 1993.

3 **Erik Bedard, Seattle Mariners**
Bedard averaged 10.93 strikeouts per nine innings for the Orioles in 2007, the best among big league starters.

4 **Cole Hamels, Philadelphia Phillies**
In 2007, his second season in the bigs, Hamels finished in the NL's top 10 in wins (15), ERA (3.39), and strikeouts (177).

5 **Scott Kazmir, Tampa Bay Rays**
The 24-year-old Kazmir was second in the majors with 239 strikeouts in 2007.

Johan Santana

MAJOR LEAGUE TEAMS

NATIONAL LEAGUE	AMERICAN LEAGUE
Arizona Diamondbacks	Baltimore Orioles
Atlanta Braves	Boston Red Sox
Chicago Cubs	Chicago White Sox
Cincinnati Reds	Cleveland Indians
Colorado Rockies	Detroit Tigers
Florida Marlins	Kansas City Royals
Houston Astros	Los Angeles Angels
Los Angeles Dodgers	Minnesota Twins
Milwaukee Brewers	New York Yankees
New York Mets	Oakland Athletics
Philadelphia Phillies	Seattle Mariners
Pittsburgh Pirates	Tampa Bay Rays
San Diego Padres	Texas Rangers
San Francisco Giants	Toronto Blue Jays
St. Louis Cardinals	
Washington Nationals	

? DID YOU KNOW?

In 2007, the Detroit Tigers' Curtis Granderson and the Philadelphia Phillies' Jimmy Rollins became the third and fourth players in history to have 20 or more doubles, triples, home runs, and stolen bases in a season.

GAME TIME

Record Start

Who is the only pitcher in MLB history to throw a no-hitter, start a World Series game, be a Rookie of the Year, and be an All-Star in his first two full seasons?

To find out, fill in the answers to the clues, then read down the highlighted columns.

Part of ERA

Take over for the starter

Posada or Sosa

Get to second on a hit

162 games

Fans' seats

Hot corner

Fielders

Point

ANSWERS ON PAGE 190

BASEBALL

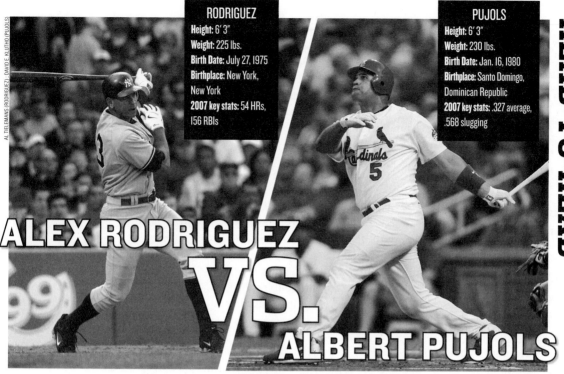

AL TIELEMANS (RODRIGUEZ); DAVID E. KLUTHO (PUJOLS)

RODRIGUEZ
Height: 6' 3"
Weight: 225 lbs.
Birth Date: July 27, 1975
Birthplace: New York, New York
2007 key stats: 54 HRs, 156 RBIs

PUJOLS
Height: 6' 3"
Weight: 230 lbs.
Birth Date: Jan. 16, 1980
Birthplace: Santo Domingo, Dominican Republic
2007 key stats: .327 average, .568 slugging

ALEX RODRIGUEZ VS. ALBERT PUJOLS

Two of baseball's hardest-hitting sluggers face off

New York Yankees, third baseman	**Team/Position**	St. Louis Cardinals, first baseman
First overall, Seattle Mariners, 1993	**Drafted**	13th round, St. Louis Cardinals, 1999
15th season: .306, 518 home runs, 1,503 RBIs, 1,501 runs, .578 slugging percentage	**Career Stats***	Eighth season: .332, 282 home runs, 861 RBIs, 847 runs, .620 slugging percentage
11-time All-Star; Gold Glove Awards (two, as a shortstop); Silver Slugger Awards (nine); AL Batting Champ (1996); AL MVP (2003, 2005, 2007)	**Awards**	Six-time All-Star; NL Rookie of the Year (2001); NL Batting Champ (2003); Silver Slugger Awards (three); NL MVP (2005)
A-Rod is an imposing batter, hitting for average and power. He's also a threat to steal a base. In the field, the former Gold Glove shortstop has settled in at third base.	**Scouting Report**	Pujols hits the ball to all fields and is very patient at the plate (592 career walks). The slugger has also become one of the best defensive first basemen in the NL.
New Yorkers won't embrace A-Rod until he comes through in the postseason and leads the Yankees to a World Series.	**Something to Prove**	Pujols has been slowed by nagging injuries, which make fans wonder how much longer he can be an offensive machine.
"By the time Alex is finished playing, he's going to hold all the records, including home runs. He's honest and serious about his business." — Carlos Beltran, outfielder, New York Mets	**What Others Say About Him**	"Pujols has no glaring weaknesses and he doesn't chase many bad pitches." — Tony Gwynn, Hall of Famer
	Who's Better	Our Pick: Pujols is a more complete player than A-Rod. He has tremendous power, rarely strikes out, and comes through in the clutch. He also has superb defensive skills.

* Through 2007 season

■ **Josh Beckett,** *pitcher, b. May 15, 1980, Spring, Texas.* When Beckett was picked second overall by the Florida Marlins in the 1999 draft, he was the first high school pitcher to be selected in the first round. Today, at 51–26, Beckett has the most wins of any MLB pitcher since the start of 2005. Twenty of those wins came in 2007, making Beckett the big leagues' first 20-game winner in two years. And it took him only 29 starts to rack up those 20 wins for the Boston Red Sox. He also had the sixth-lowest ERA at 3.27.

Matt Holliday

ROBERT BECK

■ **Matt Holliday,** *leftfielder, b. January 15, 1980, Stillwater, Oklahoma.* Holliday shined as the NL's hitting sensation in 2007, and led the Colorado Rockies to their first-ever appearance in the World Series. He was tops in the league in batting average (.340), hits (216), RBIs (137), extra-base hits (92), total bases (386), and doubles (50), and ranked in the top five in home runs (36), slugging (.607), and runs (120).

■ **Miguel Cabrera,** *third baseman, b. April 18, 1983, Maracay, Venezuela.* It seems like every year Cabrera is hitting new career highs, and 2007 was no different. He finished among NL leaders across the board, and led the Florida Marlins in home runs (34), RBIs (119), walks (79), on-base percentage (.401), and slugging percentage (.565). He also finished second in hits (188) and batting average (.320), and finished third in runs (91) and doubles (38). Cabrera is the third-youngest player to reach 500 RBIs, and also the third-youngest player to have four straight seasons with over 100 RBIs.

World Series Most Valuable Players

Year	Player		Year	Player		Year	Player
2007	Mike Lowell, Bos		1990	Jose Rijo, Cin		1972	Gene Tenace, Oak
2006	David Eckstein, StL		1989	Dave Stewart, Oak		1971	Roberto Clemente, Pitt
2005	Jermaine Dye, Chi (AL)		1988	Orel Hershiser, LA		1970	Brooks Robinson, Bal
2004	Manny Ramirez, Bos		1987	Frank Viola, Min		1969	Donn Clendenon, NY (NL)
2003	Josh Beckett, Fla		1986	Ray Knight, NY (NL)		1968	Mickey Lolich, Det
2002	Troy Glaus, Ana		1985	Bret Saberhagen, KC		1967	Bob Gibson, StL
2001	Randy Johnson, Ari; Curt Schilling, Ari		1984	Alan Trammell, Det		1966	Frank Robinson, Bal
			1983	Rick Dempsey, Bal		1965	Sandy Koufax, LA
2000	Derek Jeter, NY (AL)		1982	Darrell Porter, StL		1964	Bob Gibson, StL
1999	Mariano Rivera, NY (AL)		1981	Ron Cey, LA; Steve Yeager, LA; Pedro Guerrero, LA		1963	Sandy Koufax, LA
1998	Scott Brosius, NY (AL)					1962	Ralph Terry, NY (AL)
1997	Livan Hernandez, Fla		1980	Mike Schmidt, Phil		1961	Whitey Ford, NY (AL)
1996	John Wetteland, NY (AL)		1979	Willie Stargell, Pitt		1960	Bobby Richardson, NY (AL)
1995	Tom Glavine, Atl		1978	Bucky Dent, NY (AL)		1959	Larry Sherry, LA
1994	Series canceled due to labor dispute		1977	Reggie Jackson, NY (AL)		1958	Bob Turley, NY (AL)
			1976	Johnny Bench, Cin		1957	Lew Burdette, Mil
1993	Paul Molitor, Tor		1975	Pete Rose, Cin		1956	Don Larsen, NY (AL)
1992	Pat Borders, Tor		1974	Rollie Fingers, Oak		1955	Johnny Podres, Bklyn
1991	Jack Morris, Min		1973	Reggie Jackson, Oak			

World Series Results

2007	Boston (AL) 4, Colorado (NL) 0
2006	St. Louis (NL) 4, Detroit (AL) 1
2005	Chicago (AL) 4, Houston (NL) 0
2004	Boston (AL) 4, St. Louis (NL) 0
2003	Florida (NL) 4, New York (AL) 2
2002	Anaheim (AL) 4, San Francisco (NL) 3
2001	Arizona (NL) 4, New York (AL) 3
2000	New York (AL) 4, New York (NL) 1
1999	New York (AL) 4, Atlanta (NL) 0
1998	New York (AL) 4, San Diego (NL) 0
1997	Florida (NL) 4, Cleveland (AL) 3
1996	New York (AL) 4, Atlanta (NL) 2
1995	Atlanta (NL) 4, Cleveland (AL) 2
1994	Series canceled due to labor dispute
1993	Toronto (AL) 4, Philadelphia (NL) 2
1992	Toronto (AL) 4, Atlanta (NL) 2
1991	Minnesota (AL) 4, Atlanta (NL) 3
1990	Cincinnati (NL) 4, Oakland (AL) 0
1989	Oakland (AL) 4, San Francisco (NL) 0
1988	Los Angeles (NL) 4, Oakland (AL) 1
1987	Minnesota (AL) 4, St. Louis (NL) 3
1986	New York (NL) 4, Boston (AL) 3
1985	Kansas City (AL) 4, St. Louis (NL) 3
1984	Detroit (AL) 4, San Diego (NL) 1
1983	Baltimore (AL) 4, Philadelphia (NL) 1
1982	St. Louis (NL) 4, Milwaukee (AL) 3
1981	Los Angeles (NL) 4, New York (AL) 2
1980	Philadelphia (NL) 4, Kansas City (AL) 2
1979	Pittsburgh (NL) 4, Baltimore (AL) 3
1978	New York (AL) 4, Los Angeles (NL) 2
1977	New York (AL) 4, Los Angeles (NL) 2
1976	Cincinnati (NL) 4, New York (AL) 0
1975	Cincinnati (NL) 4, Boston (AL) 3
1974	Oakland (AL) 4, Los Angeles (NL) 1
1973	Oakland (AL) 4, New York (NL) 3
1972	Oakland (AL) 4, Cincinnati (NL) 3
1971	Pittsburgh (NL) 4, Baltimore (AL) 3
1970	Baltimore (AL) 4, Cincinnati (NL) 1
1969	New York (NL) 4, Baltimore (AL) 1
1968	Detroit (AL) 4, St. Louis (NL) 3
1967	St. Louis (NL) 4, Boston (AL) 3
1966	Baltimore (AL) 4, Los Angeles (NL) 0
1965	Los Angeles (NL) 4, Minnesota (AL) 3
1964	St. Louis (NL) 4, New York (AL) 3
1963	Los Angeles (NL) 4, New York (AL) 0
1962	New York (AL) 4, San Francisco (NL) 3
1961	New York (AL) 4, Cincinnati (NL) 1
1960	Pittsburgh (NL) 4, New York (AL) 3
1959	Los Angeles (NL) 4, Chicago (AL) 2
1958	New York (AL) 4, Milwaukee (NL) 3
1957	Milwaukee (NL) 4, New York (AL) 3
1956	New York (AL) 4, Brooklyn (NL) 3
1955	Brooklyn (NL) 4, New York (AL) 3
1954	New York (NL) 4, Cleveland (AL) 0
1953	New York (AL) 4, Brooklyn (NL) 2
1952	New York (AL) 4, Brooklyn (NL) 3
1951	New York (AL) 4, New York (NL) 2
1950	New York (AL) 4, Philadelphia (NL) 0
1949	New York (AL) 4, Brooklyn (NL) 1
1948	Cleveland (AL) 4, Boston (NL) 2
1947	New York (AL) 4, Brooklyn (NL) 3
1946	St. Louis (NL) 4, Boston (AL) 3
1945	Detroit (AL) 4, Chicago (NL) 3
1944	St. Louis (NL) 4, St. Louis (AL) 2
1943	New York (AL) 4, St. Louis (NL) 1
1942	St. Louis (NL) 4, New York (AL) 1
1941	New York (AL) 4, Brooklyn (NL) 1
1940	Cincinnati (NL) 4, Detroit (AL) 3
1939	New York (AL) 4, Cincinnati (NL) 0
1938	New York (AL) 4, Chicago (NL) 0
1937	New York (AL) 4, New York (NL) 1
1936	New York (AL) 4, New York (NL) 2
1935	Detroit (AL) 4, Chicago (NL) 2
1934	St. Louis (NL) 4, Detroit (AL) 3
1933	New York (NL) 4, Washington (AL) 1
1932	New York (AL) 4, Chicago (NL) 0
1931	St. Louis (NL) 4, Philadelphia (AL) 3
1930	Philadelphia (AL) 4, St. Louis (NL) 2
1929	Philadelphia (AL) 4, Chicago (NL) 1
1928	New York (AL) 4, St. Louis (NL) 0
1927	New York (AL) 4, Pittsburgh (NL) 0
1926	St. Louis (NL) 4, New York (AL) 3
1925	Pittsburgh (NL) 4, Washington (AL) 3
1924	Washington (AL) 4, New York (NL) 3
1923	New York (AL) 4, New York (NL) 2
1922	New York (NL) 4, New York (AL) 0; 1 tie
1921	New York (NL) 5, New York (LA) 3
1920	Cleveland (AL) 5, Brooklyn (NL) 2
1919	Cincinnati (NL) 5, Chicago (AL) 3
1918	Boston (AL) 4, Chicago (NL) 2
1917	Chicago (AL) 4, New York (NL) 2
1916	Boston (AL) 4, Brooklyn (NL) 1
1915	Boston (AL) 4, Philadelphia (NL) 1
1914	Boston (NL) 4, Philadelphia (AL) 0
1913	Philadelphia (AL) 4, New York (NL) 1
1912	Boston (AL) 4, New York (NL) 3; 1 tie
1911	Philadelphia (AL) 4, New York (NL) 2
1910	Philadelphia (AL) 4, Chicago (NL) 1
1909	Pittsburgh (NL) 4, Detroit (AL) 3
1908	Chicago (NL) 4, Detroit (AL) 1
1907	Chicago (NL) 4, Detroit (AL) 0; 1 tie
1906	Chicago (AL) 4, Chicago (NL) 2
1905	New York (NL) 4, Philadelphia (AL) 1
1904	No series
1903	Boston (AL) 5, Pittsburgh (NL) 3

League Championship Series Results

NATIONAL LEAGUE		AMERICAN LEAGUE	
2007	Colorado (WC) 4, Arizona (W) 0	2007	Boston (E) 4, Cleveland (C) 3
2006	St. Louis (C) 4, New York (E) 3	2006	Detroit (WC) 4, Oakland (W) 0
2005	Houston (WC) 4, St. Louis (C) 2	2005	Chicago (C) 4, Los Angeles (W) 1
2004	St. Louis (C) 4, Houston (WC) 3	2004	Boston (WC) 4, New York (E) 3
2003	Florida (WC) 4, Chicago (C) 3	2003	New York (E) 4, Boston (WC) 3
2002	San Francisco (WC) 4, St. Louis (C) 1	2002	Anaheim (WC) 4, Minnesota (C) 1
2001	Arizona (W) 4, Atlanta (E) 1	2001	New York (E) 4, Seattle (W) 1
2000	New York (WC) 4, St. Louis (C) 1	2000	New York (E) 4, Seattle (WC) 2
1999	Atlanta (E) 4, New York (WC) 2	1999	New York (E) 4, Boston (WC) 1
1998	San Diego (W) 4, Atlanta (E) 2	1998	New York (E) 4, Cleveland (C) 2
1997	Florida (WC) 4, Atlanta (E) 2	1997	Cleveland (C) 4, Baltimore (E) 2
1996	Atlanta (E) 4, St. Louis (C) 3	1996	New York (E) 4, Baltimore (WC) 1
1995	Atlanta (E) 4, Cincinnati (C) 0	1995	Cleveland (C) 4, Seattle (W) 2
1994	Playoffs canceled due to labor dispute	1994	Playoffs canceled due to labor dispute
1993	Philadelphia (E) 4, Atlanta (W) 2	1993	Toronto (E) 4, Chicago (W) 2
1992	Atlanta (W) 4, Pittsburgh (E) 3	1992	Toronto (E) 4, Oakland (W) 2
1991	Atlanta (W) 4, Pittsburgh (E) 3	1991	Minnesota (W) 4, Toronto (E) 1
1990	Cincinnati (W) 4, Pittsburgh (E) 2	1990	Oakland (W) 4, Boston (E) 0
1989	San Francisco (W) 4, Chicago (E) 1	1989	Oakland (W) 4, Toronto (E) 1
1988	Los Angeles (W) 4, New York (E) 3	1988	Oakland (W) 4, Boston (E) 0
1987	St. Louis (E) 4, San Francisco (W) 3	1987	Minnesota (W) 4, Detroit (E) 1
1986	New York (E) 4, Houston (W) 2	1986	Boston (E) 4, California (W) 3
1985	St. Louis (E) 4, Los Angeles (W) 2	1985	Kansas City (W) 4, Toronto (E) 3
1984	San Diego (W) 3, Chicago (E) 2	1984	Detroit (E) 3, Kansas City (W) 0
1983	Philadelphia (E) 3, Los Angeles (W) 1	1983	Baltimore (E) 3, Chicago (W) 1
1982	St. Louis (E) 3, Atlanta (W) 0	1982	Milwaukee (E) 3, California (W) 2
1981	Los Angeles (W) 3, Montreal (E) 2	1981	New York (E) 3, Oakland (W) 0
1980	Philadelphia (E) 3, Houston (W) 2	1980	Kansas City (W) 3, New York (E) 0
1979	Pittsburgh (E) 3, Cincinnati (W) 0	1979	Baltimore (E) 3, California (W) 1
1978	Los Angeles (W) 3, Philadelphia (E) 1	1978	New York (E) 3, Kansas City (W) 1
1977	Los Angeles (W) 3, Philadelphia (E) 1	1977	New York (E) 3, Kansas City (W) 2
1976	Cincinnati (W) 3, Philadelphia (E) 0	1976	New York (E) 3, Kansas City (W) 2
1975	Cincinnati (W) 3, Pittsburgh (E) 0	1975	Boston (E) 3, Oakland (W) 0
1974	Los Angeles (W) 3, Pittsburgh (E) 1	1974	Oakland (W) 3, Baltimore (E) 1
1973	New York (E) 3, Cincinnati (W) 2	1973	Oakland (W) 3, Baltimore (E) 2
1972	Cincinnati (W) 3, Pittsburgh (E) 2	1972	Oakland (W) 3, Detroit (E) 2
1971	Pittsburgh (E) 3, San Francisco (W) 1	1971	Baltimore (E) 3, Oakland (W) 0
1970	Cincinnati (W) 3, Pittsburgh (E) 0	1970	Baltimore (E) 3, Minnesota (W) 0
1969	New York (E) 3, Atlanta (W) 0	1969	Baltimore (E) 3, Minnesota (W) 0

KEY: E=East; W=West; C=Central; WC=Wild Card

All-Star Game Results

DATE	WINNER	SCORE	SITE	DATE	WINNER	SCORE	SITE
7-10-07	American	5–4	AT&T Park, SF	7-11-67	National	2–1	Anaheim Stadium, Cal
7-11-06	American	3–2	PNC Park, Pitt	7-12-66	National	2–1	Busch Stadium, StL
7-12-05	American	7–5	Comerica Park, Det	7-13-65	National	6–5	Metropolitan Stadium, Min
7-13-04	American	9–4	Minute Maid Park, Hou	7-7-64	National	7–4	Shea Stadium, NY
7-15-03	American	7–6	U.S. Cellular Field, Chi	7-9-63	National	5–3	Municipal Stadium, Cle
7-9-02	Tie (11 inn)	7–7	Miller Park, Mil	7-30-62	American	9–4	Wrigley Field, Chi
7-10-01	American	4–1	Safeco Field, Sea	7-10-62	National	3–1	D.C. Stadium, Wash
7-11-00	American	6–3	Turner Field, Atl	7-31-61	Tie	1–1	Fenway Park, Bos
7-13-99	American	4–1	Fenway Park, Bos	7-11-61	National	5–4	Candlestick Park, SF
7-7-98	American	13–8	Coors Field, Col	7-13-60	National	6–0	Yankee Stadium, NY
7-8-97	American	3–1	Jacobs Field, Cle	7-11-60	National	5–3	Municipal Stadium, KC
7-9-96	National	6–0	Veterans Stadium, Phil	8-3-59	American	5–3	Memorial Coliseum, LA
7-11-95	National	3–2	The Ballpark in Arlington, Tex	7-7-59	National	5–4	Forbes Field, Pitt
7-12-94	National	8–7	Three Rivers Stadium, Pitt	7-8-58	American	4–3	Memorial Stadium, Bal
7-13-93	American	9–3	Camden Yards, Bal	7-9-57	American	6–5	Sportsman's Park, StL
7-14-92	American	13–6	Jack Murphy Stadium, SD	7-10-56	National	7–3	Griffith Stadium, Wash
7-9-91	American	4–2	SkyDome, Tor	7-12-55	National	6–5	County Stadium, Mil
7-10-90	American	2–0	Wrigley Field, Chi	7-13-54	American	11–9	Municipal Stadium, Cle
7-11-89	American	5–3	Anaheim Stadium, Cal	7-14-53	National	5–1	Crosley Field, Cin
7-12-88	American	2–1	Riverfront Stadium, Cin	7-8-52	National	3–2	Shibe Park, Phil
7-14-87	National	2–0	Oakland Coliseum, Oak	7-10-51	National	8–3	Briggs Stadium, Det
7-15-86	American	3–2	Astrodome, Hou	7-11-50	National	4–3	Comiskey Park, Chi
7-16-85	National	6–1	Metrodome, Min	7-12-49	American	11–7	Ebbets Field, Bklyn
7-10-84	National	3–1	Candlestick Park, SF	7-13-48	American	5–2	Sportsman's Park, StL
7-6-83	American	13–3	Comiskey Park, Chi	7-8-47	American	2–1	Wrigley Field, Chi
7-13-82	National	4–1	Olympic Stadium, Mon	7-9-46	American	12–0	Fenway Park, Bos
8-9-81	National	5–4	Municipal Stadium, Cle	1945	No game due to wartime travel restrictions		
7-8-80	National	4–2	Dodger Stadium, LA	7-11-44	National	7–1	Forbes Field, Pitt
7-17-79	National	7–6	Kingdome, Sea	7-13-43	American	5–3	Shibe Park, Phil
7-11-78	National	7–3	Jack Murphy Stadium, SD	7-6-42	American	3–1	Polo Grounds, NY
7-19-77	National	7–5	Yankee Stadium, NY	7-8-41	American	7–5	Briggs Stadium, Det
7-13-76	National	7–1	Veterans Stadium, Phil	7-10-40	National	4–0	Sportsman's Park, StL
7-15-75	National	6–3	County Stadium, Mil	7-11-39	American	3–1	Yankee Stadium, NY
7-23-74	National	7–2	Three Rivers Stadium, Pitt	7-6-38	National	4–1	Crosley Field, Cin
7-24-73	National	7–1	Royals Stadium, KC	7-7-37	American	8–3	Griffith Stadium, Wash
7-25-72	National	4–3	Atlanta Stadium, Atl	7-7-36	National	4–3	Braves Field, Bos
7-13-71	American	6–4	Tiger Stadium, Det	7-8-35	American	4–1	Municipal Stadium, Cle
7-14-70	National	5–4	Riverfront Stadium, Cin	7-10-34	American	9–7	Polo Grounds, NY
7-23-69	National	9–3	RFK Memorial Stadium, Wash	7-6-33	American	4–2	Comiskey Park, Chi
7-9-68	National	1–0	Astrodome, Hou				

All-Star Game: Most Valuable Players

Year	Player	League	Year	Player	League	Year	Player	League
2007	Ichiro Suzuki, Sea	AL	1991	Cal Ripken, Jr., Bal	AL	1975	Bill Madlock, Chi;	NL
2006	Michael Young, Tex	AL	1990	Julio Franco, Tex	AL		Jon Matlack, NY	NL
2005	Miguel Tejada, Bal	AL	1989	Bo Jackson, KC	AL	1974	Steve Garvey, LA	NL
2004	Alfonso Soriano, Tex	AL	1988	Terry Steinbach, Oak	AL	1973	Bobby Bonds, SF	NL
2003	Garret Anderson, Ana	AL	1987	Tim Raines, Mon	NL	1972	Joe Morgan, Cin	NL
2002	None selected		1986	Roger Clemens, Bos	AL	1971	Frank Robinson, Bal	AL
2001	Cal Ripken, Jr., Bal	AL	1985	LaMarr Hoyt, SD	NL	1970	Carl Yastrzemski, Bos	AL
2000	Derek Jeter, NY	AL	1984	Gary Carter, Mon	NL	1969	Willie McCovey, SF	NL
1999	Pedro Martinez, Bos	AL	1983	Fred Lynn, Cal	AL	1968	Willie Mays, SF	NL
1998	Roberto Alomar, Bal	AL	1982	Dave Concepcion, Cin	NL	1967	Tony Perez, Cin	NL
1997	Sandy Alomar, Cle	AL	1981	Gary Carter, Mon	NL	1966	Brooks Robinson, Bal	AL
1996	Mike Piazza, LA	NL	1980	Ken Griffey, Cin	NL	1965	Juan Marichal, SF	NL
1995	Jeff Conine, Fla	NL	1979	Dave Parker, Pitt	NL	1964	Johnny Callison, Phil	NL
1994	Fred McGriff, Atl	NL	1978	Steve Garvey, LA	NL	1963	Willie Mays, SF	NL
1993	Kirby Puckett, Min	AL	1977	Don Sutton, LA	NL	1962	Maury Wills, LA;	NL
1992	Ken Griffey Jr., Sea	AL	1976	George Foster, Cin	NL		Leon Wagner, LA	AL

Regular Season: Most Valuable Players

Philadelphia Phillies shortstop Jimmy Rollins was named the 2007 NL MVP.

BOB ROSATO

YEAR	PLAYER, TEAM	POSITION
2007	Jimmy Rollins, Phil	Shortstop
2006	Ryan Howard, Phil	First Base
2005	Albert Pujols, StL	First Base
2004	Barry Bonds, SF	Outfield
2003	Barry Bonds, SF	Outfield
2002	Barry Bonds, SF	Outfield
2001	Barry Bonds, SF	Outfield
2000	Jeff Kent, SF	Second Base
1999	Chipper Jones, Atl	Third Base
1998	Sammy Sosa, Chi	Outfield
1997	Larry Walker, Col	Outfield
1996	Ken Caminiti, SD	Third Base
1995	Barry Larkin, Cin	Shortstop
1994	Jeff Bagwell, Hou	First Base
1993	Barry Bonds, SF	Outfield
1992	Barry Bonds, Pitt	Outfield
1991	Terry Pendleton, Atl	Third Base
1990	Barry Bonds, Pitt	Outfield
1989	Kevin Mitchell, SF	Outfield
1988	Kirk Gibson, LA	Outfield
1987	Andre Dawson, Chi	Outfield
1986	Mike Schmidt, Phil	Third Base
1985	Willie McGee, StL	Outfield
1984	Ryne Sandberg, Chi	Second Base
1983	Dale Murphy, Atl	Outfield
1982	Dale Murphy, Atl	Outfield
1981	Mike Schmidt, Phil	Third Base
1980	Mike Schmidt, Phil	Third Base
1979	Keith Hernandez, StL;	First Base
	Willie Stargell, Pitt	First Base
1978	Dave Parker, Pitt	Outfield
1977	George Foster, Cin	Outfield
1976	Joe Morgan, Cin	Second Base
1975	Joe Morgan, Cin	Second Base
1974	Steve Garvey, LA	First Base
1973	Pete Rose, Cin	Outfield
1972	Johnny Bench, Cin	Catcher
1971	Joe Torre, StL	Third Base
1970	Johnny Bench, Cin	Catcher
1969	Willie McCovey, SF	First Base
1968	Bob Gibson, StL	Pitcher
1967	Orlando Cepeda, StL	First Base
1966	Roberto Clemente, Pitt	Outfield
1965	Willie Mays, SF	Outfield
1964	Ken Boyer, StL	Third Base
1963	Sandy Koufax, LA	Pitcher
1962	Maury Wills, LA	Shortstop
1961	Frank Robinson, Cin	Outfield
1960	Dick Groat, Pitt	Shortstop
1959	Ernie Banks, Chi	Shortstop

YEAR	PLAYER, TEAM	POSITION
1958	Ernie Banks, Chi	Shortstop
1957	Hank Aaron, Mil	Outfield
1956	Don Newcombe, Bklyn	Pitcher
1955	Roy Campanella, Bklyn	Catcher
1954	Willie Mays, NY	Outfield
1953	Roy Campanella, Bklyn	Catcher
1952	Hank Sauer, Chi	Outfield
1951	Roy Campanella, Bklyn	Catcher
1950	Jim Konstanty, Phil	Pitcher
1949	Jackie Robinson, Bklyn	Second Base
1948	Stan Musial, StL	Outfield
1947	Bob Elliott, Bos	Third Base
1946	Stan Musial, StL	First Base, Outfield
1945	Phil Cavarretta, Chi	First Base
1944	Marty Marion, StL	Shortstop
1943	Stan Musial, StL	Outfield
1942	Mort Cooper, StL	Pitcher
1941	Dolph Camilli, Bklyn	First Base
1940	Frank McCormick, Cin	First Base
1939	Bucky Walters, Cin	Pitcher
1938	Ernie Lombardi, Cin	Catcher
1937	Joe Medwick, StL	Outfield
1936	Carl Hubbell, NY	Pitcher
1935	Gabby Hartnett, Chi	Catcher
1934	Dizzy Dean, StL	Pitcher
1933	Carl Hubbell, NY	Pitcher
1932	Chuck Klein, Phil	Outfield
1931	Frankie Frisch, StL	Second Base
1930	No selection	
1929	Rogers Hornsby, Chi	Second Base
1928	Jim Bottomley, StL	First Base
1927	Paul Waner, Pitt	Outfield
1926	Bob O'Farrell, StL	Catcher
1925	Rogers Hornsby, StL	Second Base, Manager
1924	Dazzy Vance, Bklyn	Pitcher
1915–23	No selections	
1914	Johnny Evers, Bos	Second Base
1913	Jake Daubert, Bklyn	First Base
1912	Larry Doyle, NY	Second Base
1911	Wildfire Schulte, Chi	Outfield

Regular Season: Most Valuable Players (cont.)

YEAR	PLAYER, TEAM	POSITION	YEAR	PLAYER, TEAM	POSITION
2007	Alex Rodriguez, NY	Third Base	1957	Mickey Mantle, NY	Outfield
2006	Justin Morneau, Min	First Base	1956	Mickey Mantle, NY	Outfield
2005	Alex Rodriguez, NY	Third Base	1955	Yogi Berra, NY	Catcher
2004	Vladimir Guerrero, Ana	Outfield	1954	Yogi Berra, NY	Catcher
2003	Alex Rodriguez, Tex	Shortstop	1953	Al Rosen, Cle	Third Base
2002	Miguel Tejada, Oak	Shortstop	1952	Bobby Shantz, Phil	Pitcher
2001	Ichiro Suzuki, Sea	Outfield	1951	Yogi Berra, NY	Catcher
2000	Jason Giambi, Oak	First Base	1950	Phil Rizzuto, NY	Shortstop
1999	Ivan Rodriguez, Tex	Catcher	1949	Ted Williams, Bos	Outfield
1998	Juan Gonzalez, Tex	Outfield	1948	Lou Boudreau, Cle	Shortstop
1997	Ken Griffey, Jr., Sea	Outfield	1947	Joe DiMaggio, NY	Outfield
1996	Juan Gonzalez, Tex	Outfield	1946	Ted Williams, Bos	Outfield
1995	Mo Vaughn, Bos	First Base	1945	Hal Newhouser, Det	Pitcher
1994	Frank Thomas, Chi	First Base	1944	Hal Newhouser, Det	Pitcher
1993	Frank Thomas, Chi	First Base	1943	Spud Chandler, NY	Pitcher
1992	Dennis Eckersley, Oak	Pitcher	1942	Joe Gordon, NY	Second Base
1991	Cal Ripken, Jr., Bal	Shortstop	1941	Joe DiMaggio, NY	Outfield
1990	Rickey Henderson, Oak	Outfield	1940	Hank Greenberg, Det	Outfield
1989	Robin Yount, Mil	Outfield	1939	Joe DiMaggio, NY	Outfield
1988	Jose Canseco, Oak	Outfield	1938	Jimmie Foxx, Bos	First Base
1987	George Bell, Tor	Outfield	1937	Charlie Gehringer, Det	Second Base
1986	Roger Clemens, Bos	Pitcher	1936	Lou Gehrig, NY	First Base
1985	Don Mattingly, NY	First Base	1935	Hank Greenberg, Det	First Base
1984	Willie Hernandez, Det	Pitcher	1934	Mickey Cochrane, Det	Catcher
1983	Cal Ripken, Jr., Bal	Shortstop	1933	Jimmie Foxx, Phil	First Base
1982	Robin Yount, Mil	Shortstop	1932	Jimmie Foxx, Phil	First Base
1981	Rollie Fingers, Mil	Pitcher	1931	Lefty Grove, Phil	Pitcher
1980	George Brett, KC	Third Base	1930	No selection	
1979	Don Baylor, Cal	Outfield, DH	1929	No selection	
1978	Jim Rice, Bos	Outfield, DH	1928	Mickey Cochrane, Phil	Catcher
1977	Rod Carew, Min	First Base	1927	Lou Gehrig, NY	First Base
1976	Thurman Munson, NY	Catcher	1926	George Burns, Cle	First Base
1975	Fred Lynn, Bos	Outfield	1925	Roger Peckinpaugh, Wash	Shortstop
1974	Jeff Burroughs, Tex	Outfield	1924	Walter Johnson, Wash	Pitcher
1973	Reggie Jackson, Oak	Outfield	1923	Babe Ruth, NY	Outfield
1972	Dick Allen, Chi	First Base	1922	George Sisler, StL	First Base
1971	Vida Blue, Oak	Pitcher	1915–21	No selections	
1970	Boog Powell, Bal	First Base	1914	Eddie Collins, Phil	Second Base
1969	Harmon Killebrew, Min	Third Base, First Base	1913	Walter Johnson, Wash	Pitcher
1968	Denny McLain, Det	Pitcher	1912	Tris Speaker, Bos	Outfield
1967	Carl Yastrzemski, Bos	Outfield	1911	Ty Cobb, Det	Outfield
1966	Frank Robinson, Bal	Outfield			
1965	Zoilo Versalles, Min	Shortstop			
1964	Brooks Robinson, Bal	Third Base			
1963	Elston Howard, NY	Catcher			
1962	Mickey Mantle, NY	Outfield			
1961	Roger Maris, NY	Outfield			
1960	Roger Maris, NY	Outfield			
1959	Nellie Fox, Chi	Second Base			
1958	Jackie Jensen, Bos	Outfield			

1973 MVP winner
Reggie Jackson

Regular Season: Rookies of the Year

NATIONAL LEAGUE

2007	Ryan Braun, Mil (3B)	1986	Todd Worrell, StL (P)	1966	Tommy Helms, Cin (2B)
2006	Hanley Ramirez, Fla (SS)	1985	Vince Coleman, StL (OF)	1965	Jim Lefebvre, LA (2B)
2005	Ryan Howard, Phi (1B)	1984	Dwight Gooden, NY (P)	1964	Dick Allen, Phil (3B)
2004	Jason Bay, Pitt (OF)	1983	Darryl Strawberry, NY (OF)	1963	Pete Rose, Cin (2B)
2003	Dontrelle Willis, Fla (P)	1982	Steve Sax, LA (2B)	1962	Ken Hubbs, Chi (2B)
2002	Jason Jennings, Col (P)	1981	Fernando Valenzuela, LA (P)	1961	Billy Williams, Chi (OF)
2001	Albert Pujols, StL (OF)	1980	Steve Howe, LA (P)	1960	Frank Howard, LA (OF)
2000	Rafael Furcal, Atl (SS)	1979	Rick Sutcliffe, LA (P)	1959	Willie McCovey, SF (1B)
1999	Scott Williamson, Cin (P)	1978	Bob Horner, Atl (3B)	1958	Orlando Cepeda, SF (1B)
1998	Kerry Wood, Chi (P)	1977	Andre Dawson, Mon (OF)	1957	Jack Sanford, Phil (P)
1997	Scott Rolen, Phil (3B)	1976	Pat Zachry, Cin (P);	1956	Frank Robinson, Cin (OF)
1996	Todd Hollandsworth, LA (OF)		Butch Metzger, SD (P)	1955	Bill Virdon, StL (OF)
1995	Hideo Nomo, LA (P)	1975	John Montefusco, SF (P)	1954	Wally Moon, StL (OF)
1994	Raul Mondesi, LA (OF)	1974	Bake McBride, StL (OF)	1953	Junior Gilliam, Bklyn (2B)
1993	Mike Piazza, LA (C)	1973	Gary Matthews, SF (OF)	1952	Joe Black, Bklyn (P)
1992	Eric Karros, LA (1B)	1972	Jon Matlack, NY (P)	1951	Willie Mays, NY (OF)
1991	Jeff Bagwell, Hou (3B)	1971	Earl Williams, Atl (C)	1950	Sam Jethroe, Bos (OF)
1990	David Justice, Atl (OF)	1970	Carl Morton, Mon (P)	1949	Don Newcombe, Bklyn (P)
1989	Jerome Walton, Chi (OF)	1969	Ted Sizemore, LA (2B)	1948*	Alvin Dark, Bos (SS)
1988	Chris Sabo, Cin (3B)	1968	Johnny Bench, Cin (C)	1947*	Jackie Robinson, Bklyn (1B)
1987	Benito Santiago, SD (C)	1967	Tom Seaver, NY (P)		

AMERICAN LEAGUE

2007	Dustin Pedroia, Bos (2B)	1987	Mark McGwire, Oak (1B)	1968	Stan Bahnsen, NY (P)
2006	Justin Verlander, Det (P)	1986	Jose Canseco, Oak (OF)	1967	Rod Carew, Min (2B)
2005	Huston Street, Oak (P)	1985	Ozzie Guillen, Chi (SS)	1966	Tommie Agee, Chi (OF)
2004	Bobby Crosby, Oak (SS)	1984	Alvin Davis, Sea (1B)	1965	Curt Blefary, Bal (OF)
2003	Angel Berroa, KC (SS)	1983	Ron Kittle, Chi (OF)	1964	Tony Oliva, Min (OF)
2002	Eric Hinske, Tor (3B)	1982	Cal Ripken, Jr., Bal (SS)	1963	Gary Peters, Chi (P)
2001	Ichiro Suzuki, Sea (OF)	1981	Dave Righetti, NY (P)	1962	Tom Tresh, NY (SS)
2000	Kazuhiro Sasaki, Sea (P)	1980	Joe Charboneau, Cle (OF)	1961	Don Schwall, Bos (P)
1999	Carlos Beltran, KC (OF)	1979	Alfredo Griffin, Tor (SS);	1960	Ron Hansen, Bal (SS)
1998	Ben Grieve, Oak (OF)		John Castino, Min (3B)	1959	Bob Allison, Wash (OF)
1997	Nomar Garciaparra, Bos (SS)	1978	Lou Whitaker, Det (2B)	1958	Albie Pearson, Wash (OF)
1996	Derek Jeter, NY (SS)	1977	Eddie Murray, Bal (DH)	1957	Tony Kubek, NY (OF, SS)
1995	Marty Cordova, Min (OF)	1976	Mark Fidrych, Det (P)	1956	Luis Aparicio, Chi (SS)
1994	Bob Hamelin, KC (DH)	1975	Fred Lynn, Bos (OF)	1955	Herb Score, Cle (P)
1993	Tim Salmon, Cal (OF)	1974	Mike Hargrove, Tex (1B)	1954	Bob Grim, NY (P)
1992	Pat Listach, Mil (SS)	1973	Al Bumbry, Bal (OF)	1953	Harvey Kuenn, Det (SS)
1991	Chuck Knoblauch, Min (2B)	1972	Carlton Fisk, Bos (C)	1952	Harry Byrd, Phil (P)
1990	Sandy Alomar, Jr., Cle (C)	1971	Chris Chambliss, Cle (1B)	1951	Gil McDougald, NY (3B)
1989	Gregg Olson, Bal (P)	1970	Thurman Munson, NY (C)	1950	Walt Dropo, Bos (1B)
1988	Walt Weiss, Oak (SS)	1969	Lou Piniella, KC (OF)	1949	Roy Sievers, StL (OF)

* One selection for both leagues

Regular Season: Cy Young Award Winners

YEAR	NATIONAL LEAGUE PITCHER	W–L	SV	ERA
2007	Jake Peavy, SD	19–6	0	2.54
2006	Brandon Webb, Ari	16–8	0	3.10
2005	Chris Carpenter, StL	21–5	0	2.83
2004	Roger Clemens, Hou	18–4	0	2.98
2003	Eric Gagne, LA	2–3	55	1.20
2002	Randy Johnson, Ari	24–5	0	2.32
2001	Randy Johnson, Ari	21–6	0	2.49
2000	Randy Johnson, Ari	19–7	0	2.64
1999	Randy Johnson, Ari	17–9	0	2.48
1998	Tom Glavine, Atl	20–6	0	2.47
1997	Pedro Martinez, Mon	17–8	0	1.90
1996	John Smoltz, Atl	24–8	0	2.94
1995	Greg Maddux, Atl	19–2	0	1.63
1994	Greg Maddux, Atl	16–6	0	1.56
1993	Greg Maddux, Atl	20–10	0	2.36
1992	Greg Maddux, Chi	20–11	0	2.18
1991	Tom Glavine, Atl	20–11	0	2.55
1990	Doug Drabek, Pitt	22–6	0	2.76
1989	Mark Davis, SD	4–3	44	1.85
1988	Orel Hershiser, LA	23–8	1	2.26
1987	Steve Bedrosian, Phil	5–3	40	2.83
1986	Mike Scott, Hou	18–10	0	2.22
1985	Dwight Gooden, NY	24–4	0	1.53
1984*	Rick Sutcliffe, Chi	16–1	0	2.69
1983	John Denny, Phil	19–6	0	2.37
1982	Steve Carlton, Phil	23–11	0	3.10
1981	Fernando Valenzuela, LA	13–7	0	2.48
1980	Steve Carlton, Phil	24–9	0	2.34
1979	Bruce Sutter, Chi	6–6	37	2.23
1978	Gaylord Perry, SD	21–6	0	2.72
1977	Steve Carlton, Phil	23–10	0	2.64
1976	Randy Jones, SD	22–14	0	2.74
1975	Tom Seaver, NY	22–9	0	2.38
1974	Mike Marshall, LA	15–12	21	2.42
1973	Tom Seaver, NY	19–10	0	2.08
1972	Steve Carlton, Phil	27–10	0	1.97
1971	Ferguson Jenkins, Chi	24–13	0	2.77
1970	Bob Gibson, StL	23–7	0	3.12
1969	Tom Seaver, NY	25–7	0	2.21
1968**	Bob Gibson, StL	22–9	0	1.12
1967	Mike McCormick, SF	22–10	0	2.85
1966	Sandy Koufax, LA (NL)	27–9	0	1.73
1965	Sandy Koufax, LA (NL)	26–8	2	2.04
1964	Dean Chance, LA (AL)	20–9	4	1.65
1963**	Sandy Koufax, LA (NL)	25–5	0	1.88
1962	Don Drysdale, LA (NL)	25–9	1	2.83
1961	Whitey Ford, NY (AL)	25–4	0	3.21
1960	Vernon Law, Pitt (NL)	20–9	0	3.08
1959	Early Wynn, Chi (AL)	22–10	0	3.17
1958	Bob Turley, NY (AL)	21–7	1	2.97
1957	Warren Spahn, Mil (NL)	21–11	3	2.69
1956**	Don Newcombe, Bklyn (NL)	27–7	0	3.06

YEAR	AMERICAN LEAGUE PITCHER	W–L	SV	ERA
2007	C.C. Sabathia, Cle	19–7	0	3.21
2006	Johan Santana, Min	19–6	0	2.77
2005	Bartolo Colon, LA	21–8	0	3.48
2004	Johan Santana, Min	20–6	0	2.61
2003	Roy Halladay, Tor	22–7	0	3.25
2002	Barry Zito, Oak	23–5	0	2.75
2001	Roger Clemens, NY	20–3	0	3.51
2000	Pedro Martinez, Bos	18–6	0	1.74
1999	Pedro Martinez, Bos	23–4	0	1.55
1998	Roger Clemens, Tor	20–6	0	2.65
1997	Roger Clemens, Tor	21–7	0	2.05
1996	Pat Hentgen, Tor	20–10	0	3.22
1995	Randy Johnson, Sea	18–2	0	2.48
1994	David Cone, KC	16–5	0	2.94
1993	Jack McDowell, Chi	22–10	0	3.37
1992**	Dennis Eckersley, Oak	7–1	51	1.91
1991	Roger Clemens, Bos	18–10	0	2.62
1990	Bob Welch, Oak	27–6	0	2.95
1989	Bret Saberhagen, KC	23–6	0	2.16
1988	Frank Viola, Min	24–7	0	2.64
1987	Roger Clemens, Bos	20–9	0	2.97
1986**	Roger Clemens, Bos	24–4	0	2.48
1985	Bret Saberhagen, KC	20–6	0	2.87
1984**	Willie Hernandez, Det	9–3	32	1.92
1983	LaMarr Hoyt, Chi	24–10	0	3.66
1982	Pete Vuckovich, Mil	18–6	0	3.34
1981**	Rollie Fingers, Mil	6–3	28	1.04
1980	Steve Stone, Bal	25–7	0	3.23
1979	Mike Flanagan, Bal	23–9	0	3.08
1978	Ron Guidry, NY	25–3	0	1.74
1977	Sparky Lyle, NY	13–5	26	2.17
1976	Jim Palmer, Bal	22–13	0	2.51
1975	Jim Palmer, Bal	23–11	1	2.09
1974	Catfish Hunter, Oak	25–12	0	2.49
1973	Jim Palmer, Bal	22–9	1	2.40
1972	Gaylord Perry, Cle	24–16	1	1.92
1971**	Vida Blue, Oak	24–8	0	1.82
1970	Jim Perry, Min	24–12	0	3.03
1969	Denny McLain, Det;	24–9	0	2.80
	Mike Cuellar, Bal	23–11	0	2.38
1968**	Denny McLain, Det	31–6	0	1.96
1967	Jim Lonborg, Bos	22–9	0	3.16

C.C. Sabathia

* NL Games only. Sutcliffe pitched 15 games with the Cleveland Indians before being traded to the Chicago Cubs.
** Won the MVP and Cy Young Awards in the same season.
Note: One award was presented to both leagues from 1956–66.

AL TIELEMANS

Regular Season: Career Individual Batting

GAMES

Pete Rose	3,562
Carl Yastrzemski	3,308
Hank Aaron	3,298
Rickey Henderson	3,081
Ty Cobb	3,035
Eddie Murray	3,026
Stan Musial	3,026
Cal Ripken Jr.	3,001
Willie Mays	2,992
Barry Bonds	2,986
Dave Winfield	2,973
Rusty Staub	2,951
Brooks Robinson	2,896
Robin Yount	2,856
Al Kaline	2,834
Rafael Palmeiro	2,831
Harold Baines	2,830
Eddie Collins	2,826
Reggie Jackson	2,820
Frank Robinson	2,808
Honus Wagner	2,792

AT BATS

Pete Rose	14,053
Hank Aaron	12,364
Carl Yastrzemski	11,988
Cal Ripken Jr.	11,551
Ty Cobb	11,429
Eddie Murray	11,336
Robin Yount	11,008
Dave Winfield	11,003
Stan Musial	10,972
Rickey Henderson	10,961
Willie Mays	10,881
Craig Biggio	10,876
Paul Molitor	10,835
Brooks Robinson	10,654
Rafael Palmeiro	10,472
Honus Wagner	10,430
George Brett	10,349
Lou Brock	10,332
Cap Anson	10,278
Luis Aparicio	10,230
Tris Speaker	10,195

HOME RUNS

Barry Bonds	762
Hank Aaron	755
Babe Ruth	714
Willie Mays	660
Sammy Sosa	609
Ken Griffey Jr.*	593
Frank Robinson	586
Mark McGwire	583
Harmon Killebrew	573
Rafael Palmeiro	569
Reggie Jackson	563
Mike Schmidt	548
Mickey Mantle	536
Jimmie Foxx	534
Willie McCovey	521
Ted Williams	521
Eddie Mathews	512
Ernie Banks	512
Mel Ott	511
Eddie Murray	504

RUNS BATTED IN

Hank Aaron	2,297
Babe Ruth	2,213
Cap Anson	2,076
Barry Bonds	1,996
Lou Gehrig	1,995
Stan Musial	1,951
Ty Cobb	1,938
Jimmie Foxx	1,922
Eddie Murray	1,917
Willie Mays	1,903
Mel Ott	1,860
Carl Yastrzemski	1,844
Ted Williams	1,839
Rafael Palmeiro	1,835
Dave Winfield	1,833
Al Simmons	1,827
Frank Robinson	1,812
Honus Wagner	1,732
Reggie Jackson	1,702
Cal Ripken Jr.	1,695

SLUGGING PERCENTAGE**

Babe Ruth	.690
Ted Williams	.634
Lou Gehrig	.632
Jimmie Foxx	.609
Barry Bonds	.607
Hank Greenberg	.605
Manny Ramirez*	.593
Mark McGwire	.588
Joe DiMaggio	.579
Vladimir Guerrero*	.579
Alex Rodriguez*	.578
Rogers Hornsby	.577
Jim Thome*	.565
Larry Walker	.565
Albert Belle	.564
Johnny Mize	.562
Juan Gonzalez*	.561
Frank Thomas*	.561
Carlos Delgado*	.549
Stan Musial	.559
Ken Griffey Jr.*	.553

STOLEN BASES

Rickey Henderson	1,406
Lou Brock	938
Billy Hamilton	912
Ty Cobb	892
Tim Raines	808
Vince Coleman	752
Eddie Collins	745
Max Carey	738
Honus Wagner	722
Joe Morgan	689
Willie Wilson	668
Bert Campaneris	649
Otis Nixon	620
Kenny Lofton*	622
George Davis	616
Tom Brown	615
Dummy Hoy	594
Maury Wills	586
George Van Haltren	583
Ozzie Smith	580
Hugh Duffy	574

ON-BASE PERCENTAGE**

Ted Williams	.482
Babe Ruth	.469
Barry Bonds	.444
Lou Gehrig	.442
Todd Helton*	.430
Jimmie Foxx	.425
Ty Cobb	.424
Rogers Hornsby	.424
Frank Thomas*	.421
Mickey Mantle	.422
Edgar Martinez	.418
Stan Musial	.417
Tris Speaker	.417
Wade Boggs	.415
Jason Giambi*	.411
Bobby Abreu*	.408
Manny Ramirez*	.409
Mel Ott	.410
Mickey Cochrane	.409
Hank Greenberg	.409

TOTAL BASES

Hank Aaron	6,856
Stan Musial	6,134
Willie Mays	6,066
Barry Bonds	5,976
Ty Cobb	5,859
Babe Ruth	5,793
Pete Rose	5,752
Carl Yastrzemski	5,539
Eddie Murray	5,397
Rafael Palmeiro	5,388
Frank Robinson	5,373
Dave Winfield	5,221
Cal Ripken Jr.	5,168
Tris Speaker	5,101
Lou Gehrig	5,060
George Brett	5,044
Mel Ott	5,041
Jimmie Foxx	4,956
Ted Williams	4,884
Honus Wagner	4,862

STRIKEOUTS

Reggie Jackson	2,597
Sammy Sosa	2,194
Jim Thome*	2,043
Andres Galarraga	2,003
Jose Canseco	1,942
Willie Stargell	1,936
Mike Schmidt	1,883
Fred McGriff	1,882
Tony Perez	1,867
Dave Kingman	1,816
Bobby Bonds	1,757
Craig Biggio	1,753
Dale Murphy	1,748
Lou Brock	1,730
Mickey Mantle	1,710
Harmon Killebrew	1,699
Chili Davis	1,698
Dwight Evans	1,697
Rickey Henderson	1,694
Dave Winfield	1,686

All stats through 2007 season.
* On a 40-man roster on Opening Day 2008   ** Minimum 5,000 at bats

Regular Season: Career Individual Batting (cont.)

All-time hits king
Pete Rose

DOUBLES

Tris Speaker	792
Pete Rose	746
Stan Musial	725
Ty Cobb	723
George Brett	665
Craig Biggio	668
Nap Lajoie	657
Carl Yastrzemski	646
Honus Wagner	640
Hank Aaron	624
Paul Molitor	605
Paul Waner	605
Cal Ripken Jr.	603
Barry Bonds	601
Rafael Palmeiro	585
Robin Yount	583
Cap Anson	581
Wade Boggs	578
Charlie Gehringer	574
Eddie Murray	560

TRIPLES

Sam Crawford	309
Ty Cobb	297
Honus Wagner	252
Jake Beckley	243
Roger Connor	233
Tris Speaker	222
Fred Clarke	220
Dan Brouthers	205
Joe Kelley	194
Paul Waner	191
Bid McPhee	188
Eddie Collins	187
Ed Delahanty	185
Sam Rice	184
Jesse Burkett	182
Ed Konetchy	182
Edd Roush	182
Buck Ewing	178
Rabbit Maranville	177
Stan Musial	177

HITS

Pete Rose	4,256
Ty Cobb	4,191
Hank Aaron	3,771
Stan Musial	3,630
Tris Speaker	3,514
Carl Yastrzemski	3,419
Cap Anson	3,418
Honus Wagner	3,415
Paul Molitor	3,319
Eddie Collins	3,315
Willie Mays	3,283
Eddie Murray	3,255
Nap Lajoie	3,242
Cal Ripken Jr.	3,184
George Brett	3,154
Paul Waner	3,152
Robin Yount	3,142
Tony Gwynn	3,141
Dave Winfield	3,110
Rickey Henderson	3,055

BATTING AVERAGE**

Ty Cobb	.367
Rogers Hornsby	.358
Ed Delahanty	.346
Tris Speaker	.345
Ted Williams	.344
Billy Hamilton	.344
Dan Brouthers	.342
Harry Heilmann	.342
Babe Ruth	.342
Willie Keeler	.341
Bill Terry	.341
Lou Gehrig	.340
George Sisler	.340
Jesse Burkett	.338
Tony Gwynn	.338
Nap Lajoie	.338
Al Simmons	.334
Cap Anson	.333
Eddie Collins	.333
Paul Waner	.333

RUNS

Rickey Henderson	2,295
Ty Cobb	2,245
Barry Bonds	2,227
Hank Aaron	2,174
Babe Ruth	2,174
Pete Rose	2,165
Willie Mays	2,062
Cap Anson	1,996
Stan Musial	1,949
Lou Gehrig	1,888
Tris Speaker	1,882
Mel Ott	1,859
Frank Robinson	1,829
Eddie Collins	1,821
Carl Yastrzemski	1,816
Ted Williams	1,798
Paul Molitor	1,782
Craig Biggio	1,776
Charlie Gehringer	1,774
Jimmie Foxx	1,751
Honus Wagner	1,736

BASES ON BALLS

Barry Bonds	2,558
Rickey Henderson	2,190
Babe Ruth	2,062
Ted Williams	2,019
Joe Morgan	1,865
Carl Yastrzemski	1,845
Mickey Mantle	1,733
Mel Ott	1,708
Frank Thomas*	1,628
Eddie Yost	1,614
Darrell Evans	1,605
Stan Musial	1,599
Pete Rose	1,566
Harmon Killebrew	1,559
Lou Gehrig	1,508
Mike Schmidt	1,507
Eddie Collins	1,499
Willie Mays	1,464
Jimmie Foxx	1,452
Eddie Mathews	1,444

All stats through 2007 season.
* On a 40-man roster on Opening Day 2008   ** Minimum 5,000 at bats

HEINZ KLUETMEIER

Regular Season: Career Individual Pitching

GAMES	
Jesse Orosco	1,252
Mike Stanton	1,178
John Franco	1,119
Dennis Eckersley	1,071
Hoyt Wilhelm	1,070
Dan Plesac	1,064
Kent Tekulve	1,050
Jose Mesa	1,022
Lee Smith	1,022
Mike Timlin*	1,011
Mike Jackson	1,005
Goose Gossage	1,002
Roberto Hernandez	1,010
Lindy McDaniel	987
Rollie Fingers	944
Todd Jones*	937
Gene Garber	931
Cy Young	906
Sparky Lyle	899
Jim Kaat	898

LOSSES	
Cy Young	316
Pud Galvin	310
Nolan Ryan	292
Walter Johnson	279
Phil Niekro	274
Gaylord Perry	265
Don Sutton	256
Jack Powell	254
Eppa Rixey	251
Bert Blyleven	250
Bobby Mathews	248
Robin Roberts	245
Warren Spahn	245
Steve Carlton	244
Early Wynn	244
Jim Kaat	237
Frank Tanana	236
Gus Weyhing	232
Tommy John	231
Bob Friend	230

WINNING PERCENTAGE	
Al Spalding	.796
Spud Chandler	.717
Pedro Martinez*	.692
Whitey Ford	.690
Dave Foutz	.690
Bob Caruthers	.688
Don Gullett	.686
Lefty Grove	.680
Johan Santana*	.679
Joe Wood	.672
Babe Ruth	.671
Roy Halladay*	.669
Jay Hughes	.669
Bill Hoffer	.667
Vic Raschi	.667
Larry Corcoran	.665
Roy Oswalt*	.665
Christy Mathewson	.665
Sam Leever	.660
Tim Hudson*	.659

INNINGS PITCHED	
Cy Young	7,356.0
Jim Galvin	6,003.1
Walter Johnson	5,914.2
Phil Niekro	5,404.1
Nolan Ryan	5,386.0
Gaylord Perry	5,350.1
Don Sutton	5,282.1
Warren Spahn	5,243.2
Steve Carlton	5,217.1
Pete Alexander	5,190.0
Kid Nichols	5,056.1
Tim Keefe	5,047.2
Bert Blyleven	4,970.0
Bobby Mathews	4,956.0
Roger Clemens	4,916.2
Greg Maddux*	4,814.1
Mickey Welch	4,802.0
Tom Seaver	4,782.2
Christy Mathewson	4,780.2
Tommy John	4,710.1

San Diego Padres starting pitcher Greg Maddux

WINS	
Cy Young	511
Walter Johnson	417
Pete Alexander	373
Christy Mathewson	373
Pud Galvin	364
Warren Spahn	363
Kid Nichols	361
Roger Clemens	354
Greg Maddux*	347
Tim Keefe	342
Steve Carlton	329
John Clarkson	328
Eddie Plank	326
Nolan Ryan	324
Don Sutton	324
Phil Niekro	318
Gaylord Perry	314
Tom Seaver	311
Charley Radbourn	309
Mickey Welch	307

All stats through 2007 season.

Note: Career pitching stats are based on a minimum of 100 decisions and 1,000 innings pitched.

* On a 40-man roster on Opening Day 2008

Regular Season: Career Individual Pitching (cont.)

SAVES		SHUTOUTS		STRIKEOUTS	
Trevor Hoffman*	524	Walter Johnson	110	Nolan Ryan	5,714
Lee Smith	478	Pete Alexander	90	Roger Clemens	4,672
Mariano Rivera*	443	Christy Mathewson	79	Randy Johnson*	4,616
John Franco	424	Cy Young	76	Steve Carlton	4,136
Dennis Eckersley	379	Eddie Plank	69	Bert Blyleven	3,701
Jeff Reardon	367	Warren Spahn	63	Tom Seaver	3,640
Billy Wagner*	358	Nolan Ryan	61	Don Sutton	3,574
Randy Myers	347	Tom Seaver	61	Gaylord Perry	3,534
Rollie Fingers	341	Bert Blyleven	60	Walter Johnson	3,509
John Wetteland	330	Don Sutton	58	Phil Niekro	3,342
Roberto Hernandez	326	Pud Galvin	57	Greg Maddux*	3,273
Troy Percival*	324	Ed Walsh	57	Ferguson Jenkins	3,192
Jose Mesa	321	Bob Gibson	56	Bob Gibson	3,117
Rick Aguilera	318	Three Finger Brown	55	Curt Schilling*	3,016
Robb Nen	314	Steve Carlton	55	Pedro Martinez*	3,030
Tom Henke	311	Jim Palmer	53	John Smoltz*	2,975
Goose Gossage	310	Gaylord Perry	53	Jim Bunning	2,855
Jeff Montgomery	304	Juan Marichal	52	Mickey Lolich	2,832
Doug Jones	303	Rube Waddell	50	Cy Young	2,803
Todd Jones*	301	Vic Willis	50	Frank Tanana	2,773

EARNED RUN AVERAGE		COMPLETE GAMES		BASES ON BALLS	
Ed Walsh	1.82	Cy Young	749	Nolan Ryan	2,795
Addie Joss	1.89	Pud Galvin	646	Steve Carlton	1,833
Jack Pfiester	2.02	Tim Keefe	554	Phil Niekro	1,809
Joe Wood	2.03	Walter Johnson	531	Early Wynn	1,775
Jim Devlin	2.05	Kid Nichols	531	Bob Feller	1,764
Mordecai Brown	2.06	Bobby Mathews	525	Bobo Newsom	1,732
John Ward	2.10	Mickey Welch	525	Amos Rusie	1,707
Christy Matthewson	2.13	Charley Radbourn	489	Charlie Hough	1,665
Al Spalding	2.14	John Clarkson	485	Roger Clemens	1,580
Rube Waddell	2.16	Tony Mullane	468	Gus Weyhing	1,566
Walter Johnson	2.17	Jim McCormick	466	Red Ruffing	1,541
Orval Overall	2.23	Gus Weyhing	448	Tom Glavine*	1,463
Jake Weimer	2.23	Pete Alexander	437	Bump Hadley	1,442
Ed Reulbach	2.28	Christy Mathewson	434	Warren Spahn	1,434
Babe Ruth	2.28	Jack Powell	422	Earl Whitehill	1,431
Will White	2.28	Eddie Plank	410	Randy Johnson*	1,422
Jim Scott	2.30	Will White	394	Tony Mullane	1,408
Tommy Bond	2.31	Amos Rusie	393	Sad Sam Jones	1,396
Reb Russell	2.33	Vic Willis	388	Jack Morris	1,390
Andy Coakley	2.35	Tommy Bond	386	Tom Seaver	1,390

Regular Season: Individual Batting, Single Season

HITS		BATTING AVERAGE		DOUBLES	
Ichiro Suzuki, 2004	262	Hugh Duffy, 1894	.440	Earl Webb, 1931	67
George Sisler, 1920	257	Tip O'Neill, 1887	.435	George Burns, 1926	64
Lefty O'Doul, 1929	254	Ross Barnes, 1876	.429	Joe Medwick, 1936	64
Bill Terry, 1930	254	Nap Lajoie, 1901	.427	Hank Greenberg, 1934	63
Al Simmons, 1925	253	Willie Keeler, 1897	.424	Paul Waner, 1932	62
Rogers Hornsby, 1922	250	Rogers Hornsby, 1924	.424	Charlie Gehringer, 1936	60
Chuck Klein, 1930	250	George Sisler, 1922	.420	Tris Speaker, 1923	59
Ty Cobb, 1911	248	Ty Cobb, 1911	.420	Chuck Klein, 1930	59
George Sisler, 1922	246	Tuck Turner, 1894	.416	Todd Helton, 2000	59
Ichiro Suzuki, 2001	242	Fred Dunlap, 1884	.412	Billy Herman, 1936	57
Heinie Manush, 1928	241	Jesse Burkett, 1896	.410	Billy Herman, 1935	57
Babe Herman, 1930	241	Ed Delahanty, 1899	.410	Carlos Delgado, 2000	57

All stats through 2007 season.

Note: Career pitching stats are based on a minimum of 100 decisions and 1,000 innings pitched. Single-season batting stats are based on a minimum of 3.1 plate appearances per game.

* On a 40-man roster on Opening Day 2008

TRIPLES	
Chief Wilson, 1912	31
Dave Orr, 1886	31
Heinie Reitz, 1894	31
Perry Werden, 1893	29
Sam Thompson, 1894	28
Harry Davis, 1897	28
Jimmy Williams, 1899	28
George Davis, 1893	27
Sam Thompson, 1894	27
John Reilly, 1890	26
George Treadway, 1894	26
Joe Jackson, 1912	26
Sam Crawford, 1914	26

HOME RUNS	
Barry Bonds, 2001	73
Mark McGwire, 1998	70
Sammy Sosa, 1998	66
Mark McGwire, 1999	65
Sammy Sosa, 2001	64
Sammy Sosa, 1999	63
Roger Maris, 1961	61
Babe Ruth, 1927	60
Babe Ruth, 1921	59
Jimmie Foxx, 1932	58
Hank Greenberg, 1938	58
Mark McGwire, 1997	58
Ryan Howard, 2006	58

TOTAL BASES	
Babe Ruth, 1921	457
Rogers Hornsby, 1922	450
Lou Gehrig, 1927	447
Chuck Klein, 1930	445
Jimmie Foxx, 1932	438
Stan Musial, 1948	429
Sammy Sosa, 2001	425
Hack Wilson, 1930	423
Chuck Klein, 1932	420
Luis Gonzalez, 2001	419
Lou Gehrig, 1930	419

RUNS BATTED IN	
Hack Wilson, 1930	191
Lou Gehrig, 1931	184
Hank Greenberg, 1937	183
Lou Gehrig, 1927	175
Jimmie Foxx, 1938	175
Lou Gehrig, 1930	174
Babe Ruth, 1921	171
Chuck Klein, 1930	170
Hank Greenberg, 1935	170
Jimmie Foxx, 1932	169

STRIKEOUTS	
Ryan Howard, 2007	199
Adam Dunn, 2004	195
Adam Dunn, 2006	194
Bobby Bonds, 1970	189
Jose Hernandez, 2002	188
Bobby Bonds, 1969	187
Preston Wilson, 2000	187
Rob Deer, 1987	186
Pete Incaviglia, 1986	185
Jose Hernandez, 2001	185
Jim Thome, 2001	185

RUNS	
Billy Hamilton, 1894	198
Tom Brown, 1891	177
Babe Ruth, 1921	177
Tip O'Neill, 1887	167
Lou Gehrig, 1936	167
Billy Hamilton, 1895	166
Willie Keeler, 1894	165
Joe Kelley, 1894	165
Arlie Latham, 1887	163
Babe Ruth, 1928	163
Lou Gehrig, 1931	163

STOLEN BASES	
Hugh Nicol, 1887	138
Rickey Henderson, 1982	130
Arlie Latham, 1887	129
Lou Brock, 1974	118
Charlie Comiskey, 1887	117
John Ward, 1887	111

Billy Hamilton, 1889	111
Billy Hamilton, 1891	111
Vince Coleman, 1985	110
Arlie Latham, 1888	109
Vince Coleman, 1987	109

BASES ON BALLS	
Barry Bonds, 2004	232
Barry Bonds, 2002	198
Barry Bonds, 2001	177
Babe Ruth, 1923	170
Ted Williams, 1947	162
Ted Williams, 1949	162
Mark McGwire, 1998	162
Ted Williams, 1946	156
Eddie Yost, 1956	151
Barry Bonds, 1996	151
Babe Ruth, 1920	150

SLUGGING PERCENTAGE	
Barry Bonds, 2001	.863
Babe Ruth, 1920	.847
Babe Ruth, 1921	.846
Barry Bonds, 2004	.812
Barry Bonds, 2002	.799
Babe Ruth, 1927	.772
Lou Gehrig, 1927	.765
Babe Ruth, 1923	.764
Rogers Hornsby, 1925	.756
Mark McGwire, 1998	.752
Jeff Bagwell, 1994	.750

Note: Single-season batting stats are based on a minimum of 3.1 plate appearances per game.

DID YOU KNOW?

Despite being outscored by a total of 20 runs during the 2007 season, the Arizona Diamondbacks had the best record in the NL (90–72).

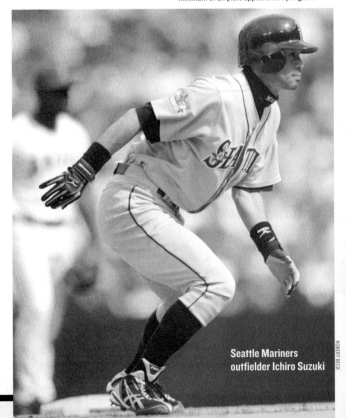

Seattle Mariners outfielder Ichiro Suzuki

ROBERT BECK

Regular Season: Individual Pitching, Single Season

GAMES

Mike Marshall, 1974	106
Kent Tekulve, 1979	94
Salomon Torres, 2006	94
Mike Marshall, 1973	92
Kent Tekulve, 1978	91
Wayne Granger, 1969	90
Mike Marshall, 1979	90
Kent Tekulve, 1987	90
Jim Brower, 2004	89
Mark Eichhorn, 1987	89
Steve Kline, 2001	89
Paul Quantrill, 2003	89
Julian Tavarez, 1997	89

GAMES STARTED

Will White, 1879	75
Pud Galvin, 1883	75
Jim McCormick, 1880	74
Charley Radbourn, 1884	73
Guy Hecker, 1884	73
Pud Galvin, 1884	72
John Clarkson, 1889	72
John Clarkson, 1885	70
Bill Hutchison, 1892	70
Matt Kilroy, 1887	69

INNINGS PITCHED

Will White, 1878	680.0
Charley Radbourn, 1884	678.2
Guy Hecker, 1884	670.2
Jim McCormick, 1880	657.2
Jim Galvin, 1883	656.1
Jim Galvin, 1884	636.1
Charley Radbourn, 1883	632.1
John Clarkson, 1885	623.0
Jim Devlin, 1876	622.0
Bill Hutchison, 1892	622.0

WINS

Charley Radbourn, 1884	59
John Clarkson, 1885	53
Guy Hecker, 1884	52
John Clarkson, 1889	49
Charley Radbourn, 1883	48
Charlie Buffinton, 1884	48
Al Spalding, 1876	47
John Ward, 1879	47
Pud Galvin, 1883	46
Pud Galvin, 1884	46
Matt Kilroy, 1887	46

LOSSES

John Coleman, 1883	48
Will White, 1880	42
Larry McKeon, 1884	41
George Bradley, 1879	40
Jim McCormick, 1879	40
Henry Porter, 1888	37
Kid Carsey, 1891	37
George Cobb, 1892	37
Stump Weidman, 1886	36
Bill Hutchison, 1892	36

WINNING PERCENTAGE

Roy Face, 1959	.947
Johnny Allen, 1937	.938
Phil Regan, 1966	.933
Perry Werden, 1884	.923
Larry Twitchell, 1887	.917
Greg Maddux, 1995	.905
Randy Johnson, 1995	.900
Ron Guidry, 1978	.893
Freddie Fitzsimmons, 1940	.889
Lefty Grove, 1931	.886
Bob Stanley, 1978	.882
Preacher Roe, 1951	.880

SAVES

Bobby Thigpen, 1990	57
Eric Gagne, 2003	55
John Smoltz, 2002	55
Randy Myers, 1993	53
Trevor Hoffman, 1998	53
Mariano Rivera, 2004	53
Eric Gagne, 2002	52
Dennis Eckersley, 1992	51
Rod Beck, 1998	51
Mariano Rivera, 2001	50
Francisco Cordero, 2004	49
Dennis Eckersley, 1990	48
Rod Beck, 1993	48
Jeff Shaw, 1998	48

EARNED RUN AVERAGE

Tim Keefe, 1880	0.86
Dutch Leonard, 1914	0.96
Mordecai Brown, 1906	1.04
Bob Gibson, 1968	1.12
Christy Mathewson, 1909	1.14
Walter Johnson, 1913	1.14
Jack Pfiester, 1907	1.15
Addie Joss, 1908	1.16
Carl Lundgren, 1907	1.17
Denny Driscoll, 1882	1.21

SHUTOUTS

George Bradley, 1876	16
Pete Alexander, 1916	16
Jack Coombs, 1910	13
Bob Gibson, 1968	13
Pud Galvin, 1884	12
Ed Morris, 1886	12
Pete Alexander, 1915	12
Tommy Bond, 1879	11
Charley Radbourn, 1884	11
Dave Foutz, 1886	11
Christy Mathewson, 1908	11
Ed Walsh, 1908	11
Walter Johnson, 1913	11
Sandy Koufax, 1963	11
Dean Chance, 1964	11

COMPLETE GAMES

Will White, 1879	75
Charley Radbourn, 1884	73
Jim McCormick, 1880	72

Pittsburgh Pirates hurler Kent Tekulve

JOHN IACONO

Pud Galvin, 1883	72
Guy Hecker, 1884	72
Pud Galvin, 1884	71
Tim Keefe, 1883	68
John Clarkson, 1885	68
John Clarkson, 1889	68
Bill Hutchison, 1892	67

STRIKEOUTS

Matt Kilroy, 1886	513
Toad Ramsey, 1886	499
Hugh Daily, 1884	483
Dupee Shaw, 1884	451
Charley Radbourn, 1884	441
Charlie Buffinton, 1884	417
Guy Hecker, 1884	385
Nolan Ryan, 1973	383
Sandy Koufax, 1965	382
Bill Sweeney, 1884	374

BASES ON BALLS

Amos Rusie, 1890	289
Mark Baldwin, 1889	274
Amos Rusie, 1892	270
Amos Rusie, 1891	262
Mark Baldwin, 1890	249
Jack Stivetts, 1891	232
Mark Baldwin, 1891	227
Phil Knell, 1891	226
Bob Barr, 1890	219
Amos Rusie, 1893	218

Note: Single-season pitching stats are based on a minimum of 1.0 innings pitched per game.

Regular Season: Individual Batting, Single Game

MOST RUNS		
7	Guy Hecker, Lou	Aug. 15, 1886

MOST HITS		
7	Wilbert Robinson, Bal	June 10, 1892
7	Rennie Stennett, Pitt	Sept. 16, 1975

MOST HOME RUNS		
4	Bobby Lowe, Bos (NL)	May 30, 1894
4	Ed Delahanty, Phil	July 13, 1896
4	Lou Gehrig, NY (AL)	June 3, 1932
4	Gil Hodges, Bklyn	Aug. 31, 1950
4	Joe Adcock, Mil (NL)	July 31, 1954
4	Rocky Colavito, Cle	June 10, 1959
4	Willie Mays, SF	April 30, 1961
4	Mike Schmidt, Phi	April 17, 1976
4	Bob Horner, Atl	July 6, 1986
4	Mark Whiten, StL	Sept. 7, 1993
4	Mike Cameron, Sea	May 2, 2002
4	Shawn Green, LA	May 23, 2002
4	Carlos Delgado, Tor	Sept. 25, 2003

MOST GRAND SLAMS		
2	Tony Lazzeri, NY (AL)	May 24, 1936
2	Jim Tabor, Bos (AL)	July 4, 1939
2	Rudy York, Bos (AL)	July 27, 1946
2	Jim Gentile, Bal	May 9, 1961
2	Tony Cloninger, Atl	July 3, 1966
2	Jim Northrup, Det	June 24, 1968
2	Frank Robinson, Bal	June 26, 1970
2	Robin Ventura, Chi (AL)	Sept. 4, 1995
2	Chris Hoiles, Bal	Aug. 14, 1998
2	Fernando Tatis, StL	April 23, 1999
2	Nomar Garciaparra, Bos	May 10, 1999
2	Bill Mueller, Bos	July 29, 2003

MOST RBIS		
12	Jim Bottomley, StL	Sept. 16, 1924
12	Mark Whiten, StL	Sept. 7, 1993

Regular Season: Individual Pitching, Single Game

MOST INNINGS PITCHED		
26	Leon Cadore, Bklyn	May 1, 1920
26	Joe Oeschger, Bos (NL)	May 1, 1920

MOST RUNS ALLOWED		
24	Al Travers, Det	May 18, 1912

MOST HITS ALLOWED		
36	Jack Wadsworth, Lou	Aug. 17, 1894

MOST WILD PITCHES		
6	J.R. Richard, Hou	April 10, 1979
6	Phil Niekro, Atl	Aug. 14, 1979
6	Bill Gullickson, Mon	April 10, 1982

MOST STRIKEOUTS		
20	Roger Clemens, Bos	April 29, 1986
20	Roger Clemens, Bos	Sept. 18, 1996
20	Kerry Wood, Chi (NL)	May 6, 1998
20	Randy Johnson, Ari	May 8, 2001

MOST WALKS ALLOWED		
16	Bill George, NY (NL)	May 30, 1887
16	George Van Haltren, Chi (NL)	June 27, 1887
16	Henry Gruber, Cle	April 19, 1890
16	Bruno Haas, Phil (AL)	June 2, 1915

LEGENDS

Rod Carew

■ **Rod Carew,** *second baseman, b. October 1, 1945, Gatun, Panama.* With a career 3,053 hits, Carew was a magician with the bat. After being named the AL Rookie of the Year in 1967, he became the league MVP in 1977. He hit over .300 in 15 seasons in a row with the Minnesota Twins and the California Angels and won seven batting titles. He is also famous for stealing home, which he did 17 times in his career. Carew was inducted into the Hall of Fame in 1991.

■ **Cal Ripken Jr.,** *shortstop, b. August 24, 1960, Havre de Grace, Maryland.* Inducted to the Hall of Fame in 2007, Ripken is considered one of the best shortstops to ever play the game. He appeared in a whopping 2,632 straight games for the Baltimore Orioles, breaking Lou Gehrig's 56-year-old record of 2,130. He logged 3,184 hits and 431 homers in his career. Ripken was named the AL Rookie of the Year in 1982 and was a two-time AL MVP.

JOHN KENNEY

Notable Achievements

Longest Hitting Streaks

NATIONAL LEAGUE		
PLAYER, TEAM	**YEAR**	**G**
Willie Keeler, Bal	1897	44
Pete Rose, Cin	1978	44
Bill Dahlen, Chi	1894	42
Tommy Holmes, Bos	1945	37
Jimmy Rollins, Phil	2005-06	36
Billy Hamilton, Phil	1894	38
Luis Castillo, Fla	2002	35
Fred Clarke, Lou	1895	35
Chase Utley, Phil	2006	35
Benito Santiago, SD	1987	34
George Davis, NY	1893	33
Rogers Hornsby, StL	1922	33

AMERICAN LEAGUE		
PLAYER, TEAM	**YEAR**	**G**
Joe DiMaggio, NY	1941	56
George Sisler, StL	1922	41
Ty Cobb, Det	1911	40
Paul Molitor, Mil	1987	39
Ty Cobb, Det	1917	35
Ty Cobb, Det	1912	34
George Sisler, StL	1925	34
John Stone, Det	1930	34
George McQuinn, StL	1938	34
Dom DiMaggio, Bos	1949	34
Hal Chase, NY	1907	33
Heinie Manush, Wash	1933	33

Triple Crown Winners*

NATIONAL LEAGUE				
PLAYER, TEAM	**YEAR**	**HR**	**RBI**	**BA**
Paul Hines, Prov	1878	4	50	.358
Hugh Duffy, Bos	1894	18	145	.438
Heinie Zimmerman, Chi	1912	14	103	.372
Rogers Hornsby, StL	1922	42	152	.401
Rogers Hornsby, StL	1925	39	143	.403
Chuck Klein, Phil	1933	28	120	.368
Joe Medwick, StL	1937	31	154	.374

AMERICAN LEAGUE				
PLAYER, TEAM	**YEAR**	**HR**	**RBI**	**BA**
Nap Lajoie, Phil	1901	14	125	.422
Ty Cobb, Det	1909	9	115	.377
Jimmie Foxx, Phil	1933	48	163	.356
Lou Gehrig, NY	1934	49	165	.363
Ted Williams, Bos	1942	36	137	.356
Ted Williams, Bos	1947	32	114	.343
Mickey Mantle, NY	1956	52	130	.353
Frank Robinson, Bal	1966	49	122	.316
Carl Yastrzemski, Bos	1967	44	121	.326

Triple Crown Pitchers**

NATIONAL LEAGUE					
PLAYER, TEAM	**YEAR**	**W**	**L**	**SO**	**ERA**
Tommy Bond, Bos	1877	40	17	170	2.11
Hoss Radbourn, Prov	1884	60	12	441	1.38
Tim Keefe, NY	1888	35	12	333	1.74
John Clarkson, Bos	1889	49	19	284	2.73
Amos Rusie, NY	1894	36	13	195	2.78
Christy Mathewson, NY	1905	31	8	206	1.27
Christy Mathewson, NY	1908	37	11	259	1.43
Grover Alexander, Phil	1915	31	10	241	1.22
Grover Alexander, Phil	1916	33	12	167	1.55
Grover Alexander, Phil	1917	30	13	201	1.86
Hippo Vaughn, Chi	1918	22	10	148	1.74
Grover Alexander, Chi	1920	27	14	173	1.91
Dazzy Vance, Bklyn	1924	28	6	262	2.16
Bucky Walters, Cin	1939	27	11	137	2.29
Sandy Koufax, LA	1963	25	5	306	1.88
Sandy Koufax, LA	1965	26	8	382	2.04
Sandy Koufax, LA	1966	27	9	317	1.73
Steve Carlton, Phil	1972	27	10	310	1.97
Dwight Gooden, NY	1985	24	4	268	1.53
Randy Johnson, Ari	2002	24	5	334	2.32

AMERICAN LEAGUE					
PLAYER, TEAM	**YEAR**	**W**	**L**	**SO**	**ERA**
Cy Young, Bos	1901	33	10	158	1.62
Rube Waddell, Phil	1905	26	11	287	1.48
Walter Johnson, Wash	1913	36	7	303	1.09
Walter Johnson, Wash	1918	23	13	162	1.27
Walter Johnson, Wash	1924	23	7	158	2.72
Lefty Grove, Phil	1930	28	5	209	2.54
Lefty Grove, Phil	1931	31	4	175	2.06
Lefty Gomez, NY	1934	26	5	158	2.33
Lefty Gomez, NY	1937	21	11	194	2.33
Hal Newhouser, Det	1945	25	9	212	1.81
Roger Clemens, Tor	1997	21	7	292	2.05
Roger Clemens, Tor	1998	20	6	271	2.64
Pedro Martinez, Bos	1999	23	4	313	2.07
Johan Santana, Min	2006	19	6	245	2.77

 DID YOU KNOW?

In 2007, Alex Rodriguez of the New York Yankees became the fifth AL player to win three MVP awards, joining Jimmie Foxx, Joe DiMaggio, Yogi Berra, and Mickey Mantle.

* Player who leads in three categories: home runs, RBIs, and batting average. ** Pitcher who leads in three categories: wins, strikeouts, and ERA.

Notable Achievements
(cont.)

Consecutive Games Played, 500 or More Games

Cal Ripken Jr.	2,632
Lou Gehrig	2,130
Everett Scott	1,307
Steve Garvey	1,207
Billy Williams	1,117
Joe Sewell	1,103
Miguel Tejada	1,069
Stan Musial	895
Eddie Yost	829
Gus Suhr	822
Nellie Fox	798
Pete Rose	745
Dale Murphy	740
Richie Ashburn	730
Ernie Banks	717
Pete Rose	678
Earl Averill	673
Frank McCormick	652
Sandy Alomar, Sr.	648
Eddie Brown	618
Roy McMillan	585
George Pinckney	577
Steve Brodie	574
Aaron Ward	565
Alex Rodriguez	546
Candy LaChance	540
Buck Freeman	535
Fred Luderus	533
Clyde Milan	511
Charlie Gehringer	511
Vada Pinson	508
Tony Cuccinello	504
Charlie Gehringer	504
Omar Moreno	503

POWER RANKINGS

↑ Best Base Stealers

1 Jose Reyes, New York Mets
Reyes led the majors in steals in 2006 and 2007.

Jose Reyes

2 Carl Crawford, Tampa Bay Rays
Crawford is the only player in the majors with 100 stolen bases and less than 20 caught stealings in 2006 and 2007.

3 Juan Pierre, Los Angeles Dodgers
Through 2007, Pierre led all active players in career stolen bases (389).

4 Hanley Ramirez, Florida Marlins
Ramirez was one of four players with back-to-back 50-steal seasons in 2006 and 2007.

5 Chone Figgins, Los Angeles Angels
Figgins led the big leagues with 62 steals in 2005, and had 93 steals over the next two seasons.

6 Dave Roberts, San Francisco Giants
Roberts doesn't reach base as often as some base stealers, but he still has had 30 stolen bases in six of the past seven seasons.

7 Jimmy Rollins, Philadelphia Phillies
Rollins stole 118 bases from 2005–07, and led all players with at least 100 steals with an 88.1 percent success rate in that span.

8 Shane Victorino, Philadelphia Phillies
In 2007, Victorino was the only player in the majors with 30-plus steals and a 90 percent stolen base success rate.

9 Ichiro Suzuki, Seattle Mariners
Ichiro had 115 steals from 2005–07, and was caught only 18 times in that span.

10 Brian Roberts, Baltimore Orioles
Roberts is rapidly improving as a base stealer, swiping a career-high 50 bases in 2007.

Unassisted Triple Plays

PLAYER, TEAM	DATE	POS	OPP	OPP BATTER
Neal Ball, Cle	July 19, 1909	SS	Bos	Amby McConnell
Bill Wambsganss, Cle	Oct. 10, 1920	2B	Bklyn	Clarence Mitchell
George Burns, Bos	Sept. 14, 1923	1B	Cle	Frank Brower
Ernie Padgett, Bos	Oct. 6, 1923	SS	Phil	Walter Holke
Glenn Wright, Pitt	May 7, 1925	SS	StL	Jim Bottomley
Jimmy Cooney, Chi	May 30, 1927	SS	Pitt	Paul Waner
Johnny Neun, Det	May 31, 1927	1B	Cle	Homer Summa
Ron Hansen, Wash	July 30, 1968	SS	Cle	Joe Azcue
Mickey Morandini, Phil	Sept. 20, 1992	2B	Pitt	Jeff King
John Valentin, Bos	July 15, 1994	SS	Min	Marc Newfield
Randy Velarde, Oak	May 29, 2000	2B	NYY	Shane Spencer
Rafael Furcal, Atl	May 10, 2003	SS	StL	Woody Williams
Troy Tulowitzki, Col	April 29, 2007	SS	Atl	Chipper Jones
Asdrubal Cabrera, Cle	May 12, 2008	2B	Tor	Lyle Overbay

Wacky Math

Digits 0 to 9 have been replaced with letters. Use logic and the math problems to determine which letters represent which numbers. In the text, replace the letters on the spaces with numbers to reveal some wacky MLB trivia.

B	E	I	A	B	F	C	G
+B	×H	+C	+D	×B	−H	×A	×B
J	H	EA	A	J	E	BE	ED

A	B	C	D	E	F	G	H	I	J

Trevor Hoffman

1 On September EH, BDDI, the Dodgers trailed the Padres by J in the bottom of the F th. Then Los Angeles (who were last in the league in home runs) hit J home runs in a span of G pitches to tie the game. They hit them off Jon Adkins and Trevor Hoffman, who had given up A homers all season to the previous JAB hitters they'd faced in a combined EHD appearances. Then, having fallen behind in the top of the ED th, the Dodgers hit E more homer in the bottom of the ED th to claim the win.

2 In BDDC, the Red Sox scored EE runs or more in A straight postseason games (games I and C of the ALCS and Game E of the World Series). Prior to that, they'd done that E time in all EDC of their regular seasons combined — that's about EI,GDD games.

3 With EC pitches in the EC th inning of the C/C/BDDC Mets–Astros game, Billy Wagner collected his EC th save of the year.

ANSWERS ON PAGE 190

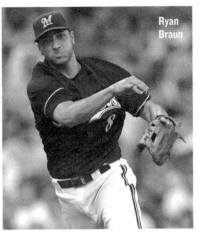

Ryan Braun

■ **Ryan Braun,** *leftfielder, b. November 17, 1973, Mission Hills, California.* Braun had a monster first season in the big leagues. The 2007 NL Rookie of the Year batted .324 with 34 homers, 97 RBIs, and 15 stolen bases, with a slugging percentage of .634, the highest of all time for a rookie. He ranked in the top five among NL rookies in nearly every category, including home runs, RBIs, runs, hits, batting average, and stolen bases.

Dioner Navarro

■ **Dioner Navarro,** *catcher, b. February 9, 1984, Caracas, Venezuela.* Navarro bounced back from a bad first half of 2007 and finished with the third-best average for starting AL catchers (.285). He also ended the year with the third-best slugging percentage (.475) for major league catchers. At only 24, this switch hitter has many seasons left to truly develop as a serious threat.

Jeremy Hermida

■ **Jeremy Hermida,** *rightfielder, b. January 30, 1984, Marietta, Georgia.* In 2007, Hermida set career highs in just about every offensive category. In the 72 games after the All-Star break, he batted .340 with 10 home runs and 36 RBIs. Insiders predict big things out of Hermida, a first-round draft pick who hit a grand slam in his first Major League at bat. As long as he can stay healthy, he is likely to fulfill all those expectations.

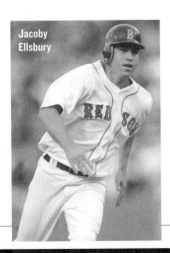

Jacoby Ellsbury

■ **Jacoby Ellsbury,** *centerfielder, b. September 11, 1983, Madras, Oregon.* Ellsbury flip-flopped between the big leagues and the minors in 2007, until he was called up in the ALCS. Ellsbury started in every postseason game after that. He batted .438 during Boston's run for the pennant and became the first rookie to hit two doubles in the same inning of a World Series game. Ellsbury is also one of only four rookies to hit three doubles in a World Series game, and only the third rookie to have four hits in a World Series game.

1 Until 2006, Rey Ordonez held the record for the most games played by an undrafted player from the Independent Northern League. Which current player holds the record now?

A. J.D. Drew

B. Kevin Millar

C. George Sherrill

Rey Ordonez

2 In 1961, MLB expanded its season to 162 games. How many games were in a season before then?

A. 150

B. 160

C. 154

3 True or False: Dustin Pedroia is the first player to lead off a World Series with a homer.

A. True

B. False

Dustin Pedroia

4 Jimmy Rollins holds the record for the longest hit streak among active players. How long was it?

A. 36

B. 33

C. 44

5 What is the minimum number of innings required for a game to be considered regulation length?

A. 7

B. 5

C. 6

6 Going into 2008, the Chicago Cubs hadn't won a World Series since 1908. Their streak of 99 seasons without a title is the longest in the majors. Which team comes in second with a streak of 59 seasons without a title?

A. Baltimore Orioles

B. San Diego Padres

C. Cleveland Indians

7 True or False: Ichiro Suzuki has finished with at least 200 hits in each of his first seven MLB seasons.

A. True

B. False

Ichiro Suzuki

8 Of the stadiums below, which two are closest to each other?

A. Yankee Stadium and Shea Stadium (New York)

B. AT&T Park and McAfee Coliseum (San Francisco and Oakland)

C. Wrigley Field and U.S. Cellular Field (Chicago)

9 Who is the only pitcher to have ever thrown a perfect game in the World Series?

A. Cy Young

B. Don Larsen

C. Randy Johnson

10 Shortstop Jose Reyes of the New York Mets led the NL in stolen bases in 2005, 2006, and 2007. How many total steals did he have in that span?

A. 202

B. 210

C. 195

Jose Reyes

Old Rivalries and New Stars

When the best NBA regular season in years ends in a showdown between the two greatest rivals in the sport, we can only thank the basketball gods. In a stirring finals that flashed back to some of the NBA's classic matchups, the Boston Celtics downed their ancient foes, the Los Angeles Lakers, in six games.

The two legendary teams hadn't faced each other in the finals since 1987, when forward Larry Bird squared off against point guard Magic Johnson. This time, it was forward Paul Pierce versus shooting guard Kobe Bryant. Pierce returned the Celtics to glory, in an inspiring baseline-to-baseline performance that led to a 131–92 title-clinching victory. Pierce won the finals MVP award. Boston won its 17th title. Fans won simply by watching.

While old rivals revisited history, young players like Chris Paul made some of their own. Two seasons ago, Paul was a star in the making. Now he's a supernova. Last year, the young court general led the league in assists (11.6) and steals (2.7) per game and finished second in MVP voting. Paul knows the game. He reads defenses well, which opens up the floor for his layups and runners. He also dishes to teammates for uncontested shots. But watch CP3 on the fast break, where his speed, decision making, and playground flair are on full display. No one is on the same level. Paul was named to the All-NBA first team last year and led his team, the New Orleans Hornets, to the Southwest Division championship.

The Hornets weren't the only team to thrive in the Western Conference in the 2007–08 season. Heavyweights such as the San Antonio Spurs and Phoenix Suns excelled playing different styles (defensive and offensive, respectively). But what made the season exciting was the competitiveness of the entire West. It seemed like the race for the playoffs began after the All-Star break, with squads moving up and down the standings every night and each game taking on more and more importance. Two weeks before the end of the season, not one Western Conference team had locked up a playoff spot. Only 6.5 games separated the eighth-place team from the first.

When the dust settled, favorites like the Houston Rockets and the Dallas Mavericks were still in the running. But so were many up-and-comers. The Utah Jazz emerged as one of the best young squads. The Golden State Warriors, the darlings of 2007, missed out, even though they finished with a record of 48–34. It was a remarkable year capped off by an equally remarkable finish.

Celtics captain Paul Pierce outplayed Kobe Bryant for his first NBA title.

BOB ROSATO

Dishing out a league-high 11.6 assists a game, New Orleans Hornets point guard Chris Paul reached new heights in 2007–08.

NBA TEAMS

EASTERN CONFERENCE

Atlanta Hawks 2
Boston Celtics 1
Charlotte Bobcats 1
Chicago Bulls 3
Cleveland Cavaliers 2
Detroit Pistons 2
Indiana Pacers 4
Miami Heat 3
Milwaukee Bucks 4

New Jersey Nets 1
New York Knicks 3
Orlando Magic 1
Philadelphia 76ers 3
Toronto Raptors 2
Washington Wizards 4

WESTERN CONFERENCE

Dallas Mavericks
Denver Nuggets
Golden State Warriors
Houston Rockets
Los Angeles Clippers
Los Angeles Lakers
Memphis Grizzlies
Minnesota Timberwolves
New Orleans Hornets

Phoenix Suns
Portland Trail Blazers
Sacramento Kings
San Antonio Spurs
Seattle SuperSonics
Utah Jazz

GAME TIME

Tele-Trades

Kevin Garnett played for the Minnesota Timberwolves when he earned the 2003–04 NBA MVP award. In 2007, Minnesota traded Garnett, making him the ninth MVP to be traded by the team he was playing for when he won the award. Who are the others?

To find out, decipher the coded names below. Each number in a name stands for one of the letters found with it on the telephone. You determine which one. A number may represent a different letter each time it's used. For instance, the code for TRADE would be 8 7 2 3 3. The 3 stands for D the first time it's used and E the next.

‾ ‾ ‾ ‾ ‾ ‾ ‾ ‾ ‾ ‾ ‾ ‾ ‾ ‾
9 4 5 8 2 4 2 6 2 3 7 5 2 4 6
(traded by the San Francisco Warriors, 1965; and the 76ers, 1968)

‾ ‾ ‾ ‾ ‾ ‾ ‾ ‾ ‾ ‾ ‾ ‾ ‾
6 7 2 2 7 7 6 2 3 7 8 7 6 6
(Cincinnati Royals, 1970)

‾ ‾ ‾ ‾ ‾ ‾ ‾ ‾ ‾ - ‾ ‾ ‾ ‾ ‾ ‾
5 2 7 3 3 6 2 2 3 8 5 5 2 2 2 2 7 (Bucks, 1975)

‾ ‾ ‾ ‾ ‾ ‾ ‾ ‾ ‾
2 6 2 6 2 2 3 6 6 (Buffalo Braves, midseason 1976–77)

‾ ‾ ‾ ‾ ‾ ‾ ‾ ‾ ‾ ‾
3 2 8 3 2 6 9 3 6 7 (Celtics, 1982)

‾ ‾ ‾ ‾ ‾ ‾ ‾ ‾ ‾ ‾ ‾
6 6 7 3 7 6 2 5 6 6 3 (Rockets, 1982; 76ers, 1986)

‾ ‾ ‾ ‾ ‾ ‾ ‾ ‾ ‾ , ‾ ‾ ‾ ‾ ‾
7 4 2 7 8 4 5 5 3 6 6 3 2 5 (Lakers, 2004)

‾ ‾ ‾ ‾ ‾ ‾ ‾ ‾ ‾ ‾ ‾
2 5 5 3 6 4 8 3 7 7 6 6 (76ers, midseason 2006–07)

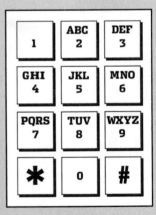

	ABC	DEF
1	2	3
GHI	JKL	MNO
4	5	6
PQRS	TUV	WXYZ
7	8	9
*	0	#

ANSWERS ON PAGE 190

BRYANT
Height: 6′ 6″
Weight: 205 lbs.
Birth Date: Aug. 23, 1978
Birthplace: Philadelphia, PA
2008 key stats: 28.3 ppg, 5.4 apg, 6.3 rpg

JAMES
Height: 6′ 5″
Weight: 250 lbs.
Birth Date: Dec. 30, 1984
Birthplace: Toledo, OH
2008 key stats: 27.3 ppg, 6.6 apg, 6.9 rpg

KOBE BRYANT VS. LEBRON JAMES

The league's two biggest stars go one-on-one

Kobe Bryant		LeBron James
Los Angeles Lakers, guard	**Team/Position**	Cleveland Cavaliers, forward
13th pick, Charlotte Hornets, 1996 (traded to Lakers after he refused to play for Charlotte)	**Drafted**	First overall, Cleveland Cavaliers, 2003
13th season: 25 ppg, 5.3 rpg, 4.6 apg	**Career Stats***	Sixth season: 27.3 ppg, 6.9 rpg, 6.6 apg
10-time All-Star; 10-time All-NBA; eight-time All-Defensive selection; All-Star MVP (2001–02, 2006–07); NBA MVP (2007–08)	**Awards and Accomplishments**	Four-time All-Star; four-time All-NBA; NBA scoring champion (2007–08); All-Star MVP (2005–06, 2007–08); Rookie of the Year (2003-04)
A tenacious competitor who performs best in the clutch, Bryant can create his own shot or blow past defenders to the rim. When he gets hot, he's impossible to stop.	**Scouting Report**	An explosive all-around player, James can go over, past, or through anyone in the league. His jump shot needs work but he makes up for it with furious drives and sensational passing.
Historically a one-man show, Bryant matured last year by playing team ball. The Lakers made the finals. But can he become a true leader and guide his team to a title before he retires?	**Something to Prove**	James needs to show he can win the games that matter. He and the Cavs are a perennial playoff threat (they made it to the finals in 2006–2007), but have fallen a hair short of greatness.
"He's the greatest player right now in our league, and probably top three or five in the history of the game," says Boston Celtics coach Doc Rivers.	**What Others Say About Him**	"There isn't a player who does everything like he does," says Cavs coach Mike Brown. "He doesn't just score. He doesn't just get people easy shots. He doesn't just rebound. He defends."
	Who's Better	James. He possesses a court vision as well as an ability (and willingness) to dish the ball. Give him a decent supporting cast and he'll be polishing championship rings in no time.

* Through 2007–08 season

NBA Champions

SEASON	CHAMPION	SERIES	RUNNER-UP	WINNING COACH	FINALS MVP
2007-08	Boston Celtics	4-2	LA Lakers	Doc Rivers	Paul Pierce, Bos
2006-07	San Antonio	4-0	Cleveland	Gregg Popovich	Tony Parker, SA
2005-06	Miami	4-2	Dallas	Pat Riley	Dwyane Wade, Mia
2004-05	San Antonio	4-3	Detroit	Gregg Popovich	Tim Duncan, SA
2003-04	Detroit	4-1	LA Lakers	Larry Brown	Chauncey Billups, Det
2002-03	San Antonio	4-2	New Jersey	Gregg Popovich	Tim Duncan, SA
2001-02	LA Lakers	4-0	New Jersey	Phil Jackson	Shaquille O'Neal, LA
2000-01	LA Lakers	4-1	Philadelphia	Phil Jackson	Shaquille O'Neal, LA
1999-00	LA Lakers	4-2	Indiana	Phil Jackson	Shaquille O'Neal, LA
1998-99	San Antonio	4-1	New York	Gregg Popovich	Tim Duncan, SA
1997-98	Chicago	4-2	Utah	Phil Jackson	Michael Jordan, Chi
1996-97	Chicago	4-2	Utah	Phil Jackson	Michael Jordan, Chi
1995-96	Chicago	4-2	Seattle	Phil Jackson	Michael Jordan, Chi
1994-95	Houston	4-0	Orlando	Rudy Tomjanovich	Hakeem Olajuwon, Hou
1993-94	Houston	4-3	New York	Rudy Tomjanovich	Hakeem Olajuwon, Hou
1992-93	Chicago	4-2	Phoenix	Phil Jackson	Michael Jordan, Chi
1991-92	Chicago	4-2	Portland	Phil Jackson	Michael Jordan, Chi
1990-91	Chicago	4-1	LA Lakers	Phil Jackson	Michael Jordan, Chi
1989-90	Detroit	4-1	Portland	Chuck Daly	Isiah Thomas, Det
1988-89	Detroit	4-0	LA Lakers	Chuck Daly	Joe Dumars, Det
1987-88	LA Lakers	4-3	Detroit	Pat Riley	James Worthy, LA
1986-87	LA Lakers	4-2	Boston	Pat Riley	Magic Johnson, LA
1985-86	Boston	4-2	Houston	K.C. Jones	Larry Bird, Bos
1984-85	LA Lakers	4-2	Boston	Pat Riley	Kareem Abdul-Jabbar, LA
1983-84	Boston	4-3	LA Lakers	K.C. Jones	Larry Bird, Bos
1982-83	Philadelphia	4-0	LA Lakers	Billy Cunningham	Moses Malone, Phil
1981-82	LA Lakers	4-2	Philadelphia	Pat Riley	Magic Johnson, LA
1980-81	Boston	4-2	Houston	Bill Fitch	Cedric Maxwell, Bos
1979-80	LA Lakers	4-2	Philadelphia	Paul Westhead	Magic Johnson, LA
1978-79	Seattle	4-1	Washington	Lenny Wilkens	Dennis Johnson, Sea
1977-78	Washington	4-3	Seattle	Dick Motta	Wes Unseld, Wash
1976-77	Portland	4-2	Philadelphia	Jack Ramsay	Bill Walton, Port
1975-76	Boston	4-2	Phoenix	Tom Heinsohn	Jo Jo White, Bos
1974-75	Golden State	4-0	Washington	Al Attles	Rick Barry, GS
1973-74	Boston	4-3	Milwaukee	Tom Heinsohn	John Havlicek, Bos
1972-73	New York	4-1	LA Lakers	Red Holzman	Willis Reed, N.Y.
1971-72	LA Lakers	4-1	New York	Bill Sharman	Wilt Chamberlain, LA
1970-71	Milwaukee	4-0	Baltimore	Larry Costello	Lew Alcindor*, Mil
1969-70	New York	4-3	LA Lakers	Red Holzman	Willis Reed, N.Y.
1968-69	Boston	4-3	LA Lakers	Bill Russell	Jerry West, LA
1967-68	Boston	4-2	LA Lakers	Bill Russell	—
1966-67	Philadelphia	4-2	San Francisco	Alex Hannum	—
1965-66	Boston	4-3	LA Lakers	Red Auerbach	—
1964-65	Boston	4-1	LA Lakers	Red Auerbach	—
1963-64	Boston	4-1	San Francisco	Red Auerbach	—
1962-63	Boston	4-2	LA Lakers	Red Auerbach	—
1961-62	Boston	4-3	LA Lakers	Red Auerbach	—
1960-61	Boston	4-1	St. Louis	Red Auerbach	—
1959-60	Boston	4-3	St. Louis	Red Auerbach	—
1958-59	Boston	4-0	Minneapolis	Red Auerbach	—
1957-58	St. Louis	4-2	Boston	Alex Hannum	—
1956-57	Boston	4-3	St. Louis	Red Auerbach	—
1955-56	Philadelphia	4-1	Ft. Wayne	George Senesky	—
1954-55	Syracuse	4-3	Ft. Wayne	Al Cervi	—
1953-54	Minneapolis	4-3	Syracuse	John Kundla	—
1952-53	Minneapolis	4-1	New York	John Kundla	—
1951-52	Minneapolis	4-3	New York	John Kundla	—
1950-51	Rochester	4-3	New York	Les Harrison	—
1949-50	Minneapolis	4-2	Syracuse	John Kundla	—
1948-49	Minneapolis	4-2	Washington	John Kundla	—
1947-48	Baltimore	4-2	Philadelphia	Buddy Jeannette	—
1946-47	Philadelphia	4-1	Chicago	Ed Gottlieb	—

Note: The NBA did not name a Finals MVP from 1946-47 to 1967-68.
* Alcindor changed his name to Kareem Abdul-Jabbar after the 1970-71 season.

Dirk Nowitzki

■ **Dirk Nowitzki,** *forward, b. June 19, 1978, Würzburg, Germany.* The scruffy Dallas Mavericks star comes from a family of athletes. His father, Jörg, was on the German national handball team. His sister, Silke, was a track-and-field champ. But the towering Nowitzki took after mom, Helen, who played for her country's national basketball team. Good thing. Nowitzki is now one of the premier players in the NBA, a lights-out shooter and steady rebounder who can play near the basket or stretch defenses with his three-point range. A seven-time All-Star and the first European player to win the NBA's MVP award (2007), Nowitzki passed Rolando Blackman in 2007–08 to become the Mavs' all-time leading scorer.

■ **Gilbert Arenas,** *b. January 6, 1982, Tampa, Florida.* Basketball's clown prince suffered a setback last year, sidelined by a knee injury and criticized by those who branded him a selfish, shot-happy bust. But you can be sure Arenas, a three-time All-Star, will only use the negativity as fuel. Arenas wears number zero to remind him of how many minutes critics said he'd play in college at Arizona. When Mike Krzyzewski cut the strong, speedy guard from the national team, Arenas unloaded 54 points on Team USA assistant Mike D'Antoni and the Phoenix Suns. Note to opponents: Never tick off a guy whose sizzling scoring earned him the nickname "Hibachi."

■ **Manu Ginóbili,** *shooting guard, b. July 28, 1977, Bahía Blanca, Argentina.* A vital cog on several championship San Antonio teams, Ginóbili wasn't drafted until the 57th pick in 1999. He's now considered one of the great draft heists of all time. The dynamic Spurs guard plays without fear. Whether it's knifing to the basket, nailing a key shot with the game on the line, or coming off the bench to give his team a lift, Ginóbili does whatever it takes to win. An All-NBA selection and winner of the Sixth Man of the Year Award in 2008, Ginóbili had career highs in points (19.5 ppg), assists (4.5 apg), and rebounds (4.8 rpg) last season. He and Bill Bradley are the only players to win an NBA title, a Euroleague championship, and an Olympic gold medal.

■ **Deron Williams,** *point guard, b. June 26, 1984, Parkersburg, West Virginia.* It didn't take long for Williams to make his mark in the NBA. In just his second season, the University of Illinois product was handed the reins to the Utah Jazz, a team living in the shadow of legendary ex-point guard John Stockton. Williams didn't blink. He ran the offense like a veteran, using pinpoint passes, well-oiled fast breaks, and, yes, a Stockton-esque pick-and-roll with power forward Carlos Boozer to turn Utah into a playoff contender again. In the 2007–2008 season, Williams got only better, averaging 18.8 points and 10.5 assists per game. The Beehive State will never forget Stockton, but Williams could turn out to be equally memorable.

NBA All-Time Individual Leaders

Scoring

MOST POINTS, CAREER		
PLAYER	POINTS	AVERAGE
Kareem Abdul-Jabbar	38,387	24.6
Karl Malone	36,928	25.0
Michael Jordan	32,292	30.1
Wilt Chamberlain	31,419	30.1
Moses Malone	27,409	20.6
Elvin Hayes	27,313	21.0
Hakeem Olajuwon	26,946	21.8
Oscar Robertson	26,710	25.7
Dominique Wilkins	26,668	24.8
John Havlicek	26,395	20.8

HIGHEST SCORING AVERAGE, CAREER		
PLAYER	AVERAGE	GAMES
Michael Jordan	30.1	1,072
Wilt Chamberlain	30.1	1,045
Allen Iverson	27.9	747
Elgin Baylor	27.4	846
LeBron James*	27.3	391
Jerry West	27.0	932
Bob Pettit	26.4	792
George Gervin	26.2	791
Oscar Robertson	25.7	1,040
Shaquille O'Neal*	25.9	98

* Active in 2007–08   Note: Minimum 400 games or 10,000 points

MOST POINTS, GAME			
PLAYER, TEAM	PTS	OPPONENT	DATE
Wilt Chamberlain, Phil	100	NY	3-2-62
Kobe Bryant, LAL	81	Tor	1-22-06
Wilt Chamberlain, Phil	73	Chi	1-13-62
Wilt Chamberlain, SF	73	NY	11-16-62
David Thompson, Den	73	Det	4-9-78
Wilt Chamberlain, SF	72	LAC	11-3-62
Elgin Baylor, LAL	71	NY	11-15-60
David Robinson, SA	71	LAC	4-24-94
Wilt Chamberlain, SF	70	Syr	3-10-63
Michael Jordan, Chi	69	Cle	3-28-90

HIGHEST FIELD GOAL PERCENTAGE, CAREER	
PLAYER	PERCENTAGE
Artis Gilmore	.599

Note: Minimum 2,000 field goals made.

HIGHEST FREE-THROW PERCENTAGE, CAREER	
PLAYER	PERCENTAGE
Mark Price	.904

Note: Minimum 1,200 free throws made.

Michael Jordan

JOHN BIEVER

3-Point Field Goals

MOST 3-POINT FIELD GOALS, CAREER	
PLAYER	3-POINT FIELD GOALS
Reggie Miller	2,560

MOST 3-POINT FIELD GOALS, GAME			
PLAYER	3-POINT FGS	OPPONENT	DATE
Kobe Bryant, LAL	12	Sea	1-7-03
Donyell Marshall, Tor	12	Phil	3-13-05

Note: 3-point field goals have only been an official stat since the 1979–80 season.

Steals

MOST STEALS, CAREER	
PLAYER	STEALS
John Stockton	3,265

MOST STEALS, GAME			
PLAYER	STEALS	OPPONENT	DATE
Kendall Gill, NJ	11	Mia	4-3-99
Larry Kenon, SA	11	KC	12-26-76

Note: Steals have only been an official stat since the 1973–74 season.

Rebounds

MOST REBOUNDS, CAREER		
PLAYER	REBOUNDS	AVERAGE
Wilt Chamberlain	23,924	22.9
Bill Russell	21,620	22.5
Kareem Abdul-Jabbar	17,440	11.2
Elvin Hayes	16,279	12.5
Moses Malone	16,212	12.2
Karl Malone	14,968	10.1
Robert Parish	14,715	9.1
Nate Thurmond	14,464	15.0
Walt Bellamy	14,241	13.7
Wes Unseld	13,769	14.0

NBA All-Time Individual Leaders (cont.)

MOST REBOUNDS, GAME			
PLAYER, TEAM	REB	OPPONENT	DATE
Wilt Chamberlain, Phil	55	Bos	11-24-60
Bill Russell, Bos	51	Syr	2-5-60
Bill Russell, Bos	49	Phil	11-16-57
Bill Russell, Bos	49	Det	3-11-65
Wilt Chamberlain, Phil	45	Syr	2-6-60
Wilt Chamberlain, Phil	45	LA	1-21-61

Assists

MOST ASSISTS, CAREER	
PLAYER	ASSISTS
John Stockton	15,806
Mark Jackson	10,334
Magic Johnson	10,141
Oscar Robertson	9,887
Isiah Thomas	9,061

MOST ASSISTS, GAME			
PLAYER, TEAM	ASSISTS	OPPONENT	DATE
Scott Skiles, Orl	30	Den	12-30-90

Blocks

MOST BLOCKS, CAREER	
PLAYER	BLOCKS
Hakeem Olajuwon	3,830
Dikembe Mutombo	3,230
Kareem Abdul-Jabbar	3,189
Mark Eaton	3,064
David Robinson	2,954

MOST BLOCKS, GAME			
PLAYER, TEAM	BLOCKS	OPPONENT	DATE
Elmore Smith, LAL	17	Port	10-28-73

Note: Blocks have only been an official stat since the 1973–74 season.

Hakeem Olajuwon

Most Valuable Players: Maurice Podoloff Trophy

SEASON	PLAYER, TEAM
2007–08	Kobe Bryant, LA Lakers
2006–07	Dirk Nowitzki, Dallas
2005–06	Steve Nash, Phoenix
2004–05	Steve Nash, Phoenix
2003–04	Kevin Garnett, Minnesota
2002–03	Tim Duncan, San Antonio
2001–02	Tim Duncan, San Antonio
2000–01	Allen Iverson, Philadelphia
1999–00	Shaquille O'Neal, LA Lakers
1998–99	Karl Malone, Utah
1997–98	Michael Jordan, Chicago
1996–97	Karl Malone, Utah
1995–96	Michael Jordan, Chicago
1994–95	David Robinson, San Antonio
1993–94	Hakeem Olajuwon, Houston
1992–93	Charles Barkley, Phoenix
1991–92	Michael Jordan, Chicago
1990–91	Michael Jordan, Chicago
1989–90	Magic Johnson, LA Lakers
1988–89	Magic Johnson, LA Lakers
1987–88	Michael Jordan, Chicago
1986–87	Magic Johnson, LA Lakers
1985–86	Larry Bird, Boston
1984–85	Larry Bird, Boston
1983–84	Larry Bird, Boston
1982–83	Moses Malone, Philadelphia
1981–82	Moses Malone, Houston
1980–81	Julius Erving, Philadelphia
1979–80	Kareem Abdul-Jabbar, LA Lakers
1978–79	Moses Malone, Houston
1977–78	Bill Walton, Portland
1976–77	Kareem Abdul-Jabbar, LA Lakers
1975–76	Kareem Abdul-Jabbar, LA Lakers
1974–75	Bob McAdoo, Buffalo
1973–74	Kareem Abdul-Jabbar, Milwaukee
1972–73	Dave Cowens, Boston
1971–72	Kareem Abdul-Jabbar, Milwaukee
1970–71	Lew Alcindor*, Milwaukee
1969–70	Willis Reed, New York
1968–69	Wes Unseld, Baltimore
1967–68	Wilt Chamberlain, Philadelphia
1966–67	Wilt Chamberlain, Philadelphia
1965–66	Wilt Chamberlain, Philadelphia
1964–65	Bill Russell, Boston
1963–64	Oscar Robertson, Cincinnati
1962–63	Bill Russell, Boston
1961–62	Bill Russell, Boston
1960–61	Bill Russell, Boston
1959–60	Wilt Chamberlain, Philadelphia
1958–59	Bob Pettit, St. Louis
1957–58	Bill Russell, Boston
1956–57	Bob Cousy, Boston
1955–56	Bob Pettit, St. Louis

* Alcindor changed his name to Kareem Abdul-Jabbar after the 1970–71 season.

Rookie of the Year: Eddie Gottlieb Trophy

SEASON	PLAYER	TEAM
2007–08	Kevin Durant	Seattle
2006–07	Brandon Roy	Portland
2005–06	Chris Paul	New Orleans
2004–05	Emeka Okafor	Charlotte
2003–04	LeBron James	Cleveland
2002–03	Amare Stoudemire	Phoenix
2001–02	Pau Gasol	Memphis
2000–01	Mike Miller	Orlando
1999–00	Steve Francis	Houston
	Elton Brand	Chicago
1998–99	Vince Carter	Toronto
1997–98	Tim Duncan	San Antonio
1996–97	Allen Iverson	Philadelphia
1995–96	Damon Stoudamire	Toronto
1994–95	Jason Kidd	Dallas
	Grant Hill	Detroit
1993–94	Chris Webber	Golden State
1992–93	Shaquille O'Neal	Orlando
1991–92	Larry Johnson	Charlotte
1990–91	Derrick Coleman	New Jersey
1989–90	David Robinson	San Antonio
1988–89	Mitch Richmond	Golden State
1987–88	Mark Jackson	New York
1986–87	Chuck Person	Indiana
1985–86	Patrick Ewing	New York
1984–85	Michael Jordan	Chicago
1983–84	Ralph Sampson	Houston
1982–83	Terry Cummings	San Diego
1981–82	Buck Williams	New Jersey
1980–81	Darrell Griffith	Utah
1979–80	Larry Bird	Boston
1978–79	Phil Ford	Kansas City
1977–78	Walter Davis	Phoenix
1976–77	Adrian Dantley	Buffalo
1975–76	Alvan Adams	Phoenix
1974–75	Keith Wilkes	Golden State
1973–74	Ernie DiGregorio	Buffalo
1972–73	Bob McAdoo	Buffalo
1971–72	Sidney Wicks	Portland
1970–71	Dave Cowens	Boston
	Geoff Petrie	Portland
1969–70	Lew Alcindor*	Milwaukee
1968–69	Wes Unseld	Baltimore
1967–68	Earl Monroe	Baltimore
1966–67	Dave Bing	Detroit
1965–66	Rick Barry	San Francisco
1964–65	Willis Reed	New York
1963–64	Jerry Lucas	Cincinnati
1962–63	Terry Dischinger	Chicago
1961–62	Walt Bellamy	Chicago
1960–61	Oscar Robertson	Cincinnati

* Alcindor changed his name to Kareem Abdul-Jabbar after the 1970–71 season.

Kevin Garnett

GREG NELSON

SEASON	PLAYER	TEAM
1959–60	Wilt Chamberlain	Philadelphia
1958–59	Elgin Baylor	Minneapolis
1957–58	Woody Sauldsberry	Philadelphia
1956–57	Tom Heinsohn	Boston
1955–56	Maurice Stokes	Rochester
1954–55	Bob Pettit	Milwaukee
1953–54	Ray Felix	Baltimore
1952–53	Don Meineke	Ft. Wayne

Defensive Player of the Year

SEASON	PLAYER	TEAM
2007–08	Kevin Garnett	Boston
2006–07	Marcus Camby	Denver
2005–06	Ben Wallace	Detroit
2004–05	Ben Wallace	Detroit
2003–04	Ron Artest	Indiana
2002–03	Ben Wallace	Detroit
2001–02	Ben Wallace	Detroit
2000–01	Dikembe Mutombo	Philadelphia/Atlanta
1999–00	Alonzo Mourning	Miami
1998–99	Alonzo Mourning	Miami
1997–98	Dikembe Mutombo	Atlanta
1996–97	Dikembe Mutombo	Atlanta
1995–96	Gary Payton	Seattle
1994–95	Dikembe Mutombo	Denver
1993–94	Hakeem Olajuwon	Houston
1992–93	Hakeem Olajuwon	Houston
1991–92	David Robinson	San Antonio
1990–91	Dennis Rodman	Detroit
1989–90	Dennis Rodman	Detroit
1988–89	Mark Eaton	Utah
1987–88	Michael Jordan	Chicago
1986–87	Michael Cooper	LA Lakers
1985–86	Alvin Robertson	San Antonio
1984–85	Mark Eaton	Utah
1983–84	Sidney Moncrief	Milwaukee
1982–83	Sidney Moncrief	Milwaukee

Sixth Man of the Year

SEASON	PLAYER	TEAM
2007–08	Manu Ginobili	San Antonio
2006–07	Leandro Barbosa	Phoenix
2005–06	Mike Miller	Memphis
2004–05	Ben Gordon	Chicago
2003–04	Antawn Jamison	Dallas
2002–03	Bobby Jackson	Sacramento
2001–02	Corliss Williamson	Detroit
2000–01	Aaron McKie	Philadelphia
1999–00	Rodney Rogers	Phoenix
1998–99	Darrell Armstrong	Orlando
1997–98	Danny Manning	Phoenix
1996–97	John Starks	New York
1995–96	Toni Kukoc	Chicago
1994–95	Anthony Mason	New York
1993–94	Dell Curry	Charlotte
1992–93	Clifford Robinson	Portland
1991–92	Detlef Schrempf	Indiana
1990–91	Detlef Schrempf	Indiana
1989–90	Ricky Pierce	Milwaukee
1988–89	Eddie Johnson	Phoenix
1987–88	Roy Tarpley	Dallas
1986–87	Ricky Pierce	Milwaukee
1985–86	Bill Walton	Boston
1984–85	Kevin McHale	Boston
1983–84	Kevin McHale	Boston
1982–83	Bobby Jones	Philadelphia

Ben Gordon

Hedo Turkoglu

Most Improved Player

SEASON	PLAYER	TEAM
2007–08	Hedo Turkoglu	Orlando
2006–07	Monta Ellis	Golden State
2005–06	Boris Diaw	Phoenix Suns
2004–05	Bobby Simmons	LA Clippers
2003–04	Zach Randolph	Portland
2002–03	Gilbert Arenas	Golden State
2001–02	Jermaine O'Neal	Indiana
2000–01	Tracy McGrady	Orlando
1999–00	Jalen Rose	Indiana
1998–99	Darrell Armstrong	Orlando
1997–98	Alan Henderson	Atlanta
1996–97	Isaac Austin	Miami
1995–96	Gheorghe Muresan	Washington
1994–95	Dana Barros	Philadelphia
1993–94	Don MacLean	Washington
1992–93	Mahmoud Abdul-Rauf	Denver
1991–92	Pervis Ellison	Washington
1990–91	Scott Skiles	Orlando
1989–90	Rony Seikaly	Miami
1988–89	Kevin Johnson	Phoenix
1987–88	Kevin Duckworth	Portland
1986–87	Dale Ellis	Seattle
1985–86	Alvin Robertson	San Antonio

Allen Iverson

Kareem
Abdul-Jabbar

Techn

First-Round Draft Picks

Who was the first NBA player to be drafted first overall without ever playing high school or college ball in the U.S.?

To find out, draw a straight line (a ruler helps) connecting the NBA first-round draft picks in column A with the team that picked them in column B. If you match the players and teams correctly, each line will cross off one letter. Unscramble the remaining letters to answer the question.

Shaquille O'Neal •

Kareem Abdul-Jabbar •

LeBron James •

Magic Johnson •

Tim Duncan •

Patrick Ewing •

Allen Iverson •

Greg Oden •

• Milwaukee Bucks

• San Antonio Spurs

• Portland Trail Blazers

• New York Knicks

• Orlando Magic

• Los Angeles Lakers

• Philadelphia 76ers

• Cleveland Cavaliers

J G A K M O Y I D W U N L E O

ANSWERS ON PAGE 190

NBA All-Star Game Results

YEAR	RESULT	SITE	WINNING COACH	MOST VALUABLE PLAYER
2008	East 134, West 128	New Orleans, LA	Doc Rivers	LeBron James, Cleveland
2007	West 153, East 132	Las Vegas, NV	Mike D'Antoni	Kobe Bryant, LA Lakers
2006	East 122, West 120	Houston, TX	Flip Saunders	LeBron James, Cleveland
2005	East 125, West 115	Denver, CO	Stan Van Gundy	Allen Iverson, Philadelphia
2004	West 136, East 132	Los Angeles, CA	Flip Saunders	Shaquille O'Neal, LA Lakers;
2003	West 155, East 145 (2 OT)	Atlanta, GA	Rick Adelman	Kevin Garnett, Minnes
2002	West 135, East 120	Philadelphia, PA	Don Nelson	Kobe Bryant, LA Lakers
2001	East 111, West 110	Washington, DC	Larry Brown	Allen Iverson, Philadelphia
2000	West 137, East 126	Oakland, CA	Phil Jackson	Shaquille O'Neal, LA Lakers; Tim Duncan, San Antonio
1999	Canceled due to lockout			
1998	East 135, West 114	New York, NY	Larry Bird	Michael Jordan, Chicago
1997	East 132, West 120	Cleveland, OH	Doug Collins	Glen Rice, Charlotte
1996	East 129, West 118	San Antonio, TX	Phil Jackson	Michael Jordan, Chicago
1995	West 139, East 112	Phoenix, AZ	Paul Westphal	Mitch Richmond, Sacramento
1994	East 127, West 118	Minneapolis, MN	Lenny Wilkens	Scottie Pippen, Chicago
1993	West 135, East 132	Salt Lake City, UT	Paul Westphal	Karl Malone, Utah; John Stockton, Utah
1992	West 153, East 113	Orlando, FL	Don Nelson	Magic Johnson, LA Lakers
1991	East 116, West 114	Charlotte, NC	Chris Ford	Charles Barkley, Philadelphia
1990	East 130, West 113	Miami, FL	Chuck Daly	Magic Johnson, LA Lakers
1989	West 143, East 134	Houston, TX	Pat Riley	Karl Malone, Utah
1988	East 138, West 133	Chicago, IL	Mike Fratello	Michael Jordan, Chicago
1987	West 154, East 149 (OT)	Seattle, WA	Pat Riley	Tom Chambers, Seattle
1986	East 139, West 132	Dallas, TX	K.C. Jones	Isiah Thomas, Detroit
1985	West 140, East 129	Indianapolis, IN	Pat Riley	Ralph Sampson, Houston
1984	East 154, West 145 (OT)	Denver, CO	K.C. Jones	Isiah Thomas, Detroit
1983	East 132, West 123	Los Angeles, CA	Billy Cunningham	Julius Erving, Philadelphia
1982	East 120, West 118	East Rutherford, NJ	Bill Fitch	Larry Bird, Boston
1981	East 123, West 120	Cleveland, OH	Billy Cunningham	Nate Archibald, Boston
1980	East 144, West 135 (OT)	Washington, DC	Billy Cunningham	George Gervin, San Antonio
1979	West 134, East 129	Detroit, MI	Lenny Wilkens	David Thompson, Denver
1978	East 133, West 125	Atlanta, GA	Billy Cunningham	Randy Smith, Buffalo
1977	West 125, East 124	Milwaukee, WI	Larry Brown	Julius Erving, Philadelphia
1976	East 123, West 109	Philadelphia, PA	Tom Heinsohn	Dave Bing, Washingto
1975	East 108, West 102	Phoenix, AZ	K.C. Jones	Walt Frazier, New York
1974	West 134, East 123	Seattle, WA	Larry Costello	Bob Lanier, Detroit
1973	East 104, West 84	Chicago, IL	Tom Heinsohn	Dave Cowens, Boston
1972	West 112, East 110	Los Angeles, CA	Bill Sharman	Jerry West, LA Lakers
1971	West 108, East 107	San Diego, CA	Larry Costello	Lenny Wilkens, Seattle
1970	East 142, West 135	Philadelphia, PA	Red Holzman	Willis Reed, New York
1969	East 123, West 112	Baltimore, MD	Gene Shue	Oscar Robertson, Cincinnati
1968	East 144, West 124	New York, NY	Alex Hannum	Hal Greer, Philadelphia
1967	West 135, East 120	San Francisco, CA	Fred Schaus	Rick Barry, San Francisco
1966	East 137, West 94	Cincinnati, OH	Red Auerbach	Adrian Smith, Cincinnati
1965	East 124, West 123	St. Louis, MO	Red Auerbach	Jerry Lucas, Cincinnati
1964	East 111, West 107	Boston, MA	Red Auerbach	Oscar Robertson, Cincinnati
1963	East 115, West 108	Los Angeles, CA	Red Auerbach	Bill Russell, Boston
1962	West 150, East 130	St. Louis, MO	Fred Schaus	Bob Pettit, St. Louis
1961	West 153, East 131	Syracuse, NY	Paul Seymour	Oscar Robertson, Cincinnati
1960	East 125, West 115	Philadelphia, PA	Red Auerbach	Wilt Chamberlain, Philadelphia
1959	West 124, East 108	Detroit, MI	Ed Macauley	Bob Pettit, St. Louis; Elgin Baylor, Minnesota
1958	East 130, West 118	St. Louis, MO	Red Auerbach	Bob Pettit, St. Louis
1957	East 109, West 97	Boston, MA	Red Auerbach	Bob Cousy, Boston
1956	West 108, East 94	Rochester, NY	Charley Eckman	Bob Pettit, St. Louis
1955	East 100, West 91	New York, NY	Al Cervi	Bill Sharman, Boston
1954	East 98, West 93 (OT)	New York, NY	Joe Lapchick	Bob Cousy, Boston
1953	West 79, East 75	Ft. Wayne, IN	John Kundla	George Mikan, Minnesota
1952	East 108, West 91	Boston, MA	Al Cervi	Paul Arizin, Philadelphia
1951	East 111, West 94	Boston, MA	Joe Lapchick	Ed Macauley, Boston

No. 1 NBA Draft Choices

YEAR	PLAYER	TEAM	SCHOOL/COUNTRY
2008	Derrick Rose	Chicago	Memphis
2007	Greg Oden	Portland	Ohio State
2006	Andrea Bargnani	Toronto	Italy
2005	Andrew Bogut	Milwaukee	Utah
2004	Dwight Howard	Orlando	SW Atlanta Christian Academy (GA)
2003	LeBron James	Cleveland	St. Vincent-St. Mary HS (OH)
2002	Yao Ming	Houston	China
2001	Kwame Brown	Washington	Glynn Academy
2000	Kenyon Martin	New Jersey Nets	Cincinnati
1999	Elton Brand	Chicago Bulls	Duke
1998	Michael Olowokandi	Los Angeles Clippers	Pacific (Cal.)
1997	Tim Duncan	San Antonio	Wake Forest
1996	Allen Iverson	Philadelphia	Georgetown
1995	Joe Smith	Golden State	Maryland
1994	Glenn Robinson	Milwaukee	Purdue
1993	Chris Webber	Orlando	Michigan
1992	Shaquille O'Neal	Orlando	Louisiana State
1991	Larry Johnson	Charlotte	Nevada–Las Vegas
1990	Derrick Coleman	New Jersey	Syracuse
1989	Pervis Ellison	Sacramento	Louisville
1988	Danny Manning	LA Clippers	Kansas
1987	David Robinson	San Antonio	Navy
1986	Brad Daugherty	Cleveland	North Carolina
1985	Patrick Ewing	New York	Georgetown
1984	Hakeem Olajuwon	Houston	Houston
1983	Ralph Sampson	Houston	Virginia
1982	James Worthy	LA Lakers	North Carolina
1981	Mark Aguirre	Dallas	DePaul
1980	Joe Barry Carroll	Golden State	Purdue
1979	Magic Johnson	LA Lakers	Michigan State
1978	Mychal Thompson	Portland	Minnesota
1977	Kent Benson	Milwaukee	Indiana
1976	John Lucas	Houston	Maryland
1975	David Thompson	Atlanta	North Carolina State
1974	Bill Walton	Portland	UCLA
1973	Doug Collins	Philadelphia	Illinois State
1972	LaRue Martin	Portland	Loyola–Chicago
1971	Austin Carr	Cleveland	Notre Dame
1970	Bob Lanier	Detroit	St. Bonaventure
1969	Lew Alcindor*	Milwaukee	UCLA
1968	Elvin Hayes	Houston	Houston
1967	Jimmy Walker	Detroit	Providence
1966	Cazzie Russell	New York	Michigan
1965	Fred Hetzel	San Francisco	Davidson College
1964	Jim Barnes	New York	University of Texas at El Paso
1963	Art Heyman	New York	Duke University
1962	Bill McGill	Chicago	University of Utah
1961	Walt Bellamy	Chicago	Indiana University
1960	Oscar Robertson	Cincinnati	University of Cincinnati
1959	Bob Boozer	Cincinnati	Kansas State University
1958	Elgin Baylor	Minneapolis	Seattle University
1957	Hot Rod Hundley	Cincinnati	West Virginia University
1956	Si Green	Rochester	Duquesne University
1955	Dick Ricketts	St. Louis	Duquesne University
1954	Frank Selvy	Baltimore	Furman University
1953	Ray Felix	Baltimore	Long Island University
1952	Mark Workman	Milwaukee	West Virginia University
1951	Gene Melchiorre	Baltimore	Bradley University
1950	Chuck Share	Boston	Bowling Green State University

Derrick Rose

DAVID BERGMAN

* Alcindor changed his name to Kareem Abdul-Jabbar after the 1970–71 season.

■ **Charles Barkley,** *forward, b. February 20, 1963, Leeds, Alabama.* With his short, robust frame and glass-cleaning prowess, Barkley was dubbed the Round Mound of Rebound during his college days at Auburn. Barkley entered the league in 1984 and soon proved himself to also be an explosive scorer and elite defender. He quickly earned a new nickname, this one far more respectful: Sir Charles. In his career with the Philadelphia 76ers, Phoenix Suns, and Houston Rockets, the hotheaded Barkley racked up technical fouls to go with a bundle of awards. He was a league MVP in 1993 and an 11-time All-NBA player, and he won two Olympic gold medals with the Dream Team, leading all players in scoring. He finished his career as one of only four players in NBA history to tally 20,000 points, 10,000 rebounds, and 4,000 assists.

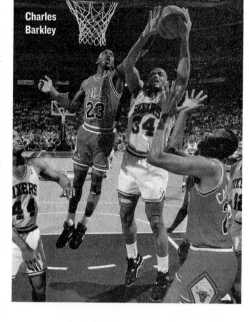

Charles Barkley

■ **Bernard King,** *forward, b. December 4, 1956, Brooklyn, New York.* Only a special player averages 24.2 points his rookie season. One of the most potent offensive weapons ever to grace the court, King had long arms, a whip-quick release, and an excellent postgame. For seven straight seasons, King shot .500 or better from the field. His peak came in 1984, when he led the New York Knicks to the Eastern Conference finals. The following year, King averaged a league-best 32.9 points, and on Christmas Day beat his old team, the New Jersey Nets, with a 60-point outburst. That year was also marked by disaster when King blew out his knee. It took him three years to bounce back. But he did, with the Washington Bullets, after changing his game to become an all-around player. King earned a third trip to the All-Star game in 1991, his last season.

↑ RANKINGS

POWER

Steve Nash

Best Three-point Shooters

1 **Steve Nash, PG, Phoenix Suns**
This superstar shoots threes better than most players shoot twos (47 percent last season).

2 **Ray Allen, SG, Boston Celtics**
With over 2,250 career threes, Allen is one of the best ever.

3 **Peja Stojakovic, G/F, New Orleans Hornets**
This Serbian marksman is deadly from behind the arc.

4 **Mike Miller, G/F, Memphis Grizzlies**
In three consecutive games last year, Miller hit a combined 23 threes.

5 **Rashard Lewis, F, Orlando Magic**
At 6′ 10″, Lewis launches with ease from long distances.

6 **Jason Kapono, G/F, Toronto Raptors**
This shoot-out champ made a blistering 48.3 percent of his threes last year.

7 **Kyle Korver, SF, Philadelphia 76ers**
His quick release and high-arcing shot result in big buckets.

8 **Jason Richardson, G/F, Charlotte Bobcats**
This shooter bombs away and scores in bunches.

9 **Daniel Gibson, G, Cleveland Cavaliers**
"Boobie" has emerged as one of the NBA's clutch three-point men.

10 **Raja Bell, SG, Phoenix Suns**
This utility player is always dangerous from downtown.

Michael Beasley

■ **Michael Beasley,** *forward, b. January 9, 1989, Frederick, Maryland.* In high school, the goofy Beasley once put a dead rat in a teacher's desk drawer as a prank. He'll have to keep the Bart Simpson antics in check when he makes the jump to the NBA. The athletic left-hander wowed scouts with his mid-post game, quick first step, and smooth jumper, and was taken second overall in the 2008 NBA Draft by the Miami Heat. Often compared to Carmelo Anthony, Beasley was so polished offensively during his one year at Kansas State, it's hard to imagine he won't make an immediate impact at the pro level.

■ **Kevin Durant,** *forward, b. September 29, 1988, Washington, D.C.* Excellent speed, good handle, an enormous wingspan, and soft hands make young Sonics star Durant a tough cover for any opponent. His three-point range doesn't help. The second pick in the 2007 NBA Draft out of Texas, Durant averaged 20.3 points and nearly a block a game in his debut season, good enough to win Rookie of the Year honors. And he saved the best for last: Against Golden State in the final game of the regular season, he erupted for 42 points, 13 rebounds, and six assists. There's only more to come.

Kevin Durant

■ **Al Horford,** *center-forward, b. June 3, 1986, Puerto Plata, Dominican Republic.* Horford knows how to win. He played on two NCAA championship teams at Florida, and in his first season as a pro, he helped take Atlanta to the playoffs, where the Hawks nearly upset the champion Celtics in a knockdown seven-game series. Throughout his rookie NBA season, he showed maturity beyond his years. A graceful athlete and powerful inside presence with excellent rebounding and defensive skills, Horford also displayed some scoring pop that should improve in the future. His rock-solid presence in the post gives the Hawks a foundation to build on.

■ **Greg Oden,** *center, b. January 22, 1988, Buffalo, New York.* Unfortunately, Oden missed his entire rookie season due to knee surgery. After spending one year at Ohio State, Oden was the top pick in the 2007 NBA draft. He didn't play a minute for the Portland Trail Blazers, but when he comes back, everyone will see what makes Oden so special. The seven-footer is destined to be a dominant player in the NBA for years to come. Oden is a menacing presence in the paint, a ferocious shot blocker, rebounder, and inside finisher whom scouts compare to Bill Russell. Yikes!

1 What was the nickname of triple-double machine and All-Star guard Lafayette Lever?
A. Hot Shot
B. Fat
C. Laffy Taffy

2 Who was the Houston Rockets' first-ever first-round pick in 1967?
A. Elvin Hayes
B. Rudy Tomjanovich
C. Pat Riley

3 In what sport other than basketball is Boston Celtics star Kevin Garnett a devoted fan of?
A. Swimming
B. Soccer
C. Tennis

4 True or False: Hall of Famer "Pistol" Pete Maravich got his nickname because of his ability to hit three-pointers.
A. True
B. False

Lafayette Lever

5 Where was the first professional basketball game played?
A. At a YMCA in Springfield, Massachusetts
B. In a cage in Trenton, New Jersey
C. At the Houston Astrodome

6 Who was the first black athlete to play in the NBA?
A. Nat "Sweetwater" Clifton
B. Earl Lloyd
C. Earl "The Goat" Manigault

7 True of False: Although 7'7" Manute Bol and Gheorghe Muresan share the distinction of being the tallest men to ever play in the NBA, they never competed against each other until they faced off in a charity arm-wrestling contest in Turkey in 2003.
A. True
B. False

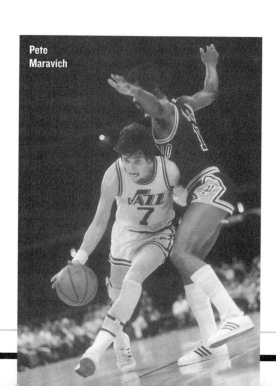
Pete Maravich

1.B,2.C,3.B,4.B,5.B,6.B,7.B

Reaching New Heights

In 2008, the WNBA bounded into its 12th season with a buzz around the game like never before. The reason? An influx of new talent.

Many believe the 2008 WNBA draft will go down in history. It started with former Tennessee star Candace Parker, drafted first overall by the Los Angeles Sparks. Parker made national news by becoming the first woman to win the McDonald's High School All-American Slam Dunk Contest. She beat out the likes of Josh Smith, who would win a slam dunk title of his own — in the NBA. After winning two national titles with the Lady Vols, Parker again made history in 2008. The junior became the first woman to leave school early for the WNBA.

But the talent didn't stop there. Second overall pick Sylvia Fowles (drafted by the Chicago Sky) led LSU to four straight Final Fours and is already drawing comparisons to another former Tiger, Shaquille O'Neal. After Fowles went Stanford's Candice Wiggins (Minnesota Lynx), who wrapped up her collegiate career as one of the greatest players in Pac 10 history. Such was the depth of the draft that Maryland's Laura Harper, the 2006 Final Four MVP, wasn't selected until the 10th pick.

Former LSU star Silvia Fowles was drafted number 2 by the Chicago Sky.

GARY DINEEN/NBAE/GETTY IMAGES

As in the NBA, the balance of power is tilted in favor of the WNBA's Western Conference, which the league hopes will lead to fantastic playoff chases. Los Angeles is now the league's powerhouse, featuring a frontcourt combo of Parker and Lisa Leslie. But they're hardly the only dynamic duo. The Phoenix Mercury are led by Diana Taurasi and Cappie Pondexter, while guard Sue Bird and 2007 MVP Lauren Jackson give the Seattle Storm a phenomenal inside-outside game.

Moreover, the WNBA hopes to coast on the recent success of the women's college game. The 2008 women's NCAA Tournament was the most viewed in ESPN history, with ratings up 30 percent from the previous year. That's good news for the WNBA, which needs plenty of star power to market the league.

The 2008 season tipped off with a sold-out game between the Sparks and the Mercury. It was the debut of Parker, and the game drew about 60 percent more TV viewers than the 2007 opener. The WNBA recorded 14 sellouts in the month of May alone, a league record.

The WNBA also welcomed a new team in Atlanta, which played before a sold-out crowd of more than 10,000 people in its first home game. Its nickname is a perfect choice for a league that's thinking lofty thoughts these days: The Dream.

After missing the entire 2007 season, three-time league MVP Lisa Leslie returned in 2008 and ignited the Los Angeles Sparks.

True or False?

The WNBA began with eight teams in 1997. Since then, nine teams have been added, two have moved, and four have folded. Do you know who's come and gone? Find out by deciding if each statement in the maze is true or false.

Start

The Miami Sol became the CT Sun in 2003. **F** **T**

The Mystics and the Lynx both entered the league in 1999. **T** **F**

The Cleveland Rockers were the first of two inaugural teams to fold. **F** **T**

The Chicago Sky is the youngest franchise. **F** **T**

The Portland Fire played for four years. **F** **T**

Finish

ANSWERS ON PAGE 190

DID YOU KNOW?
Houston Comets guard Cynthia Cooper was named finals MVP in each of the WNBA's first four years.

WNBA: All-Time Leaders

POINTS			
PLAYER	GP	PTS	AVG
Lisa Leslie	317	5,588	17.6
Tina Thompson	313	5,072	16.2
Katie Smith	297	4,762	16.0
Sheryl Swoopes	275	4,508	16.4
Lauren Jackson	216	4,438	19.4
Yolanda Griffith	289	4,064	14.1
Chamique Holdsclaw	225	3,975	17.7
Nykesha Sales	278	3,955	14.2
Tangela Smith	329	3,925	11.9
Vickie Johnson	357	3,904	10.9

SCORING AVERAGE					
PLAYER	GP	FG	FT	PTS	AVG
Seimone Augustus	78	656	324	1,700	21.8
Cynthia Cooper	124	802	758	2,601	21.0
Diana Taurasi	142	962	518	2,798	19.7
Lauren Jackson	229	1,559	1,017	4,438	19.4
Cappie Pondexter	72	488	304	1,382	19.2
Chamique Holdsclaw	225	1,531	855	3,975	17.7
Lisa Leslie	317	2,073	1,324	5,588	17.6
Tamika Catchings	189	1,017	885	3,216	17.0
Alana Beard	139	838	468	2,303	16.6
Sheryl Swoopes	275	1,690	892	4,508	16.4

Seimone Augustus

Sue Bird

3-POINT FIELD-GOAL PERCENTAGE			
PLAYER	3FGM	3FGA	PCT
Sidney Spencer	68	142	.479
Laurie Koehn	78	168	.464
Jennifer Azzi	158	345	.458
Kristen Rasmussen	51	122	.418
Sandy Brondello	114	278	.410
Jackie Stiles	65	160	.406
Eva Nemcova	131	326	.402
Jamie Carey	59	148	.399
Korie Hlede	83	209	.397
Shanna Crossley	122	308	.396

ASSISTS			
PLAYER	GP	A	AVG
Ticha Penicheiro	315	1,889	6.0
Teresa Weatherspoon	254	1,338	5.3
Dawn Staley	263	1,337	5.1
Shannon Johnson	296	1,235	4.2
Sue Bird	206	1,157	5.6
Vickie Johnson	357	1,045	2.9
Sheryl Swoopes	275	927	3.4
Nikki Teasley	186	923	5.0
Tamecka Dixon	313	890	2.8
Andrea Stinson	272	810	3.0

KEY: GP=games played; PTS=points; AVG=average; FG=field goals; FT=free throws; 3FGM=3-point field goals made; 3FGA=3-point field goals attempted; PCT=percentage; A=assists

■ **Diana Taurasi,** *guard, b. June 11, 1982, Chino, California.* Entering the league in 2004 as the top overall draft pick, Taurasi knew about winning. She was part of three straight national championships at Connecticut and won a gold medal in 2004 as part of Team USA. Phoenix failed to make the playoffs her first three seasons, but broke through in 2007. Teamed with Cappie Pondexter and Penny Taylor, the high-scoring Taurasi led the Mercury to the WNBA title and established them as a force for many years to come.

Diana Taurasi

ROSS D. FRANKLIN/AP

■ **Seimone Augustus,** *guard, b. April 30, 1984, Baton Rouge, Louisiana.* A Louisiana legend, Augustus led her Baton Rouge high school to two state titles, then took LSU to three straight Final Fours. After the Minnesota Lynx drafted her with the first pick in 2006, Augustus was named Rookie of the Year and finished second in league scoring in 2007, pouring in 22.9 points per game.

■ **Candace Parker,** *forward, b. April 19, 1986, St. Louis, Missouri.* Parker won two national titles in her three years at Tennessee. During the 2008 championship run, Parker played through an excruciating injury after she separated her shoulder. Just over a month later, Parker played in her first WNBA game as a member of the Los Angeles Sparks and picked up where she left off. A week into the season, she was already considered a candidate for league MVP.

WNBA: All-Time Leaders (cont.)

REBOUNDS			
PLAYER	GP	REB	AVG
Lisa Leslie	317	2,961	9.3
Yolanda Griffith	289	2,326	8.0
Margo Dydek	321	2,140	6.7
Tina Thompson	313	2,092	6.6
Taj McWilliams-Franklin	283	1,984	7.3
Chamique Holdsclaw	225	1,862	8.3
Natalie Williams	221	1,832	8.3
Wendy Palmer	311	1,825	5.9
Lauren Jackson	229	1,835	8.0
Tangela Smith	329	1,734	5.3

STEALS			
PLAYER	GP	STL	AVG
Sheryl Swoopes	275	614	2.23
Ticha Penicheiro	315	605	1.92
Nykesha Sales	278	490	1.76
Yolanda Griffith	278	496	1.72

Tamika Catchings	189	487	2.58
Teresa Weatherspoon	254	465	1.83
Lisa Leslie	317	449	1.42
Sheri Sam	307	426	1.39
Shannon Johnson	296	429	1.45
DeLisha Milton-Jones	278	414	1.49

BLOCKS			
PLAYER	GP	BLK	AVG
Margo Dydek	321	877	2.73
Lisa Leslie	317	729	2.30
Lauren Jackson	229	472	2.06
Tangela Smith	329	431	1.31
Ruth Riley	232	367	1.58
Tammy Sutton-Brown	236	348	1.47
Elena Baranova	209	320	1.53
Yolanda Griffith	289	311	1.08
Taj McWilliams-Franklin	283	310	1.10

KEY: GP=games played; REB=rebounds; AVG=average; STL=steals; BLK=blocks

WNBA Champions

YEAR	CHAMPION	RUNNER-UP	FINALS MVP
2007	Phoenix Mercury	Detroit Shock	Cappie Pondexter
2006	Detroit Shock	Sacramento Monarchs	Deanna Nolan
2005	Sacramento Monarchs	Connecticut Sun	Yolanda Griffith
2004	Seattle Storm	Connecticut Sun	Betty Lennox
2003	Detroit Shock	Los Angeles Sparks	Ruth Riley
2002	Los Angeles Sparks	New York Liberty	Lisa Leslie
2001	Los Angeles Sparks	Charlotte Sting	Lisa Leslie
2000	Houston Comets	New York Liberty	Cynthia Cooper
1999	Houston Comets	New York Liberty	Cynthia Cooper
1998	Houston Comets	Phoenix Mercury	Cynthia Cooper
1997	Houston Comets	New York Liberty	Cynthia Cooper

WNBA All-Star Game Results

YEAR	RESULT	SITE	WINNING COACH	MVP
2007	East 103, West 99	Washington, DC	Bill Laimbeer	Cheryl Ford
2006	East 98, West 82	New York, NY	Mike Thibault	Katie Douglas
2005	West 122, East 99	Uncasville, CT	Van Chancellor	Sheryl Swoopes
2004	No All-Star Game			
2003	West 84, East 75	New York, NY	Michael Cooper	Nikki Teasley
2002	West 81, East 76	Washington, DC	Michael Cooper	Lisa Leslie
2001	West 80, East 72	Orlando, FL	Van Chancellor	Lisa Leslie
2000	West 73, East 61	Phoenix, AZ	Van Chancellor	Tina Thompson
1999	West 79, East 61	New York, NY	Van Chancellor	Lisa Leslie

TRIVIA

1 Which of these is NOT a WNBA franchise?
A. Washington Mystics
B. Sacramento Monarchs
C. Houston Oilers

2 Los Angeles Sparks star Lisa Leslie missed the entire 2007 WNBA season. Why did she take the year off?
A. Had a baby
B. Had a torn ACL
C. Worked as a model in Europe

3 The two-time WNBA champion Detroit Shock are coached by which former Detroit Piston?
A. Isiah Thomas
B. Bill Laimbeer
C. Joe Dumars

4 In what month are the WNBA finals played?
A. September
B. October
C. November

5 True or False: Women's basketball great Rebecca Lobo is married to a former SPORTS ILLUSTRATED writer.
A. True
B. False

Rebecca Lobo

WNBA: Awards

Lauren Jackson

MVP

YEAR	PLAYER, TEAM
2007	Lauren Jackson, Seattle Storm
2006	Lisa Leslie, Los Angeles Sparks
2005	Sheryl Swoopes, Houston Comets
2004	Lisa Leslie, Los Angeles Sparks
2003	Lauren Jackson, Seattle Storm
2002	Sheryl Swoopes, Houston Comets
2001	Lisa Leslie, Los Angeles Sparks
2000	Sheryl Swoopes, Houston Comets
1999	Yolanda Griffith, Sacramento Monarchs
1998	Cynthia Cooper, Houston Comets
1997	Cynthia Cooper, Houston Comets

ROOKIE OF THE YEAR

YEAR	PLAYER, TEAM
2007	Armintie Price, Chicago Sky
2006	Seimone Augustus, Minnesota Lynx
2005	Temeka Johnson, Washington Mystics
2004	Diana Taurasi, Phoenix Mercury
2003	Cheryl Ford, Detroit Shock
2002	Tamika Catchings, Indiana Fever
2001	Jackie Stiles, Portland Fire
2000	Betty Lennox, Minnesota Lynx
1999	Chamique Holdsclaw, Washington Mystics
1998	Tracy Reid, Charlotte Sting

Armintie Price

DEFENSIVE PLAYER OF THE YEAR

YEAR	PLAYER, TEAM
2007	Lauren Jackson, Seattle Storm
2006	Tamika Catchings, Indiana Fever
2005	Tamika Catchings, Indiana Fever
2004	Lisa Leslie, Los Angeles Sparks
2003	Sheryl Swoopes, Houston Comets
2002	Sheryl Swoopes, Houston Comets
2001	Debbie Black, Miami Sol
2000	Sheryl Swoopes, Houston Comets
1999	Yolanda Griffith, Sacramento Monarchs
1998	Teresa Weatherspoon, New York Liberty
1997	Teresa Weatherspoon, New York Liberty

MOST IMPROVED PLAYER

YEAR	PLAYER, TEAM
2007	Janel McCarville, New York Liberty
2006	Erin Buescher, Sacramento Monarchs
2005	Nicole Powell, Sacramento Monarchs
2004	Kelly Miller, Indiana Fever; Wendy Palmer, Connecticut Sun
2003	Michelle Snow, Houston Comets
2002	Coco Miller, Washington Mystics
2001	Janeth Arcain, Houston Comets
2000	Tari Phillips, New York Liberty

■ **Natalie Williams,** *forward, b. November 30, 1970, Long Beach, California.* Williams might be the best all-around athlete in WNBA history. Not only a star basketball player at UCLA, Williams also led the Bruins to two national titles in volleyball (1990, 1991) as national Player of The Year both times. The third overall pick of the 1999 draft by the Utah Starzz, this four-time WNBA All-Star had her best season in 2000, averaging a league-high 11.6 rebounds to go along with 18.7 points, fourth-best in the WNBA. For her accomplishments, Williams was nominated to be a member of the WNBA All-Decade Team in 2006.

Natalie Williams

■ **Rebecca Lobo,** *forward, b. October 6, 1973, Hartford, Connecticut.* One of the original WNBA icons, Lobo was for many years the face of women's basketball. She won a national championship at UConn in 1995 and a gold medal a year later in the Olympics. Lobo grew so famous she even got to go jogging with President Bill Clinton. In the WNBA's inaugural season in 1997, Lobo was assigned to the New York Liberty. A member of the All-WNBA second team, she led the Liberty to the first WNBA finals, where New York fell to the Houston Comets. After twice tearing her ACL, Lobo retired in 2003.

■ **Nancy Lieberman,** *point guard, b. July 1, 1958, Brooklyn, New York.* Before Lieberman even stepped onto a WNBA court, she was already a member of the Naismith Memorial Basketball Hall of Fame. One of the pioneers of women's basketball, "Lady Magic" developed her toughness playing on the streets of New York City. In college, she led Old Dominion to AIAW national titles in back-to-back seasons, with the Lady Monarchs going 72-2 in that span. Having previously played in several professional leagues, Lieberman was drafted in 1997 at the age of 38. She played just one season before being named G.M. and head coach of the Detroit Shock.

WNBA: All-Time No. 1 Draft Picks

YEAR	NAME	TEAM	SCHOOL/COUNTRY
2008	Candace Parker	Los Angeles	Tennessee
2007	Lindsey Harding	Phoenix	Duke
2006	Seimone Augustus	Minnesota	LSU
2005	Janel McCarville	Charlotte	Minnesota
2004	Diana Taurasi	Phoenix	UConn
2003	LaToya Thomas	Cleveland	Mississippi St.
2002	Sue Bird	Seattle	UConn
2001	Lauren Jackson	Seattle	Australia
2000	Ann Wauters	Cleveland	Belgium
1999	Chamique Holdsclaw	Washington	Tennessee
1998	Margo Dydek	Utah	Poland
1997	Dena Head	Utah	Tennessee

The Year of the Upset

Shocking upsets by small schools over traditional powerhouses? Must be March Madness, right? No, not anymore. The college football landscape is also dotted with Cinderellas. Just look at the Fiesta Bowl. Non-BCS schools (Utah and Boise State) have won twice in the past three years.

Or better yet, look at the 2007 season — the Year of the Upset. The craziness began right away. On September 1, Division I-AA Appalachian State pulled off one of the biggest stunners in college sports history, beating No. 5 Michigan 34–32 in the Big House. The Mountaineers' Julian Rauch hit a go-ahead 24-yard field goal with 26 seconds remaining, and a last-second field goal block by ASU safety Corey Lynch secured a victory for the ages. It was the season's biggest surprise — for about a month.

In October, 41-point underdog Stanford

Appalachian State tailback Kevin Richardson silenced Michigan and the Big House with an historic upset.

defeated USC, 24–23, in the L.A. Coliseum. Backup QB Tavita Pritchard completed two fourth-down passes on Stanford's final drive. The last one was a 10-yarder to wide receiver Mark Bradford with 49 seconds left for the win.

It appeared that order was restored in November. Football powers LSU and Ohio State were on track to play each other for the national title. Turns out the fun was just beginning. The Buckeyes were defeated by unranked Illinois, and the Tigers dropped a triple-overtime heartbreaker to Arkansas that pushed both Ohio State and LSU out of the national title picture. Temporarily.

After all the upsets in November, West Virginia and Missouri appeared destined to square off in New Orleans. But the No. 2 Mountaineers were stunned in their season finale by a Pittsburgh team that entered the game 4–7. Missouri's loss to Oklahoma in the Big 12 Championship was less surprising, but no one expected the Tigers to be so dominated by the Sooners, who won 38–17.

That left the door open for Ohio State and LSU again. Ohio State scored on the fourth

LSU running back Jacob Hester rushed for 86 yards and one TD as the Tigers dominated Ohio State to win the national championship.

play of the game — a 65-yard touchdown run by Chris "Beanie" Wells. The Buckeyes added a field goal to make it 10–0. Then, just like the regular season, the game was turned on its head. The Tigers scored 31 unanswered points and smothered the Ohio State offense to become the first two-loss national champion.

Because of all the turmoil, nine different teams were ranked second in the country at some point during the season. What accounts for all the upsets? Some point to the NCAA limit of total scholarships. Others claim that offensive schemes like the spread have helped athletically inferior teams compete with the big boys. But none of these theories holds up under scrutiny. In the end, no one really knows. Big surprise.

Paths to Greatness

Follow the paths to discover what each college football award is for and who won it in 2007. Paths go under and over one another.

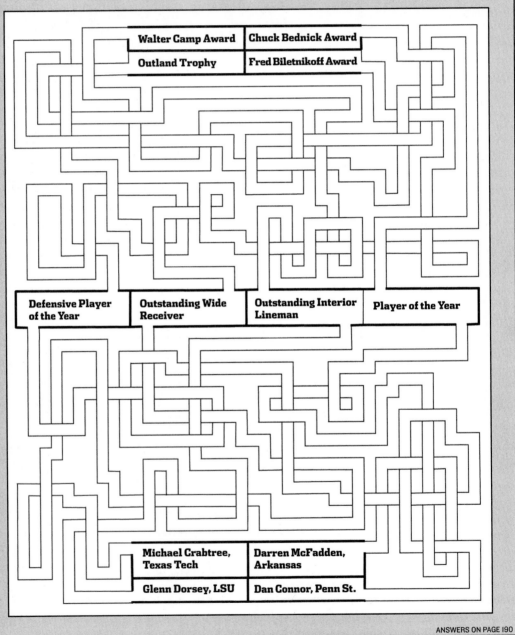

Walter Camp Award | Chuck Bednick Award
Outland Trophy | Fred Biletnikoff Award

Defensive Player of the Year | Outstanding Wide Receiver | Outstanding Interior Lineman | Player of the Year

Michael Crabtree, Texas Tech | Darren McFadden, Arkansas
Glenn Dorsey, LSU | Dan Connor, Penn St.

ANSWERS ON PAGE 190

■ **Tim Tebow,** *quarterback, b. August 14, 1987, St. Augustine, Florida.* When Tebow decided to sign with Florida, Gators fans could only dream about what the quarterback might accomplish in coach Urban Meyer's spread offense. Those dreams have become a reality. As a freshman, Tebow backed up Chris Leak and was mostly used in goal-line situations. A 6'3", 235-pound wrecking ball, Tebow rushed for eight touchdowns, propelling Florida to a national title. In 2007, Tebow took over the starting role and became the first major college quarterback to rush and pass for over 20 touchdowns. He finished with a remarkable 32 TDs through the air and another 23 on the ground. Tebow became the first sophomore to win a Heisman.

Tim Tebow

HEINZ KLUETMEIER

■ **Chase Daniel,** *quarterback, b. October 7, 1986, Southlake, Texas.* Overlooked by many big-time schools because of his height (he's 6'0"), Daniel was happily welcomed to Missouri by coach Gary Pinkel. He exploded onto the college football scene as a sophomore, throwing for more than 3,500 yards and 28 touchdowns. With defenses keying on Daniel in 2007, the junior compiled 4,170 passing yards, fifth-best in the nation, and threw for another 33 TDs. Both were school records. He finished fourth in the Heisman voting, the highest for a Tiger in nearly 70 years. After flirting with leaving for the NFL, Daniel returned for his senior season to finish what he started.

College Football: National Championships

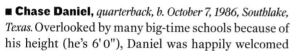

YEAR	CHAMPION	RECORD	HEAD COACH	YEAR	CHAMPION	RECORD	HEAD COACH
2007	LSU	10-2	Les Miles	1984	Brigham Young	13-0-0	LaVell Edwards
2006	Florida	13-1	Urban Meyer	1983	Miami (Florida)	11-1-0	Howard Schnellenberger
2005	Texas	13-0	Mack Brown	1982	Penn State	11-1-0	Joe Paterno
2004	USC	13-0	Pete Carroll	1981	Clemson	12-0-0	Danny Ford
2003	USC	12-1	Pete Carroll	1980	Georgia	12-0-0	Vince Dooley
(split)	LSU	13-1	Nick Saban	1979	Alabama	12-0-0	Bear Bryant
2002	Ohio State	14-0	Jim Tressel	1978	Alabama	11-1-0	Bear Bryant
2001	Miami (Florida)	12-0	Larry Coker	(split)	USC (UPI)	12-1-0	John Robinson
2000	Oklahoma	13-0	Bob Stoops	1977	Notre Dame	11-1-0	Dan Devine
1999	Florida State	12-0	Bobby Bowden	1976	Pittsburgh	12-0-0	Johnny Majors
1998	Tennessee	13-0	Phillip Fulmer	1975	Oklahoma	11-1-0	Barry Switzer
1997	Michigan	12-0	Lloyd Carr	1974	Oklahoma (AP)	11-0-0	Barry Switzer
(split)	Nebraska (ESPN)	13-0	Tom Osborne	(split)	USC (UPI)	10-1-1	John McKay
1996	Florida	12-1	Steve Spurrier	1973	Notre Dame	11-0-0	Ara Parseghian
1995	Nebraska	12-0-0	Tom Osborne	(split)	Alabama (UPI)	11-1-0	Bear Bryant
1994	Nebraska	13-0-0	Tom Osborne	1972	USC	12-0-0	John McKay
1993	Florida State	12-1-0	Bobby Bowden	1971	Nebraska	13-0-0	Bob Devaney
1992	Alabama	13-0-0	Gene Stallings	1970	Nebraska	11-0-1	Bob Devaney
1991	Miami (Florida)	12-0-0	Dennis Erickson	(split)	Texas (UPI)	10-1-0	Darrell Royal
(split)	Washington (CNN)	12-0-0	Don James	1969	Texas	11-0-0	Darrell Royal
1990	Colorado	11-1-1	Bill McCartney	1968	Ohio State	10-0-0	Woody Hayes
(split)	Georgia Tech (UPI)	11-0-1	Bobby Ross	1967	USC	10-1-0	John McKay
1989	Miami (Florida)	11-1-0	Dennis Erickson	1966	Notre Dame	9-0-1	Ara Parseghian
1988	Notre Dame	12-0-0	Lou Holtz	1965	Alabama	9-1-1	Bear Bryant
1987	Miami (Florida)	12-0-0	Jimmy Johnson	(split)	Michigan State (UPI)	10-1-0	Duffy Daugherty
1986	Penn State	12-0-0	Joe Paterno	1964	Alabama	10-1-0	Bear Bryant
1985	Oklahoma	11-1-0	Barry Switzer	1963	Texas	11-0-0	Darrell Royal

Note: National Championship selectors: The Associated Press (AP), 1936–present; United Press International (UPI), 1958–90; USA Today/CNN (CNN), 1991–96; USA Today/ESPN (ESPN), 1997–present. In 1996, the NCAA introduced overtime to break ties.

College Football: National Championships (cont.)

YEAR	CHAMPION	RECORD	HEAD COACH	YEAR	CHAMPION	RECORD	HEAD COACH
1962	USC	11-0-0	John McKay	(split)	Stanford (D)(H)	10-0-1	Pop Warner
1961	Alabama	11-0-0	Bear Bryant	1925	Alabama (H)	10-0-0	Wallace Wade
1960	Minnesota	8-2-0	Murray Warmath	(split)	Dartmouth (D)	8-0-0	Jesse Hawley
1959	Syracuse	11-0-0	Ben Schwartzwalder	1924	Notre Dame	10-0-0	Knute Rockne
1958	Louisiana State	11-0-0	Paul Dietzel	1923	Illinois	8-0-0	Bob Zuppke
1957	Auburn	10-0-0	Shug Jordan	1922	Cornell	8-0-0	Gil Dobie
(split)	Ohio State (UPI)	9-1-0	Woody Hayes	1921	Cornell	8-0-0	Gil Dobie
1956	Oklahoma	10-0-0	Bud Wilkinson	1920	California	9-0-0	Andy Smith
1955	Oklahoma	11-0-0	Bud Wilkinson	1919	Harvard	9-0-1	Bob Fisher
1954	Ohio State	10-0-0	Woody Hayes	1918	Pittsburgh	4-1-0	Pop Warner
(split)	UCLA (UPI)	9-0-0	Red Sanders	1917	Georgia Tech	9-0-0	John Heisman
1953	Maryland	10-1-0	Jim Tatum	1916	Pittsburgh	8-0-0	Pop Warner
1952	Michigan State	9-0-0	Biggie Munn	1915	Cornell	9-0-0	Al Sharpe
1951	Tennessee	10-1-0	Robert Neyland	1914	Army	9-0-0	Charley Daly
1950	Oklahoma	10-1-0	Bud Wilkinson	1913	Harvard	9-0-0	Percy Haughton
1949	Notre Dame	10-0-0	Frank Leahy	1912	Harvard	9-0-0	Percy Haughton
1948	Michigan	9-0-0	Bennie Oosterbaan	1911	Princeton	8-0-2	Bill Roper
1947	Notre Dame	9-0-0	Frank Leahy	1910	Harvard	8-0-1	Percy Haughton
(split)	Michigan	10-0-0	Fritz Crisler	1909	Yale	10-0-0	Howard Jones
1946	Notre Dame	8-0-1	Frank Leahy	1908	Pennsylvania	11-0-1	Sol Metzger
1945	Army	9-0-0	Red Blaik	1907	Yale	9-0-1	Bill Knox
1944	Army	9-0-0	Red Blaik	1906	Princeton	9-0-1	Bill Roper
1943	Notre Dame	9-1-0	Frank Leahy	1905	Chicago	10-0-0	Amos Alonzo Stagg
1942	Ohio State	9-1-0	Paul Brown	1904	Pennsylvania	12-0-0	Carl Williams
1941	Minnesota	8-0-0	Bernie Bierman	1903	Princeton	11-0-0	Art Hillebrand
1940	Minnesota	8-0-0	Bernie Bierman	1902	Michigan	11-0-0	Fielding Yost
1939	Texas A&M (AP)	11-0-0	Homer Norton	1901	Michigan	11-0-0	Fielding Yost
(split)	USC (D)	8-0-2	Howard Jones	1900	Yale	12-0-0	Malcolm McBride
1938	TCU (AP)	11-0-0	Dutch Meyer	1899	Harvard	10-0-1	Benjamin H. Dibblee
(split)	Notre Dame (D)	8-1-0	Elmer Layden	1898	Harvard	11-0-0	W. Cameron Forbes
1937	Pittsburgh	9-0-1	Jock Sutherland	1897	Pennsylvania	15-0-0	George W. Woodruff
1936	Minnesota	7-1-0	Bernie Bierman	1896	Princeton	10-0-1	Garrett Cochran
1935	Minnesota (H)	8-0-0	Bernie Bierman	1895	Pennsylvania	14-0-0	George W. Woodruff
(split)	SMU (D)	12-1-0	Matty Bell	1894	Yale	16-0-0	William C. Rhodes
1934	Minnesota	8-0-0	Bernie Bierman	1893	Princeton	11-0-0	Tom Trenchard
1933	Michigan	8-0-0	Harry Kipke	1892	Yale	13-0-0	Walter Camp
1932	USC (H)	10-0-0	Howard Jones	1891	Yale	13-0-0	Walter Camp
(split)	Michigan (D)	8-0-0	Harry Kipke	1890	Harvard	11-0-0	G. Stewart/G. Adams
1931	USC	10-1-0	Howard Jones	1889	Princeton	10-0-0	Edgar Poe
1930	Notre Dame	10-0-0	Knute Rockne	1888	Yale	13-0-0	Walter Camp
1929	Notre Dame	9-0-0	Knute Rockne	1887	Yale	9-0-0	Harry W. Beecher
1928	Georgia Tech (H)	10-0-0	Bill Alexander	1886	Yale	9-0-1	Robert N. Corwin
(split)	USC (D)	9-0-1	Howard Jones	1885	Princeton	9-0-0	Charles DeCamp
1927	Illinois	7-0-1	Bob Zuppke	1884	Yale	8-0-1	Eugene L. Richards
1926	Alabama (H)	9-0-1	Wallace Wade	1883	Yale	8-0-0	Ray Tompkins

Note: National Championship selectors: Helms Athletic Foundation (H), 1883–1935; The Dickinson System (D), 1924–40; The Associated Press (AP), 1936–present; United Press International (UPI), 1958–90.

College Football: Major Bowl Game Results

ROSE BOWL

DATE	RESULT	DATE	RESULT	DATE	RESULT
1-1-08	USC 35, Illinois 10	1-2-95	Penn State 38, Oregon 20	1-1-82	Washington 28, Iowa 0
1-1-07	USC 32, Michigan 18	1-1-94	Wisconsin 21, UCLA 16	1-1-81	Michigan 23, Washington 6
1-4-06	Texas 41, USC 38	1-1-93	Michigan 38, Washington 31	1-1-80	USC 17, Ohio State 16
1-1-05	Texas 38, Michigan 37	1-1-92	Washington 34, Michigan 14	1-1-79	USC 17, Michigan 10
1-1-04	USC 28, Michigan 14	1-1-91	Washington 46, Iowa 34	1-2-78	Washington 27, Michigan 20
1-1-03	Oklahoma 34, Washington State 14	1-1-90	USC 17, Michigan 10	1-1-77	USC 14, Michigan 6
1-3-02	Miami 37, Nebraska 14	1-2-89	Michigan 22, USC 14	1-1-76	UCLA 23, Ohio State 10
1-1-01	Washington 34, Purdue 24	1-1-88	Michigan State 20, USC 17	1-1-75	USC 18, Ohio State 17
1-1-00	Wisconsin 17, Stanford 9	1-1-87	Arizona State 22, Michigan 15	1-1-74	Ohio State 42, USC 21
1-1-99	Wisconsin 38, UCLA 31	1-1-86	UCLA 45, Iowa 28	1-1-73	USC 42, Ohio State 17
1-1-98	Michigan 21, Washington State 16	1-1-85	USC 20, Ohio State 17	1-1-72	Stanford 13, Michigan 12
1-1-97	Ohio State 20, Arizona State 17	1-2-84	UCLA 45, Illinois 9	1-1-71	Stanford 27, Ohio State 17
1-1-96	USC 41, Northwestern 32	1-1-83	UCLA 24, Michigan 14	1-1-70	USC 10, Michigan 3

College Football: Major Bowl Game Results (cont.)

ROSE BOWL (cont.)

DATE	RESULT	DATE	RESULT	DATE	RESULT
1-1-69	Ohio State 27, USC 16	1-1-49	Northwestern 20, California 14	1-1-29	Georgia Tech 8, California 7
1-1-68	USC 14, Indiana 3	1-1-48	Michigan 49, USC 0	1-2-28	Stanford 7, Pittsburgh 6
1-2-67	Purdue 14, USC 13	1-1-47	Illinois 45, UCLA 14	1-1-27	Stanford 7, Alabama 7
1-1-66	UCLA 14, Michigan State 12	1-1-46	Alabama 34, USC 14	1-1-26	Alabama 20, Washington 19
1-1-65	Michigan 34, Oregon State 7	1-1-45	USC 25, Tennessee 0	1-1-25	Notre Dame 27, Stanford 10
1-1-64	Illinois 17, Washington 7	1-1-44	USC 29, Washington 0	1-1-24	Washington 14, Navy 14
1-1-63	USC 42, Wisconsin 37	1-1-43	Georgia 9, UCLA 0	1-1-23	USC 14, Penn State 3
1-1-62	Minnesota 21, UCLA 3	1-1-42	Oregon State 20, Duke 16	1-2-22	California 0, Washington & Jefferson 0
1-2-61	Washington 17, Minnesota 7	1-1-41	Stanford 21, Nebraska 13	1-1-21	California 28, Ohio State 0
1-1-60	Washington 44, Wisconsin 8	1-1-40	USC 14, Tennessee 0	1-1-20	Harvard 7, Oregon 6
1-1-59	Iowa 38, California 12	1-2-39	USC 7, Duke 3	1-1-19	Great Lakes 17, Mare Island 0
1-1-58	Ohio State 10, Oregon 7	1-1-38	California 13, Alabama 0	1-1-18	Mare Island 19, Camp Lewis 7
1-1-57	Iowa 35, Oregon State 19	1-1-37	Pittsburgh 21, Washington 0	1-1-17	Oregon 14, Pennsylvania 0
1-2-56	Michigan State 17, UCLA 14	1-1-36	Stanford 7, SMU 0	1-1-16	Washington State 14, Brown 0
1-1-55	Ohio State 20, USC 7	1-1-35	Alabama 29, Stanford 13	1-1-02	Michigan 49, Stanford 0
1-1-54	Michigan State 28, UCLA 20	1-1-34	Columbia 7, Stanford 0		
1-1-53	USC 7, Wisconsin 0	1-2-33	USC 35, Pittsburgh 0		
1-1-52	Illinois 40, Stanford 7	1-1-32	USC 21, Tulane 12		
1-1-51	Michigan 14, California 6	1-1-31	Alabama 24, Washington State 0		
1-2-50	Ohio State 17, California 14	1-1-30	USC 47, Pittsburgh 14		

Note: From 1903 to 1915, no Rose Bowl football game was held. In 1903, polo replaced football. From 1904 to 1915, chariot races were held. Football returned in 1916.

ORANGE BOWL

DATE	RESULT	DATE	RESULT
1-3-08	Kansas 24, Virginia Tech 21	1-1-71	Nebraska 17, LSU 12
1-2-07	Louisville 24, Wake Forest 13	1-1-70	Penn State 10, Missouri 3
1-3-06	Penn State 26, Florida State 23	1-1-69	Penn State 15, Kansas 14
1-4-05	USC 55, Oklahoma 19	1-1-68	Oklahoma 26, Tennessee 24
1-1-04	Miami (Florida) 16, Florida State 14	1-2-67	Florida 27, Georgia Tech 12
1-2-03	USC 38, Iowa 17	1-1-66	Alabama 39, Nebraska 28
1-2-02	Florida 56, Maryland 23	1-1-65	Texas 21, Alabama 17
1-3-01	Oklahoma 13, Florida State 2	1-1-64	Nebraska 13, Auburn 7
1-1-00	Michigan 35, Alabama 34 (OT)	1-1-63	Alabama 17, Oklahoma 0
1-2-99	Florida 31, Syracuse 10	1-1-62	LSU 25, Colorado 7
1-2-98	Nebraska 42, Tennessee 17	1-2-61	Missouri 21, Navy 14
12-31-96	Nebraska 41, Virginia Tech 21	1-1-60	Georgia 14, Missouri 0
1-1-96	Florida State 31, Notre Dame 26	1-1-59	Oklahoma 21, Syracuse 6
1-1-95	Nebraska 24, Miami (Florida) 17	1-1-58	Oklahoma 48, Duke 21
1-1-94	Florida State 18, Nebraska 16	1-1-57	Colorado 27, Clemson 21
1-1-93	Florida State 27, Nebraska 14	1-2-56	Oklahoma 20, Maryland 6
1-1-92	Miami (Florida) 22, Nebraska 0	1-1-55	Duke 34, Nebraska 7
1-1-91	Colorado 10, Notre Dame 9	1-1-54	Oklahoma 7, Maryland 0
1-1-90	Notre Dame 21, Colorado 6	1-1-53	Alabama 61, Syracuse 6
1-2-89	Miami (Florida) 23, Nebraska 3	1-1-52	Georgia Tech 17, Baylor 14
1-1-88	Miami (Florida) 20, Oklahoma 14	1-1-51	Clemson 15, Miami (Florida) 14
1-1-87	Oklahoma 42, Arkansas 8	1-2-50	Santa Clara 21, Kentucky 13
1-1-86	Oklahoma 25, Penn State 10	1-1-49	Texas 41, Georgia 28
1-1-85	Washington 28, Oklahoma 17	1-1-48	Georgia Tech 20, Kansas 14
1-2-84	Miami (Florida) 31, Nebraska 30	1-1-47	Rice 8, Tennessee 0
1-1-83	Nebraska 21, LSU 20	1-1-46	Miami (Florida) 13, Holy Cross 6
1-1-82	Clemson 22, Nebraska 15	1-1-45	Tulsa 26, Georgia Tech 12
1-1-81	Oklahoma 18, Florida State 17	1-1-44	LSU 19, Texas A&M 14
1-1-80	Oklahoma 24, Florida State 7	1-1-43	Alabama 37, Boston College 21
1-1-79	Oklahoma 31, Nebraska 24	1-1-42	Georgia 40, TCU 26
1-2-78	Arkansas 31, Oklahoma 6	1-1-41	Mississippi State 14, Georgetown 7
1-1-77	Ohio State 27, Colorado 10	1-1-40	Georgia Tech 21, Missouri 7
1-1-76	Oklahoma 14, Michigan 6	1-2-39	Tennessee 17, Oklahoma 0
1-1-75	Notre Dame 13, Alabama 11	1-1-38	Auburn 6, Michigan State 0
1-1-74	Penn State 16, LSU 9	1-1-37	Duquesne 13, Mississippi State 12
1-1-73	Nebraska 40, Notre Dame 6	1-1-36	Catholic 20, Mississippi 19
1-1-72	Nebraska 38, Alabama 6	1-1-35	Bucknell 26, Miami (Florida) 0

College Football: Major Bowl Game Results (cont.)

SUGAR BOWL

DATE	RESULT	DATE	RESULT
1-1-08	Georgia 41, Hawaii 10	1-1-71	Tennessee 34, Air Force 13
1-3-07	LSU 41, Notre Dame 14	1-1-70	Mississippi 27, Arkansas 22
1-2-06	West Virginia 38, Georgia 35	1-1-69	Arkansas 16, Georgia 2
1-3-05	Auburn 16, Virginia Tech 13	1-1-68	LSU 20, Wyoming 13
1-4-04	LSU 21, Oklahoma 14	1-2-67	Alabama 34, Nebraska 7
1-1-03	Georgia 26, Florida State 13	1-1-66	Missouri 20, Florida 18
1-1-02	LSU 47, Illinois 34	1-1-65	LSU 13, Syracuse 10
1-2-01	Miami (Florida) 37, Florida 20	1-1-64	Alabama 12, Mississippi 7
1-4-00	Florida State 46, Virginia Tech 29	1-1-63	Mississippi 17, Arkansas 13
1-1-99	Ohio State 24, Texas A&M 14	1-1-62	Alabama 10, Arkansas 3
1-1-98	Florida State 31, Ohio State 14	1-2-61	Mississippi 14, Rice 6
1-2-97	Florida 52, Florida State 20	1-1-60	Mississippi 21, LSU 0
12-31-95	Virginia Tech 28, Texas 10	1-1-59	LSU 7, Clemson 0
1-2-95	Florida State 23, Florida 17	1-1-58	Mississippi 39, Texas 7
1-1-94	Florida 41, West Virginia 7	1-1-57	Baylor 13, Tennessee 7
1-1-93	Alabama 34, Miami (Florida) 13	1-2-56	Georgia Tech 7, Pittsburgh 0
1-1-92	Notre Dame 39, Florida 28	1-1-55	Navy 21, Mississippi 0
1-1-91	Tennessee 23, Virginia 22	1-1-54	Georgia Tech 42, West Virginia 19
1-1-90	Miami (Florida) 33, Alabama 25	1-1-53	Georgia Tech 24, Mississippi 7
1-2-89	Florida State 13, Auburn 7	1-1-52	Maryland 28, Tennessee 13
1-1-88	Auburn 16, Syracuse 16	1-1-51	Kentucky 13, Oklahoma 7
1-1-87	Nebraska 30, LSU 15	1-2-50	Oklahoma 35, LSU 0
1-1-86	Tennessee 35, Miami (Florida) 7	1-1-49	Oklahoma 14, North Carolina 6
1-1-85	Nebraska 28, LSU 10	1-1-48	Texas 27, Alabama 7
1-2-84	Auburn 9, Michigan 7	1-1-47	Georgia 20, North Carolina 10
1-1-83	Penn State 27, Georgia 23	1-1-46	Oklahoma State 33, Saint Mary's 13
1-1-82	Pittsburgh 24, Georgia 20	1-1-45	Duke 29, Alabama 26
1-1-81	Georgia 17, Notre Dame 10	1-1-44	Georgia Tech 20, Tulsa 18
1-1-80	Alabama 24, Arkansas 9	1-1-43	Tennessee 14, Tulsa 7
1-1-79	Alabama 14, Penn State 7	1-1-42	Fordham 2, Missouri 0
1-2-78	Alabama 35, Ohio State 6	1-1-41	Boston College 19, Tennessee 13
1-1-77	Pittsburgh 27, Georgia 3	1-1-40	Texas A&M 14, Tulane 13
12-31-75	Alabama 13, Penn State 6	1-2-39	TCU 15, Carnegie Mellon 7
12-31-74	Nebraska 13, Florida 10	1-1-38	Santa Clara 6, LSU 0
12-31-73	Notre Dame 24, Alabama 23	1-1-37	Santa Clara 21, LSU 14
12-31-72	Oklahoma 14, Penn State 0	1-1-36	TCU 3, LSU 2
1-1-72	Oklahoma 40, Auburn 22	1-1-35	Tulane 20, Temple 14

COTTON BOWL

DATE	RESULT	DATE	RESULT
1-1-08	Missouri 38, Arizona 7	1-1-91	Miami (Florida) 46, Texas 3
1-1-07	Auburn 17, Nebraska 14	1-1-90	Tennessee 31, Arkansas 27
1-2-06	Alabama 13, Texas Tech 10	1-2-89	UCLA 17, Arkansas 3
1-1-05	Tennessee 38, Texas A&M 7	1-1-88	Texas A&M 35, Notre Dame 10
1-2-04	Mississippi 31, Oklahoma State 28	1-1-87	Ohio State 28, Texas A&M 12
1-1-03	Texas 35, LSU 20	1-1-86	Texas A&M 36, Auburn 16
1-1-02	Oklahoma 10, Arkansas 3	1-1-85	Boston College 45, Houston 28
1-1-01	Kansas State 35, Tennessee 21	1-2-84	Georgia 10, Texas 9
1-1-00	Arkansas 27, Texas 6	1-1-83	SMU 7, Pittsburgh 3
1-1-99	Texas 38, Mississippi State 11	1-1-82	Texas 14, Alabama 12
1-1-98	UCLA 29, Texas A&M 23	1-1-81	Alabama 30, Baylor 2
1-1-97	BYU 19, Kansas State 15	1-1-80	Houston 17, Nebraska 14
1-1-96	Colorado 38, Oregon 6	1-1-79	Notre Dame 35, Houston 34
1-2-95	USC 55, Texas Tech 14	1-2-78	Notre Dame 38, Texas 10
1-1-94	Notre Dame 24, Texas A&M 21	1-1-77	Houston 30, Maryland 21
1-1-93	Notre Dame 28, Texas A&M 3	1-1-76	Arkansas 31, Georgia 10
1-1-92	Florida State 10, Texas A&M 2	1-1-75	Penn State 41, Baylor 20

■ **Charlie Ward,** *quarterback, b. October 12, 1970, Thomasville, Georgia.* Ward accomplished more in 1993 than most athletes do in a lifetime. In the spring, he helped lead the Florida State basketball team to the NCAA Tournament's Elite Eight. In the fall, he won the school's first football national championship. Starring in a shotgun offense nicknamed the "Fast Break," Ward completed almost 70 percent of his passes and infuriated defenses with his scrambling ability. Florida State went 11–1 and defeated Nebraska in the 1994 Orange Bowl for the national title. FSU's first Heisman winner, Ward compiled 27 TD passes and nearly 3,400 total yards. Considered too small by NFL scouts, Ward went on to have a successful career in the NBA.

■ **Randy Moss,** *wide receiver, b. February 13, 1977, Rand, West Virginia.* Moss's brilliant college career

Randy Moss

of almost didn't happen. He had his scholarship to Notre Dame revoked in 1995 after he was charged with beating a high school classmate. He ended up at Florida State, but was thrown off the team for violating probation. One of the greatest players in college football history walked on to the Marshall team in his home state of West Virginia. In his two years with the Thundering Herd, Moss put up astronomical statistics: 168 catches, 3,467 receiving yards and 53 touchdowns. In 1997, he set a Division I single-season record with 25 TD grabs. In 2007, Moss set the NFL record for most touchdown receptions in a season (23) as a member of the New England Patriots.

■ **George Gipp,** *halfback, b. February 18, 1895, Laurium, Michigan, d. December 14, 1920, South Bend, Indiana.* Gipp died when he was 25, but he will live forever in college football lore. On his deathbed, Gipp instructed Notre Dame coach Knute Rockne to tell his players to "win one for the Gipper." Rockne used the line before the 1928 Army game, and the phrase was immortalized in the 1940 movie *Knute Rockne, All American.* Gipp had never played organized football when he arrived at Notre Dame, but was spotted by Rockne as he practiced drop-kicking footballs. Gipp racked up a combined 4,100 rushing and passing yards and helped the Irish to undefeated seasons in 1919 and 1920.

AL TIELEMANS

College Football: Major Bowl Game Results (cont.)

COTTON BOWL (cont.)

DATE	RESULT	DATE	RESULT
1-1-74	Nebraska 19, Texas 3	1-1-63	LSU 13, Texas 0
1-1-73	Texas 17, Alabama 13	1-1-62	Texas 12, Mississippi 7
1-1-72	Penn State 30, Texas 6	1-2-61	Duke 7, Arkansas 6
1-1-71	Notre Dame 24, Texas 11	1-1-60	Syracuse 23, Texas 14
1-1-70	Texas 21, Notre Dame 17	1-1-59	TCU 0, Air Force 0
1-1-69	Texas 36, Tennessee 13	1-1-58	Navy 20, Rice 7
1-1-68	Texas A&M 20, Alabama 16	1-1-57	TCU 28, Syracuse 27
12-31-66	Georgia 24, SMU 9	1-2-56	Mississippi 14, TCU 13
1-1-66	LSU 14, Arkansas 7	1-1-55	Georgia Tech 14, Arkansas 6
1-1-65	Arkansas 10, Nebraska 7	1-1-54	Rice 28, Alabama 6
1-1-64	Texas 28, Navy 6	1-1-53	Texas 16, Tennessee 0

College Football: Major Bowl Game Results (cont.)

COTTON BOWL (cont.)

DATE	RESULT	DATE	RESULT
1-1-52	Kentucky 20, TCU 7	1-1-44	Texas 7, Randolph Field 7
1-1-51	Tennessee 20, Texas 14	1-1-43	Texas 14, Georgia Tech 7
1-2-50	Rice 27, North Carolina 13	1-1-42	Alabama 29, Texas A&M 21
1-1-49	SMU 21, Oregon 13	1-1-41	Texas A&M 13, Fordham 12
1-1-48	SMU 13, Penn State 13	1-1-40	Clemson 6, Boston College 3
1-1-47	Arkansas 0, LSU 0	1-2-39	St. Mary's (CA) 20, Texas Tech 13
1-1-46	Texas 40, Missouri 27	1-1-38	Rice 28, Colorado 14
1-1-45	Oklahoma State 34, TCU 0	1-1-37	TCU 16, Marquette 6

FIESTA BOWL

DATE	RESULT	DATE	RESULT
1-2-08	West Virginia 48, Oklahoma 28	1-2-89	Notre Dame 34, West Virginia 21
1-2-07	Boise State 43, Oklahoma 42 (OT)	1-1-88	Florida State 31, Nebraska 28
1-2-06	Ohio State 34, Notre Dame 20	1-2-87	Penn State 14, Miami (Florida) 10
1-1-05	Utah 35, Pittsburgh 7	1-1-86	Michigan 27, Nebraska 23
1-2-04	Ohio State 35, Kansas St. 28	1-1-85	UCLA 39, Miami (Florida) 37
1-3-03	Ohio State 31, Miami (Florida) 24	1-2-84	Ohio State 28, Pittsburgh 23
1-1-02	Oregon 38, Colorado 16	1-1-83	Arizona State 32, Oklahoma 21
1-1-01	Oregon State 41, Notre Dame 9	1-1-82	Penn State 26, USC 10
1-2-00	Nebraska 31, Tennessee 21	12-26-80	Penn State 31, Ohio State 19
1-4-99	Tennessee 23, Florida State 16	12-25-79	Pittsburgh 16, Arizona 10
12-31-97	Kansas State 35, Syracuse 18	12-25-78	Arkansas 10, UCLA 10
1-1-97	Penn State 38, Texas 15	12-25-77	Penn State 42, Arizona State 30
1-2-96	Nebraska 62, Florida 24	12-25-76	Oklahoma 41, Wyoming 7
1-2-95	Colorado 41, Notre Dame 24	12-26-75	Arizona State 17, Nebraska 14
1-1-94	Arizona 29, Miami (Florida) 0	12-28-74	Oklahoma State 16, BYU 6
1-1-93	Syracuse 26, Colorado 22	12-21-73	Arizona State 28, Pittsburgh 7
1-1-92	Penn State 42, Tennessee 17	12-23-72	Arizona State 49, Missouri 35
1-1-91	Louisville 34, Alabama 7	12-27-71	Arizona State 45, Florida State 38
1-1-90	Florida State 41, Nebraska 17		

BCS NATIONAL CHAMPIONSHIP GAME

DATE	RESULT
1-7-08	LSU 38, Ohio State 24
1-8-07	Florida 41, Ohio State 14

NCAA Division I-AA Football Championships

YEAR	WINNER	RUNNER-UP	SCORE	YEAR	WINNER	RUNNER-UP	SCORE
2007	Appalachian State	Delaware	49–21	1992	Marshall	Youngstown State	31–28
2006	Appalachian State	Massachusetts	28–17	1991	Youngstown State	Marshall	25–17
2005	Appalachian State	Northern Iowa	21–16	1990	Georgia Southern	Nevada-Reno	36–13
2004	James Madison	Montana	31–21	1989	Georgia Southern	Stephen F. Austin	37–34
2003	Delaware	Colgate	40–0	1988	Furman	Georgia Southern	17–12
2002	Western Kentucky	McNeese State	34–14	1987	Louisiana Monroe	Marshall	43–42
2001	Montana	Furman	13–6	1986	Georgia Southern	Arkansas State	48–21
2000	Georgia Southern	Montana	27–25	1985	Georgia Southern	Furman	44–42
1999	Georgia Southern	Youngstown State	59–24	1984	Montana State	Louisiana Tech	19–6
1998	Massachusetts	Georgia Southern	55–43	1983	Southern Illinois	Western Carolina	43–7
1997	Youngstown State	McNeese State	10–9	1982	Eastern Kentucky	Delaware	17–14
1996	Marshall	Montana	49–29	1981	Idaho State	Eastern Kentucky	34–23
1995	Montana	Marshall	22–20	1980	Boise State	Eastern Kentucky	31–29
1994	Youngstown State	Boise State	28–14	1979	Eastern Kentucky	Lehigh	30–7
1993	Youngstown State	Marshall	17–5	1978	Florida A&M	Massachusetts	35–28

Heisman Memorial Trophy Award Winners

Awarded to the nation's best college player by the Downtown Athletic Club (DAC) of New York City. The trophy is named after John W. Heisman, who coached Georgia Tech to the national championship in 1917 and later served as DAC athletic director.

YEAR	WINNER, COLLEGE	RUNNER-UP, COLLEGE
2007	Tim Tebow*, Florida	Darren McFadden, Arkansas
2006	Troy Smith, Ohio State	Darren McFadden, Arkansas
2005	Reggie Bush, USC	Vince Young, Texas
2004	Matt Leinart**†, USC	Adrian Peterson, Oklahoma
2003	Jason White**, Oklahoma	Larry Fitzgerald, Pittsburgh
2002	Carson Palmer, USC	Brad Banks, Iowa
2001	Eric Crouch, Nebraska	Rex Grossman, Florida
2000	Chris Weinke, Florida State	Josh Heupel, Oklahoma
1999	Ron Dayne, Wisconsin	Joe Hamilton, Georgia Tech
1998	Ricky Williams, Texas	Michael Bishop, Kansas State
1997	Charles Woodson†, Michigan	Peyton Manning, Tennessee
1996	Danny Wuerffel†, Florida	Troy Davis, Iowa State
1995	Eddie George, Ohio State	Tommie Frazier, Nebraska
1994	Rashaan Salaam, Colorado	Ki-Jana Carter, Penn State
1993	Charlie Ward†, Florida State	Heath Shuler, Tennessee
1992	Gino Torretta, Miami (Florida)	Marshall Faulk, San Diego State
1991	Desmond Howard**, Michigan	Casey Weldon, Florida State
1990	Ty Detmer**, BYU	Raghib Ismail, Notre Dame
1989	Andre Ware**, Houston	Anthony Thompson, Indiana
1988	Barry Sanders**, Oklahoma State	Rodney Peete, USC
1987	Tim Brown, Notre Dame	Don McPherson, Syracuse
1986	Vinny Testaverde, Miami (Florida)	Paul Palmer, Temple
1985	Bo Jackson, Auburn	Chuck Long, Iowa
1984	Doug Flutie, Boston College	Keith Byars, Ohio State
1983	Mike Rozier, Nebraska	Steve Young, BYU
1982	Herschel Walker**, Georgia	John Elway, Stanford
1981	Marcus Allen, USC	Herschel Walker, Georgia
1980	George Rogers, South Carolina	Hugh Green, Pittsburgh
1979	Charles White, USC	Billy Sims, Oklahoma
1978	Billy Sims**, Oklahoma	Chuck Fusina, Penn State
1977	Earl Campbell, Texas	Terry Miller, Oklahoma State
1976	Tony Dorsett†, Pittsburgh	Ricky Bell, USC
1975	Archie Griffin, Ohio State	Chuck Muncie, California
1974	Archie Griffin**, Ohio State	Anthony Davis, USC
1973	John Cappelletti, Penn State	John Hicks, Ohio State
1972	Johnny Rodgers, Nebraska	Greg Pruitt, Oklahoma
1971	Pat Sullivan, Auburn	Ed Marinaro, Cornell
1970	Jim Plunkett, Stanford	Joe Theismann, Notre Dame
1969	Steve Owens, Oklahoma	Mike Phipps, Purdue
1968	O.J. Simpson, USC	Leroy Keyes, Purdue
1967	Gary Beban, UCLA	O.J. Simpson, USC
1966	Steve Spurrier, Florida	Bob Griese, Purdue
1965	Mike Garrett, USC	Howard Twilley, Tulsa
1964	John Huarte, Notre Dame	Jerry Rhome, Tulsa
1963	Roger Staubach**, Navy	Billy Lothridge, Georgia Tech
1962	Terry Baker, Oregon State	Jerry Stovall, LSU

* Sophomore   ** Junior (all others were seniors)
† Winners who played for national championship teams the same year

Heisman Memorial Trophy Award Winners (cont.)

YEAR	WINNER, COLLEGE	RUNNER-UP, COLLEGE
1961	Ernie Davis, Syracuse	Bob Ferguson, Ohio State
1960	Joe Bellino, Navy	Tom Brown, Minnesota
1959	Billy Cannon, LSU	Rich Lucas, Penn State
1958	Pete Dawkins, Army	Randy Duncan, Iowa
1957	John David Crow, Texas A&M	Alex Karras, Iowa
1956	Paul Hornung, Notre Dame	Johnny Majors, Tennessee
1955	Howard Cassady, Ohio State	Jim Swink, TCU
1954	Alan Ameche, Wisconsin	Kurt Burris, Oklahoma
1953	John Lattner, Notre Dame	Paul Giel, Minnesota
1952	Billy Vessels, Oklahoma	Jack Scarbath, Maryland
1951	Dick Kazmaier, Princeton	Hank Lauricella, Tennessee
1950	Vic Janowicz**, Ohio State	Kyle Rote, SMU
1949	Leon Hartt†, Notre Dame	Charlie Justice, North Carolina
1948	Doak Walker**, SMU	Charlie Justice, North Carolina
1947	John Lujack†, Notre Dame	Bob Chappius, Michigan
1946	Glenn Davis, Army	Charley Trippi, Georgia
1945	Doc Blanchard**†, Army	Glenn Davis, Army
1944	Les Horvath, Ohio State	Glenn Davis, Army
1943	Angelo Bertelli, Notre Dame	Bob Odell, Pennsylvania
1942	Frank Sinkwich, Georgia	Paul Governali, Columbia
1941	Bruce Smith†, Minnesota	Angelo Bertelli, Notre Dame
1940	Tom Harmon, Michigan	John Kimbrough, Texas A&M
1939	Nile Kinnick, Iowa	Tom Harmon, Michigan
1938	Davey O'Brien†, TCU	Marshall Goldberg, Pittsburgh
1937	Clint Frank, Yale	Byron White, Colorado
1936	Larry Kelley, Yale	Sam Francis, Nebraska
1935	Jay Berwanger, Chicago	Monk Meyer, Army

** Juniors (all others were seniors)
† Winners who played for national championship teams the same year

↑ RANKINGS Best Programs

POWER

1 **USC (754 wins):** Since 2002, USC has had three Heisman Trophy winners, two AP national titles, and one BCS title.

2 **LSU (692 wins):** In 2007, the Tigers became the first two-time champs since the creation of the BCS.

3 **Ohio State (797 wins):** The 2002 national champs are 23–1 over the last two regular seasons, but were clobbered in the BCS Championship Game both times.

4 **Florida (628 wins):** The Gators had a disappointing 2007, but they never lack for talent — like 2007 Heisman winner Tim Tebow.

5 **Oklahoma (779 wins):** Like the Buckeyes, the Sooners have won a national title in the last decade, but lost in two other championship games.

6 **Texas (820 wins):** Won the 2005 title in dramatic fashion over USC, but that was with a once-in-a-lifetime quarterback named Vince Young.

7 **Georgia (713 wins):** The Bulldogs have played in three SEC championship games over the last six years, and many believe they deserved to play for the 2007 national title.

8 **Auburn (676 wins):** Ignored by the BCS despite a 13–0 record in 2004, the Tigers had beaten Alabama six straight times entering 2008.

9 **Michigan (869 wins):** Coach Rich Rodriguez will attempt to restore Michigan to past glory.

10 **Tennessee (771 wins):** The Volunteers rebounded to win a combined 19 games in 2006 and 2007 after a disastrous 5–6 campaign in 2005.

2005 Heisman winner Reggie Bush of USC

PETER READ MILLER

1 Which distinction can Michigan lay claim to?

A. A Wolverines coach invented the forward pass.

B. It's the winningest program in college football history.

C. The team was the first to wear plastic helmets.

The Big House at Michigan

2 What is the Rutgers football program famous for?

A. One of its professors created the word "touchdown."

B. The team played in the first college game.

C. Engineering students designed the first goal posts.

3 Which school is known as "Tailback U" for its many great running backs?

A. Ohio State

B. Oklahoma

C. USC

4 How many players are allowed on a football field at one time?

A. 11

B. 22

C. 33

5 Which current SEC head coach won the 1966 Heisman Trophy as a Florida quarterback?

A. Urban Meyer

B. Phil Fulmer

C. Steve Spurrier

6 Clemson's stadium is known as "Death Valley." Which SEC school has a stadium that goes by the same nickname?

A. Florida

B. Georgia

C. LSU

7 When was overtime introduced to major college football?

A. 1976

B. 1986

C. 1996

8 What official record does Oklahoma State's Barry Sanders still hold?

A. Single-season rushing record

B. Longest run from scrimmage

C. Most missed tackles

9 What material is the outer layer of the Heisman Trophy made of?

A. Copper

B. Granite

C. Bronze

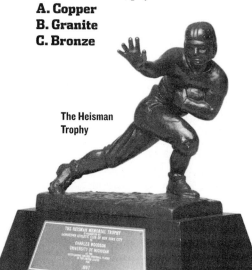

The Heisman Trophy

1.B, 2.B, 3.C, 4.B, 5.C, 6.C, 7.C, 8.A, 9.C

A Thrilling Finish

Everybody wondered the same thing after the 2008 Final Four's first night: What happened to March Madness? An event that built its reputation on buzzer-beaters, Cinderellas, and loads of drama supplied little of all three. Prior to the title game, 30 of the 63 games played were decided by 15 or more points — including both national semifinal games.

Tiny Davidson College provided a glimmer of hope by advancing to the Elite Eight. But that hope was extinguished when the No. 10 seed lost to Kansas, by missing a potential game-winning three at the buzzer.

Television ratings were way down, and although history was made (never before had all No. 1 seeds reached the Final Four), no one seemed particularly excited. The regular season was short on surprises. Memphis set an NCAA record with 38 wins in a single season, mostly by chewing up on lesser competition, and the teams in the Final Four entered the season's last weekend with a combined record of 143–9. So by the time Kansas and Memphis squared off for the title on April 7, most fans were just happy to see the basketball season come to an end. Little did they know that one of the greatest games in college basketball history was about to unfold.

After a seesaw first half, the Jayhawks led 33–28 at the intermission. But Kansas couldn't match Memphis' intensity coming out of the break, and the Tigers' superstar freshman guard, Derrick Rose, took over. During a 10–0 run, Rose scored eight of the team's points. And then, with just over four minutes left, Rose hit a fadeaway bank shot as the shot clock expired. It looked as if this would be Memphis' year.

At the 2:12 mark, the Jayhawks were down by nine. But after a crucial steal of an inbounds pass, Kansas scored five points in a span of eight seconds. The Jayhawks then had no choice but to foul Memphis and hope for a miracle against one of the worst free throw-shooting teams in the country. The Tigers missed four of five shots from the charity stripe down the stretch to give Kansas one last chance. With 10.8 seconds to go and the Jayhawks down by three, Kansas guard Sherron Collins rushed up the floor, stumbled, and shoveled the ball to teammate Mario Chalmers, who launched a rainbow three-pointer. It dropped through the hoop with 2.1 seconds left and sent the game into overtime as the Alamodome broke into chaos. Shell-shocked, Memphis couldn't muster a fight in the extra period.

The final score: 75–68, Kansas. The hero: Mario Chalmers.

Mario Chalmers's three-point shot capped off a furious Kansas comeback.

BOB ROSATO

UCLA forward Kevin Love was named first-team All-America after averaging 17.5 points and 10.6 rebounds as a freshman.

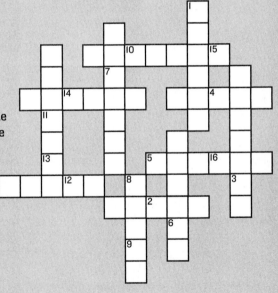

↑ RANKINGS   Best Coaches

POWER

1 **Rick Pitino, Louisville** The only coach to lead three different teams to the Final Four has rebuilt the Cardinals.

2 **Roy Williams, North Carolina** In five years at his alma mater, Williams has won over 80 percent of his games and a national title in 2005.

3 **Ben Howland, UCLA** In his five years, the Bruins have gone to three straight Final Fours.

4 **John Calipari , Memphis** The offensive guru has gone 104–10 in the last three years.

5 **Bill Self, Kansas** Has won big everywhere he's gone. Now people will finally stop asking if he can win the Big One.

6 **Mike Krzyzewski, Duke** Still a legend, but advancing past the Sweet 16 just once in the past seven years is cause for concern.

7 **Tom Izzo, Michigan State** Once went to four Final Fours in seven years, but recent NCAA trips have been disappointing.

8 **Bruce Pearl, Tennessee** This sparkplug has turned a dormant program into an SEC giant.

9 **Bob Huggins, West Virginia** Sure, he's got personal issues, but boy can he coach and recruit. Cincinnati looks foolish for forcing him out.

10 **Tony Bennett, Washington State** Transformed a Pac 10 doormat into a power virtually overnight.

BOB ROSATO

Mike Krzyzewski

GAME TIME

Making History

Who is the only University of Kansas men's basketball coach to own a losing record?

To find out, place the last names of these NCAA basketball coaches into the grid so they crisscross like a crossword. Then write the letters in the numbered boxes on the spaces with the same number.

Mike DAVIS   Jim CALHOUN
Jeff JONES   Billy DONOVAN
Thad MATTA   Leon KRUGER
Bruce WEBER   Rick MAJERUS
Steve FISHER   Rick PITINO
Bob KNIGHT   Rom PENDERS

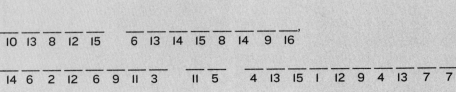

__ __ __ __ __ __ __ __ __ __ __ __ __ ,
10 13 8 12 15 6 13 14 15 8 14 9 16

__ __ __ __ __ __ __ __ __ __ __ __ __ __ __ __ __ __ __ __ .
14 6 2 12 6 9 11 3 11 5 4 13 15 1 12 9 4 13 7 7

ANSWERS ON PAGE 190

NCAA Men's Division I: All-Time Single-Season Leaders

POINTS						
PLAYER, SCHOOL	YEAR	GP	FG	3FG	FT	PTS
Pete Maravich, LSU	1970	31	522	—	337	1,381
Elvin Hayes, Houston	1968	33	519	—	176	1,214
Frank Selvy, Furman	1954	29	427	—	355	1,209
Pete Maravich, LSU	1969	26	433	—	282	1,148
Pete Maravich, LSU	1968	26	432	—	274	1,138
Bo Kimble, Loyola Marymount	1990	32	404	92	231	1,131
Hersey Hawkins, Bradley	1988	31	377	87	284	1,125
Austin Carr, Notre Dame	1970	29	444	—	218	1,106
Austin Carr, Notre Dame	1971	29	430	—	241	1,101
Otis Birdsong, Houston	1977	36	452	—	186	1,090

SCORING AVERAGE						
PLAYER, SCHOOL	YEAR	GP	FG	FT	PTS	AVG
Pete Maravich, LSU	1970	31	522	337	1,381	44.5
Pete Maravich, LSU	1969	26	433	282	1,148	44.2
Pete Maravich, LSU	1968	26	432	274	1,138	43.8
Frank Selvy, Furman	1954	29	427	355	1,209	41.7
Johnny Neumann, Mississippi	1971	23	366	191	923	40.1
Freeman Williams, Portland State	1977	26	417	176	1,010	38.8
Billy McGill, Utah	1962	26	394	221	1,009	38.8
Calvin Murphy, Niagara	1968	24	337	242	916	38.2
Austin Carr, Notre Dame	1970	29	444	218	1,106	38.1
Austin Carr, Notre Dame	1971	29	430	241	1,101	38.0

Bo Kimble

REBOUND AVERAGE (BEFORE 1973)				
PLAYER, SCHOOL	YEAR	GP	REB	AVG
Charlie Slack, Marshall	1955	21	538	25.6
Leroy Wright, Pacific	1959	26	652	25.1
Art Quimby, Connecticut	1955	25	611	24.4
Charlie Slack, Marshall	1956	22	520	23.6
Ed Conlin, Fordham	1953	26	612	23.5

REBOUND AVERAGE (SINCE 1973)				
PLAYER, SCHOOL	YEAR	GP	REB	AVG
Kermit Washington, American Univ.	1973	25	511	20.4
Marvin Barnes, Providence	1973	30	571	19.0
Marvin Barnes, Providence	1974	32	597	18.7
Pete Padgett, Nevada	1973	26	462	17.8
Jim Bradley, Northern Illinois	1973	24	426	17.8

Note: Freshmen became eligible for varsity play before the 1972–73 season.

ASSISTS			
PLAYER, SCHOOL	YEAR	GP	A
Mark Wade, UNLV	1987	38	406
Avery Johnson, Southern Univ.	1988	30	399
Anthony Manuel, Bradley	1988	31	373
Avery Johnson, Southern Univ.	1987	31	333
Mark Jackson, St. John's (NY)	1986	32	328

KEY: GP=games played; FG=field goals; 3FG=3-point field goals; FT=free throws; PTS=points; AVG=average; REB=rebounds; A=assists

ANDY HAYT

All-Time Single-Season Leaders (cont.)

FIELD GOAL PERCENTAGE				
PLAYER, SCHOOL	**YEAR**	**FGM**	**FGA**	**PCT**
Steve Johnson, Oregon State	1981	235	315	74.6
Dwayne Davis, Florida	1989	179	248	72.2
Keith Walker, Utica	1985	154	216	71.3
Steve Johnson, Oregon State	1980	211	297	71.0
Adam Mark, Belmont	2002	150	212	70.8

FREE THROW PERCENTAGE				
PLAYER, SCHOOL	**YEAR**	**FTM**	**FTA**	**PCT**
Blake Ahearn, Missouri State*	2004	117	120	97.5
Ryan Toolson, Utah Valley Sate	2006	96	99	97.0
Derek Raivio, Gonzaga	2006	146	152	96.1
Craig Collins, Penn State	1985	94	98	95.9
A.J. Graves, Butler	2006	137	143	95.8

* formerly Southwest Missouri State

3-POINT FIELD GOAL PERCENTAGE				
PLAYER, SCHOOL	**YEAR**	**3FGM**	**3FGA**	**PCT**
Glenn Tropf, Holy Cross	1988	52	82	63.4
Sean Wightman, Western Michigan	1992	48	76	63.2
Keith Jennings, East Tennessee State	1991	84	142	59.2
Dave Calloway, Monmouth	1989	48	82	58.5
Steve Kerr, Arizona	1988	114	199	57.3

Derek Raivo

KEY: FGM=field goals made; FGA=field goals attempted; PCT=percentage; FTM=free throws made; FTA=free throws attempted; 3FGM=3-point field goals made; 3FGA=3-point field goals attempted

TRIVIA

1 What did the game's creator, Dr. James Naismith, use as the first basketball hoop?
A. Laundry basket
B. Hula hoop
C. Peach basket

2 What was UCLA center Lew Alcindor known as after a name change in 1971?
A. Kareem Abdul-Jabbar
B. Muhammad Ali
C. Mahmoud Abdul-Rauf

3 What is the nickname of legendary coach Bob Knight?
A. The Admiral
B. The General
C. Sergeant Slaughter

4 Which is NOT a difference between the NBA and college basketball?
A. Length of game
B. Location of three-point line
C. Size of basketball

5 What do Kentucky, Villanova, and Davidson all have in common?
A. The nickname "Wildcats"
B. All located in Kentucky
C. Each play in the SEC

6 What is the name for the Duke student section?
A. Hell's Belles
B. Devil Dogs
C. Cameron Crazies

Lew Alcindor

1.C, 2.A, 3.B, 4.C, 5.A, 6.C

■ **Tyler Hansbrough**, *forward, b. November 3, 1985, Poplar Bluff, Missouri*. When Hansbrough announced he would be returning for his senior season, there was just one thought on his mind: the 2009 national championship. And no one wants it more than the man they call "Psycho T." The 2008 National Player of the Year averaged 22.6 points per game and 10.2 rebounds for the Tar Heels in 2008, dominating the paint all year long. But UNC came up just short of winning it all in 2007 and 2008, leaving a bitter taste in his mouth.

■ **Stephen Curry**, *guard, b. March 14, 1988, Charlotte, North Carolina*. The son of former NBA sharpshooter Dell Curry, he was the baby-faced star of the 2008 Big Dance. Scoring 25.1 points per game over the season (fifth best in the country), Curry willed No. 10 seed Davidson to the Elite Eight with wins over Gonzaga, Georgetown, and Wisconsin. Against the Hoyas, Curry's shooting helped Davidson erase a 17-point second-half deficit. The sophomore averaged 32 points per game during the tourney.

Tyler Hansbrough

JOHN BIEVER

■ **Hasheem Thabeet**, *center, b. February 16, 1987, Dar es Salaam, Tanzania*. He didn't start playing the game until he was 16, but now Thabeet has a chance to join the likes of Emeka Okafor and Hilton Armstrong in a long line of great Connecticut big men. The 7' 3" giant from Tanzania with a 7' 5" wingspan has turned into a shot-blocking machine for the Huskies. In 2007–08, the sophomore ranked second in blocks in the nation (4.5 swats per game). He also averaged 10.5 points and 7.9 boards. And if he develops his feel for the game even further, the sky's the limit.

All-Time Single-Season Leaders (cont.)

STEALS			
PLAYER, SCHOOL	YEAR	GP	STL
Desmond Cambridge, Alabama A&M	2002	29	160
Mookie Blaylock, Oklahoma	1988	39	150
Aldwin Ware, Florida A&M	1988	29	142
Darron Brittman, Chicago State	1986	28	139
John Linehan, Providence	2002	31	139

BLOCKS			
PLAYER, SCHOOL	YEAR	GP	BLK
David Robinson, Navy	1986	35	207
Shawn James, Northeastern	2006	30	196
Mickell Gladness, Alabama A&M	2006	30	188
Adonal Foyle, Colgate	1997	28	180
Keith Closs, Central Conn. State	1996	28	178

KEY: GP=games played; STL=steals; BLK=blocks

NCAA Men's Division I: Championship Results

YEAR	WINNER	SCORE	RUNNER-UP	THIRD PLACE	FOURTH PLACE	WINNING COACH
2008	Kansas	75–68(OT)	Memphis	UCLA*	North Carolina*	Bill Self
2007	Florida	84–75	Ohio State	UCLA*	Georgetown*	Billy Donovan
2006	Florida	73–57	UCLA	George Mason*	LSU*	Billy Donovan
2005	North Carolina	75–70	Illinois	Michigan State*	Louisville*	Roy Williams
2004	Connecticut	82–73	Georgia Tech	Duke*	Oklahoma State*	Jim Calhoun
2003	Syracuse	81–78	Kansas	Texas*	Marquette*	Jim Boeheim
2002	Maryland	64–52	Indiana	Kansas*	Oklahoma*	Gary Williams
2001	Duke	82–72	Arizona	Maryland*	Michigan State*	Mike Krzyzewski
2000	Michigan State	89–76	Florida	Wisconsin*	North Carolina*	Tom Izzo
1999	Connecticut	77–74	Duke	Michigan State*	Ohio State*	Jim Calhoun
1998	Kentucky	78–69	Utah	Stanford*	North Carolina*	Tubby Smith
1997	Arizona	84–79(OT)	Kentucky	Minnesota*	North Carolina*	Lute Olson
1996	Kentucky	76–67	Syracuse	Vacated**	Mississippi State*	Rick Pitino
1995	UCLA	89–78	Arkansas	North Carolina*	Oklahoma State*	Jim Harrick
1994	Arkansas	76–72	Duke	Arizona*	Florida*	Nolan Richardson
1993	North Carolina	77–71	Vacated**	Kansas*	Kentucky*	Dean Smith
1992	Duke	71–51	Vacated**	Cincinnati*	Indiana*	Mike Krzyzewski
1991	Duke	72–65	Kansas	UNLV*	North Carolina*	Mike Krzyzewski
1990	UNLV	103–73	Duke	Arkansas*	Georgia Tech*	Jerry Tarkanian
1989	Michigan	80–79(OT)	Seton Hall	Duke*	Illinois*	Steve Fisher
1988	Kansas	83–79	Oklahoma	Arizona*	Duke*	Larry Brown
1987	Indiana	83–79	Syracuse	UNLV*	Providence*	Bobby Knight
1986	Louisville	74–73	Duke	Kansas*	LSU*	Denny Crum
1985	Villanova	72–69	Georgetown	St. John's (NY)*	Vacated**	Rollie Massimino
1984	Georgetown	66–64	Houston	Kentucky*	Virginia*	John Thompson
1983	North Carolina State	84–75	Houston	Georgia*	Louisville*	Jim Valvano
1982	North Carolina	54–52	Georgetown	Houston*	Louisville*	Dean Smith
1981	Indiana	63–62	North Carolina	Virginia	LSU	Bobby Knight
1980	Louisville	63–50	Vacated**	Purdue	Iowa	Denny Crum
1979	Michigan State	59–54	Indiana State	DePaul	Penn	Jud Heathcote
1978	Kentucky	75–64	Duke	Arkansas	Notre Dame	Joe Hall
1977	Marquette	94–88	North Carolina	UNLV	UNC-Charlotte	Al McGuire
1976	Indiana	67–59	Michigan	UCLA	Rutgers	Bobby Knight
1975	UCLA	86–68	Kentucky	Louisville	Syracuse	John Wooden
1974	North Carolina State	92–85	Marquette	UCLA	Kansas	Norm Sloan
1973	UCLA	76–64	Memphis State	Indiana	Providence	John Wooden
1972	UCLA	87–66	Florida State	North Carolina	Louisville	John Wooden
1971	UCLA	81–76	Vacated**	Vacated**	Kansas	John Wooden
1970	UCLA	68–62	Jacksonville	New Mexico State	St. Bonaventure	John Wooden
1969	UCLA	80–69	Purdue	Drake	North Carolina	John Wooden
1968	UCLA	92–72	North Carolina	Ohio State	Houston	John Wooden
1967	UCLA	78–55	Dayton	Houston	North Carolina	John Wooden
1966	Texas Western	79–64	Kentucky	Duke	Utah	Don Haskins
1965	UCLA	72–65	Michigan	Princeton	Wichita State	John Wooden
1964	UCLA	91–80	Duke	Michigan	Kansas State	John Wooden
1963	Loyola (Ill.)	98–83	Cincinnati	Duke	Oregon State	George Ireland
1962	Cincinnati	60–58(OT)	Ohio State	Wake Forest	UCLA	Edwin Jucker
1961	Cincinnati	71–59	Ohio State	Vacated**	Utah	Edwin Jucker
1960	Ohio State	70–65(OT)	California	Cincinnati	NYU	Fred Taylor
1959	California	75–55	West Virginia	Cincinnati	Louisville	Pete Newell
1958	Kentucky	71–70	Seattle	Temple	Kansas State	Adolph Rupp
1957	North Carolina	84–72	Kansas	San Francisco	Michigan State	Frank McGuire
1956	San Francisco	83–71	Iowa	Temple	SMU	Phil Woolpert
1955	San Francisco	77–63	La Salle	Colorado	Iowa	Phil Woolpert
1954	La Salle	92–76	Bradley	Penn State	USC	Kenneth Loeffler
1953	Indiana	69–68	Kansas	Washington	LSU	Branch McCracken
1952	Kansas	80–63	St. John's (NY)	Illinois	Santa Clara	Forrest Allen
1951	Kentucky	68–58	Kansas State	Illinois	Oklahoma State	Adolph Rupp
1950	City College of NY	71–68	Bradley North	Carolina State	Baylor	Nat Holman
1949	Kentucky	46–36	Oklahoma State	Illinois	Oregon State	Adolph Rupp
1948	Kentucky	58–42	Baylor	Holy Cross	Kansas State	Adolph Rupp
1947	Holy Cross	58–47	Oklahoma	Texas	City College of NY	Alvin Julian
1946	Oklahoma A&M	43–40	North Carolina	Ohio St.	California	Hank Iba
1945	Oklahoma A&M	49–45	NYU	Arkansas*	Ohio State*	Hank Iba
1944	Utah	42–40(OT)	Dartmouth	Iowa State*	Ohio State*	Vadal Peterson
1943	Wyoming	46–34	Georgetown	Texas*	DePaul*	Everett Shelton
1942	Stanford	53–38	Dartmouth	Colorado*	Kentucky*	Everett Dean
1941	Wisconsin	39–34	Washington State	Pittsburgh*	Arkansas*	Harold Foster
1940	Indiana	60–42	Kansas	Duquesne*	USC*	Branch McCracken
1939	Oregon	46–33	Ohio St.	Oklahoma*	Villanova*	Howard Hobson

* Tied for third place. ** Student-athletes representing St. Joseph's (Pennsylvania) in 1961, Villanova in 1971, Western Kentucky in 1971, UCLA in 1980, Memphis State in 1985, Michigan in 1992 and 1993, and Massachusetts in 1996 were declared ineligible subsequent to the tournament.

NCAA Final Four Most Outstanding Players

YEAR	WINNER, SCHOOL	YEAR	WINNER, SCHOOL	YEAR	WINNER, SCHOOL
2008	Mario Chalmers, Kansas	1984	Patrick Ewing, Georgetown	1960	Jerry Lucas, Ohio State
2007	Corey Brewer, Florida	1983	Akeem Olajuwon, Houston*	1959	Jerry West, West Virginia*
2006	Joakim Noah, Florida	1982	James Worthy, North Carolina	1958	Elgin Baylor, Seattle*
2005	Sean May, North Carolina	1981	Isiah Thomas, Indiana	1957	Wilt Chamberlain, Kansas*
2004	Emeka Okafor, Connecticut	1980	Darrell Griffith, Louisville	1956	Hal Lear, Temple*
2003	Carmelo Anthony, Syracuse	1979	Earvin Johnson, Michigan State	1955	Bill Russell, San Francisco
2002	Juan Dixon, Maryland	1978	Jack Givens, Kentucky	1954	Tom Gola, La Salle
2001	Shane Battier, Duke	1977	Butch Lee, Marquette	1953	B.H. Born, Kansas*
2000	Mateen Cleaves, Michigan State	1976	Kent Benson, Indiana	1952	Clyde Lovellette, Kansas
1999	Richard Hamilton, Connecticut	1975	Richard Washington, UCLA	1951	Bill Spivey, Kentucky
1998	Jeff Sheppard, Kentucky	1974	David Thompson, N.C. State	1950	Irwin Dambrot, CCNY
1997	Miles Simon, Arizona	1973	Bill Walton, UCLA	1949	Alex Groza, Kentucky
1996	Tony Delk, Kentucky	1972	Bill Walton, UCLA	1948	Alex Groza, Kentucky
1995	Ed O'Bannon, UCLA	1971	Howard Porter, Villanova*†	1947	George Kaftan, Holy Cross
1994	Corliss Williamson, Arkansas	1970	Sidney Wicks, UCLA	1946	Bob Kurland, Oklahoma A&M
1993	Donald Williams, North Carolina	1969	Lew Alcindor, UCLA**	1945	Bob Kurland, Oklahoma A&M
1992	Bobby Hurley, Duke	1968	Lew Alcindor, UCLA**	1944	Arnie Ferrin, Utah
1991	Christian Laettner, Duke	1967	Lew Alcindor, UCLA**	1943	Ken Sailors, Wyoming
1990	Anderson Hunt, UNLV	1966	Jerry Chambers, Utah*	1942	Howard Dallmar, Stanford
1989	Glen Rice, Michigan	1965	Bill Bradley, Princeton*	1941	John Kotz, Wisconsin
1988	Danny Manning, Kansas	1964	Walt Hazzard, UCLA	1940	Marv Huffman, Indiana
1987	Keith Smart, Indiana	1963	Art Heyman, Duke	1939	Jimmy Hull, Ohio State*
1986	Pervis Ellison, Louisville	1962	Paul Hogue, Cincinnati		
1985	Ed Pinckney, Villanova	1961	Jerry Lucas, Ohio State*		

* Not a member of the championship-winning team.
† Record later vacated.
** Alcindor changed his name to Kareem Abdul-Jabbar after the 1970–71 NBA season.

LEGENDS

Bill Walton

■ **Bill Walton,** *center, b. November 5, 1952, San Diego, California.* Now famous for being a loud and occasionally obnoxious TV commentator, the guy with the curly red hair was one of the best collegians to ever pick up a basketball. Walton, a three-time National Player of the Year at UCLA who averaged 20.3 points per game and 15.7 rebounds over his career, was at his finest in crunch time. In the 1972 title game, he racked up 24 points and 20 boards in a UCLA victory. In the 1973 title game, he had 44 points (on 21-of-22 shooting) in a game for the ages.

■ **Larry Johnson,** *forward, b. March 14, 1969, Tyler, Texas.* The UNLV Runnin' Rebels were the bad boys of college basketball, and Johnson was the team's gold-toothed leader. The powerful and mobile Johnson combined with future NBA players Greg Anthony and Stacey Augmon to form one of the greatest teams ever. The 1990 Rebels cruised through the Big Dance and crushed Duke by 30 points in the title game. A year later, UNLV went 34–0 before falling to the same Blue Devils in the Final Four.

■ **Carmelo Anthony,** *forward, b. May 29, 1984, New York, New York.* Hype swirled around the McDonald's All-American well before he stepped onto the Syracuse campus. A 6'8", 220-pound forward as just a freshman, Anthony made his opponents look like kids on the basketball court. He averaged over 20 points and 10 boards in 2003–04 and led Syracuse to the program's first national title with a near-triple double in the championship game.

RICH CLARKSON

Summitt Reaches the Top

Entering Tennessee's Elite Eight matchup with Texas A&M, it appeared no one could stop the Lady Vols' march to back-to-back national championships. Tennessee had the best player (Candace Parker) and coach (Pat Summitt) in the country, and easily defeated its first three NCAA tournament opponents.

Then the unthinkable happened — the Lady Vols started to look vulnerable. In the first half against the Aggies, Parker dislocated her left shoulder not once, but twice. She returned in the second half wearing a brace and helped the Lady Vols advance to the Final Four. But awaiting Tennessee and its gimpy star was LSU, which had accounted for one of its two losses during the season.

Parker and her teammates struggled throughout, but in true March Madness style, Tennessee guard Alexis Hornbuckle put back a missed layup with 0.7 seconds left for a 47–46 victory, setting off a wild celebration. Next up: Stanford, the *other* team to beat Tennessee in 2007–08. This time, the Lady Vols didn't leave anything to chance, crushing the Cardinal 64–48 thanks to Parker's 17 points and nine boards.

The win gave Tennessee coach Pat Summitt a mind-boggling eight national titles, just two short of the NCAA record of 10, set by UCLA legend John Wooden. It was just the latest accomplishment in an amazing career that started 34 years ago, almost by chance.

Fresh out of college in 1974 and just 22 years old, Summitt was offered an assistant coaching position at Tennessee. Her big break came just two weeks later, when then-coach Margaret Hutson decided to take a sabbatical. Just like that, Pat Summitt, barely older than her players, was the head coach of the Tennessee Lady Vols.

Summitt's first two teams had respectable seasons, winning 16 games apiece. Since then, every other Lady Vols team has won at least 20 games. The 1997–98 squad went 39–0 and locked up Summitt's sixth NCAA title.

During her time on the bench, Summitt has accumulated an astounding 983 career wins, more than any man or woman in NCAA history. She's also coached some of the game's greatest players, most recently Shyra Ely, Tamika Catchings, and Chamique Holdsclaw. Because of her astounding success, Summitt has become a college basketball icon, one both feared and loved.

A two-time Wooden Award winner as player of the year, Candace Parker led Tennessee to back-to-back national titles.

DAMIAN STROHMEYER

Connecticut forward Maya Moore set the school record for most points scored by a freshman (678) and was named Big East Player of the Year in 2007–08.

NCAA Women's Division I: Single-Season Leaders

POINTS			
PLAYER	**YEAR**	**GP**	**PTS**
Jackie Stiles, Missouri St.	2001	35	1,062
Cindy Brown, Long Beach St.	1987	35	974
Genia Miller, Cal St. Fullerton	1991	33	969
Sheryl Swoopes, Texas Tech	1993	34	955
Andrea Congreaves, Mercer	1992	28	925
Wanda Ford, Drake	1986	30	919
Chamique Holdsclaw, Tennessee	1998	39	915
Barbara Kennedy, Clemson	1982	31	908
Patricia Hoskins, Mississippi Val.	1989	27	908
LaTaunya Pollard, Long Beach St.	1983	31	907

Jackie Stiles

SCORING AVERAGE							
PLAYER	**YEAR**	**GP**	**FG**	**3FG**	**FT**	**PTS**	**AVG**
Patricia Hoskins, Mississippi Val.	1989	27	345	13	205	908	33.6
Andrea Congreaves, Mercer	1992	28	353	77	142	925	33.0
Deborah Temple, Delta St.	1984	28	373	—	127	873	31.2
Andrea Congreaves, Mercer	1993	26	390	51	150	805	31.0
Wanda Ford, Drake	1986	30	390	—	139	919	30.6
Anucha Brown, Northwestern	1985	28	341	—	173	855	30.5
LeChandra LeDay, Grambling	1988	28	334	36	146	850	30.4
Jackie Stiles, Missouri St.	2001	35	365	65	267	1,062	30.3
Kim Perrot, La.-LaFayette	1990	28	309	95	128	841	30.0

Lachelle Lyles

REBOUND AVERAGE				
PLAYER	**YEAR**	**GP**	**REB**	**AVG**
Rosina Pearson, Bethune-Cookman	1985	26	480	18.5
Wanda Ford, Drake	1985	30	534	17.8
Katie Beck, East Tenn. St.	1988	25	441	17.6
DeShawne Blocker, East Tenn. St.	1994	26	450	17.3
Patricia Hoskins, Mississippi Valley St.	1987	28	476	17.0
Lachelle Lyles, Southeast Mo. St.	2007	31	527	17.0
Wanda Ford, Drake	1986	30	506	16.9
Patricia Hoskins, Mississippi Valley St.	1989	27	440	16.3
Joy Kellogg, Oklahoma City	1984	23	373	16.2
Deborah Mitchell, Mississippi College	1983	28	447	16.0
Courtney Paris, Oklahoma	2007	33	526	15.9

ASSISTS			
PLAYER	**YEAR**	**GP**	**A**
Suzie McConnell, Penn St.	1987	30	355
Suzie McConnell, Penn St.	1986	32	338
Tine Freil, Pacific	1990	29	321
Neacole Hall, Alabama St.	1989	29	319
Neacole Hall, Alabama St.	1988	28	318

KEY: GP=games played; PTS=points; FG=field goals; 3FG=3-point field goals; FT=free throws; AVG=average; REB=rebounds; A=assists

NCAA Women's Division I:
Single-Season Leaders (cont.)

FIELD-GOAL PERCENTAGE					
PLAYER	YEAR	GP	FGM	FGA	PCT
Myndee Larsen, Southern Utah	1998	28	249	344	72.4
Chantelle Anderson, Vanderbilt	2001	34	292	404	72.3
Deneka Knowles, Southeastern La.	1996	26	199	276	72.1
Barbara Farris, Tulane	1998	27	151	210	71.9
Renay Adams, Tennessee Tech	1991	30	185	258	71.7

FREE-THROW PERCENTAGE					
PLAYER	YEAR	GP	FTM	FTA	PCT
Adrienne Squire, Penn St.	2006	29	80	83	96.4
Shanna Zolman, Tennessee	2004	35	88	92	95.7
Ginny Doyle, Richmond	1992	29	96	101	95.0
Jill Marano, La Salle	2003	29	88	93	94.6
Sue Bird, Connecticut	2002	39	98	104	94.2

3-POINT FIELD-GOAL PERCENTAGE					
PLAYER	YEAR	GP	3FGM	3FGA	PCT
Heather Donlon, Fordham	1990	29	50	87	57.5
Kathy Halligan, Creighton	1992	32	72	130	55.4
Alicia Ratay, Notre Dame	2001	36	81	148	54.7
Jill Morton, Louisville	2000	27	69	129	53.5
K.C. Cowgill, Missouri St.	2005	33	74	139	53.2

KEY: GP=games played; FGM=free goals made; FGA=free goals attempted; PCT=percentage; FTM=free throws made
FTA=free throws attempted: 3FGM=3-point field goals made; 3FGA=3-point field goals attempted

NCAA Women's Division I: Championship Results

Pat Summitt

YEAR	WINNER	SCORE	RUNNER-UP	WINNING COACH
2008	Tennessee	64–48	Stanford	Pat Summitt
2007	Tennessee	59–46	Rutgers	Pat Summitt
2006	Maryland	78–75(OT)	Duke	Brenda Frese
2005	Baylor	84–62	Michigan State	Kim Mulkey-Robertson
2004	Connecticut	70–61	Tennessee	Geno Auriemma
2003	Connecticut	73–68	Tennessee	Geno Auriemma
2002	Connecticut	82–70	Oklahoma	Geno Auriemma
2001	Notre Dame	68–66	Purdue	Muffet McGraw
2000	Connecticut	71–52	Tennessee	Geno Auriemma
1999	Purdue	62–45	Duke	Carolyn Peck
1998	Tennessee	93–75	Louisiana Tech	Pat Summitt
1997	Tennessee	68–59	Old Dominion	Pat Summitt
1996	Tennessee	83–65	Georgia	Pat Summitt
1995	Connecticut	70–64	Tennessee	Geno Auriemma
1994	North Carolina	60–59	Louisiana Tech	Sylvia Hatchell
1993	Texas Tech	84–82	Ohio State	Marsha Sharp
1992	Stanford	78–62	Western Kentucky	Tara VanDerveer
1991	Tennessee	70–67(OT)	Virginia	Pat Summitt
1990	Stanford	88–81	Auburn	Tara VanDerveer
1989	Tennessee	76–60	Auburn	Pat Summitt
1988	Louisiana Tech	56–54	Auburn	Leon Barmore
1987	Tennessee	67–44	Louisiana Tech	Pat Summitt
1986	Texas	97–81	USC	Jody Conradt
1985	Old Dominion	70–65	Georgia	Marianne Stanley
1984	USC	72–61	Tennessee	Linda Sharp
1983	USC	69–67	Louisiana Tech	Linda Sharp
1982	Louisiana Tech	76–62	Cheyney State	Sonja Hogg/Leon Barmore

NCAA Women's Division I: Single-Season Leaders (cont.)

STEALS			
PLAYER	**YEAR**	**GP**	**STL**
Natalie White, Florida A&M	1995	30	191
Natalie White, Florida A&M	1994	28	172
Heidi Caruso, Lafayette	1993	28	168
Ticha Penicheiro, Old Dominion	1997	36	161
Ticha Penicheiro, Old Dominion	1998	32	161

BLOCKS			
PLAYER	**YEAR**	**GP**	**BLK**
Amie Williams, Jackson St.	2003	29	152
Michelle Wilson, Texas Southern	1989	27	151
Alison Bales, Duke	2007	34	151
Sandora Irvin, TCU	2005	33	150
Denise Hogue, Col. of Charleston	1992	28	147

Alison Bales

KEY: GP=games played; STL=steals; BLK=blocks

TODAY'S STARS

Andrea Riley

■ **Andrea Riley,** *guard, b. July 22, 1988, Dallas, Texas.* Ever wonder where Riley got those crazy dribbling skills? Look no further than her father, Roosevelt, who played for the Harlem Globetrotters. The 5'5" Oklahoma State guard is used to working in crowded spaces, too; she has nine siblings. As a sophomore last season, Riley carried the Cowgirls to their first Sweet 16 appearance since 1991, hitting a free throw with 0.7 seconds remaining in OT for a 73–72 second-round victory over Florida State. She also scored 23.1 points per game, fifth-best in the nation.

■ **Courtney Paris,** *center, b. September 21, 1987, San Jose, California.* The daughter of former San Francisco 49ers offensive lineman Bubba Paris, Courtney excels at shoving bodies out of her way just like dad. This two-time Big 12 Player of the Year and three-time Big 12 Defensive Player of the Year led the nation in rebounding last season, grabbing 15 boards a game for Oklahoma. She also contributed 18.6 points and swatted 108 shots. With Courtney teaming with her identical twin sister, Ashley, in the post, Oklahoma entered the 2008–09 season with one of the best frontcourts in the nation.

■ **Maya Moore,** *forward, b. June 11, 1989, Jefferson City, Missouri.* The nation's No. 1 recruit coming out of high school, Moore lived up to all the hype as a UConn freshman in 2007–08. The first Big East frosh — male or female — to be named conference Player of the Year, Moore played through bad knees and a bruised tailbone to become the Big East's all-time freshman scoring leader (678 points). Stunned by Stanford in the Final Four after winning 36 games last season, the Huskies are expecting bigger and better things from Moore as a sophomore.

1 Where did Tennessee coach Pat Summitt attend college?
A. Tennessee
B. Vanderbilt
C. Tennessee—Martin

Pat Summitt

2 The WNBA Draft is held one day after what event?
A. Women's NCAA Tournament
B. Men's NBA Draft
C. July 4ᵗʰ

3 In what country was UConn coach Geno Auriemma born?
A. Australia
B. Italy
C. Canada

Geno Auriemma

4 Which team did shock jock Don Imus offend in 2007, sparking a national controversy?
A. DePaul
B. St. John's
C. Rutgers

5 What is smaller in the women's game than the men's?
A. Height of hoop
B. Size of ball
C. Length of court

6 What was the nickname for the 2008 national championship game between Stanford's Candice Wiggins and Tennessee's Candace Parker?
A. Fire vs. Ice
B. Ace vs. Ice
C. Thunder vs. Lightning

7 When was the first women's NCAA Tournament?
A. 1962
B. 1972
C. 1982

8 Which former Texas Tech player scored 47 points to win the 1993 national title game?
A. Sue Bird
B. Sheryl Swoopes
C. Swin Cash

9 Who was the first female to win the McDonald's High School Slam Dunk Contest?
A. Candace Parker
B. Lisa Leslie
C. Sylvia Fowles

10 What is Rutgers guard Epiphanny Prince's claim to fame?
A. Little sister of NBA's Tayshaun Prince
B. Scored over 100 points in a single high school game
C. First NCAA female player over 7 feet tall

Epiphanny Prince

Candice Wiggins

1.C; 2.A; 3.B; 4.C; 5.B; 6.B; 7.C; 8.B; 9.A; 10.B

NCAA Women's Division I: Most Outstanding Players

YEAR	WINNER, SCHOOL	YEAR	WINNER, SCHOOL	YEAR	WINNER, SCHOOL
2008	Candace Parker, Tennessee	1999	Ukari Figgs, Purdue	1990	Jennifer Azzi, Stanford
2007	Candace Parker, Tennessee	1998	Chamique Holdsclaw, Tennessee	1989	Bridgette Gordon, Tennessee
2006	Laura Harper, Maryland	1997	Chamique Holdsclaw, Tennessee	1988	Erica Westbrooks, Louisiana Tech
2005	Sophia Young, Baylor	1996	Michelle Marciniak, Tennessee	1987	Tonya Edwards, Tennessee
2004	Diana Taurasi, Connecticut	1995	Rebecca Lobo, Connecticut	1986	Clarissa Davis, Texas
2003	Diana Taurasi, Connecticut	1994	Charlotte Smith, North Carolina	1985	Tracy Claxton, Old Dominion
2002	Swin Cash, Connecticut	1993	Sheryl Swoopes, Texas Tech	1984	Cheryl Miller, Southern California
2001	Ruth Riley, Notre Dame	1992	Molly Goodenbour, Stanford	1983	Cheryl Miller, Southern California
2000	Shea Ralph, Connecticut	1991	Dawn Staley, Virginia	1982	Janice Lawrence, Louisiana Tech

GAME TIME

From C To Shining C

Carrie Moore, Crystal Kelly, Courtney Paris, and Chrissy Givens (C something similar about their names?) were the top four 2006–07 NCAA women's basketball leaders in what category?

To find out, write the letter of the Division I school found in each state on the space provided. Then sort the states from west to east so the letters reveal the answer to the trivia question.

North Carolina	Nebraska	Utah	New Jersey	Ohio	California	Louisiana
____	____	____	____	____	____	____

B — Clemson   L — Vanderbilt
C — Weber State   N — Wake Forest
D — Auburn   O — Creighton
E — DePaul   P — Villanova
G — Seton Hall   R — Tulane
I — Xavier   S — Stanford
K — Syracuse   U — Baylor

West ____ ____ ____ ____ ____ ____ ____ East

ANSWERS ON PAGE 190

■ **Chamique Holdsclaw,** *forward, b. August 9, 1977, Flushing, New York.* Billed as the female Michael Jordan after winning four state titles at Christ the King High School in Queens, New York, Holdsclaw came to Knoxville and collected three national championships (1996, 1997, 1998). Scoring 20.4 points and grabbing 8.8 rebounds per game over her career, she finished as the SEC's all-time leading scorer (3,025) and rebounder (1,295) for men and women. She became the first women's basketball player to win the prestigious Sullivan Award in 1998, given to the nation's top amateur athlete. Holdsclaw was also the top overall pick in the 2001 WNBA Draft.

Chamique Holdsclaw

■ **Jackie Stiles,** *guard, b. December 21, 1978, Kansas City, Kansas.* Stiles grew up in the tiny town of Claflin, Kansas (population: 700). As a young player, she would force herself to make 1,000 shots a day, and it wasn't long before her hard work paid off. She finished her career at Missouri State (then known as Southwest Missouri State) as the leading scorer in Division I women's NCAA history, with 3,393 points. And Stiles saved her best for last, combining for 73 points in victories over Duke and Washington to reach the women's Final Four as a senior. Stiles's little sister, Roxy, has followed in Jackie's footsteps and is now a junior at Missouri State.

Cheryl Miller

■ **Cheryl Miller,** *forward, b. January 3, 1964, Riverside, California.* The older sister of NBA legend Reggie Miller, Cheryl is arguably the most important player in women's college basketball history. Like her brother, Miller could always attract the spotlight with her brash style of play. She played with an athleticism that was never before seen in the women's game. Miller led USC to the 1983 and 1984 NCAA championships and averaged 23.6 points per game over her career. In 1986, SPORTS ILLUSTRATED called Miller the country's best college basketball player — male or female.

Young Stars to the Rescue

The rivalry's already been billed as the Magic Johnson–Larry Bird of hockey. And if Sidney Crosby and Alexander Ovechkin live up to that kind of hype, it'll be very good news for a league still recovering from the 2004–2005 lockout. So far, so good.

During the 2005–06 campaign, each put up one of the best rookie seasons in league history. The first pick of the 2005 NHL Draft, Sid the Kid notched 102 points as an 18-year-old center for the Pittsburgh Penguins, but was nevertheless outdone by his 20-year-old Washington Capitals counterpart from Russia. Ovechkin, the No. 1 pick of the 2004 draft, tallied 106 points and was awarded the Calder Trophy as the top rookie.

A year later, Crosby struck back. He led the league in scoring (120 points) and assists (84) and earned a Hart Trophy as league MVP, all the while looking like a young Wayne Gretzky. He was the award's second-youngest winner, behind only Gretzky himself. As for Alexander the Great, he finished with only 92 points.

In 2007–08, it was Ovechkin's turn to shine again. While Crosby played in just 53 games due to a high ankle sprain that nagged him all season long, the Capitals left wing not only led the league in points (112) and goals (65), he became the first player since 1996 to score over 60 goals. For his efforts, Ovechkin was awarded the Hart Trophy, not to mention a 13-year, $124-million contract extension, the richest deal in NHL history.

Perhaps more importantly, both players took their teams to new heights in 2007–08. Ovechkin sparked a late-season surge that resulted in the Capitals' first postseason appearance since 2003. Not to be outdone, Crosby matched Ovechkin's accomplishment, leading the Penguins to the playoffs, then did him one better. While the Caps were bounced in the first round by Philadelphia, Pittsburgh caught fire in the postseason and landed in its first Stanley Cup finals since 1992.

But there the Penguins were overmatched by a vastly more experienced Detroit Red Wings club that cruised to the league's best regular season (115 points). The Wings won the first two games by a combined score of 7–0. The Pens staged a big comeback in a Game 5 triple-overtime win, but fell just short of another miracle in Game 6 and lost the series. For the Red Wings, it was their 11th Stanley Cup. So maybe it's not Magic–Bird just yet — after their first two seasons, both had NBA rings — but Ovechkin and Crosby are the twin stars of a league on the mend. The two phenoms are carrying the hopes of their teams as well as the NHL.

Capitals left wing Alex Ovechkin finished the 2007–08 season with 112 points.

LOU CAPOZZOLA

DAVID F. KLUTHO

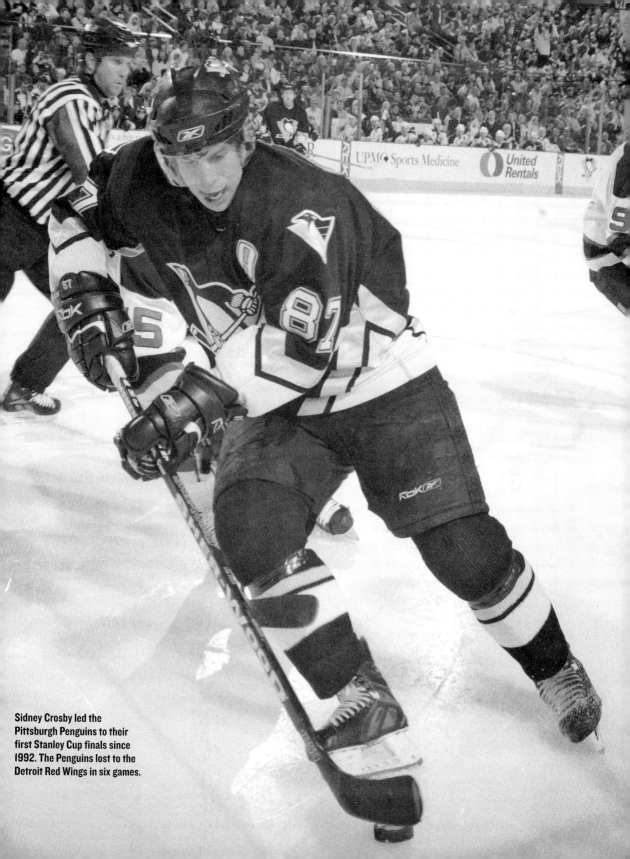

Sidney Crosby led the Pittsburgh Penguins to their first Stanley Cup finals since 1992. The Penguins lost to the Detroit Red Wings in six games.

POWER RANKINGS

Best Centers

Vincent Lecavalier

1 **Sidney Crosby, Pittsburgh Penguins**
Hailed as the next Wayne Gretzky, Crosby is already the game's best center.

2 **Joe Thornton, San Jose Sharks**
Led the league in assists each of the past three seasons.

3 **Vincent Lecavalier, Tampa Bay Lightning**
Scored 92 goals over the last two seasons.

4 **Evegeni Malkin, Pittsburgh Penguins**
Picked up the slack for injured Crosby in 2008 and finished second in points (106).

5 **Jason Spezza, Ottawa Senators**
Averaged 90 points over the past three seasons.

6 **Marc Savard, Boston Bruins**
This late bloomer was third in assists (63) during 2007–08.

7 **Joe Sakic, Colorado Avalanche**
One of the all-time greats, he missed 38 games last season.

8 **Pavel Datsyuk, Detroit Red Wings**
Ranked second in NHL assists (66) in 2007–08 season.

9 **Eric Staal, Carolina Hurricanes**
After winning the Stanley Cup in 2005–06, production has fallen.

10 **Henrik Sedin, Vancouver Canucks**
Finished fourth in assists two seasons in a row.

NHL TEAMS

EASTERN CONFERENCE	WESTERN CONFERENCE
Atlanta Thrashers	Anaheim Ducks
Boston Bruins	Calgary Flames
Buffalo Sabres	Chicago Blackhawks
Carolina Hurricanes	Colorado Avalanche
Florida Panthers	Columbus Blue Jackets
Montreal Canadiens	Dallas Stars
New Jersey Devils	Detroit Red Wings
New York Islanders	Edmonton Oilers
New York Rangers	Los Angeles Kings
Ottawa Senators	Minnesota Wild
Philadelphia Flyers	Nashville Predators
Pittsburgh Penguins	Phoenix Coyotes
Tampa Bay Lightning	San Jose Sharks
Toronto Maple Leafs	St. Louis Blues
Washington Capitals	Vancouver Canucks

LOU CAPOZZOLA

? DID YOU KNOW?
Edmonton Oilers defenseman Sheldon Souray's slap shot has been measured to be more than 102 miles per hour.

GAME TIME

One for the Record Books

Decipher this NHL record by fitting the right boxes into the empty spaces. Black squares are spaces between words, and words wrap from one line to the next.

J		O	M	I	R		J	A		■		H	
	■		S	■			F	T	E		T	H	
O	N	S	E	C			I	V	E			I	R	T
Y			O	A	L		S	E	A	S			I	N
2			7	■	T			N	G		M	I	
G	A	R	T	N	E		■		R	E	C	O	

| F | I |
| U | T |

| A | D |
| ■ | C |

| - | G |
| O | O |

| T | H |
| O | N |

| Y | I |
| R | S |

| K | E |
| R | D |

| A | R |
| H | I |

| G | R |
| E | N |

ANSWERS ON PAGE 190

Stanley Cup Results

Awarded annually to the team that wins the NHL's best-of-seven final-round playoffs. The Stanley Cup is the oldest trophy for which professional athletes in North America compete. It was donated in 1893 by Frederick Arthur, Lord Stanley of Preston.

SEASON	CHAMPION	FINALIST	GAMES PLAYED IN FINAL
2007–08	Detroit Red Wings	Pittsburgh Penguins	6
2006–07	Anaheim Ducks	Ottawa Senators	5
2005–06	Carolina Hurricanes	Edmonton Oilers	7
2004–05	Season canceled because of lockout		
2003–04	Tampa Bay Lightning	Calgary Flames	7
2002–03	New Jersey Devils	Anaheim Mighty Ducks	7
2001–02	Detroit Red Wings	Carolina Hurricanes	5
2000–01	Colorado Avalanche	New Jersey Devils	7
1999–00	New Jersey Devils	Dallas Stars	6
1998–99	Dallas Stars	Buffalo Sabres	6
1997–98	Detroit Red Wings	Washington Capitals	4
1996–97	Detroit Red Wings	Philadelphia Flyers	4
1995–96	Colorado Avalanche	Florida Panthers	4
1994–95	New Jersey Devils	Detroit Red Wings	4
1993–94	New York Rangers	Vancouver Canucks	7
1992–93	Montreal Canadiens	Los Angeles Kings	5
1991–92	Pittsburgh Penguins	Chicago Blackhawks	4
1990–91	Pittsburgh Penguins	Minnesota North Stars	6
1989–90	Edmonton Oilers	Boston Bruins	5
1988–89	Calgary Flames	Montreal Canadiens	6
1987–88	Edmonton Oilers	Boston Bruins	4
1986–87	Edmonton Oilers	Philadelphia Flyers	7
1985–86	Montreal Canadiens	Calgary Flames	5
1984–85	Edmonton Oilers	Philadelphia Flyers	5
1983–84	Edmonton Oilers	New York Islanders	5
1982–83	New York Islanders	Edmonton Oilers	4
1981–82	New York Islanders	Vancouver Canucks	4
1980–81	New York Islanders	Minnesota North Stars	5
1979–80	New York Islanders	Philadelphia Flyers	6
1978–79	Montreal Canadiens	New York Rangers	5
1977–78	Montreal Canadiens	Boston Bruins	6
1976–77	Montreal Canadiens	Boston Bruins	4
1975–76	Montreal Canadiens	Philadelphia Flyers	4
1974–75	Philadelphia Flyers	Buffalo Sabres	6
1973–74	Philadelphia Flyers	Boston Bruins	6
1972–73	Montreal Canadiens	Chicago Blackhawks	6
1971–72	Boston Bruins	New York Rangers	6
1970–71	Montreal Canadiens	Chicago Blackhawks	7
1969–70	Boston Bruins	St. Louis Blues	4
1968–69	Montreal Canadiens	St. Louis Blues	4
1967–68	Montreal Canadiens	St. Louis Blues	4
1966–67	Toronto Maple Leafs	Montreal Canadiens	6
1965–66	Montreal Canadiens	Detroit Red Wings	6
1964–65	Montreal Canadiens	Chicago Blackhawks	7
1963–64	Toronto Maple Leafs	Detroit Red Wings	7
1962–63	Toronto Maple Leafs	Detroit Red Wings	5
1961–62	Toronto Maple Leafs	Chicago Blackhawks	6
1960–61	Chicago Blackhawks	Detroit Red Wings	6
1959–60	Montreal Canadiens	Toronto Maple Leafs	4

Stanley Cup Results (cont.)

SEASON	CHAMPION	FINALIST	GAMES PLAYED IN FINAL
1958-59	Montreal Canadiens	Toronto Maple Leafs	5
1957-58	Montreal Canadiens	Boston Bruins	6
1956-57	Montreal Canadiens	Boston Bruins	5
1955-56	Montreal Canadiens	Detroit Red Wings	5
1954-55	Detroit Red Wings	Montreal Canadiens	7
1953-54	Detroit Red Wings	Montreal Canadiens	7
1952-53	Montreal Canadiens	Boston Bruins	5
1951-52	Detroit Red Wings	Montreal Canadiens	4
1950-51	Toronto Maple Leafs	Montreal Canadiens	5
1949-50	Detroit Red Wings	New York Rangers	7
1948-49	Toronto Maple Leafs	Detroit Red Wings	4
1947-48	Toronto Maple Leafs	Detroit Red Wings	4
1946-47	Toronto Maple Leafs	Montreal Canadiens	6
1945-46	Montreal Canadiens	Boston Bruins	5
1944-45	Toronto Maple Leafs	Detroit Red Wings	7
1943-44	Montreal Canadiens	Chicago Blackhawks	4
1942-43	Detroit Red Wings	Boston Bruins	4
1941-42	Toronto Maple Leafs	Detroit Red Wings	7
1940-41	Boston Bruins	Detroit Red Wings	4
1939-40	New York Rangers	Toronto Maple Leafs	6
1938-39	Boston Bruins	Toronto Maple Leafs	5
1937-38	Chicago Blackhawks	Toronto Maple Leafs	4
1936-37	Detroit Red Wings	New York Rangers	5
1935-36	Detroit Red Wings	Toronto Maple Leafs	4
1934-35	Montreal Maroons	Toronto Maple Leafs	3
1933-34	Chicago Blackhawks	Detroit Red Wings	4
1932-33	New York Rangers	Toronto Maple Leafs	4
1931-32	Toronto Maple Leafs	New York Rangers	3
1930-31	Montreal Canadiens	Chicago Blackhawks	5
1929-30	Montreal Canadiens	Boston Bruins	2
1928-29	Boston Bruins	New York Rangers	2
1927-28	New York Rangers	Montreal Maroons	5
1926-27	Ottawa Senators	Boston Bruins	4
1925-26	Montreal Maroons	Victoria Cougars	4
1924-25	Victoria Cougars	Montreal Canadiens	4
1923-24*	Montreal Canadiens	Vancouver Maroons, Calgary Tigers	2, 2
1922-23**	Ottawa Senators	Edmonton Eskimos, Vancouver Maroons	2, 4
1921-22	Toronto St. Pats	Vancouver Millionaires	5
1920-21	Ottawa Senators	Vancouver Millionaires	5
1919-20	Ottawa Senators	Seattle Metropolitans	5
1918-19***	No decision	No decision	5
1917-18	Toronto Arenas	Vancouver Millionaires	5
1916-17	Seattle Metropolitans	—	—
1915-16	Montreal Canadiens	—	—
1914-15	Vancouver Millionaires	—	—
1913-14	Toronto Blueshirts	—	—
1912-13	Quebec Bulldogs	—	—
1911-12	Quebec Bulldogs	—	—
1910-11	Ottawa Senators	—	—

* In 1923-24, the Montreal Canadiens beat the Vancouver Maroons in two games and the Calgary Tigers in two games.
** In 1922-23, the Ottawa Senators beat the Edmonton Eskimos in two games and the Vancouver Maroons in four games.
*** In 1918-19, the Montreal Canadiens traveled to meet the Seattle Metropolitans. After five games had been played — the teams were tied at two wins apiece and one tie — the series was called off by the local Department of Health because of an influenza epidemic that led to the death of Canadiens defenseman Joe Hall.

Stanley Cup Results (cont.)

SEASON	CHAMPION	FINALIST	GAMES PLAYED IN FINAL
1909–10	Montreal Wanderers	—	—
1908–09	Ottawa Senators	—	—
1907–08	Montreal Wanderers	—	—
1906–07	Montreal Wanderers (Mar.)	—	—
1906–07	Kenora Thistles (Jan.)	—	—
1905–06	Montreal Wanderers (Mar.)	—	—
1905–06	Ottawa Silver Seven (Feb.)	—	—
1904–05	Ottawa Silver Seven	—	—
1903–04	Ottawa Silver Seven	—	—
1902–03	Ottawa Silver Seven (Mar.)	—	—
1902–03	Montreal A.A.A. (Feb.)	—	—
1901–02	Montreal A.A.A. (Mar.)	—	—
1901–02	Winnipeg Victorias (Jan.)	—	—
1900–01	Winnipeg Victorias	—	—
1899–00	Montreal Shamrocks	—	—
1898–99	Montreal Shamrocks (Mar.)	—	—
1898–99	Montreal Victorias (Feb.)	—	—
1897–98	Montreal Victorias	—	—
1896–97	Montreal Victorias	—	—
1895–96	Montreal Victorias (Dec.)	—	—
1895–96	Winnipeg Victorias (Feb.)	—	—
1894–95	Montreal Victorias	—	—
1893–94	Montreal A.A.A.	—	—
1892–93	Montreal A.A.A.	—	—

The Stanley Cup

TRIVIA

1 Which was not a member of the inaugural NHL franchises known as the "Original Six"?
A. Boston Bruins
B. New York Rangers
C. Philadelphia Flyers

2 True or False: The 2004–05 lockout was the first in NHL history.
A. True
B. False

3 Which city is known as "Hockeytown"?
A. Pittsburgh
B. Detroit
C. Buffalo

4 What is Wayne Gretzky's nickname?
A. The Dominator
B. The Great One
C. The Beastmaster

5 Which team has won the most Stanley Cups of any franchise?
A. Detroit
B. Toronto
C. Montreal

1.C 2.B 3.B 4.B 5.C

■ **Jarome Iginla,** *right wing, b. July 1, 1977, Edmonton, Alberta, Canada.* After five seasons in the league, Iginla became a star for the Calgary Flames in 2002, scoring 52 goals and totaling 96 points, both tops in the NHL. A year later, he was named the NHL's first-ever black team captain. A year after that, Iginla tied for the league lead in goals and, more importantly, led the Flames to their first Stanley Cup Finals since 1989. Iginla scored 98 points in 2007–08 (third-most in the NHL) and was named a finalist for the Hart Trophy for the third time.

Jarome Iginla

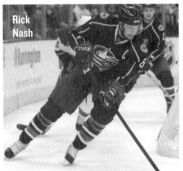
Rick Nash

■ **Rick Nash,** *left wing, b. June 16, 1984, Brampton, Ontario, Canada.* As the first overall pick in the 2002 NHL draft, Nash immediately took a starring role on the Columbus Blue Jackets. In just his second year, Nash led the league in goals (41). He went to his third All-Star Game in 2007–08, finishing with 69 points and 38 goals. Nash is also the cover athlete of the video game NHL 2K9.

■ **Evgeni Nabokov,** *goaltender, b. July 25, 1975, Kamenogorsk, Kazakhstan.* After four solid seasons to start his career, it appeared Nabokov had flamed out during the 2005–06 season. His goals-against average skyrocketed to 3.10, and he found himself riding the San Jose Sharks' bench. But the past two seasons Nabokov has come back stronger than ever, winning a league-leading 46 games for the Sharks in 2007–08. With a 2.14 GAA that tied for third in the NHL, Nabokov was nominated for the Vezina Trophy, awarded to the top goalie.

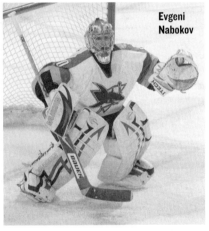
Evgeni Nabokov

Henrik Lundqvist

■ **Henrik Lundqvist,** *goaltender, b. March 2, 1982, Are, Sweden.* Lundqvist burst onto the scene in 2005–06 by winning 30 games in just 50 starts for the New York Rangers. That same year, he also led Sweden to a gold medal in the Olympics. Playing in front of the harsh New York media, Lundqvist nevertheless earned the nickname "King Henrik" for his regal netminding. In 2007–08, he was nominated for the Vezina Trophy for the third consectuive year.

Conn Smythe Trophy (Past 20 Seasons)

Awarded to the Most Valuable Player of the Stanley Cup playoffs, as selected by the Professional Hockey Writers Association. The trophy was named for the former coach, general manager, president, and owner of the Toronto Maple Leafs.

Detroit Red Wings left wing Henrik Zetterberg

SEASON	WINNER
2007–08	Henrik Zetterberg, Detroit Red Wings
2006–07	Scott Niedermayer, Anaheim Ducks
2005–06	Cam Ward, Carolina Hurricanes
2003–04	Brad Richards, Tampa Bay Lightning
2002–03	Jean-Sebastien Giguere, Anaheim Mighty Ducks
2001–02	Nicklas Lidstrom, Detroit Red Wings
2000–01	Patrick Roy, Colorado Avalanche
1999–00	Scott Stevens, New Jersey Devils
1998–99	Joe Nieuwendyk, Dallas Stars
1997–98	Steve Yzerman, Detroit Red Wings
1996–97	Mike Vernon, Detroit Red Wings
1995–96	Joe Sakic, Colorado Avalanche
1994–95	Claude Lemieux, New Jersey Devils
1993–94	Brian Leetch, New York Rangers
1992–93	Patrick Roy, Montreal Canadiens
1991–92	Mario Lemieux, Pittsburgh Penguins
1990–91	Mario Lemieux, Pittsburgh Penguins
1989–90	Bill Ranford, Edmonton Oilers
1988–89	Al MacInnis, Calgary Flames
1987–88	Wayne Gretzky, Edmonton Oilers

Hart Memorial Trophy (Past 20 Seasons)

Awarded annually "to the player adjudged to be the most valuable to his team." The original trophy was donated by Dr. David A. Hart, father of Cecil Hart, former manager-coach of the Montreal Canadiens.

SEASON	WINNER
2007–08	Alexander Ovechkin, Washington Capitals
2006–07	Sidney Crosby, Pittsburgh Penguins
2005–06	Joe Thornton, San Jose Sharks
2003–04	Martin St. Louis, Tampa Bay Lightning
2002–03	Peter Forsberg, Colorado Avalanche
2001–02	Jose Theodore, Montreal Canadiens
2000–01	Joe Sakic, Colorado Avalanche
1999–00	Chris Pronger, St. Louis Blues
1998–99	Jaromir Jagr, Pittsburgh Penguins
1997–98	Dominik Hasek, Buffalo Sabres
1996–97	Dominik Hasek, Buffalo Sabres
1995–96	Mario Lemieux, Pittsburgh Penguins
1994–95	Eric Lindros, Philadelphia Flyers
1993–94	Sergei Fedorov, Detroit Red Wings
1992–93	Mario Lemieux, Pittsburgh Penguins
1991–92	Mark Messier, New York Rangers
1990–91	Brett Hull, St. Louis Blues
1989–90	Mark Messier, Edmonton Oilers
1988–89	Wayne Gretzky, Los Angeles Kings
1987–88	Mario Lemieux, Pittsburgh Penguins

Art Ross Trophy (Past 20 Seasons)

Awarded annually "to the player who leads the league in scoring points at the end of the regular season." The trophy was presented to the NHL in 1947 by Arthur Howie Ross, former manager-coach of the Boston Bruins. If two or more players are tied, the tie-breakers, in order, are: (1) player with most goals, (2) player with fewer games played, (3) player who scored the first goal of the season.

SEASON	WINNER	POINTS
2007–08	Alexander Ovechkin, Washington Capitals	112
2006–07	Sidney Crosby, Pittsburgh Penguins	120
2005–06	Joe Thornton, San Jose Sharks	125
2003–04	Martin St. Louis, Tampa Bay Lightning	94
2002–03	Peter Forsberg, Colorado Avalanche	106
2001–02	Jarome Iginla, Calgary Flames	96
2000–01	Jaromir Jagr, Pittsburgh Penguins	121
1999–00	Jaromir Jagr, Pittsburgh Penguins	96
1998–99	Jaromir Jagr, Pittsburgh Penguins	127
1997–98	Jaromir Jagr, Pittsburgh Penguins	102
1996–97	Mario Lemieux, Pittsburgh Penguins	122
1995–96	Mario Lemieux, Pittsburgh Penguins	161
1994–95	Jaromir Jagr, Pittsburgh Penguins	70
1993–94	Wayne Gretzky, Los Angeles Kings	130
1992–93	Mario Lemieux, Pittsburgh Penguins	160
1991–92	Mario Lemieux, Pittsburgh Penguins	131
1990–91	Wayne Gretzky, Los Angeles Kings	163
1989–90	Wayne Gretzky, Los Angeles Kings	142
1988–89	Mario Lemieux, Pittsburgh Penguins	199
1987–88	Mario Lemieux, Pittsburgh Penguins	168

Note: The 2004–2005 season was cancelled because of a lockout.

Lady Byng Memorial Trophy (Past 20 Seasons)

Awarded annually "to the player adjudged to have exhibited the best type of sportsmanship and gentlemanly conduct combined with a high standard of playing ability." Lady Byng, who first presented the trophy in 1925, was the wife of Canada's governor-general. She donated a second trophy in 1936 because the first one was given permanently to Frank Boucher of the New York Rangers, who had won it seven times in eight seasons.

SEASON	WINNER	SEASON	WINNER
2007–08	Pavel Datsyuk, Detroit Red Wings	1996–97	Paul Kariya, Anaheim Mighty Ducks
2006–07	Pavel Datsyuk, Detroit Red Wings	1995–96	Paul Kariya, Anaheim Mighty Ducks
2005–06	Pavel Datsyuk, Detroit Red Wings	1994–95	Ron Francis, Pittsburgh Penguins
2003–04	Brad Richards, Tampa Bay Lightning	1993–94	Wayne Gretzky, Los Angeles Kings
2002–03	Alexander Mogilny, Toronto Maple Leafs	1992–93	Pierre Turgeon, New York Islanders
2001–02	Ron Francis, Carolina Hurricanes	1991–92	Wayne Gretzky, Los Angeles Kings
2000–01	Joe Sakic, Colorado Avalanche	1990–91	Wayne Gretzky, Los Angeles Kings
1999–00	Pavol Demitra, St. Louis Blues	1989–90	Brett Hull, St. Louis Blues
1998–99	Wayne Gretzky, New York Rangers	1988–89	Joe Mullen, Calgary Flames
1997–98	Ron Francis, Pittsburgh Penguins	1987–88	Mats Naslund, Montreal Canadiens

James Norris Memorial Trophy (Past 20 Seasons)

Awarded annually "to the defense player who demonstrates throughout the season the greatest all-around ability in the position." James Norris was the former owner-president of the Detroit Red Wings.

Detroit Red Wings defenseman Nicklas Lidstrom

DAVID E. KLUTHO

SEASON	WINNER	SEASON	WINNER
2007–08	Nicklas Lidstrom, Detroit Red Wings		
2006–07	Nicklas Lidstrom, Detroit Red Wings		
2005–06	Nicklas Lidstrom, Detroit Red Wings		
2003–04	Scott Niedermayer, New Jersey Devils		
2002–03	Nicklas Lidstrom, Detroit Red Wings		
2001–02	Nicklas Lidstrom, Detroit Red Wings		
2000–01	Nicklas Lidstrom, Detroit Red Wings		
1999–00	Chris Pronger, St. Louis Blues	1992–93	Chris Chelios, Chicago Blackhawks
1998–99	Al MacInnis, St. Louis Blues	1991–92	Brian Leetch, New York Rangers
1997–98	Rob Blake, Los Angeles Kings	1990–91	Ray Bourque, Boston Bruins
1996–97	Brian Leetch, New York Rangers	1989–90	Ray Bourque, Boston Bruins
1995–96	Chris Chelios, Chicago Blackhawks	1988–89	Chris Chelios, Montreal Canadiens
1994–95	Paul Coffey, Detroit Red Wings	1987–88	Ray Bourque, Boston Bruins
1993–94	Ray Bourque, Boston Bruins		

Calder Memorial Trophy (Past 20 Seasons)

Awarded annually "to the player selected as the most proficient in his first year of competition in the National Hockey League." Frank Calder was a former NHL president. Sergei Makarov, who won the award in 1989–90, was the oldest recipient of the trophy, at 31. If a player is 26 or older as of September 15 of a season, he is no longer eligible to win the award.

SEASON	WINNER	SEASON	WINNER
2007–08	Patrick Kane, Chicago Blackhawks	1996–97	Bryan Berard, New York Islanders
2006–07	Evgeni Malkin, Pittsburgh Penguins	1995–96	Daniel Alfredsson, Ottawa Senators
2005–06	Alexander Ovechkin, Washington Capitals	1994–95	Peter Forsberg, Quebec Nordiques
2003–04	Andrew Raycroft, Boston Bruins	1993–94	Martin Brodeur, New Jersey Devils
2002–03	Barret Jackman, St. Louis Blues	1992–93	Teemu Selanne, Winnipeg Jets
2001–02	Dany Heatley, Atlanta Thrashers	1991–92	Pavel Bure, Vancouver Canucks
2000–01	Evgeni Nabokov, San Jose Sharks	1990–91	Ed Belfour, Chicago Blackhawks
1999–00	Scott Gomez, New Jersey Devils	1989–90	Sergei Makarov, Calgary Flames
1998–99	Chris Drury, Colorado Avalanche	1988–89	Brian Leetch, New York Rangers
1997–98	Sergei Samsonov, Boston Bruins	1987–88	Joe Nieuwendyk, Calgary Flames

Vezina Trophy (Past 20 Seasons)

Martin Brodeur

Awarded annually "to the goalkeeper adjudged to be the best at his position." The trophy was named for Georges Vezina, an outstanding goalie for the Montreal Canadiens who collapsed during a game on November 28, 1925, and died four months later of tuberculosis. The general managers of the NHL teams vote on the award.

SEASON	WINNER
2007–08	Martin Brodeur, New Jersey Devils
2006–07	Martin Brodeur, New Jersey Devils
2005–06	Miikka Kiprusoff, Calgary Flames
2003–04	Martin Brodeur, New Jersey Devils
2002–03	Martin Brodeur, New Jersey Devils
2001–02	Jose Theodore, Montreal Canadiens
2000–01	Dominik Hasek, Buffalo Sabres
1999–00	Olaf Kolzig, Washington Capitals
1998–99	Dominik Hasek, Buffalo Sabres
1997–98	Dominik Hasek, Buffalo Sabres
1996–97	Dominik Hasek, Buffalo Sabres
1995–96	Jim Carey, Washington Capitals
1994–95	Dominik Hasek, Buffalo Sabres
1993–94	Dominik Hasek, Buffalo Sabres
1992–93	Ed Belfour, Chicago Blackhawks
1991–92	Patrick Roy, Montreal Canadiens
1990–91	Ed Belfour, Chicago Blackhawks
1989–90	Patrick Roy, Montreal Canadiens
1988–89	Patrick Roy, Montreal Canadiens
1987–88	Grant Fuhr, Edmonton Oilers

LOU CAPOZZOLA

Selke Trophy (Past 20 Seasons)

Awarded annually "to the forward who best excels in the defensive aspects of the game." The trophy was named for Frank J. Selke, the architect of the Montreal Canadiens dynasty that won the Stanley Cup five consecutive times in the late 1950s. The winner is selected by a vote of the Professional Hockey Writers Association.

SEASON	WINNER	SEASON	WINNER
2007–08	Pavel Datsyuk, Detroit Red Wings	1996–97	Michael Peca, Buffalo Sabres
2006–07	Rod Brind'Amour, Carolina Hurricanes	1995–96	Sergei Fedorov, Detroit Red Wings
2005–06	Rod Brind'Amour, Carolina Hurricanes	1994–95	Ron Francis, Pittsburgh Penguins
2003–04	Kris Draper, Detroit Red Wings	1993–94	Sergei Fedorov, Detroit Red Wings
2002–03	Jere Lehtinen, Dallas Stars	1992–93	Doug Gilmour, Toronto Maple Leafs
2001–02	Michael Peca, New York Islanders	1991–92	Guy Carbonneau, Montreal Canadiens
2000–01	John Madden, New Jersey Devils	1990–91	Dirk Graham, Chicago Blackhawks
1999–00	Steve Yzerman, Detroit Red Wings	1989–90	Rick Meagher, St. Louis Blues
1998–99	Jere Lehtinen, Dallas Stars	1988–89	Guy Carbonneau, Montreal Canadiens
1997–98	Jere Lehtinen, Dallas Stars	1987–88	Guy Carbonneau, Montreal Canadiens

DID YOU KNOW?

The trio of actors who played the infamous Hanson brothers in the classic film *Slapshot* had a combined 34 years of professional hockey experience.

NHL: Career Records

POINTS						
PLAYER	**YRS**	**GP**	**G**	**A**	**PTS**	**AVG**
Wayne Gretzky, Edm, LA, StL, NYR	20	1,487	894	1,963	2,857	1.921
Mark Messier, Edm, Van, NYR	25	1,756	694	1,193	1,887	1.075
Gordie Howe, Det, Hart	26	1,767	801	1,049	1,850	1.047
Ron Francis, Hart, Pitt, Car, Tor	23	1,731	549	1,249	1,798	1.039
Marcel Dionne, Det, LA, NYR	18	1,348	731	1,040	1,771	1.314

GOALS				
PLAYER	**YRS**	**GP**	**G**	**AVG**
Wayne Gretzky, Edm, LA, StL, NYR	20	1,487	894	.601
Gordie Howe, Det, Hart	26	1,767	801	.453
Brett Hull, Cal, StL, Dal, Det	19	1,264	741	.586
Marcel Dionne, Det, LA, NYR	18	1,348	731	.542
Phil Esposito, Chi, Bos, NYR	18	1,282	717	.559

ASSISTS				
PLAYER	**YRS**	**GP**	**G**	**AVG**
Wayne Gretzky, Edm, LA, StL, NYR	20	1,487	1,963	1.320
Ron Francis, Hart, Pitt, Car, Tor	23	1,731	1,249	.721
Mark Messier, Edm, NYR, Van	25	1,756	1,193	.679
Ray Bourque, Bos, Col	22	1,612	1,169	.725
Paul Coffey, Edm, Pitt, LA, Det, Hart, Phi, Chi, Car, Bos	21	1,409	1,135	.806

KEY: YRS=years; GP=games played; G=goals; A=assists; PTS=points; AVG=average

Wayne Gretzky

Brett Hull

NHL: Career Records (cont.)

Goaltending

WINS

GOALTENDER	W	L	T
Patrick Roy, Mtl, Col	551	315	131
Martin Brodeur, NJ	494	263	105
Ed Belfour, Chi, SJ, Dal, Tor, Fla	484	320	111
Terry Sawchuk, Det, Bos, Tor, LA, NYR	447	330	172
Curtis Joseph, StL, Edm, Tor, Det, Phoe	446	341	90

Patrick Roy

SHUTOUTS

GOALTENDER	YRS	GP	SO
Terry Sawchuk, Det, Bos, Tor, LA, NYR	21	971	103
George Hainsworth, Mtl, Tor	11	465	94
Martin Brodeur, NJ	14	891	92
Glenn Hall, Det, Chi, StL	18	906	84
Jacques Plante, Mtl, NYR, StL, Tor, Bos	18	837	82

GOALS-AGAINST AVERAGE (PRE-1950)

GOALTENDER	YRS	GP	GA	GAA
George Hainsworth, Mtl, Tor	11	465	937	1.91
Alex Connell, Ott, Det, NYA, Mtl M	12	417	830	1.91
Chuck Gardiner, Chi	7	316	664	2.0
Lorne Chabot, NYR, Tor, Mtl, Chi, Mtl M, NYA	11	411	861	2.04
Tiny Thompson, Bos, Det	12	553	1,183	2.08

GOALS-AGAINST AVERAGE (POST-1950)

GOALTENDER	YRS	GP	GA	GAA
Martin Brodeur, NJ	14	891	1,931	2.20
Dominik Hasek, Chi, Buf, Det, Ott	15	694	1,488	2.21
Ken Dryden, Mtl	8	397	870	2.24
Jacques Plante, Mtl, NYR, StL, Tor, Bos	18	837	1,965	2.38
Chris Osgood, Det, NYI, StL	13	621	1,455	2.45

Note: Minimum 350 games played. Goals-against average equals goals against per 60 minutes played

KEY: W=wins; L=losses; T=ties; YRS=years; GP=games played; SO=shutouts; GA=goals against; GAA=goals-against average

Dominik Hasek

DID YOU KNOW?

In Game 6 of the 1964 Stanley Cup, Toronto Maple Leafs defenseman Bob Baun took a shot in the foot, breaking his right ankle. Baun came back to score an overtime goal and force a Game 7. The Leafs won that game and the Cup.

■ **Steve Yzerman,** *center, b. May 9, 1965, Cranbook, British Columbia.* Known as just "The Captain" or "Stevie Y" in Detroit, Yzerman led the Red Wings to three Stanley Cups in his 22 seasons. Yzerman, Detroit's captain from 1986 to his retirement, was a true warrior. He recovered from major knee surgery during the 2002–03 season and took a puck to the face in 2004 that required four and a half hours of surgery. A 10-time All-Star, Yzerman finished sixth all-time in points (1,755). He retired in 2006 and now holds a position in the team's front office.

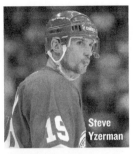

Steve Yzerman

■ **Ron Francis,** *center, b. March 1, 1963, Sault Ste. Marie, Ontario, Canada.* Like Yzerman, Francis was a player of incredible durability. In a career that spanned 23 seasons, Francis finished third all-time in games played (1,731). Nicknamed "The Quiet Superstar," Francis made everybody around him better, as evidenced by his 1,249 career assists, second only to Wayne Gretzky. A two-time Stanley Cup winner with the Pittsburgh Penguins (1991, 1992), Francis also led the Carolina Hurricanes on their surprise run to the 2002 Finals. Francis retired in 2005 at the age of 42.

Ron Francis

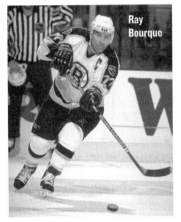

Ray Bourque

■ **Ray Bourque,** *defenseman, b. December 28, 1960, Montreal, Quebec, Canada.* After 20-plus seasons with the Boston Bruins and a record 1,826 games without a championship, Bourque became the story of the 2000–01 season when a trade to the Colorado Avalanche gave him a shot at the Stanley Cup. Sure enough, Bourque ended his streak and helped the Avalanche to the 2001 title. Loyal to his Boston roots, Bourque flew the Cup back to Beantown for a celebration in City Hall. He never played again, finishing first in career points by a defenseman (1,579).

Maurice Richard

■ **Maurice "Rocket" Richard,** *right wing, b. August 4, 1921, Montreal, Quebec, Canada; d. May 27, 2000.* Nicknamed "the Rocket" for his blazing speed, Montreal's hometown hero was a legend for the Canadiens. Just 5' 10" and 170 pounds, Richard was known for his intense demeanor and ferocious play. He won eight Stanley Cups in his 18 years with the team and retired with a then-record 544 regular-season goals. One of the NHL's greatest players ever, he was listed No. 62 on the Associated Press's list of the Top 100 athletes of the 20th century.

All in the Family

The largest group of brothers to play in the NHL came from the Sutter family. From 1976 to 2001, at least one of the six Sutters was playing in the league.

1 Begin at the dot below each brother's name. Follow the vertical line downward until you reach a horizontal line.

2 Travel along the horizontal line until you reach another vertical line, then follow that line downward again.

3 You must take the new path at every intersection, always traveling down, left, or right. If you follow the paths correctly, you'll discover something about each of the brothers.

Clockwise from top left: Ron, Rich, Brent, Darryl, Brian, Duane

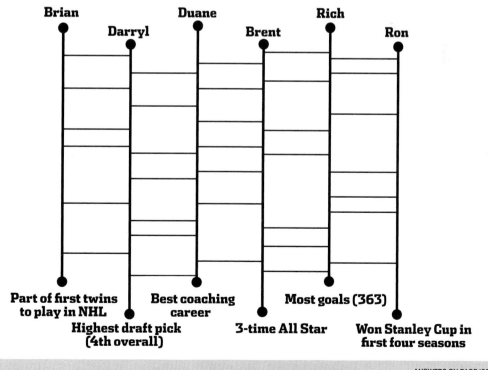

Brian — Part of first twins to play in NHL

Darryl — Highest draft pick (4th overall)

Duane — Best coaching career

Brent — 3-time All Star

Rich — Most goals (363)

Ron — Won Stanley Cup in first four seasons

ANSWERS ON PAGE 190

Getting Their Kicks

Soccer fans in the U.S. have waited a long time for their sport to get some respect. It's finally happening. In 2007, MLS brought in a new breed of foreign players, exported several homegrown stars, and fielded an increasing number of competitive teams. The league now grows U.S. talent. And the results can be seen throughout the world.

Take the Houston Dynamo. The club won over thousands of fans and turned into a dynasty by capturing its second MLS Cup in two years. In November, the Dynamo beat the New England Revolution 2–1 in the finals, with Houston's exceptional Canadian midfielder Dwayne De Rosario heading home the clinching goal. De Rosario was named finals MVP. And Houston's roster of domestic stars provided more firepower throughout the season. U.S. national team players Brian Ching and Ricardo Clark, along with Nate Jaqua, made the Dynamo a force.

A further sign of MLS's maturity was the creation of amateur programs for teams to scout youth players. Soccer-specific stadiums also went up in Colorado and expansion town Toronto. Nearly half the MLS teams now play in the smaller, nicer European-style stadiums, which boost attendance and revenue.

Maybe the best indication of the rising health of MLS was the arrival of a certain Englishman named David Beckham. The international superstar signed with the Los Angeles Galaxy in a record $250 million deal. In his first season, Beckham was limited by injury but brought global attention to the league. And he wasn't the only talented foreigner to make waves. Newcomers Juan Pablo Ángel and Cuauhtémoc Blanco became top players. Brazilian danger man Luciano Emilio partnered with slick Argentine playmaker Christian Gómez to lead D.C. United to a Supporters' Shield title for most regular-season points. Emilio was voted league MVP after scoring 20 goals.

But it wasn't a one-way street. After honing their skills in MLS, some of the best U.S. players departed for bigger venues overseas. Jaqua left for Austria. Clint Dempsey signed with Fulham in the English Premiership and has scored several key goals for his new team. And the most famous young player in the U.S., Freddy Adu, played part of the season for Real Salt Lake, then packed his bags for Benfica in the Portuguese first division.

With the continued success of MLS and U.S. youth teams, the future looks bright for the sport. Soccer may not be a U.S. pastime yet, but the game continues to attract more people every year.

In his first MLS season, Brazilian star Emilio scored a league-leading 20 goals for D.C. United.

TONY QUINN/MLS/WIREIMAGE

In 2007, Houston Dynamo forward Brian Ching tied for the team lead in goals (7) and helped them to their second straight MLS Cup.

EASTERN CONFERENCE	WESTERN CONFERENCE
Chicago Fire	Club Deportivo Chivas USA
Columbus Crew	Colorado Rapids
D.C. United	FC Dallas
Kansas City Wizards	Houston Dynamo
New York Red Bulls	Los Angeles Galaxy
New England Revolution	Real Salt Lake
Toronto FC	San Jose Earthquakes

? DID YOU KNOW?

D.C. United forward Jaime Moreno is the leading scorer in MLS history. He has the most career goals (118) and ranks fifth all-time in assists (96).

MLS STARS

■ **Landon Donovan,** *winger, b. March 4, 1982, Redlands, California.* The golden boy of U.S. soccer was stuck in a rough patch until recently. Donovan disappeared during the 2006 World Cup and, despite 13 assists in 2007, could do little to prevent his club team, the Los Angeles Galaxy, from finishing near the bottom of the MLS table. But the dynamic winger bounced back the following season and meshed nicely with David Beckham to create a dangerous scoring duo. He also upped his game on the international stage, scoring a brilliant hat trick against Ecuador in March and later breaking Eric Wynalda's all-time U.S. goals record.

■ **Juan Pablo Ángel,** *forward, b. October 24, 1975, Medellín, Colombia.* One of the most experienced strikers to play in MLS, Ángel arrived in 2007 from Premiership side Aston Villa, where he once scored 23 goals in a season. In his first year with the New York Red Bulls, Angel bagged 19 goals, good for second in the league, and led the team into the playoffs. Coach Bruce Arena couldn't believe his luck. "This guy's too good to be real," he said. Ángel has 33 caps for the Colombian national team.

Landon Donovan

WENDY LARSEN/ISIPHOTOS.COM

■ **Cuauhtémoc Blanco,** *midfielder, b. January 17, 1973, Mexico City, México.* Beckham was supposed to be the big foreign import to MLS in 2007. Blanco had other plans. The Mexican national team player brought his outsize personality to Chicago and instantly turned the Fire into contenders. Arriving mid-season, Blanco tallied four goals and seven assists in 14 games and propelled his club to the Eastern Conference Finals. Blanco's scoring celebration quickly caught on with fans: He strikes a pose in honor of Aztec ruler and namesake Cuauhtémoc, a Mexican hero who resisted the Spanish conquistadors.

MLS Cup Results

YEAR	CHAMPION	SCORE	RUNNER-UP
2007	Houston Dynamo	2-1	New England Revolution
2006	Houston Dynamo*	1-1 (OT)	New England Revolution
2005	Los Angeles Galaxy	1-0	New England Revolution
2004	D.C. United	3-2	Kansas City Wizards
2003	San Jose Earthquakes	4-2	Chicago Fire
2002	Los Angeles Galaxy	1-0 (OT)	New England Revolution
2001	San Jose Earthquakes	2-1 (OT)	Los Angeles Galaxy
2000	Kansas City Wizards	1-0	Chicago Fire
1999	D.C. United	2-0	Los Angeles Galaxy
1998	Chicago Fire	2-0	D.C. United
1997	D.C. United	2-1	Colorado Rapids
1996	D.C. United	3-2 (OT)	Los Angeles Galaxy

* Won on penalty kicks.

MLS Award Winners

YEAR	MVP	TOP GOAL SCORER	GOAL OF THE YEAR	COACH
2007	Luciano Emilio, D.C. United	Luciano Emilio, D.C. United	Cuauhtémoc Blanco, Chicago Fire	Preki, Chivas USA
2006	Christian Gomez, D.C. United	Jeff Cunningham, Real Salt Lake	Brian Ching, Real Salt Lake	Bob Bradley, Chivas USA
2005	Taylor Twellman, NE Revolution	Taylor Twellman, NE Revolution	Dwayne De Rosario, San Jose Earthquakes	Dominic Kinnear, San Jose Earthquakes
2004	Amado Guevara, NY/NJ MetroStars	Amado Guevara, NY/NJ MetroStars	Dwayne De Rosario, San Jose Earthquakes	Greg Andrulis, Columbus Crew
2003	Preki, Kansas City Wizards	Preki, Kansas City Wizards	Damani Ralph, Chicago Fire	Dave Sarachan, Chicago Fire
2002	Carlos Ruiz, LA Galaxy	Taylor Twellman, NE Revolution	Carlos Ruiz, LA Galaxy	Steve Nicol, NE Revolution
2001	Alex Pineda Chacon, Miami Fusion	Alex Pineda Chacon, Miami Fusion	Clint Mathis, NY/NJ MetroStars	Frank Yallop, San Jose Earthquakes
2000	Tony Meola, Kansas City Wizards	Mamadou Diallo, Tampa Bay Mutiny	Marcelo Balboa, Colorado Rapids	Bob Gansler, Kansas City Wizards
1999	Jason Kreis, Dallas Burn	Jason Kreis, Dallas Burn	Marco Etcheverry, D.C. United	Sigi Schmid, LA Galaxy
1998	Marco Etcheverry, D.C. United	Stern John, Columbus Crew	Brian McBride, Columbus Crew	Bob Bradley, Chicago Fire
1997	Preki, Kansas City Wizards	Preki, Kansas City Wizards	Marco Etcheverry, D.C. United	Bruce Arena, D.C. United
1996	Carlos Valderrama, Tampa Bay Mutiny	Roy Lassiter, Tampa Bay Mutiny	Eric Wynalda, San Jose Clash	Thomas Rongen, Tampa Bay Mutiny

YEAR	GOALKEEPER	DEFENDER	ROOKIE	COMEBACK PLAYER
2007	Brad Guzan, Chivas USA	Michael Parkhurst, NE Revolution	Maurice Edu, Toronto FC	Eddie Johnson, Kansas City Wizards
2006	Troy Perkins, D.C. United	Bobby Boswell, D.C. United	Jonathan Bornstein, Chivas USA	Richard Mulrooney, FC Dallas
2005	Pat Onstad, San Jose Earthquakes	Jimmy Conrad, Kansas City Wizards	Michael Parkhurst, NE Revolution	Chris Klein, Kansas City Wizards

MLS MVP X 2

Discover a record set during the 2007 MLS Cup. First write the answer to each clue on the spaces. Then transfer letters from the spaces to the boxes with the same numbers to reveal the record. Black squares separate words, and words wrap from one line to the next.

First number in 3-1-2 record
__ __ __ __
33 14 36 11

Stop the ball
__ __ __ __
25 56 53 49

Contest
__ __ __ __ __
44 53 41 47 19

2007 MLS Cup winner
__ __ __ __ __ __
57 4   35 55 31 39

Pass preceding a goal
__ __ __ __ __ __
53 24 11 34 17 29

Restart the game
__ __ __ __ __ __ __
26 42 23 28 2   6   5

This earns an indirect free kick
__ __ __ __ __ __ __
10 40 21 46 22 1   8

Second deepest defender
__ __ __ __ __ __ __
46 54 32 37 52 8   23

Possession change
__ __ __ __ __ __ __ __
18 48 9   36 15 51 20 23

4-2-4, 4-3-3, or 4-4-2
__ __ __ __ __ __ __ __ __
40 10 38 50 55 29 30 39 35

Warning
__ __ __ __ __ __ __ __ __ __
4   43 45 45 10 27   47 12 38 57

1	2	3	4	5	6		7	8		9	10	11	12	13	14	15	
16	17		18	19	20		21	22	23	24	25		26	27	28	—	29
30	31	32		33	34	35	36	37	38		39	40		41	42	43	
44	45	46		47	48	49		50	51	52		53	54	55	56	57	

ANSWERS ON PAGE 191

■ Jozy Altidore, *forward, b. November 6, 1989, Boca Raton, Florida.* The U.S. has pumped out quality defenders and midfielders for years. But forwards? Not so much, until now. Altidore is fast, powerful, and nimble — everything you want in a striker. And at 6'1", the Red Bulls' 19-year-old star is still growing. This lethal combination of size and skill made him an instant success as a rookie in 2006. After his performance in the under-20 World Cup in 2007 — Altidore notched two goals in a stunning U.S. win over Brazil — he was rewarded with a transfer to Villarreal, of the Spanish League.

Jozy Altidore

■ Michael Bradley, *midfielder, b. July 31, 1987, Princeton, New Jersey.* He may be the coach's son, but Bradley deserves his spot on the national team. The 21-year-old sees the field as well as any American in the middle has since Claudio Reyna. But Bradley's inventive passes aren't his only asset. The rugged midfielder, who plays club ball for Heerenveen in the Dutch first division, is also a tough defender who provides much-needed fire on the pitch. He performed admirably in the 2007 CONCACAF Gold Cup, helping propel the U.S. to the title.

YOUNG STARS TO WATCH

MLS Award Winners (cont.)

YEAR	GOALKEEPER	DEFENDER	ROOKIE	COMEBACK PLAYER
2004	Joe Cannon, Colorado Rapids	Robin Fraser, Columbus Crew	Clint Dempsey, NE Revolution	Brian Ching, San Jose Earthquakes
2003	Pat Onstad, San Jose Earthquakes	Carlos Bocanegra, Chicago Fire	Damani Ralph, Chicago Fire	Chris Armas, Chicago Fire
2002	Joe Cannon, San Jose Earthquakes	Carlos Bocanegra, Chicago Fire	Kyle Martino, Columbus Crew	Chris Klein, Kansas City Wizards
2001	Tim Howard, MetroStars	Jeff Agoos, San Jose Earthquakes	Rodrigo Faria, MetroStars	Troy Dayak, San Jose Earthquakes
2000	Tony Meola, Kansas City Wizards	Peter Vermes, Kansas City Wizards	Carlos Bocanegra, Chicago Fire	Tony Meola, Kansas City Wizards
1999	Kevin Hartman, LA Galaxy	Robin Fraser, LA Galaxy	Jay Heaps, Miami Fusion	Not awarded
1998	Zach Thornton, Chicago Fire	Lubos Kubik, Chicago Fire	Ben Olsen, D.C. United	Not awarded
1997	Brad Friedel, Columbus Crew	Eddie Pope, D.C. United	Mike Duhaney, Tampa Bay Mutiny	Not awarded
1996	Mark Dodd, Dallas Burn	John Doyle, San Jose Clash	Steve Ralston, Tampa Bay Mutiny	Not awarded

All-Time World Cup Scoring Leaders: Men

PLAYER, NATION	TOURNAMENTS	GOALS
Ronaldo, Brazil	1998, 2002, 2006	15
Gerd Müller, West Germany	1970, 1974	14
Just Fontaine, France	1958	13
Pelé, Brazil	1958, 1962, 1966, 1970	12
Jürgen Klinsman, Germany	1990, 1994, 1998	11
Sandor Kocsis, Hungary	1954	11
Teofilo Cubillas, Peru	1970, 1978	10
Miroslav Klose, Germany	2002, 2006	10
Gregorz Lato, Poland	1974, 1978, 1982	10
Gary Lineker, England	1986, 1990	10
Helmut Rahn, West Germany	1954, 1958	10

World Cup Results: Men

YEAR	CHAMPION	SCORE	RUNNER-UP	WINNING COACH
2006	Italy	1-1 (5-3)	France	Marcello Lippi
2002	Brazil	2-0	Germany	Luiz Felipe Scolari
1998	France	3-0	Brazil	Aime Jacquet
1994	Brazil	0-0 (3-2)	Italy	Carlos Alberto Parreira
1990	West Germany	1-0	Argentina	Franz Beckenbauer
1986	Argentina	3-2	West Germany	Carlos Bilardo
1982	Italy	3-1	West Germany	Enzo Bearzot
1978	Argentina	3-1	Netherlands	César Menotti
1974	West Germany	2-1	Netherlands	Helmut Schön
1970	Brazil	4-1	Italy	Mario Zagallo
1966	England	4-2	West Germany	Alf Ramsey
1962	Brazil	3-1	Czechoslovakia	Aymore Moreira
1958	Brazil	5-2	Sweden	Vicente Feola
1954	West Germany	3-2	Hungary	Sepp Herberger
1950	Uruguay	2-1	Brazil	Juan Lopez
1938	Italy	4-2	Hungary	Vittorio Pozzo
1934	Italy	2-1	Czechoslovakia	Vittorio Pozzo
1930	Uruguay	4-2	Argentina	Alberto Supicci

Note: The World Cup was not held in 1942 and 1946 because of World War II.

DID YOU KNOW?
Goalkeeper Mohamed Al-Deayea holds the record for caps (international appearances) by a male soccer player. He appeared in 181 games for Saudi Arabia.

Cristiano Ronaldo

■ **Cristiano Ronaldo,** *winger, b. February 5, 1985, Madeira, Portugal.* Ronaldo conquered the soccer world in 2007–08. The spiky-haired master of the stepover juked his way to 42 goals for Manchester United, leading his club to the Premiership crown and the Champion's League title. It was one of the finest pro seasons in the history of the sport. Ronaldo's scoring tally, an improbable number for a midfielder, broke the 40-year club record for a winger, set by George Best, considered the top player in Man U history. There's only more to come. Ronaldo is just 24.

■ **Lionel Messi,** *winger, b. June 24, 1987, Santa Fe, Argentina.* Watching Argentine international Messi dance past defenders, you sometimes forget he's an athlete. Messi is more of an artist, and his brand of high-speed tango recalls Diego Maradona's grace with the ball. Like the Argentine legend, Messi is blazingly quick and built low to the ground, a result of a growth hormone deficiency when he was young. But his stature gives the Barcelona standout tremendous balance and agility. Couple that with his vision and creativity and you have one of the best players in the world.

Lionel Messi

■ **Fernando Torres,** *forward, b. March 20, 1984, Madrid, Spain.* Fans at The Kop stadium in Liverpool serenade Torres in verse: "We bought the lad from sunny Spain, he gets the ball and scores again." The Liverpudlian love affair with the new No. 9 began in 2007, when the powerful Spanish striker moved to England and lit up the Premiership with 24 goals. With 33 strikes in total competition, Torres became the first Reds player to break the 30-goal mark since Robbie Fowler in 1996–97.

Fernando Torres

■ **Kaká,** *midfielder, b. April 22, 1982, Brasilia, Brazil.* A sprinter's speed and precision footwork make Kaká more or less unstoppable as an attacking midfielder. The big A.C. Milan star can rumble past opponents or fake them out of their cleats and he plays best when the stakes are high. Kaká led his club to the Champions League title in 2007 with 10 goals. His performance last season earned him soccer's two highest individual awards: the Ballon d'Or, given to the best European footballer, and FIFA's World Player of the Year.

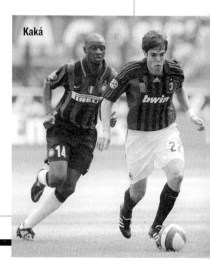

Kaká

INTERNATIONAL STARS

All-Time World Cup Scoring Leaders: Women

PLAYER, NATION	TOURNAMENTS	GOALS
Birgit Prinz, Germany	1995, 1999, 2003, 2007	14
Michelle Akers, United States	1991, 1999	12
Sun Wen, China	1991, 1995, 1999, 2003	11
Bettina Wiegmann, Germany	1991, 1995, 1999, 2003	11
Ann Kristin Aarønes, Norway	1995, 1999	10
Marta, Brazil	2003, 2007	10
Heidi Mohr, Germany	1991, 1995	10
Linda Medalen, Norway	1991, 1995, 1999	9
Hege Riise, Norway	1991, 1995, 1999, 2003	9
Abby Wambach, United States	2003, 2007	9
Liu Ailing, China	1995, 1999	8
Mia Hamm, United States	1991, 1995, 1999, 2003	8
Kristine Lilly, United States	1991, 1995, 1999, 2003, 2007	8
Marianne Pettersen, Norway	1995, 1999, 2003	8
Tiffeny Milbrett, United States	1995, 1999, 2003	7
Sissi, Brazil	1999	7

World Cup Results: Women

YEAR	CHAMPION	SCORE	RUNNER-UP	WINNING COACH
2007	Germany	2-0	Brazil	Silvia Neid
2003	Germany	2-1	Sweden	Tina Theune-Meyer
1999	United States	0-0	China	Tony DiCicco
1995	Norway	2-0	Germany	Even Pellerud
1991	United States	2-1	Norway	Anson Dorrance

Germany celebrates after winning the 2007 Women's World Cup.

SIMON BRUTY

FIFA Women's World Cup China 2007

Picture This

Soccer great Abby Wambach scored 75 goals in her first 94 games. To get a picture of how she did this, find where each of the 12 individual pieces below is in the big picture. Below each piece, write the letter of the column (circle) and row (square) where it is found. Heads up, pay attention to the order of the shapes! The letters under the pieces will spell something else about Abby's feat. Get the picture? We've found the first piece for you.

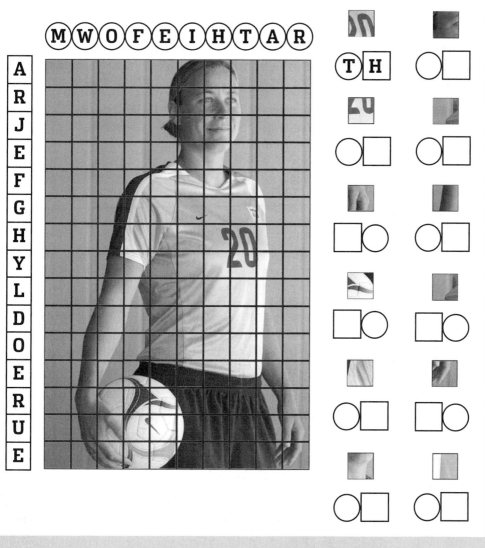

ANSWERS ON PAGE 191

JOHN TODD/ISIPHOTOS.COM

PAUL GILHAM/GETTY IMAGES (MARTA, SMITH); MICHAEL REYNOLDS/EPA (PRINZ); DAVID BERGMAN (SOLO)

■ **Marta,** *midfielder, b. February 19, 1986, Dois Riachos, Brazil.* She wears No. 10 and is compared to Pelé for good reason. This left-footed magician is considered the best women's soccer player in the world. Marta starred on the Brazilian team that won the 2007 Pan-American games, scoring 12 goals and spearheading a 5–0 rout of the U.S. in the final. Although Brazil lost to Germany in the finals of the 2007 Women's World Cup, Marta won the Golden Ball for best player and Golden Shoe for top scorer. She also plays club soccer for Umeå IK in Sweden, where she has won three league titles.

Marta

Brigit Prinz

■ **Brigit Prinz,** *forward, b. October 25, 1977, Frankfurt, Germany.* A three-time FIFA Women's World Player of the Year winner, Prinz holds the Women's World Cup all-time scoring record (14 goals). She was good enough to have attracted attention from a Serie A men's side in 2003. It may have been a publicity stunt, but it's no knock on her talent. The striker has racked up goals everywhere she's played. In the past season, she scored 22 times for her club team, FFC Frankfurt, and beat Umeå IK in the 2008 UEFA Cup finals.

■ **Kelly Smith,** *forward, b. October 29, 1978, Watford, England.* As a kid, Smith honed her skills playing on boys' teams. She even cut her hair short to disguise herself from adults who didn't want girls playing soccer. By 16, Smith was wearing an England jersey. She went to college at Seton Hall, broke scoring records, then played in the now-defunct WUSA after graduating. But injuries — a torn ACL, a broken leg, stress fractures — have held her back. When healthy, Smith is one of the deadliest strikers in the game. Now playing for her former British team, Arsenal Ladies, she showed her ability in the 2006–07 season, scoring 30 goals.

Kelly Smith

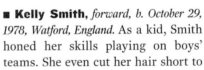

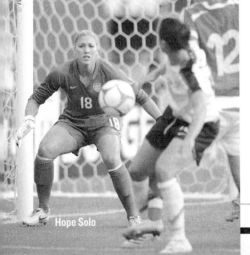

Hope Solo

■ **Hope Solo,** *goalkeeper, b. July 30, 1981, Richland, Washington.* There's no questioning Solo's athletic ability. The U.S. national team goalie was an All-America striker in high school. In college, she switched positions, and before long she was an All-America goalkeeper. A bulwark in the net at the international level, Solo only let in two goals during the 2007 Women's World Cup. Yet her coach, Greg Ryan, benched her against Brazil. The U.S. lost 4–0. Solo threw a fit. Ryan got fired. The U.S. went home to regroup.

1 True or False: The 32-panel design of pentagons and hexagons on a traditional soccer ball was created by a math professor at Belgium's Ghent University in 1970.
A. True
B. False

2 Who is the all-time leading scorer in the World Cup, with 15 goals?
A. Just Fontaine, France
B. Gerd Müller, Germany
C. Ronaldo, Brazil

3 True or False: The rules of soccer were first addressed formally in 1848, when H.C. Malden convened a meeting at Trinity College, Cambridge, with representatives from Eton, Harrow, Rugby, Winchester, and Shrewsbury.
A. True
B. False

4 Real Madrid has won a record nine Champion's League titles. Which club has won the second-most, with seven?
A. A.C. Milan
B. Liverpool
C. Ajax

5 Who holds the record for most assists in an MLS season?
A. Carlos Valderrama, 26 (2000)
B. Steve Ralston, 28 (2003)
C. Marco Etcheverry, 31 (1998)

6 What team does legendary Dutch player Ruud Gullit now coach?
A. FC Barcelona
B. Grasshopper Club Zürich
C. LA Galaxy

7 Which country hosted — and won — the first World Cup, in 1930?
A. Uruguay
B. Brazil
C. Germany

8 What is the name for the fluid Dutch system of soccer, pioneered by AFC Ajax?
A. Total Windmill
B. Total Football
C. Total Awesomeness

9 What did German goalkeeper Jens Lehmann consult before saving two penalty kicks in the quarterfinals against Argentina during the 2006 World Cup?
A. Notes about opponents' tendencies
B. A rabbit's foot that he kept in his sock
C. A crystal ball

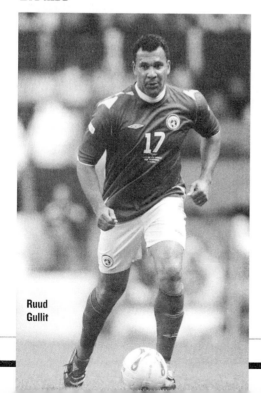
Ruud Gullit

Jens Lehmann

1.B, 2.C, 3.A, 4.A, 5.A, 6.C, 7.A, 8.B, 9.A

High-Flying Thrills

My, oh my, can that tomato fly. If the action sports world had an equivalent to Tiger or Kobe, it would be Shaun. That's Shaun White, the wispy snowboarder/skater with the flowing red hair and the circus nickname. White's known for his wild hairdo, but he's even more famous for his skill on the board. The only snowboarder to win gold at both the Olympics and the X Games, White continued his success last year by dominating just about every competition under the sun.

In August 2007, White beat out Pierre Luc Gagnon for the gold medal in skateboard vert at X Games XIII, which was also notable for Jake Brown's terrifying fall from the skate big air ramp. (Brown dropped 45 feet but was able to get up and walk away on his own.)

Next up: January 2008's Winter X Games XII, where White's frontside 1260 won the snowboard superpipe and gave him 14 X Games medals, seven of them gold. That haul matches the record Tanner Hall set by winning the ski superpipe at the same Winter X Games.

But White wasn't done. He finished first in the Swatch TTR World Snowboard Tour. He also took home the championship in skate vert in the AST Dew Tour. And he successfully defended his title at the 25th Burton U.S. Open, where he finished first in the halfpipe and became the first Burton Global Open champion. Quite a year.

White wasn't alone in establishing his dominance in action sports. Ryan Sheckler won the overall title in skateboard park in the AST Dew Tour for the third straight year. And Daniel Dhers solidified his place as the top BMX park rider, winning his second straight AST Dew Tour. Perhaps the only real surprise last year came from surfer Mick Fanning, who held off big-name stars like Kelly Slater and Andy Irons to win his first ASP world title.

Shaun White won gold in skateboard vert at X Games XIII.

DUSTIN SNIPES/ICON SMI

ACTION SPORTS

Torah Bright, *b. December 27, 1986, Cooma, Australia.* The maestra of the snowboard superpipe, Bright has racked up an impressive resumé since turning pro at age 14. In 2007, she became the first Aussie to win a gold medal at the Winter X Games. Last year, she also won the Nippon Open, finished atop the 2007 TTR Women's World Tour, and was the overall winner of the 2007 Burton Global Open Series. Bright started off as a downhill ski racer, but her older brother soon got her hooked on snowboarding. The devout Mormon lives and trains in Salt Lake City.

Torah Bright

Daniel Dhers, *b. March 25, 1985, Caracas, Venezuela.* This two-wheel trick machine hails from an unlikely spot for BMX riders (Dhers moved from Caracas to Buenos Aires, Argentina, at 16, and honed his skills there in local parks). But no one's quibbling with the results. Dhers won X Games gold in BMX park in 2007. Equally impressive are his repeat titles in the AST Dew Tour. Dhers first won the Tour in 2006 and looked just as good last year. One of the most consistent riders around, Dhers is best known for his powerful tailwhip combos.

Winter X Games Results

			MONO X	
YEAR	EVENT	GOLD	SILVER	BRONZE
2008	Skier X	Kees-Jan van der Klooster, Ned.	Tyler Walker, U.S.	Chris Devlin-Young, U.S.
2007	Skier X	Tyler Walker, U.S.	Kevin Connolly U.S.	Kees-Jan van der Klooster, Netherlands

			MOTO X	
YEAR	EVENT	GOLD	SILVER	BRONZE
2006	Best Trick	Jeremy Stenberg, U.S.	Mat Rebeaud, U.S.	Ronnie Faisst, U.S.
2005	Best Trick	Brian Deegan, U.S.	Jeff Kargola, U.S.	Dustin Miller, U.S.
2004	Best Trick	Caleb Wyatt, U.S.	Mike Metzger, U.S.	Nate Adams, U.S.
2003	Big Air	Mike Metzger, U.S.	Dane Kinnaird, Australia	Caleb Wyatt, U.S.
2002	Big Air	Brian Deegan, U.S.	Mike Jones, U.S.	Tommy Clowers, U.S.
2001	Big Air	Mike Jones, U.S.	Tommy Clowers, U.S.	Clifford Adoptante, U.S.

			SKIING – MEN	
YEAR	EVENT	GOLD	SILVER	BRONZE
2008	Skier X	Daron Rahlves, U.S.	Stanley Hayer, Canada	Casey Puckett, U.S.
2007	Skier X	Casey Puckett, U.S.	Jake Fiala, U.S.	Enak Gavaggio, France
2006	Skier X	Lars Lewen, Sweden	Reggie Crist, U.S.	Chris Del Bosco, U.S.
2005	Skier X	Reggie Crist, U.S.	Zach Crist, U.S.	Enak Gavaggio, France
2004	Skier X	Casey Puckett, U.S.	Lars Lewen, Sweden	Reggie Crist, U.S.
2003	Skier X	Lars Lewen, Sweden	Reggie Crist, U.S.	Enak Gavaggio, France
2002	Skier X	Reggie Crist, U.S.	Peter Lind, Sweden	Enak Gavaggio, France
2001	Skier X	Zach Crist, U.S.	Tomas Andersson, Sweden	Enak Gavaggio, France
2000	Skier X	Shaun Palmer, U.S.	Bill Hudson, U.S.	Zach Crist, U.S.
1999	Skier X	Enak Gavaggio, France	Shane McConkey, U.S.	Jeremy Nobis, U.S.
1998	Skier X	Denis Rey, France	Kent Kreitler, U.S.	Chris Davenport, U.S.
2008	Slopestyle	Andreas Hatveit, Norway	Jossi Wells, New Zealand	Jon Olsson, Sweden
2007	Slopestyle	Candide Thovex, France	Sammy Carlson, U.S.	Cobly West, U.S.
2006*	Best Trick	T.J. Schiller, Canada	Charles Gagnier, Canada	Andrea Hatveit, Norway
2005	Slopestyle	Charles Gagnier, Canada	Tanner Hall, U.S.	Jon Olsson, Sweden
2004	Slopestyle	Tanner Hall, U.S.	Peter Olenick, U.S.	Jon Olsson, Sweden

* Ski Slopestyle was turned into Ski Best Trick due to time considerations.

SKIING – MEN (CONT.)

YEAR	EVENT	GOLD	SILVER	BRONZE
2003	Slopestyle	Tanner Hall, U.S.	Pep Fujas, U.S.	Jon Olsson, Sweden
2002	Slopestyle	Tanner Hall, U.S.	C.R. Johnson, U.S.	Jon Olsson, Sweden
2008	SuperPipe	Tanner Hall, U.S.	Simon Dumont, U.S.	Colby West, U.S.
2007	SuperPipe	Tanner Hall, U.S.	Simon Dumont, U.S.	Peter Olenick, U.S.
2006	SuperPipe	Tanner Hall, U.S.	Laurent Favre, France	Simon Dumont, U.S.
2005	SuperPipe	Simon Dumont, U.S.	Tanner Hall, U.S.	Jon Olsson, Sweden
2004	SuperPipe	Simon Dumont, U.S.	Jon Olsson, Sweden	Peter Olenick, U.S.
2003	SuperPipe	Candide Thovex, France	Tanner Hall, U.S.	Jon Olsson, Sweden
2002	SuperPipe	Jon Olsson, Sweden	Philippe Larose, Canada	Philippe Poirier, Canada
2008	Big Air	Jon Olsson, Sweden	Charles Gagnier, Canada	Simon Dumont, U.S./Jacob Wester, Sweden
2001	Big Air	Tanner Hall, U.S.	Evan Raps, U.S.	C.R. Johnson, U.S.
2000	Big Air	Candide Thovex, France	Skogen Sprang, U.S.	Evan Raps, U.S.
1999	Big Air	J.F. Cusson, Canada	Jonny Moseley, U.S.	Vincent Dorion, Canada

SKIING – WOMEN

YEAR	EVENT	GOLD	SILVER	BRONZE
2008	Skier X	Ophelie David, France	Hedda Bernsten, Norway	Magdalena Jonsson, Sweden
2007	Skier X	Ophelie David, France	Valentine Scuotto, France	Meryll Boulangeat, France
2006	Skier X	Karin Huttary, Austria	Gro Kvinlog, Norway	Ophelie David, France
2005	Skier X	Sanna Tidstrand, Sweden	Karin Huttary, Austria	Magdalena Jonsson, Sweden
2004	Skier X	Karin Huttary, Austria	Aleisha Cline, Canada	Sanna Tidstrand, Sweden
2003	Skier X	Aleisha Cline, Canada	Karin Huttary, Austria	Cecilie Larsen, Norway
2002	Skier X	Aleisha Cline, Canada	Magdalena Jonsson, Sweden	Patti Sherman-Kauf, U.S.
2001	Skier X	Aleisha Cline, Canada	Magdalena Jonsson, Sweden	Chiara Lawrence, U.S.
2000	Skier X	Anik Demers, Canada	Chiara Lawrence, U.S.	Patti Sherman-Kauf, U.S.
1999	Skier X	Aleisha Cline, Canada	Darian Boyle, U.S.	Patti Sherman-Kauf, U.S.
2008	SuperPipe	Sarah Burke, Canada	Miriam Jaeger, Switzerland	Jen Hudak, U.S.
2007	SuperPipe	Sarah Burke, Canada	Grete Eliassen, Norway	Jen Hudak, U.S.
2006	SuperPipe	Grete Eliassen, Norway	Sarah Burke, Canada	Marie Martinod-Routin, France
2005	SuperPipe	Grete Eliassen, Norway	Sarah Burke, Canada	Kristi Leskinen, U.S.

SNOWBOARDING – MEN

YEAR	EVENT	GOLD	SILVER	BRONZE
2008	Slopestyle	Andreas Wiig, Norway	Kevin Pearce, U.S.	Shaun White, U.S
2007	Slopestyle	Andreas Wiig, Norway	Jussi Oksanen, Finland	Shaun White, U.S.
2006	Slopestyle	Shaun White, U.S.	Andreas Wiig, Norway	Danny Kass, U.S.
2005	Slopestyle	Shaun White, U.S.	Danny Kass, U.S.	Travis Rice, U.S.
2004	Slopestyle	Shaun White, U.S.	Danny Kass, U.S.	Andreas Wiig, Norway
2003	Slopestyle	Shaun White, U.S.	Jussi Oksanen, Finland	Jimi Tomer, U.S.
2002	Slopestyle	Travis Rice, U.S.	Shaun White, U.S.	Todd Richards, U.S.
2001	Slopestyle	Kevin Jones, U.S.	Todd Richards, U.S.	Jussi Oksanen, Finland
2000	Slopestyle	Kevin Jones, U.S.	Todd Richards, U.S.	Peter Line, U.S.
1999	Slopestyle	Peter Line, U.S.	Kevin Jones, U.S.	Jimmy Halopoff, U.S.
1998	Slopestyle	Ross Powers, U.S.	Kevin Jones, U.S.	Rob Kingwill, U.S.
1997	Slopestyle	Daniel Franck, Norway	Jimmy Halopoff, U.S.	Bryan Iguchi, U.S.
2008	Snowboarder X	Nate Holland, U.S.	Marcus Schai, Austria	David Speiser, Germany
2007	Snowboarder X	Nate Holland, U.S.	Xavier de le Rue, France	Seth Wescott, U.S.
2006	Snowboarder X	Nate Holland, U.S.	Marco Huser, Switzerland	Jayson Hale, U.S.
2005	Snowboarder X	Xavier de le Rue, France	Seth Wescott, U.S.	Marco Huser, Switzerland
2004	Snowboarder X	Ueli Kestenholz, Switzerland	Seth Wescott, U.S.	Xavier de le Rue, France
2003	Snowboarder X	Ueli Kestenholz, Switzerland	Xavier de le Rue, France	Michael Rosengren, U.S.
2002	Snowboarder X	Philippe Conte, Switzerland	Seth Wescott, U.S.	Berti Denervaud, Switzerland
2001	Snowboarder X	Scott Gaffney, Canada	Mark Schulz, U.S.	Seth Wescott, U.S.
2000	Snowboarder X	Drew Neilson, Canada	Scott Gaffney, Canada	Jason Ford, U.S.
1999	Snowboarder X	Shaun Palmer, U.S.	Drew Neilson, Canada	Scott Gaffney, Canada
1998	Snowboarder X	Shaun Palmer, U.S.	Jason Brown, U.S.	Seth Wescott, U.S.
1997	Snowboarder X	Shaun Palmer, U.S.	Berti Denervaud, Switzerland	Mike Basich, U.S.
2008	SuperPipe	Shaun White, U.S.	Ryoh Aono, Japan	Kevin Pearce, U.S.
2007	SuperPipe	Steve Fisher, U.S.	Shaun White, U.S.	Mason Aguirre, U.S.
2006	SuperPipe	Shaun White, U.S.	Mason Aguirre, U.S.	Scotty Lago, U.S.
2005	SuperPipe	Antti Autti, Finland	Andy Finch, U.S.	Danny Kass, U.S.
2004	SuperPipe	Steve Fisher, U.S.	Danny Kass, U.S.	Keir Dillon, U.S.

Winter X Games Results (cont.)

YEAR	EVENT	GOLD	SILVER	BRONZE
		SNOWBOARDING – MEN (CONT.)		
2003	Superpipe	Shaun White, U.S.	Danny Kass, U.S.	Markku Koski, Finland
2002	Superpipe	J.J. Thomas, U.S.	Shaun White, U.S.	Keir Dillon, U.S.
2001	Superpipe	Danny Kass, U.S.	Tommy Czeschin, U.S.	Ross Powers, U.S.
2000	Superpipe	Todd Richards, U.S.	Ross Powers, U.S.	Tommy Czeschin, U.S.
1999	Halfpipe	Jimi Scott, U.S.	Mike Michalchuk, Canada	Luke Wynen, U.S.
1998	Halfpipe	Ross Powers, U.S.	Guillaume Chastagnol, France	Todd Richards, U.S.
1997	Halfpipe	Todd Richards, U.S.	Daniel Franck, Norway	Fabien Rohrer, Switzerland
2001	Big Air	Jussi Oksanen, Finland	Todd Richards, U.S.	Josh Dirksen, U.S.
2000	Big Air	Peter Line, U.S.	Jason Borgstede, U.S.	Kevin Jones, U.S.
1999	Big Air	Kevin Sansalone, Canada	Peter Line, U.S.	Kevin Jones, U.S.
1998	Big Air	Jason Borgstede, U.S.	Ryan W. Williams, U.S.	Kevin Jones, U.S.
1997	Big Air	Jimmy Halopoff, U.S.	Steve Adkins, U.S.	Bjorn Leines, U.S.

YEAR	EVENT	GOLD	SILVER	BRONZE
		SNOWBOARDING – WOMEN		
2008	Slopestyle	Jamie Anderson, U.S.	Claudia Fliri, Austria	Spence O'Brien, Canada
2007	Slopestyle	Jamie Anderson, U.S.	Hana Beaman, U.S.	Chanelle Sladics, U.S.
2006	Slopestyle	Janna Meyen, U.S.	Hana Beaman, U.S.	Jamie Anderson, U.S.
2005	Slopestyle	Janna Meyen, U.S.	Silvia Mittermueller, Germany	Natasza Zurek, Canada
2004	Slopestyle	Janna Meyen, U.S.	Tara Dakides, U.S.	Jessica Dalpiaz, U.S.
2003	Slopestyle	Janna Meyen, U.S.	Hana Beaman, U.S.	Lindsey Jacobellis, U.S.
2002	Slopestyle	Tara Dakides, U.S.	Janna Meyen, U.S.	Barrett Christy, U.S.
2001	Slopestyle	Jaime MacLeod, U.S.	Shannon Dunn, U.S.	Marni Yamada, U.S.
2000	Slopestyle	Tara Dakides, U.S.	Jaime MacLeod, U.S.	Barrett Christy, U.S
1999	Slopestyle	Tara Dakides, U.S.	Barrett Christy, U.S.	Jaime MacLeod, U.S.
1998	Slopestyle	Jennie Waara, Sweden	Barrett Christy, U.S.	Aurelie Sayres, U.S.
1997	Slopestyle	Barrett Christy, U.S.	Cara-Beth Burnside, U.S.	Jennie Waara, Sweden

What's the Meaning of This?

What Winter X gold medalist is a character in the Microsoft XBox games Amped 2 and Amped 3?

To find out, answer the True/False questions by circling the letters in the appropriate column. If the answer to 1 were true (we're not saying it is), you'd circle the letter H. Write the circled letters on the spaces with the same numbers to reveal the answer to the question.

	TRUE	FALSE		TRUE	FALSE
1. "Railing" means making hard, fast turns.	H	C	5. A "nollie" is a jump off the nose of the board.	R	N
2. "Heel drag" happens when bindings are too close to the toe edge of the board.	L	I	6. The nose and tail of a directional board are shaped differently.	T	S
3. "Corduroy" is a non-slip fabric on top of a board.	E	G	7. "Grab" refers to how sticky snow is. "Bad grab" is wet, sticky, slow snow.	J	A
4. "Fall line" refers to one of three safe body positions a boarder should assume to control a crash.	K	O	8. A snowboard that vibrates too much during high speeds and turns is said to "chatter."	B	D

GAME TIME

___ ___ ___ ___ ___   ___ ___ ___ ___ ___
6 4 5 7 1   8 5 2 3 1 6

ANSWERS ON PAGE 191

Winter X Games Results (cont.)

YEAR	EVENT	GOLD	SILVER	BRONZE
2008	Snowboarder X	Lindsey Jacobellis, U.S.	Tanja Frieden, Switzerland	Sanja Frei, Switzerland
2007	Snowboarder X	Joanie Anderson, U.S.	Lindsey Jacobellis, U.S.	Maelie Ricker, Canada
2006	Snowboarder X	Maelle Ricker, Canada	Joanie Anderson, U.S.	Claudia Haeusermann, Switzerland
2005	Snowboarder X	Lindsey Jacobellis, U.S.	Erin Simmons, Canada	Karine Ruby, France
2004	Snowboarder X	Lindsey Jacobellis, U.S.	Karine Ruby, France	Yvonne Mueller, Switzerland
2003	Snowboarder X	Lindsey Jacobellis, U.S.	Tanja Frieden, Switzerland	Yvonne Mueller, Switzerland
2002	Snowboarder X	Ine Poetzl, Austria	Erin Simmons, Canada	Tanja Frieden, Switzerland
2001	Snowboarder X	Line Oestvold, Norway	Erin Simmons, Canada	Amy Johnson, U.S.
2000	Snowboarder X	Leslee Olson, U.S.	Carlee Baker, Canada	Line Oestvold, Norway
1999	Snowboarder X	Maelle Ricker, Canada	Leslee Olson, U.S.	Candice Drouin, Canada
1998	Snowboarder X	Tina Dixon, U.S.	Corrie Rudishauser, U.S.	Katrina Warnick, U.S.
1997	Snowboarder X	Jennie Waara, Sweden	Hillary Maybery, U.S.	Aurelie Sayres, U.S.
2008	Superpipe	Gretchen Bleiler, U.S.	Torah Bright, Australia	Kelly Clark, U.S.
2007	Superpipe	Torah Bright, Australia	Gretchen Bleiler, U.S.	Elena Hight, U.S.
2006	Superpipe	Kelly Clark, U.S.	Torah Bright, Australia	Soko Yamaoka, Japan
2005	Superpipe	Gretchen Bleiler, U.S	Doriane Vidal, France	Hannah Teter, U.S.
2004	Superpipe	Hannah Teter, U.S.	Kelly Clark, U.S.	Doriane Vidal, Franc
2003	Superpipe	Gretchen Bleiler, U.S.	Kelly Clark, U.S.	Hannah Teter, U.S.
2002	Superpipe	Kelly Clark, U.S.	Stine Brun Kjeldaas, Norway	Natasza Zurek, Canada
2001	Superpipe	Shannon Dunn, U.S.	Natasza Zurek, Canada	Fabienne Reuteler, Switzerland
2000	Superpipe	Stine Brun Kjeldaas, Norway	Barrett Christy, U.S.	Natasza Zurek, Canada
1999	Halfpipe	Michelle Taggart, U.S.	Shannon Dunn, U.S.	Cara-Beth Burnside, U.S.
1998	Halfpipe	Cara-Beth Burnside, U.S.	Michelle Taggart, U.S.	Nicola Thost, Germany
1997	Halfpipe	Shannon Dunn, U.S.	Jennie Waara, Sweden	Nicole Angelrath, Switzerland
2001	Big Air	Tara Dakides, U.S.	Barrett Christy, U.S.	Jenna Murano, U.S.
2000	Big Air	Tara Dakides, U.S.	Leah Wagner, Canada	Jessica Dalpiaz, U.S.
1999	Big Air	Barrett Christy, U.S.	Tara Dakides, U.S.	Janet Matthews, Canada
1998	Big Air	Tina Basich, U.S.	Barrett Christy, U.S.	Tara Zwink, U.S.
1997	Big Air	Barrett Christy, U.S.	Tara Zwink, U.S.	Tina Basich, U.S.

SNOWMOBILING

YEAR	EVENT	GOLD	SILVER	BRONZE
2008	SnoCross	Tucker Hibbert, U.S.	Brett Turcotte, Canada	D.J. Eckstrom, U.S.
2007	SnoCross	Tucker Hibbert, U.S.	Ryan Simons, Canada	T.J. Gulla, U.S.
2006	SnoCross	Blair Morgan, Canada	Levi LaVallee, U.S.	Ross Martin, U.S.
2005	SnoCross	Blair Morgan, Canada	Tucker Hibbert, U.S.	Steve Martin, Canada
2004	SnoCross	Michael Island, Canada	Tucker Hibbert, U.S.	Blair Morgan, Canada
2003	SnoCross	Blair Morgan, Canada	D.J. Eckstrom, U.S.	Tucker Hibbert, U.S.
2002	SnoCross	Blair Morgan, Canada	Tucker Hibbert, U.S.	Tomi Ahmasalo, Finland
2001	SnoCross	Blair Morgan, Canada	Kent Ipsen, U.S.	D.J. Eckstrom, U.S.
2000	SnoCross	Tucker Hibbert, U.S.	Blair Morgan, Canada	T.J. Gulla, U.S.
1999	SnoCross	Chris Vincent, U.S.	Blair Morgan, Canada	Trevor John, U.S.
1998	SnoCross	Toni Haikonen, Finland	Dennis Burks, U.S.	Per Berggren, Sweden
2004	HillCross	Levi LaVallee, U.S.	Justin Tate, U.S.	Carl Kuster, Canada
2003	HillCross	T.J. Gulla, U.S.	Carl Kuster, Canada	Steve Martin, Canada
2002	HillCross	Carl Kuster, Canada	Steve Martin, Canada	Rick Ward, U.S.
2001	HillCross	Carl Kuster, Canada	Vinny Clark, Canada	Matt Luczynski, U.S.

ULTRACROSS*

YEAR	GOLD	SILVER	BRONZE
2005	Marco Huser, Switzerland	Xavier de le Rue, France	Nate Holland, U.S.
	Eric Andersson, Sweden	Davey Barr, Canada	Eric Archer, U.S.
2004	Nate Holland, U.S.	Lars Lewen, Sweden	Xavier Kuhn, France
	Reggie Crist, U.S.	Xavier de le Rue, France	Drew Neilson, Canada
2003	Xavier de le Rue, France	Seth Wescott, U.S.	Ben Jacobellis, U.S.
	Kaj Zackrisson, Sweden	Peter Lind, Sweden	Lars Lewen, Sweden
2002	Seth Wescott, U.S.	Scott Gaffney, Canada	Rob Fagan, Canada
	Peter Lind, Sweden	Eric Archer, U.S.	Enak Gavaggio, France
2001	Shaun Palmer, U.S.	Jason Evans, U.S.	Pontus Staahlkloo, Sweden
	Hiroomi Takizawa, Japan	Isidor Gruener, Austria	Matt Murphy, U.S
2000	Travis McLain, U.S.	Scott Gaffney, Canada	Terry Plum, U.S.
	Peter Lind, Sweden	Sverre Liliequist, Sweden	Mike Dill, U.S.

* First athlete listed is a snowboarder; second athlete is a skier.

■ **Rodney Mullen,** *b. August 17, 1966, Gainesville, Florida.* If any action sports athlete has earned legendary status, it's Mullen. Arguably the most influential and creative skater in history, Mullen invented many of the moves popular in the sport today. In fact, one of the first tricks any skater learns — the flat-ground ollie — owes its existence to him. He's also responsible for the 360 flip and the kickflip. After turning pro at 13, Mullen joined the legendary Powell Peralta Bones Brigade team. In 34 freestyle competitions over the next decade, he was beaten only once.

■ **Bucky Lasek,** *b. December 3, 1972, Baltimore, Maryland.* Lasek got into skateboarding at age 12 after his bike was stolen. What a lucky break. Lasek was soon competing in and winning amateur skating events. After turning pro, he quickly made a name for himself as the best vert skater in the world. Lasek has won four vert golds at the X Games to go with a passel of other medals. He is a back-to-back AST Dew Tour skate vert champ.

Rodney Mullen

GRANT BRITTAIN

LEGENDS

Summer X Games Results

YEAR	EVENT	GOLD	SILVER	BRONZE
		AGGRESSIVE IN-LINE – MEN		
2003	Park	Bruno Lowe, Germany	Stephane Alfano, France	Sven Boekhorst, Netherlands
2002	Park	Jaren Grob, U.S.	Bruno Lowe, Germany	Blake Dennis, Australia
2001	Park	Jaren Grob, U.S.	Louie Zamora, U.S.	Franky Morales, U.S.
2000	Park	Sven Boekhorst, Netherlands	Jaren Grob, U.S.	Sam Fogarty, Australia
1999	Street	Nicky Adams, Canada	Blake Dennis, Australia	Aaron Feinberg, U.S.
1998	Street	Jonathan Bergeron, Canada	Marco Hintze, Mexico	Aaron Feinberg, U.S.
1997	Street	Aaron Feinberg, U.S.	Tim Ward, Australia	Chris Edwards, U.S.
1996	Street	Arlo Eisenberg, U.S.	Matt Mantz, U.S.	Chris Edwards, U.S.
1995	Street	Matt Salerno, Australia	Scott Bentley, New Zealand	Ryan Jacklone, U.S.
2004	Vert	Takeshi Yasutoko, Japan	Marco De Santi, Brazil	Eito Yasutoko, Japan
2003	Vert	Eito Yasutoko, Japan	Takeshi Yasutoko, Japan	Nel Martin, Spain
2002	Vert	Takeshi Yasutoko, Japan	Eito Yasutoko, Japan	Marc Englehart, U.S.
2001	Vert	Taig Khris, France	Takeshi Yasutoko, Japan	Shane Yost, Australia
2000	Vert	Eito Yasutoko, Japan	Takeshi Yasutoko, Japan	Cesar Mora, Australia
1999	Vert	Eito Yasutoko, Japan	Cesar Mora, Australia	Matt Salerno, Australia
1998	Vert	Cesar Mora, Australia	Matt Salerno, Australia	Taig Khris, France
1997	Vert	Tim Ward, Australia	Taig Khris, France	Chris Edwards, U.S.
1996	Vert	Rene Hulgreen, Denmark	Tom Fry, Australia	Chris Edwards, U.S.
1995	Vert	Tom Fry, Australia	Cesar Mora, Australia	Manuel Billiris, Australia
1999	Vert Triples	Sven Boekhorst, Netherlands	Mike Budnik, U.S.	Maki Komori, Japan
		Javier Bujanda, Spain	Cesar Mora, Australia	Eito Yasutoko, Japa
		Taig Khris, France	Matt Salerno, Australia	Takeshi Yasutoko, Japa
1998	Vert Triples	Paul Malina, Australia	Mike Budnik, U.S.	Sven Boekhorst, Netherlands
		Viorel Popa, U.S.	Cesar Mora, Australia	Javier Bujanda, Spain
		Sam Fogarty, Australia	Matt Salerno, Australia	Taig Khris, France
1996	Best Trick	Dion Antony, Australia	Ryan Jacklone, U.S.	Eric Schrijn, U.S.
1995	Best Trick	B. Hardin, U.S.	Ryan Jacklone, U.S.	Brooke Howard-Smith, New Zealand
1995	High Air	Chris Edwards, U.S.	Manuel Billiris, Australia	Ichi Komori, Japan

Summer X Games Results (cont.)

AGGRESSIVE IN-LINE – WOMEN

YEAR	EVENT	GOLD	SILVER	BRONZE
2003	Park	Fabiola da Silva, Brazil	Jenny Logue, United Kingdom	Martina Svobodova, Slovakia
2002	Park	Martina Svobodova, Slovakia	Jenna Downing, United Kingdom	Fallon Heffernan, U.S.
2001	Park	Martina Svobodova, Slovakia	Fallon Heffernan, U.S.	Anneke Winter, Germany
2000	Park	Fabiola da Silva, Brazil	Martina Svobodova, Slovakia	Kelly Matthews, U.S.
1999	Street	Sayaka Yabe, Japan	Kelly Matthews, U.S.	Jenny Curry, U.S.
1998	Street	Jenny Curry, U.S.	Salima Sanga, Switzerland	Sayaka Yabe, Japa
1997	Street	Sayaka Yabe, Japan	Katie Brown, U.S.	True Otis, U.S.
2001	Vert	Fabiola da Silva, Brazil	Ayumi Kawasaki, Japan	Not awarded
2000	Vert	Fabiola da Silva, Brazil	Ayumi Kawasaki, Japan	Merce Borrull, Spain
1999	Vert	Ayumi Kawasaki, Japan	Fabiola da Silva, Brazil	Maki Komori, Japan
1998	Vert	Fabiola da Silva, Brazil	Ayumi Kawasaki, Japan	Maki Komori, Japan
1997	Vert	Fabiola da Silva, Brazil	Claudia Trachsel, Switzerland	Ayumi Kawasaki, Japan
1996	Vert	Fabiola da Silva, Brazil	Jodie Tyler, Australia	Tasha Hodgson, Australia
1995	Vert	Tasha Hodgson, Australia	Angie Walton, New Zealand	Laura Connery, U.S.

BAREFOOT JUMPING

YEAR	GOLD	SILVER	BRONZE
1998	Peter Fleck, U.S.	Ron Scarpa, U.S.	Massimiliano Colosio, Italy
1997	Peter Fleck, U.S.	Evan Berger, South Africa	Warren Fine, South Africa
1996	Ron Scarpa, U.S.	Jon Kretchman, U.S.	Rael Nurick, South Africa
1995	Justin Seers, Australia	Ron Scarpa, U.S.	Rael Nurick, South Africa

BIKE STUNT

YEAR	EVENT	GOLD	SILVER	BRONZE
2006	Dirt	Corey Bohan, Australia	Ryan Nyquist, U.S.	Anthony Napolitan, U.S
2005	Dirt	Corey Bohan, Australia	Chris Doyle, U.S.	Ryan Guettler, U.S.
2004	Dirt	Corey Bohan, Australia	Chris Doyle, U.S.	T.J. Lavin, U.S.
2003	Dirt	Ryan Nyquist, U.S.	Corey Bohan, Australia	Chris Doyle, U.S.
2002	Dirt	Allan Cooke, U.S.	Ryan Nyquist, U.S.	Chris Doyle, U.S
2001	Dirt	Stephen Murray, United Kingdom	Ryan Nyquist, U.S.	T.J. Lavin, U.S.
2000	Dirt	Ryan Nyquist, U.S.	Cory Nastazio, U.S.	T.J. Lavin, U.S.
1999	Dirt	T.J. Lavin, U.S.	Brian Foster, U.S.	Ryan Nyquist, U.S.
1998	Dirt	Brian Foster, U.S.	Ryan Nyquist, U.S.	Joey Garcia, U.S.
1997	Dirt	T.J. Lavin, U.S.	Brian Foster, U.S.	Ryan Nyquist, U.S.
1996	Dirt	Joey Garcia, U.S.	T.J. Lavin, U.S.	Brian Foster, U.S.
1995	Dirt	Jay Miron, Canada	Taj Mihelich, U.S.	Joey Garcia, U.S.

Ryan
Nyquist

BO BRIDGES

KOBE BRYANT

JOHN W MCDONOUGH

Los Angeles guard KOBE BRYANT was on his game in 2007–08, leading his Lakers to the top seed in the Western Conference and the brink of an NBA championship. The Lakers lost in the finals to the Boston Celtics, but Bryant finished second in the NBA in scoring (28.3 points per game) and was named league MVP.

ADRIAN PETERSON

Minnesota Vikings running back **ADRIAN PETERSON** set an NFL single-game record when he rushed for 296 yards against San Diego. Peterson finished 2007 leading the NFC with 1,341 rushing yards and was named the Associated Press Offensive Rookie of the Year.

DAVID WRIGHT

In 2007, New York Mets third baseman DAVID WRIGHT was a front-runner for the National League MVP — until his team missed the playoffs. Wright did win a Gold Glove and a Silver Slugger award after hitting 30 home runs and 107 RBIs.

NASTIA LIUKIN

NASTIA LIUKIN, the 2007 world champ on the balance beam, won her second American Cup all-around title in New York in the first meet of the 2008 season. The win kicked off a big year for the 18-year-old, who headed to the Beijing Olympics with high hopes.

At 35 years old, Detroit Red Wings goalie CHRIS OSGOOD had an eventful 2007–08 season. First he backstopped his team to the best record in the NHL — and then he helped them to the Stanley Cup. Osgood led the league with a 2.09 goals-against average.

CHRIS OSGOOD

TYLER HANSBROUGH

N orth Carolina junior TYLER HANSBROUGH led the top-seeded Tar Heels to the 2008 Final Four, where they lost to the eventual champion, Kansas. Still, Hansbrough received his share of accolades: He was named first-team All-America as well as National Player of the Year.

TORAH BRIGHT

One of the most popular female snowboarders in the world, TORAH BRIGHT had an explosive 2007 that included six first-place finishes. The Australian won a gold medal at the 2007 X Games and was named champion of the Ticket to Ride Tour.

MICHAEL PHELPS

Since winning six gold medals at the 2004 Olympics, 22-year-old swimmer MICHAEL PHELPS has yet to slow down. At the 2007 world championships in Melbourne, Australia, he won seven gold medals, matching Mark Spitz's haul in the 1972 Munich Olympics.

TIGER WOODS

TIGER WOODS, the world's greatest golfer, just keeps getting better. He started off 2008 by winning the first three tournaments. Playing on an injured knee in June, he pulled off a gutsy playoff win at the U.S. Open for his 14th career major. Woods missed the remainder of the season after knee surgery.

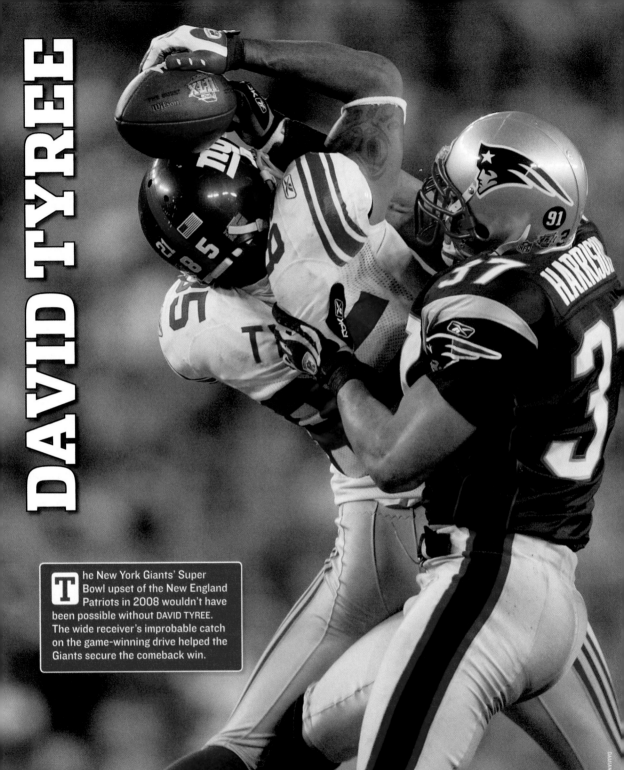

DAVID TYREE

The New York Giants' Super Bowl upset of the New England Patriots in 2008 wouldn't have been possible without DAVID TYREE. The wide receiver's improbable catch on the game-winning drive helped the Giants secure the comeback win.

DAMIAN STROHMEYER

DWAYNE DE ROSARIO

Houston Dynamo midfielder DWAYNE DE ROSARIO continued to light up the highlight reels. He scored six goals in 24 games in 2007 and had two in the postseason, including the game-winner in the MLS Cup. De Rosario led the Dynamo to its second straight Cup and also won his second MLS Cup MVP award.

SIDNEY CROSBY

Pittsburgh Penguins center SIDNEY CROSBY has lived up to all the hype. In 2008, he led the Penguins to their first Stanley Cup finals in 16 years and had a postseason-high 27 points.

FRED VUICH

JUSTINE HENIN

Tennis star JUSTINE HENIN kicked off 2008 ranked No. 1 after victories at the 2007 French and U.S. Opens. In March, she became the seventh woman to be ranked No. 1 for 12 consecutive months — and then abruptly retired in May.

BODE MILLER

In 2008, U.S. skier BODE MILLER won his second World Cup overall title. Miller finished the season with 1,409 points, 111 more points than the second-place finisher.

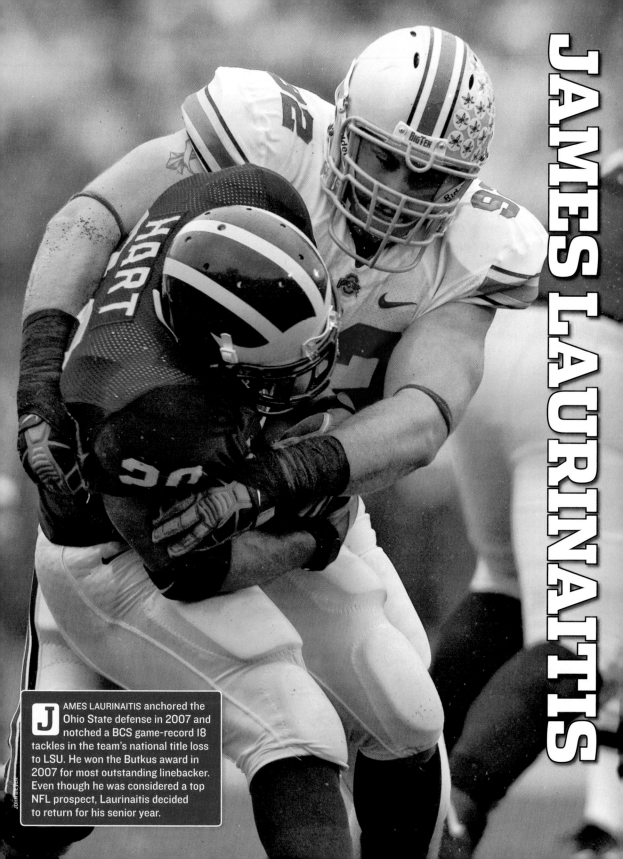

JAMES LAURINAITIS

JAMES LAURINAITIS anchored the Ohio State defense in 2007 and notched a BCS game-record 18 tackles in the team's national title loss to LSU. He won the Butkus award in 2007 for most outstanding linebacker. Even though he was considered a top NFL prospect, Laurinaitis decided to return for his senior year.

JOHN BIEVER

BUBBA HARRIS

Just 22, former BMX world champ BUBBA HARRIS is already a veteran in his sport. Last year, he nearly lost his left foot in a nasty spill on the track in Beijing. He fought back after the injury, but then broke his right foot at the Olympic trials and wasn't on the U.S. team when BMX made its Olympic debut.

KEN GRIFFEY JR.

Cincinnati Reds outfielder KEN GRIFFEY JR. further solidifed his spot in the Hall of Fame in 2008. In June, he bashed his 600th career home run, becoming the sixth player to reach that milestone.

DWIGHT HOWARD

DWIGHT HOWARD of the Orlando Magic is a dunking expert. At the 2007–08 All-Star Game, the 6′ 11″ center became the tallest player ever to win a Slam Dunk Contest. But that isn't his only specialty: He also led the NBA in rebounding, averaging 14.2 boards per game.

GREG NELSON

BOB SANDERS

PUTZIER

88

N icknamed "the Eraser" for his ability to undo a teammate's mistake, Indianapolis Colts safety BOB SANDERS won the Defensive Player of the Year award in 2007. In Week 2 of that season, he had 11 tackles and 2.5 sacks against the Tennessee Titans. He finished the year with 96 tackles.

CAPPIE PONDEXTER

Phoenix Mercury guard CAPPIE PONDEXTER averaged 23.9 points and 5.8 assists in the WNBA finals against the Detroit Shock to lead the Mercury to its first championship. She was named 2007 WNBA finals Most Valuable Player.

Boston Red Sox closer JONATHAN PAPELBON shut down opponents in 2007, notching 37 saves and 84 strikeouts. In Game 4 of the World Series, he had his biggest strikeout of the year. Papelbon got the Colorado Rockies' final batter, outfielder Seth Smith, to whiff on a high fastball, sending Boston to its second World Series victory in four years.

JONATHAN PAPELBON

MORGAN PRESSEL

At 18, MORGAN PRESSEL won the 2007 Kraft Nabisco Championship to become the youngest major winner in LPGA Tour history.

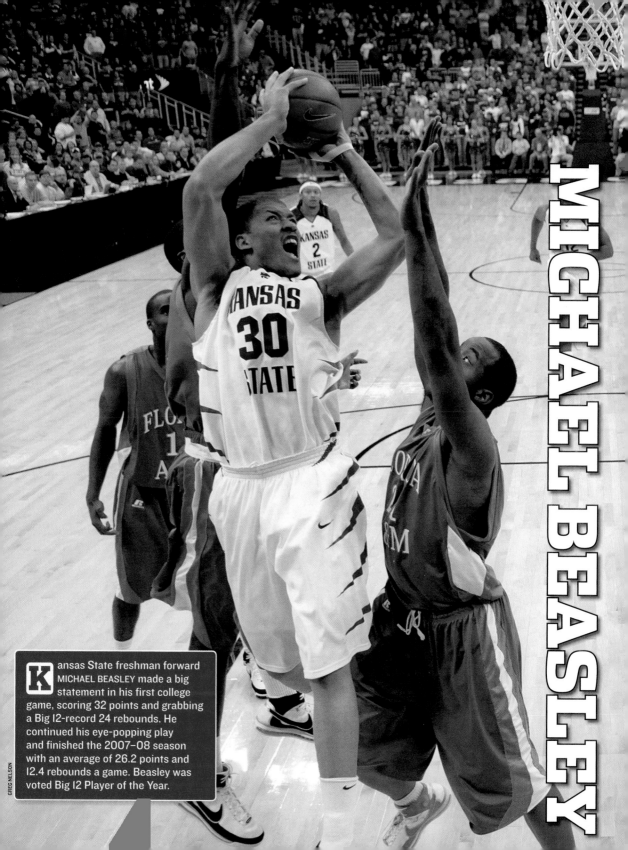

MICHAEL BEASLEY

Kansas State freshman forward MICHAEL BEASLEY made a big statement in his first college game, scoring 32 points and grabbing a Big 12-record 24 rebounds. He continued his eye-popping play and finished the 2007–08 season with an average of 26.2 points and 12.4 rebounds a game. Beasley was voted Big 12 Player of the Year.

JAKE PEAVY

an Diego Padres pitcher JAKE PEAVY unanimously won the 2007 National League Cy Young Award. He was just the second pitcher in 22 years to capture the pitching equivalent of the Triple Crown, leading the NL in victories (19), strikeouts (240), and ERA (2.54).

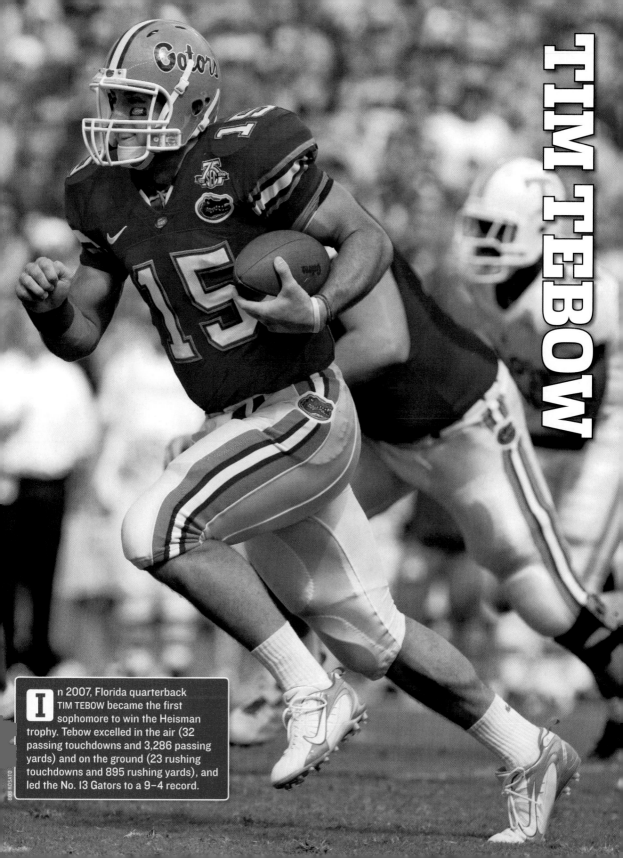

TIM TEBOW

In 2007, Florida quarterback TIM TEBOW became the first sophomore to win the Heisman trophy. Tebow excelled in the air (32 passing touchdowns and 3,286 passing yards) and on the ground (23 rushing touchdowns and 895 rushing yards), and led the No. 13 Gators to a 9–4 record.

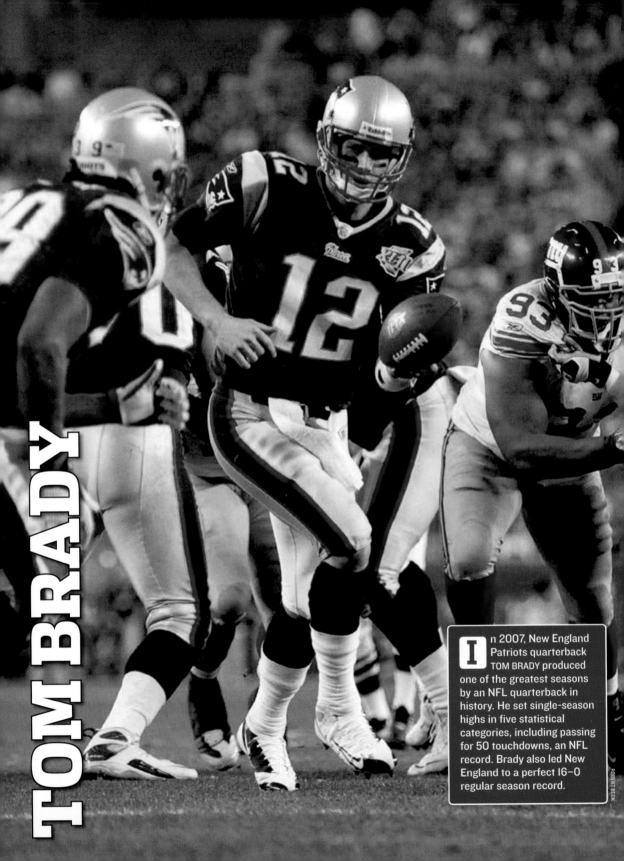

TOM BRADY

In 2007, New England Patriots quarterback TOM BRADY produced one of the greatest seasons by an NFL quarterback in history. He set single-season highs in five statistical categories, including passing for 50 touchdowns, an NFL record. Brady also led New England to a perfect 16-0 regular season record.

ROBERT BECK

A BBY WAMBACH had a busy 2007, scoring six goals in the World Cup to lead the U.S. to a third-place finish. She also scored her 76th career goal to move into the top five on the U.S. all-time list. To cap it off, she won her third U.S. Female Soccer Player of the Year honor.

ABBY WAMBACH

U Conn freshman **MAYA MOORE** led the Huskies in scoring (17.8 points per game) and 3-point shooting (42 percent). Moore, who guided UConn to the Final Four, is only the second freshman to earn a spot on the Associated Press All-America first team.

MAYA MOORE

MAO ASADA

Japanese figure skater MAO ASADA continued her rise to the elite rank in 2008 by winning gold at the world figure skating championships, a year after winning silver. Asada, who at age 12 landed a triple-triple-triple combination, also won the 2008 Four Continents Figure Skating Championships.

DALE EARNHARDT JR.

DALE EARNHARDT JR., who was winless in 2007, hoped to turn his fortunes around with a new car. After the season, he left Dale Earnhardt, Inc., the company founded by his late father, to join Rick Hendrick (*below, with Earnhardt Jr.*) and Hendrick Motorsports.

GUO JINGJING

GUO JINGJING, a two-time Olympic gold medalist, is China's diving princess. In her home country, she is a superstar who appears in advertisements, in fashion shows, and on magazine covers.

KEVIN GARNETT

Forward KEVIN GARNETT joined the Boston Celtics in the off-season in the largest single-player deal in NBA history, revitalizing a team that won only 24 games in 2006–07. Averaging 18.8 points and 9.2 rebounds per game, Garnett led the Celtics to the league's best record (66–16) and a convincing victory over the Los Angeles Lakers in the NBA finals.

Summer X Games Results (cont.)

BIKE STUNT (CONT.)

YEAR	EVENT	GOLD	SILVER	BRONZE
2003	Flatland	Simon O'Brien, Australia	Nathan Penonzek, Canada	Trevor Meyer, U.S.
2002	Flatland	Martti Kuoppa, Finland	Michael Steingraeber, Germany	Phil Dolan, United Kingdom
2001	Flatland	Martti Kuoppa, Finland	Phil Dolan, United Kingdom	Matt Wilhelm, U.S.
2000	Flatland	Martti Kuoppa, Finland	Michael Steingraeber, Germany	Phil Dolan, United Kingdom
1999	Flatland	Trevor Meyer, U.S.	Phil Dolan, United Kingdom	Nathan Penonzek, Canada
1998	Flatland	Trevor Meyer, U.S.	Andrew Faris, Canada	Martti Kuoppa, Finland
1997	Flatland	Trevor Meyer, U.S.	Nate Hanson, U.S.	Andrew Faris, Canada
2007	Park	Daniel Dhers, Venezuela	Scotty Cranmer, U.S.	Dave Mirra, U.S.
2006	Park	Scotty Cranmer, U.S.	Morgan Wade, U.S.	Daniel Dhers, Venezuela
2005	Park	Dave Mirra, U.S.	Scotty Cranmer, U.S.	Ryan Nyquist, U.S.
2004	Park	Dave Mirra, U.S.	Ryan Nyquist, U.S.	Ryan Guettler, Australia
2003	Park	Ryan Nyquist, U.S.	Gary Young, U.S.	Dave Mirra, U.S.
2002	Park	Ryan Nyquist, U.S.	Alistair Whitton, United Kingdom	Chad Kagy, U.S.
2001	Park	Bruce Crisman, U.S.	Alistair Whitton, United Kingdom	Jay Miron, Canada
2000	Park	Dave Mirra, U.S.	Markus Wilke, Germany	Ryan Nyquist, U.S.
1999	Street	Dave Mirra, U.S.	Jay Miron, Canada	Chad Kagy, U.S.
1998	Street	Dave Mirra, U.S.	Jay Miron, Canada	Dennis McCoy, U.S.
1997	Street	Dave Mirra, U.S.	Dennis McCoy, U.S.	Dave Voelker, U.S.
1996	Street	Dave Mirra, U.S.	Jay Miron, Canada	Rob Nolli, U.S.
2007	Vert	Jamie Bestwick, United Kingdom	Simon Tabron, United Kingdom	Kevin Robinson, U.S.
2006	Vert	Chad Kagy, U.S.	Jamie Bestwick, United Kingdom	Simon Tabron, United Kingdom
2005	Vert	Jamie Bestwick, United Kingdom	Chad Kagy, U.S.	Kevin Robinson, U.S.
2004	Vert	Dave Mirra, U.S.	Simon Tabron, United Kingdom	Kevin Robinson, U.S.
2003	Vert	Jamie Bestwick, United Kingdom	Dave Mirra, U.S.	Kevin Robinson, U.S.
2002	Vert	Dave Mirra, U.S.	Mat Hoffman, U.S.	Simon Tabron, United Kingdom
2001	Vert	Dave Mirra, U.S.	Jay Miron, Canada	Mat Hoffman, U.S.
2000	Vert	Jamie Bestwick, United Kingdom	Dave Mirra, U.S.	Mat Hoffman, U.S.
1999	Vert	Dave Mirra, U.S.	Jay Miron, Canada	Simon Tabron, United Kingdom
1998	Vert	Dave Mirra, U.S.	Dennis McCoy, U.S.	Simon Tabron, United Kingdom
1997	Vert	Dave Mirra, U.S.	Dennis McCoy, U.S.	Mat Hoffman, U.S.
1996	Vert	Mat Hoffman, U.S.	Dave Mirra, U.S.	Jamie Bestwick, United Kingdom
1995	Vert	Mat Hoffman, U.S.	Dave Mirra, U.S.	Jay Miron, Canada
1998	Vert Doubles	Dave Mirra, U.S.	Jay Miron, Canada	Jason Davies, United Kingdom
		Dennis McCoy, U.S.	Dave Osato, Canada	John Parker, U.S

BUNGY

YEAR	GOLD	SILVER	BRONZE
1996	Peter Bihun, Canada	Doug Anderson, Canada	Carolyn Anderson, Canada
1995	Doug Anderson, Canada	Mark Baldwin, U.S.	Todd Watkins, U.S.

DOWNHILL BMX

YEAR	GOLD	SILVER	BRONZE
2003	Brandon Meadows, U.S.	Kyle Bennett, U.S.	Michael Day, U.S.
2002	Robbie Miranda, U.S.	Kyle Bennett, U.S.	Robert de Wilde, Netherlands
2001	Brandon Meadows, U.S.	Brian Foster, U.S.	John Whipperman, U.S.

DOWNHILL IN-LINE – MEN

YEAR		GOLD	SILVER	BRONZE
1998		Patrick Naylor, U.S.	Jeremy Anderson, U.S.	Dane Lewis, U.S.
1997		Derek Downing, U.S.	Keith Turner, U.S.	B.J. Steketee, U.S.
1996		Dante Muse, U.S.	Derek Parra, U.S.	Jim Wiederhold, U.S.
1995	Combined	Derek Downing, U.S.	Jim Wiederhold, U.S.	Jondon Trevena, U.S

DOWNHILL IN-LINE – WOMEN

YEAR	GOLD	SILVER	BRONZE
1998	Julie Brandt, U.S.	Aimee Sanderson, U.S.	Theresa Cliff, U.S.
1997	Gypsy Tidwell, U.S.	Julie Brandt, U.S.	Jessica Apgar, U.S.
1996	Gypsy Tidwell, U.S.	Jennifer Jones, U.S.	Desly Hill, Australia

Summer X Games Results (cont.)

KITESKIING			
YEAR	GOLD	SILVER	BRONZE
1995	Cory Roessler, U.S.	Clarin Mustad, Norway	Thomas Jeltsch, Germany

MOUNTAIN BIKING – MEN				
YEAR	EVENT	GOLD	SILVER	BRONZE
1995	Dual Downhill	Robert Naughton, U.S.	Jurgen Beneke, Germany	Todd Tanner, U.S.
1995	Dual Slalom	Jimmy Knight, U.S.	Myles Rockwell, U.S.	Mike King, U.S.
1995	Observed Trials	Libor Karas, Czech Republic	Hans Rey, Germany	Marc Brooks, U.S.

MOUNTAIN BIKING – WOMEN				
YEAR	EVENT	GOLD	SILVER	BRONZE
1995	Dual Downhill	Cheri Elliott, U.S.	Kim Sonier, U.S.	Leigh Donovan, U.S.
1995	Dual Slalom	Leigh Donovan, U.S.	Cheri Elliott, U.S.	Giovanna Bonazzi, Italy

MOTO X				
YEAR	EVENT	GOLD	SILVER	BRONZE
2003	Big Air	Brian Deegan, U.S.	Nate Adams, U.S.	Kenny Bartram, U.S.
2002	Big Air	Mike Metzger, U.S.	Carey Hart, U.S.	Brian Deegan, U.S.
2001	Big Air	Kenny Bartram, U.S.	Dustin Miller, U.S.	Brian Deegan, U.S.
2007	Freestyle	Adam Jones, U.S.	Nate Adams, U.S.	Jeremy Stenberg, U.S.
2006	Freestyle	Travis Pastrana, U.S.	Adam Jones, U.S.	Mike Mason, U.S.
2005	Freestyle	Travis Pastrana, U.S.	Kenny Bartram, U.S.	Nate Adams, U.S.
2004	Freestyle	Nate Adams, U.S.	Travis Pastrana, U.S.	Adam Jones, U.S.
2003	Freestyle	Travis Pastrana, U.S.	Nate Adams, U.S.	Brian Deegan, U.S.
2002	Freestyle	Mike Metzger, U.S.	Kenny Bartram, U.S.	Drake McElroy, U.S.
2001	Freestyle	Travis Pastrana, U.S.	Clifford Adoptante, U.S.	Jake Windham, U.S.
2000	Freestyle	Travis Pastrana, U.S.	Tommy Clowers, U.S.	Brian Deegan, U.S.
1999	Freestyle	Travis Pastrana, U.S.	Mike Cinqmars, U.S.	Brian Deegan, U.S.

TRIVIA

1 Skateboard decks are usually made from what material?
A. **Canadian maple**
B. **Kevlar and carbon fiber**
C. **The luxuriant hardwoods of the Amazon basin**

2 True or False: In the 1970s, police issued speeding tickets to street lugers inventing the sport in the hills of Southern California.
A. **True**
B. **False**

3 What year did BMX racing become an Olympic sport?
A. **2000**
B. **2004**
C. **2008**

4 True or False: The predecessor of the modern snowmobile was an armored sleigh with a machine gun designed by aviation pioneer Igor Sikorsky and used by the Russian Army.
A. **True**
B. **False**

5 Vanessa Torres was the first female to accomplish which feat at the X Games?
A. **Compete in Motocross**
B. **Hit a 540 backside**
C. **Win gold in skateboarding**

Vanessa Torres

1.A, 2.A, 3.C, 4.A, 5.C

Summer X Games Results (cont.)

MOTO X (CONT.)

YEAR	EVENT	GOLD	SILVER	BRONZE
2007	Step Up	Ronnie Renner, U.S.	Brian Deegan, U.S.	Matt Buyten, U.S.
2006	Step Up	Matt Buyten, U.S.	Jeremy McGrath, U.S.	Brian Deegan, U.S.
2005	Step Up	Tommy Clowers, U.S.	Matt Buyten, U.S.	Jeremy McGrath, U.S.
2004	Step Up	Jeremy McGrath, U.S.	Matt Buyten, U.S.	Tommy Clowers, U.S.
2003	Step Up	Matt Buyten, U.S.	Tommy Clowers, U.S.	Ronnie Renner, U.S.
2002	Step Up	Tommy Clowers, U.S.	Mike Metzger, U.S.	Brian Deegan, U.S.
2001	Step Up	Tommy Clowers, U.S.	Travis Pastrana, U.S.	(tie) Colin Morrison, U.S.; Ronnie Renner, U.S.; Kris Rourke, U.S.; Jeremy Stenberg, U.S.
2000	Step Up	Tommy Clowers, U.S.	Kris Rourke, U.S	Brian Deegan, U.S.
2007	Super Moto	Mark Burkhart, U.S.	Jeff Ward, U.S.	David Pengree, U.S.
2006	Super Moto	Jeff Ward, U.S.	Mark Burkhart, U.S.	Doug Henry, U.S.
2005	Super Moto	Doug Henry, U.S.	Jeremy McGrath, U.S.	Chad Reed, Australia
2004	Super Moto	Ben Bostrom, U.S.	Eddy Seel, Belgium	Jeremy McGrath, U.S.
2005	Best Trick	Jeremy Stenberg, U.S.	Travis Pastrana, U.S.	Nate Adams, U.S.
2004	Best Trick	Chuck Carothers, U.S.	Nate Adams, U.S.	Travis Pastrana, U.S.

DID YOU KNOW?
The first person to a pull a backflip on a BMX bike was Jose Yanez in 1984. Yanez later went on tour with the Ringling Brothers Circus.

Travis Pastrana won gold at X Games XII in Moto X Best Trick.

SKATEBOARDING – MEN

YEAR	EVENT	GOLD	SILVER	BRONZE
2003	Park	Ryan Sheckler, U.S.	Rodil de Araujo Jr., Brazil	Chad Bartie, Australia
2002	Park	Rodil de Araujo Jr., Brazil	Wagner Ramos, Brazil	Eric Koston, U.S.
2001	Park	Rodil de Araujo Jr., Brazil	Kerry Getz, U.S.	Caine Gayle, U.S.
2000	Park	Eric Koston, U.S.	Rodil de Araujo Jr., Brazil	Kerry Getz, U.S.
2007	Street	Chris Cole, U.S.	Greg Lutzka, U.S.	Jereme Rogers, U.S.
2006	Street	Chris Cole, U.S.	Ryan Sheckler, U.S.	Andrew Reynolds, U.S.
2005	Street	Paul Rodriguez, U.S.	Greg Lutzka, U.S.	Chris Cole, U.S.
2004	Street	Paul Rodriguez, U.S.	Andrew Reynolds, U.S.	Bastien Salabanzi, France
2003	Street	Eric Koston, U.S.	Rodil de Araujo Jr., Brazil	Paul Rodriguez, U.S.
2002	Street	Rodil de Araujo Jr., Brazil	Wagner Ramos, Brazil	Kyle Berard, U.S.
2001	Street	Kerry Getz, U.S.	Eric Koston, U.S.	Chris Senn, U.S.
1999	Street	Chris Senn, U.S.	Pat Channita, U.S.	Chad Fernandez, U.S.
1998	Street	Rodil de Araujo Jr., Brazil	Andy Macdonald, U.S.	Chris Senn, U.S.
1997	Street	Chris Senn, U.S.	Andy Macdonald, U.S.	Brian Patch, U.S.
1996	Street	Rodil de Araujo Jr., Brazil	Chris Senn, U.S.	Brian Patch, U.S.
1995	Street	Chris Senn, U.S.	Tony Hawk, U.S.	Willy Santos, U.S.
2003	Street Best Trick	Chad Muska, U.S.	Rodil de Araujo, Jr., Brazil	Wagner Ramos, Brazil
2002	Street Best Trick	Rodil de Araujo Jr., Brazil	Wagner Ramos, Brazil	Dayne Brummet, U.S.
2001	Street Best Trick	Rick McCrank, Canada	Kerry Getz, U.S.	Eric Koston, U.S.
1996	Street Best Trick	Gershon Mosley, U.S.	Chris Senn, U.S.	Brian Patch, U.S.
1995	Street Best Trick	Jamie Thomas, U.S.	Gershon Mosley, U.S.	Kareem Campbell, U.S.

DANIEL OCHOA DE OLZA/AP

Summer X Games Results (cont.)

YEAR	EVENT	GOLD	SILVER	BRONZE
		SKATEBOARDING – MEN (CONT.)		
2007	Vert	Shaun White, U.S.	Pierre-Luc Gagnon, Canada	Mathias Ringstrom, Sweden
2006	Vert	Sandro Dias, Brazil	Pierre-Luc Gagnon, Canada	Bucky Lasek, U.S.
2005	Vert	Pierre-Luc Gagnon, Canada	Shaun White, U.S.	Sandro Dias, Brazil
2004	Vert	Bucky Lasek, U.S.	Pierre-Luc Gagnon, Canada	Rune Glifberg, Denmark
2003	Vert	Bucky Lasek, U.S.	Andy Macdonald, U.S.	Rune Glifberg, Denmark
2002	Vert	Pierre-Luc Gagnon, Canada	Bob Burnquist, Brazil	Rune Glifberg, Denmark
2001	Vert	Bob Burnquist, Brazil	Bucky Lasek, U.S.	Tas Pappas, Australia
2000	Vert	Bucky Lasek, U.S.	Pierre-Luc Gagnon, Canada	Colin McKay, Canada
1999	Vert	Bucky Lasek, U.S.	Andy Macdonald, U.S.	Tony Hawk, U.S.
1998	Vert	Andy Macdonald, U.S.	Giorgio Zattoni, Italy	Tony Hawk, U.S.
1997	Vert	Tony Hawk, U.S.	Rune Glifberg, Denmark	Bob Burnquist, Brazil
1996	Vert	Andy Macdonald, U.S.	Tony Hawk, U.S.	Tas Pappas, Australia
1995	Vert	Tony Hawk, U.S.	Neal Hendrix, U.S.	Rune Glifberg, Denmark
2006	Vert Best Trick	Bucky Lasek, U.S.	Max Dufour, Canada	Bob Burnquist, Brazil
2005	Vert Best Trick	Bob Burnquist, Brazil	Colin McKay, Canada	Pierre-Luc Gagnon, Canada
2004	Vert Best Trick	Sandro Dias, Brazil	Pierre-Luc Gagnon, Canada	Danny Mayer, U.S.
2003	Vert Best Trick	Tony Hawk, U.S.	Sandro Dias, Brazil	Andy Macdonald, U.S.
2002	Vert Best Trick	Pierre-Luc Gagnon, Canada	Sandro Dias, Brazil	Tony Hawk, U.S.
2001	Vert Best Trick	Matt Dove, U.S.	Tony Hawk, U.S.	Bob Burnquist, Brazil
2000	Vert Best Trick	Bob Burnquist, Brazil	Colin McKay, Canada	Andy Macdonald, U.S.
1999	Vert Best Trick	Tony Hawk, U.S.	Colin McKay, Canada	Bob Burnquist, Brazil
2005	Big Air	Danny Way, U.S.	Pierre-Luc Gagnon, Canada	Andy Macdonald, U.S.
2004	Big Air	Danny Way, U.S.	Pierre-Luc Gagnon, Canada	Andy Macdonald, U.S.
2003	Vert Doubles	Bucky Lasek, U.S.	Rune Glifberg, Denmark	Neal Hendrix, U.S.
		Bob Burnquist, Brazil	Mike Crum, U.S.	Buster Halterman, U.S.
2002	Vert Doubles	Tony Hawk, U.S.	Bob Burnquist, Brazil	Mike Crum, U.S.
		Andy Macdonald, U.S.	Bucky Lasek, U.S.	Rune Glifberg, Denmark
2001	Vert Doubles	Tony Hawk, U.S.	Mike Crum, U.S.	Mike Frazier, U.S.
		Andy Macdonald, U.S.	Chris Gentry, U.S.	Neal Hendrix, U.S.
2000	Vert Doubles	Tony Hawk, U.S.	Pierre-Luc Gagnon, Canada	Sandro Dias, Brazil
		Andy Macdonald, U.S.	Max Dufour, Canada	Cristiano Mateus, Brazil
1999	Vert Doubles	Tony Hawk, U.S.	Bucky Lasek, U.S.	Mike Crum, U.S.
		Andy Macdonald, U.S.	Brian Patch, U.S.	Rune Glifberg, Denmark
1998	Vert Doubles	Tony Hawk, U.S.	Bucky Lasek, U.S.	Bob Burnquist, Brazil
		Andy Macdonald, U.S.	Brian Patch, U.S.	Lincoln Ueda, Brazil
1997	Vert Doubles	Tony Hawk, U.S.	Mike Frazier, U.S.	Max Dufour, Canada
		Andy Macdonald, U.S.	Neal Hendrix, U.S.	Mathias Ringstrom, Sweden
1995	High Air	Danny Way, U.S.	Neal Hendrix, U.S.	Tas Pappas, Australia

Tony Hawk

Summer X Games Results (cont.)

YEAR	EVENT	GOLD	SILVER	BRONZE
2007	Street	Marisa Del Santo, U.S.	Elissa Steamer, U.S.	Amy Caron, U.S.
2006	Street	Elissa Steamer, U.S.	Lauren Perkins, U.S.	Lacey Baker, U.S.
2005	Street	Elissa Steamer, U.S.	Evelien Bouilliart, Belgium	Marissa Del Santo, U.S.
2004	Street	Elissa Steamer, U.S.	Vanessa Torres, U.S.	Lauren Perkins, U.S.
2007	Vert	Lyn-Z Adams Hawkins, U.S.	Mimi Koop, U.S.	Cara-Beth Burnside, U.S.
2006	Vert	Cara-Beth Burnside, U.S.	Mimi Koop, U.S.	Karen Jones, U.S.
2005	Vert	Cara-Beth Burnside, U.S.	Lyn-Z Adams Hawkins, U.S.	Mimi Knoop, U.S.
2004	Vert	Lyn-Z Adams Hawkins, U.S.	Cara-Beth Burnside, U.S.	Mimi Knoop, U.S.

SPORT CLIMBING – MEN

YEAR	EVENT	GOLD	SILVER	BRONZE
2002	Speed	Maxim Stenkovoy, Ukraine	Alexandre Pechekhonov, Russia	Serguei Sinitsyn, Russia
2001	Speed	Maxim Stenkovoy, Ukraine	Vladimir Zakharov, Ukraine	Chris Bloch, U.S.
2000	Speed	Vladimir Zakharov, Ukraine	Chris Bloch, U.S.	Tomasz Oleksy, Poland
1999	Speed	Aaron Shamy, U.S.	Chris Bloch, U.S.	Vladimir Netsvetaev, Russia
1998	Speed	Vladimir Netsvetaev, Russia	Aaron Shamy, U.S.	Chris Bloch, U.S.
1997	Speed	Hans Florine, U.S.	Chris Bloch, U.S.	Jason Campbell, U.S.
1996	Speed	Hans Florine, U.S.	Chris Bloch, U.S.	Tim Fairfield, U.S.
1995	Speed	Hans Florine, U.S.	Salavat Rakhmetov, Russia	Yuji Hirayama, Japan
1999	Bouldering	Chris Sharma, U.S.	Francois Petit, France	Stephane Julien, France
1998	Difficulty	Christian Core, Italy	Francois Legrand, France	Vadim Vinokur, U.S.
1997	Difficulty	Francois Legrand, France	Yuji Hirayama, Japan	Chris Sharma, U.S.
1996	Difficulty	Arnaud Petit, France	Francois Lombard, France	Cristian Brenna, Italy
1995	Difficulty	Ian Vickers, United Kingdom	Arnaud Petit, France	Francois Petit, France

SPORT CLIMBING – WOMEN

YEAR	EVENT	GOLD	SILVER	BRONZE
2002	Speed	Tori Allen, U.S.	Olga Zakharova, Ukraine	Etti Hendrawati, Indonesia
2001	Speed	Elena Repko, Ukraine	Olga Zakharova, Ukraine	Alena Ostapenko, Ukraine
2000	Speed	Etti Hendrawati, Indonesia	Elena Repko, Ukraine	Olga Zakharova, Ukraine
1999	Speed	Renata Piszczek, Poland	Olga Zakharova, Ukraine	Etti Hendrawati, Indonesia
1998	Speed	Elena Ovchinnikova, U.S.	Yuyun Yuniar, Indonesia	Venera Tchereshneva, Russia
1997	Speed	Elena Ovchinnikova, U.S.	Abby Watkins, Australia	Mi Sun Go, South Korea
1996	Speed	Cecile Le Flem, France	Elena Choumilova, Russia	Natalie Richer, France
1995	Speed	Elena Ovchinnikova, Russia	Diane Russell, U.S.	Georgia Phipps-Franklin, U.S.
1999	Bouldering	Stephanie Bodet, France	Liv Sansoz, France	Elena Choumilova, Russia
1998	Difficulty	Katie Brown, U.S.	Mi Sun Go, South Korea	Elena Choumilova, Russia
1997	Difficulty	Katie Brown, U.S.	Liv Sansoz, France	Muriel Sarkany, Belgium
1996	Difficulty	Katie Brown, U.S.	Laurence Guyon, France	Liv Sansoz, France
1995	Difficulty	Robyn Erbesfield, U.S.	Elena Ovchinnikova, Russia	Mia Axon, U.S.

STREET LUGE

YEAR	EVENT	GOLD	SILVER	BRONZE
2001	Super Mass	Brent DeKeyser, U.S.	David Rogers, U.S.	Dave Auld, U.S.
2000	Super Mass	Bob Pereyra, U.S.	Lee Dansie, United Kingdom	John Rogers, U.S.
1999	Super Mass	David Rogers, U.S.	Biker Sherlock, U.S.	Sean Slate, U.S.
1998	Super Mass	Rat Sult, U.S.	Bob Pereyra, U.S.	Todd Lehr, U.S.
1997	Super Mass	Chris Ponseti, U.S.	Biker Sherlock, U.S.	Rat Sult, U.S.
2000	Dual	Bob Ozman, U.S.	Wade Sokol, U.S.	Bob Pereyra, U.S.
1999	Dual	Dennis Derammelaere, U.S.	Lee Dansie, United Kingdom	Biker Sherlock, U.S.
1998	Dual	Biker Sherlock, U.S.	Stefan Wagner, Germany	Dave Auld, U.S.
1997	Dual	Biker Sherlock, U.S.	Dennis Derammelaere, U.S.	Darren Lott, U.S.
1996	Dual	Shawn Goulart, U.S.	Stefan Wagner, Germany	Dennis Derammelaere, U.S.
1995	Dual	Bob Pereyra, U.S.	Stefan Wagner, Germany	Shawn Goulart, U.S.
1998	Mass	Rat Sult, U.S.	Sean Slate, U.S.	Steve Fernando, U.S
1997	Mass	Biker Sherlock, U.S.	Dennis Derammelaere, U.S.	Lee Dansie, United Kingdom
1996	Mass	Biker Sherlock, U.S.	Daryl Thompson, U.S.	Dennis Derammelaere, U.S.
1995	Mass	Shawn Goulart, U.S.	Lee Dansie, United Kingdom	Stefan Wagner, Germany

Summer X Games Results (cont.)

Dallas
Friday

REDBULL-PHOTOFILES.COM

SURFING – MEN

YEAR	GOLD	SILVER	BRONZE
2007	Team USA	International	Not awarded
2006	East Coast	West Coast	Not awarded
2005	East Coast	West Coast	Not awarded
2004	East Coast	West Coast	Not awarded
2003	East Coast	West Coast	Not awarded

SURFING – WOMEN

YEAR	GOLD	SILVER	BRONZE
2007	Team USA	International	Not awarded

WAKEBOARDING – MEN

YEAR	GOLD	SILVER	BRONZE
2005	Danny Harf, U.S.	Phillip Soven, U.S.	Josh Sanders, Australia
2004	Phillip Soven, U.S.	Chad Sharpe, Canada	Parks Bonifay, U.S.
2003	Danny Harf, U.S.	Parks Bonifay, U.S.	Daniel Watkins, U.S.
2002	Danny Harf, U.S.	Darin Shapiro, U.S.	Shaun Murray, U.S
2001	Danny Harf, U.S.	Darin Shapiro, U.S.	Erik Ruck, U.S.
2000	Darin Shapiro, U.S.	Shaun Murray, U.S.	Shane Bonifay, U.S.
1999	Parks Bonifay, U.S.	Darin Shapiro, U.S.	Brannan Johnson, U.S.
1998	Darin Shapiro, U.S.	Shaun Murray, U.S.	Zane Schwenk, U.S.
1997	Jeremy Kovak, Canada	Darin Shapiro, U.S.	Parks Bonifay, U.S.
1996	Parks Bonifay, U.S.	Jeremy Kovak, Canada	Scott Byerly, U.S.

WAKEBOARDING – WOMEN

YEAR	GOLD	SILVER	BRONZE
2005	Dallas Friday, U.S.	Emily Copeland, U.S.	Tara Hamilton, U.S.
2004	Dallas Friday, U.S.	Tara Hamilton, U.S.	Maeghan Major, U.S.
2003	Dallas Friday, U.S.	Melissa Marquardt, U.S.	Emily Copeland, U.S.
2002	Emily Copeland, U.S.	Dallas Friday, U.S.	Leslie Kent, U.S.
2001	Dallas Friday, U.S.	Emily Copeland, U.S.	Tara Hamilton, U.S.
2000	Tara Hamilton, U.S.	Dallas Friday, U.S.	Maeghan Major, U.S.
1999	Maeghan Major, U.S.	Emily Copeland, U.S.	Andrea Gaytan, Mexico
1998	Andrea Gaytan, Mexico	Dana Preble, U.S.	Tara Hamilton, U.S.
1997	Tara Hamilton, U.S.	Andrea Gaytan, Mexico	Jaime Necrason, U.S.

WINDSURFING – MEN

YEAR	GOLD	SILVER	BRONZE
1995	Bjorn Dunkerbeck, Spain	Micah Buzianis, U.S.	Al Aguera, U.S.

WINDSURFING – WOMEN

YEAR	GOLD	SILVER	BRONZE
1995	Angela Cochran, U.S.	Jayne Fenner-Benedict, U.S.	Jutta Mueller, Germany

X VENTURE RACE

YEAR	GOLD	SILVER	BRONZE
1997	Team Presidio: Ian Adamson, Australia John Howard, New Zealand Andrea Spitzer, Germany	Team Endeavour: Louise Cooper-Lovelace, U.S. Neil Jones, New Zealand Jeff Mitchell, New Zealand	Team Red Hot: Sharyn Davis, Australia John Jacoby, Australia Tim Smallwood, Australia
1996	Team Kobeer: Angelika Castaneda, U.S. John Howard, New Zealand Keith Murray, New Zealand	Team Eco-Internet: Ian Adamson, Australia Robert Nagle, Ireland Vivienne Prince, U.S.	Team Mirage: Kirk Boylston, U.S. Nancy Bristow, U.S. Steve Gurney, New Zealand
1995	Team Thredbo: Jane Hall, Australia Andrew Hislop, Australia Rod Hislop, Australia John Jacoby, Australia Novak Thompson, Australia	Twin Team: Angelika Castaneda, U.S. Adrian Crane, U.S. Tom Possert, U.S. Robert Rambach, U.S. Marshall Ulrich, U.S.	Team Eco-Internet: Ian Adamson, Australia John Howard, New Zealand Keith Murray, New Zealand Robert Nagle, Ireland Cathy Sassin-Smith, U.S.

Who's Who and What's What

Which 2007 BMX rookie pulled the first-ever 1080 in competition, earning him Trick of the Year?

To find out, identify what's what on this bike. Write the letter of each part name on the appropriate space in the diagram. Transfer the letters from the diagram to the boxes with the same numbers to answer the question.

A - Block	K - Sprocket	O - Nose
C - Truck	L - Boot	P - Top tube
E - Fork	M - Crank	R - Hub
I - Grip	N - Seat clamp	S - Rear brakes

8	7	5	2

6	I	7	4	4	2	3

ANSWERS ON PAGE 191

Dew Action Sports Tour Champions

YEAR	EVENT	FIRST	SECOND	THIRD
SKATEBOARDING – MEN				
2007	Skate Park	Ryan Sheckler, U.S.	Greg Lutzka, U.S.	Rodolfo Ramos, Brazil
2006	Skate Park	Ryan Sheckler, U.S.	Jereme Rogers, U.S.	Rodolfo Ramos, Brazil
2005	Skate Park	Ryan Sheckler, U.S.	Chad Fernandez, U.S.	Greg Lutzka, U.S.
2007	Skate Vert	Shaun White, U.S.	Bucky Lasek, U.S.	Pierre-Luc Gagnon, Canada
2006	Skate Vert	Bucky Lasek, U.S.	Sandro Dias, Brazil	Bob Burnquist, Brazil
2005	Skate Vert	Bucky Lasek, U.S.	Pierre-Luc Gagnon, Canada	Andy Macdonald, U.S.
BIKE STUNT – MEN				
2007	BMX Park	Daniel Dhers, Venezuela	Mike Spinner, U.S.	Ryan Nyquist, U.S.
2006	BMX Park	Daniel Dhers, Venezuela	Scotty Cranmer, U.S.	Ryan Nyquist, U.S.
2005	BMX Park	Ryan Guettler, Australia	Scotty Cranmer, U.S.	Ryan Nyquist, U.S.
2007	BMX Vert	Jamie Bestwick, U.K.	Simon Tabron, U.K.	Steve McCann, Australia
2006	BMX Vert	Jamie Bestwick, U.K.	Chad Kagy, U.S.	Kevin Robinson, U.S.
2005	BMX Vert	Jamie Bestwick, U.K.	Kevin Robinson, U.S.	Chad Kagy, U.S.
2007	BMX Dirt	Ryan Nyquist, U.S.	Cameron White, Australia	Dennis Enarson, U.S.
2006	BMX Dirt	Anthony Napolitan, U.S.	Luke Parslow, Australia	Corey Bohan, Australia
2005	BMX Dirt	Ryan Guettler, Australia	Corey Bohan, Australia	Cameron White, Australia
MOTO X – MEN				
2007	FMX Park	Nate Adams, U.S.	Adam Jones, U.S.	Mike Mason, U.S.
2006	FMX Park	Nate Adams, U.S.	Mike Mason, U.S.	Travis Pastrana, U.S.
2005	FMX Park	Kenny Bartram, U.S.	Jeremy Stenberg, U.S.	Mike Mason, U.S.

A Tale of Two Champions

From the moment Tiger Woods came on the scene, the golf world has waited for a real challenger to emerge. No one thought his equal would be found on the LPGA Tour. Although Woods is almost six years older than Lorena Ochoa, their careers — and lives — have mirrored each other from an early age.

Both seemed destined for greatness when they were kids. A child prodigy, Woods appeared on national TV as a two-year-old and putted with comedian Bob Hope. When Ochoa was five, she begged her father to take her to the golf course with her older brothers. Three years later, she won her age group at the Junior Worlds.

Both gained national attention at a young age. At 15, Woods became the youngest U.S. Junior Amateur champion in golf history. Ochoa won her first national tournament at the age of seven. Their paths even crossed once in 1993, when a 12-year-old Ochoa took a picture with a 17-year-old Woods at a golf tournament — a photo she cherishes to this day.

And now, as pros, they dominate the competition and leave both opponents and spectators in awe. From the beginning of 2006 to the end of May 2008, Ochoa won 19 LPGA events; Woods had 18 PGA wins during that span.

Both won two majors in that time frame and were ranked No. 1.

Woods won three of his first five starts in 2008, coming in second at The Masters. His finish at Augusta was a disappointment for Woods, whom many believed would win golf's Grand Slam by claiming all four majors in one year. However, Woods came back and won the U.S. Open in thrilling fashion, capturing the tournament in a playoff. With 14 majors to his name, he remained just five short of breaking the record owned by Jack Nicklaus — Woods's ultimate goal.

Ochoa got off to an even hotter start in 2008. She won six of her first nine events, including the LPGA's first major of the year.

Woods, who is African American and Thai, has been credited with spreading the game to African Americans, whose participation in golf more than doubled between 1997 and 2003. A native of Mexico, Ochoa has also gained a huge following with her stellar game and likeable personality. After winning the Kraft Nabisco Championship in April 2008, Ochoa was serenaded by a mariachi band as she and her family leaped into the lake surrounding the 18th green. To top it off, Ochoa was named one of TIME magazine's 100 most influential people in the world, an honor not even Woods received. He'll just have to step it up in 2009.

Lorena Ochoa won six of her first nine LPGA Tour events in 2008.

MICHAEL J LEBRECHT II/DEUCE3 PHOTOGRAPHY

Having won 14 majors, Tiger Woods is five short of breaking Jack Nicklaus's record.

MIKE EHRMANN

All-Time Champions — Men: The Masters

YEAR	WINNER	YEAR	WINNER	YEAR	WINNER
2008	Trevor Immelman	1983	Seve Ballesteros	1958	Arnold Palmer
2007	Zach Johnson	1982	Craig Stadler*	1957	Doug Ford
2006	Phil Mickelson	1981	Tom Watson	1956	Jack Burke, Jr.
2005	Tiger Woods*	1980	Seve Ballesteros	1955	Cary Middlecoff
2004	Phil Mickelson	1979**	Fuzzy Zoeller*	1954	Sam Snead*
2003	Mike Weir*	1978	Gary Player	1953	Ben Hogan
2002	Tiger Woods	1977	Tom Watson	1952	Sam Snead
2001	Tiger Woods	1976	Ray Floyd	1951	Ben Hogan
2000	Vijay Singh	1975	Jack Nicklaus	1950	Jimmy Demaret
1999	Jose Maria Olazabal	1974	Gary Player	1949	Sam Snead
1998	Mark O'Meara	1973	Tommy Aaron	1948	Claude Harmon
1997	Tiger Woods	1972	Jack Nicklaus	1947	Jimmy Demaret
1996	Nick Faldo	1971	Charles Coody	1946	Herman Keiser
1995	Ben Crenshaw	1970	Billy Casper*	1943–45	No tournament
1994	Jose Maria Olazabal	1969	George Archer	1942	Byron Nelson*
1993	Bernhard Langer	1968	Bob Goalby	1941	Craig Wood
1992	Fred Couples	1967	Gay Brewer, Jr.	1940	Jimmy Demaret
1991	Ian Woosnam	1966	Jack Nicklaus*	1939	Ralph Guldahl
1990	Nick Faldo*	1965	Jack Nicklaus	1938	Henry Picard
1989	Nick Faldo*	1964	Arnold Palmer	1937	Byron Nelson
1988	Sandy Lyle	1963	Jack Nicklaus	1936	Horton Smith
1987	Larry Mize*	1962	Arnold Palmer	1935	Gene Sarazen*
1986	Jack Nicklaus	1961	Gary Player	1934	Horton Smith
1985	Bernhard Langer	1960	Arnold Palmer		
1984	Ben Crenshaw	1959	Art Wall, Jr.		

* Winner in playoff. ** Playoff cut from 18 holes to sudden death. Note: Played at Augusta National Golf Club, Augusta, Georgia.

TODAY'S STARS

Paula Creamer, *b. August 5, 1986, Mountain View, California.* Known as the "Pink Panther" for her love of the color, Creamer excelled in gymnastics and cheerleading as a youngster. But golf was her calling. She claimed her first LPGA win by the age of 18, the youngest person to win a tour event in 55 years. More recently, Creamer beat Juli Inkster in a May playoff to win the SemGroup Championship for her sixth career victory and second of 2008.

Anthony Kim, *b. June 19, 1985, Los Angeles, California.* At 22, Kim won his first PGA Tour event in March 2008 after having tied for second and third earlier in the year. The success came after a rough rookie year in 2007, in which Kim gained a bigger reputation for his fiery temper and hard-partying ways. But Kim has since turned his game around, adding veteran Mark O'Meara as a mentor.

Paula Creamer

DAVID WALBERG

Trevor Immelman, *b. December 16, 1979, Cape Town, South Africa.* Immelman's recent past has been a roller-coaster ride. He had a tumor removed from his back in December 2007 and then, just months later, was shrugging into the legendary Green Jacket as the newest Masters champion. Standing just 5' 9", he stared down Tiger Woods in the final round for a three-shot victory — just the second time a South African has won the Masters.

All-Time Champions — Men: U.S. Open

Angel Cabrera

ROBERT BECK

YEAR	WINNER
2008	Tiger Woods
2007	Angel Cabrera
2006	Geoff Ogilvy
2005	Michael Campbell
2004	Retief Goosen
2003	Jim Furyk
2002	Tiger Woods
2001	Retief Goosen*
2000	Tiger Woods
1999	Payne Stewart
1998	Lee Janzen
1997	Ernie Els
1996	Steve Jones
1995	Corey Pavin
1994	Ernie Els*
1993	Lee Janzen
1992	Tom Kite
1991	Payne Stewart*
1990	Hale Irwin*
1989	Curtis Strange
1988	Curtis Strange*
1987	Scott Simpson
1986	Ray Floyd
1985	Andy North
1984	Fuzzy Zoeller*
1983	Larry Nelson
1982	Tom Watson
1981	David Graham
1980	Jack Nicklaus
1979	Hale Irwin
1978	Andy North
1977	Hubert Green
1976	Jerry Pate
1975	Lou Graham*
1974	Hale Irwin
1973	Johnny Miller
1972	Jack Nicklaus
1971	Lee Trevino*
1970	Tony Jacklin

YEAR	WINNER
1969	Orville Moody
1968	Lee Trevino
1967	Jack Nicklaus
1966	Billy Casper*
1965	Gary Player*
1964	Ken Venturi
1963	Julius Boros*
1962	Jack Nicklaus*
1961	Gene Littler
1960	Arnold Palmer
1959	Billy Casper
1958	Tommy Bolt
1957	Dick Mayer*
1956	Cary Middlecoff
1955	Jack Fleck*
1954	Ed Furgol
1953	Ben Hogan

YEAR	WINNER
1952	Julius Boros
1951	Ben Hogan
1950	Ben Hogan*
1949	Cary Middlecoff
1948	Ben Hogan
1947	Lew Worsham*
1946	Lloyd Mangrum*
1942–45	No tournament
1941	Craig Wood
1940	Lawson Little*
1939	Byron Nelson*
1938	Ralph Guldahl
1937	Ralph Guldahl
1936	Tony Manero
1935	Sam Parks Jr.
1934	Olin Dutra
1933	Johnny Goodman

YEAR	WINNER
1932	Gene Sarazen
1931	Billy Burke*
1930	Bobby Jones
1929	Bobby Jones*
1928	Johnny Farrell*
1927	Tommy Armour*
1926	Bobby Jones
1925	Willie MacFarlane*
1924	Cyril Walker
1923	Bobby Jones*
1922	Gene Sarazen
1921	Jim Barnes
1920	Edward Ray
1919	Walter Hagen*
1917–18	No tournament
1916	Chick Evans
1915	Jerry Travers
1914	Walter Hagen
1913	Francis Ouimet*
1912	John McDermott
1911	John McDermott*
1910	Alex Smith*
1909	George Sargent
1908	Fred McLeod*
1907	Alex Ross
1906	Alex Smith
1905	Willie Anderson
1904	Willie Anderson
1903	Willie Anderson*
1902	Laurie Auchterlonie
1901	Willie Anderson*
1900	Harry Vardon
1899	Willie Smith
1898	Fred Herd
1897**	Joe Lloyd
1896**	James Foulis
1895**	Horace Rawlins

* Winner in playoff. ** Before 1898, 36 holes were played; from 1898 on, 72 holes were played.
Note: The 1990 playoff went to one hole of sudden death after an 18-hole playoff. In the 1994 playoff, Montgomerie was eliminated after 18 playoff holes, and Els beat Roberts on the 20th.

All-Time Champions — Men: British Open

YEAR	WINNER
2007	Padraig Harrington*
2006	Tiger Woods
2005	Tiger Woods
2004	Todd Hamilton*
2003	Ben Curtis
2002	Ernie Els*
2001	David Duval
2000	Tiger Woods
1999	Paul Lawrie*
1998	Mark O'Meara*
1997	Justin Leonard
1996	Tom Lehman
1995	John Daly*
1994	Nick Price
1993	Greg Norman
1992	Nick Faldo
1991	Ian Baker-Finch
1990	Nick Faldo
1989**	Mark Calcavecchia*
1988	Seve Ballesteros
1987	Nick Faldo
1986	Greg Norman

YEAR	WINNER
1985	Sandy Lyle
1984	Seve Ballesteros
1983	Tom Watson
1982	Tom Watson
1981	Bill Rogers
1980	Tom Watson
1979	Seve Ballesteros
1978	Jack Nicklaus
1977	Tom Watson
1976	Johnny Miller
1975	Tom Watson*
1974	Gary Player
1973	Tom Weiskopf
1972	Lee Trevino
1971	Lee Trevino
1970	Jack Nicklaus*
1969	Tony Jacklin
1968	Gary Player
1967	Robert DeVicenzo
1966	Jack Nicklaus
1965	Peter Thomson
1964	Tony Lema

YEAR	WINNER
1963	Bob Charles*
1962	Arnold Palmer
1961	Arnold Palmer
1960	Kel Nagle
1959	Gary Player
1958	Peter Thomson*
1957	Bobby Locke
1956	Peter Thomson
1955	Peter Thomson
1954	Peter Thomson
1953	Ben Hogan
1952	Bobby Locke
1951	Max Faulkner
1950	Bobby Locke
1949	Bobby Locke*
1948	Henry Cotton
1947	Fred Daly
1946	Sam Snead
1940–45	No tournament
1939	Richard Burton
1938	Reginald A. Whitcombe
1937	Henry Cotton

* Winner in playoff. ** Playoff cut from 18 holes to 4 holes.

YEAR	WINNER	YEAR	WINNER	YEAR	WINNER
1936	Alfred Padgham	1907	Arnaud Massy	1882	Robert Ferguson
1935	Alfred Perry	1906	James Braid	1881	Robert Ferguson
1934	Henry Cotton	1905	James Braid	1880	Robert Ferguson
1933	Denny Shute*	1904	Jack White	1879	Jamie Anderson
1932	Gene Sarazen	1903	Harry Vardon	1878	Jamie Anderson
1931	Tommy Armour	1902	Alexander Herd	1877	Jamie Anderson
1930	Bobby Jones	1901	James Braid	1876	Bob Martin†
1929	Walter Hagen	1900	John H. Taylor	1875	Willie Park
1928	Walter Hagen	1899	Harry Vardon	1874	Mungo Park
1927	Bobby Jones	1898	Harry Vardon	1873	Tom Kidd
1926	Bobby Jones	1897	Harold Hilton	1872	Tom Morris, Jr.
1925	Jim Barnes	1896	Harry Vardon*	1871	No tournament
1924	Walter Hagen	1895	John H. Taylor	1870	Tom Morris, Jr.
1923	Arthur G. Havers	1894	John H. Taylor	1869	Tom Morris, Jr.
1922	Walter Hagen	1893	William Auchterlonie	1868	Tom Morris, Jr.
1921	Jock Hutchison*	1892***	Harold Hilton	1867	Tom Morris, Sr.
1920	George Duncan	1891	Hugh Kirkaldy	1866	Willie Park
1915–19	No tournament	1890	John Ball	1865	Andrew Strath
1914	Harry Vardon	1889	Willie Park, Jr.*	1864	Tom Morris, Sr.
1913	John H. Taylor	1888	Jack Burns	1863	Willie Park
1912	Ted Ray	1887	Willie Park, Jr.	1862	Tom Morris, Sr.
1911	Harry Vardon	1886	David Brown	1861	Tom Morris, Sr.
1910	James Braid	1885	Bob Martin	1860	Willie Park
1909	John H. Taylor	1884	Jack Simpson		
1908	James Braid	1883	Willie Fernie*		

* Winner in playoff. *** Championship extended from 36 to 72 holes. † Tied, but opponent refused playoff.
Note: The first annual Open, in 1860, was open only to pro golfers. The second event was open to amateurs and pros.

GAME TIME

Holes in One

Morgan Pressel led the pack in 2007 with two holes in one. How many players tied for second with a single hole in one?

To find out, place the last name of each golfer on a line in the grid, using the letters provided (and a little logic) to determine where each goes. There can be spaces before and after names, but not between letters. If you place the names correctly, the answer to the question will be revealed in one of the columns. We're not telling which one.

Shi Hyun AHN

Julieta GRANADA

Juli INKSTER

Mi Hyun KIM

Won LEE

Leta LINDLEY

Brooke TULL

Sherri TURNER

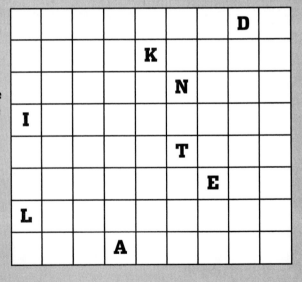

ANSWERS ON PAGE 191

All-Time Champions — Men: PGA Championship

YEAR	WINNER	YEAR	WINNER	YEAR	WINNER	YEAR	WINNER
2007	Tiger Woods*	1965	Dave Marr	1948	Ben Hogan	1931	Tom Creavy
2006	Tiger Woods	1964	Bobby Nichols	1947	Jim Ferrier	1930	Tommy Armour
2005	Phil Mickelson	1963	Jack Nicklaus	1946	Ben Hogan	1929	Leo Diegel
2004	Vijay Singh	1962	Gary Player	1945	Byron Nelson	1928	Leo Diegel
2003	Shaun Micheel	1961	Jerry Barber	1944	Bob Hamilton	1927	Walter Hagen
2002	Rich Beem	1960	Jay Hebert	1943	No tournament	1926	Walter Hagen
2001	David Toms	1959	Bob Rosburg	1942	Sam Snead	1925	Walter Hagen
2000	Tiger Woods*	1958	Dow Finsterwald	1941	Vic Ghezzi	1924	Walter Hagen
1999	Tiger Woods	1957	Lionel Hebert	1940	Byron Nelson	1923	Gene Sarazen
1998	Vijay Singh	1956	Jack Burke	1939	Henry Picard	1922	Gene Sarazen
1997	Davis Love III	1955	Doug Ford	1938	Paul Runyan	1921	Walter Hagen
1996	Mark Brooks*	1954	Chick Harbert	1937	Denny Shute	1920	Jock Hutchison
1995	Steve Elkington*	1953	Walter Burkemo	1936	Denny Shute	1919	Jim Barnes
1994	Nick Price	1952	Jim Turnesa	1935	Johnny Revolta	1917–18	No tournament
1993	Paul Azinger*	1951	Sam Snead	1934	Paul Runyan	1916	Jim Barnes
1992	Nick Price	1950	Chandler Harper	1933	Gene Sarazen		
1991	John Daly	1949	Sam Snead	1932	Olin Dutra		
1990	Wayne Grady						
1989	Payne Stewart						
1988	Jeff Sluman						
1987	Larry Nelson*						
1986	Bob Tway						
1985	Hubert Green						
1984	Lee Trevino						
1983	Hal Sutton						
1982	Raymond Floyd						
1981	Larry Nelson						
1980	Jack Nicklaus						
1979	David Graham*						
1978	John Mahaffey*						
1977**	Lanny Wadkins*						
1976	Dave Stockton						
1975	Jack Nicklaus						
1974	Lee Trevino						
1973	Jack Nicklaus						
1972	Gary Player						
1971	Jack Nicklaus						
1970	Dave Stockton						
1969	Ray Floyd						
1968	Julius Boros						
1967	Don January*						
1966	Al Geiberger						

* Winner in playoff. ** Playoff changed from 18 holes to sudden death.

Phil Mickelson

ROBERT BECK

All-Time Champions — Women: LPGA Championship

YEAR	WINNER	YEAR	WINNER	YEAR	WINNER
2008	Yani Tseng	1990	Beth Daniel	1972	Kathy Ahern
2007	Suzann Pettersen	1989	Nancy Lopez	1971	Kathy Whitworth
2006	Se Ri Pak	1988	Sherri Turner	1970	Shirley Englehorn*
2005	Annika Sorenstam	1987	Jane Geddes	1969	Betsy Rawls
2004	Annika Sorenstam	1986	Pat Bradley	1968	Sandra Post*
2003	Annika Sorenstam	1985	Nancy Lopez	1967	Kathy Whitworth
2002	Se Ri Pak	1984	Patty Sheehan	1966	Gloria Ehret
2001	Karrie Webb	1983	Patty Sheehan	1965	Sandra Haynie
2000	Juli Inkster*	1982	Jan Stephenson	1964	Mary Mills
1999	Juli Inkster	1981	Donna Caponi	1963	Mickey Wright
1998	Se Ri Pak	1980	Sally Little	1962	Judy Kimball
1997	Chris Johnson*	1979	Donna Caponi	1961	Mickey Wright
1996	Laura Davies	1978	Nancy Lopez	1960	Mickey Wright
1995	Kelly Robbins	1977	Chako Higuchi	1959	Betsy Rawls
1994	Laura Davies	1976	Betty Burfeindt	1958	Mickey Wright
1993	Patty Sheehan	1975	Kathy Whitworth	1957	Louise Suggs
1992	Betsy King	1974	Sandra Haynie	1956	Marlene Hagge*
1991	Meg Mallon	1973	Mary Mills	1955	Beverly Hanson**

* Won in playoff. The 1956, 1997, and 2000 titles were decided in sudden death; 1968 and 1970 were 18-hole playoffs. ** Won match-play final.

■ **Nick Faldo,** *b. July 18, 1957, Welwyn Garden City, England.* Now a popular commentator for CBS Sports, Faldo was one of the greatest clutch players in golf history. A winner of six major championships and 34 international events, he is best remembered for defeating Greg Norman in the 1996 Masters. Trailing by six shots entering the final round, Norman crumbled under the pressure while Faldo fired a 67 for a five-shot victory.

Nick Faldo

AL TIELEMANS

■ **Annika Sorenstam,** *b. October 9, 1970, Stockholm, Sweden.* After one of the greatest careers in LPGA history, Sorenstam announced in May that she would retire at the end of 2008. She said NFL quarterback Brett Favre's retirement speech influenced her decision. At the time of her announcement, Sorenstam had won 72 LPGA events (the record is 88) and 10 majors. In 2003, she became the first woman in 58 years to play in a PGA event.

■ **Nancy Lopez,** *b. January 6, 1957, Torrance, California.* Lopez burst onto the LPGA tour in 1978 by winning Rookie of the Year, Player of the Year, and the Vare Trophy (lowest average strokes per round) in the same season. She remains the only person to accomplish the feat. Winning three more Player of the Year titles (1979, 1985, 1988), Lopez collected 48 career victories and three major titles and became an icon of the game with her cheery persona.

All-Time Champions — Women: U.S. Women's Open

YEAR	WINNER	YEAR	WINNER	YEAR	WINNER
2007	Cristie Kerr	1981	Pat Bradley	1955	Fay Crocker
2006	Annika Sorenstam	1980	Amy Alcott	1954	Babe Zaharias
2005	Birdie Kim	1979	Jerilyn Britz	1953	Betsy Rawls*
2004	Meg Mallon	1978	Hollis Stacy	1952	Louise Suggs
2003	Hilary Lunke*	1977	Hollis Stacy	1951	Betsy Rawls
2002	Juli Inkster	1976	JoAnne Carner*	1950	Babe Zaharias
2001	Karrie Webb	1975	Sandra Palmer	1949	Louise Suggs
2000	Karrie Webb	1974	Sandra Haynie	1948	Babe Zaharias
1999	Juli Inkster	1973	Susie Berning	1947	Betty Jameson
1998	Se Ri Pak**	1972	Susie Berning	1946	Patty Berg
1997	Alison Nicholas	1971	JoAnne Carner		
1996	Annika Sorenstam	1970	Donna Caponi		
1995	Annika Sorenstam	1969	Donna Caponi		
1994	Patty Sheehan	1968	Susie Berning		
1993	Lauri Merten	1967	Catherine LaCoste		
1992	Patty Sheehan*	1966	Sandra Spuzich		
1991	Meg Mallon	1965	Carol Mann		
1990	Betsy King	1964	Mickey Wright*		
1989	Betsy King	1963	Mary Mills		
1988	Liselotte Neumann	1962	Murle Breer		
1987	Laura Davies*	1961	Mickey Wright		
1986	Jane Geddes*	1960	Betsy Rawls		
1985	Kathy Baker	1959	Mickey Wright		
1984	Hollis Stacy	1958	Mickey Wright		
1983	Jan Stephenson	1957	Betsy Rawls		
1982	Janet Anderson	1956	Kathy Cornelius*		

* Winner in playoff. ** Winner on second hole of sudden death after 18-hole playoff ended in a tie.

Women's British Open

YEAR	WINNER
2007	Lorena Ochoa
2006	Sherri Steinhauer
2005	Jeong Jang
2004	Karen Stupples
2003	Annika Sorenstam
2002	Karrie Webb
2001	Se Ri Pak

Note: Designated a major in 2001.

All-Time Champions — Women: Kraft Nabisco Championship

Karrie Webb

YEAR	WINNER	YEAR	WINNER
2008	Lorena Ochoa	1989	Juli Inkster
2007	Morgan Pressel	1988	Amy Alcott
2006	Karrie Webb	1987	Betsy King*
2005	Annika Sorenstam	1986	Pat Bradley
2004	Grace Park	1985	Alice Miller
2003	Patricia Meunier-Lebouc	1984	Juli Inkster*
2002	Annika Sorenstam	1983	Amy Alcott
2001	Annika Sorenstam	1982	Sally Little
2000	Karrie Webb	1981	Nancy Lopez
1999	Dottie Pepper	1980	Donna Caponi
1998	Pat Hurst	1979	Sandra Post
1997	Betsy King	1978	Sandra Post*
1996	Patti Sheehan	1977	Kathy Whitworth
1995	Nanci Bowen	1976	Judy Rankin
1994	Donna Andrews	1975	Sandra Palmer
1993	Helen Alfredsson	1974	Jo Ann Prentice*
1992	Dottie Mochrie*	1973	Mickey Wright
1991	Amy Alcott	1972	Jane Blalock
1990	Betsy King		

* Winner in sudden-death playoff.

Note: Designated a major in 1983; played at Mission Hills Country Club, Rancho Mirage, California.

TRIVIA

1 True or False: There is no limit to the number of clubs a player can carry in a bag.
A. True
B. False

2 A double eagle is a score of three under par on a hole. What's another bird nickname for that score?
A. Bald Eagle
B. Dodo
C. Albatross

Camilo Villegas

3 What is Colombian golfer Camilo Villegas's nickname?
A. The Snake
B. Spider-Man
C. The Avenger

4 True or False: You cannot let your club touch the ground in a sand trap before hitting the ball.
A. True
B. False

5 Where did Michelle Wie and Tiger Woods both attend college?
A. Harvard
B. Stanford
C. Duke

1.B, 2.C, 3.B, 4.A, 5.B

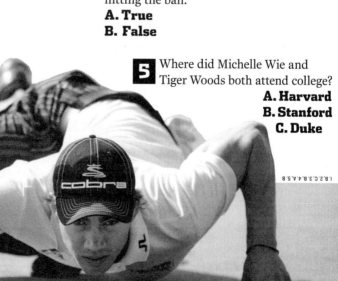

A New World

Nextel Cup champ Jimmie Johnson and his #48 car go head-to-head against Kyle Busch.

New cars. New teams. New names. It was a season of change in motor sports. The one constant? The winning ways of reigning NASCAR Nextel Cup champ Jimmie Johnson.

After starting 2007 with a crash in the Daytona 500, Johnson and his #48 Chevy quickly returned to championship form, reeling off early victories in Las Vegas, Atlanta, and Martinsville. The speedster from Southern California was looking unstoppable until a summer slump tightened up the standings. But Johnson roared back to take the checkered flag in four straight races, the first driver to pull off the feat since his teammate Jeff Gordon did it nearly a decade ago. Johnson also became the first driver since Gordon to win 10 races in one season.

It was only fitting, then, that the chase for the Cup came down to Gordon and Johnson. And it came down to the wire. In the final race of the year, Johnson finished seventh and locked up the Cup on accumulated points, making him the first driver to win back-to-back titles since — guess who? — Jeff Gordon in 1998.

If the guard was changing in NASCAR last season, so were the rides. One of the biggest developments to hit the sport in years was a new car. Dubbed the "Car of Tomorrow" and introduced before the Bristol race in March, the CoT was boxier than its sleek predecessors, which evolved from 1966 Holman Moody Ford Fairlanes. The CoT was cheaper to build, making it harder for rich teams to outspend everyone.

It was safer, too. With a smaller gas tank and a reinforced, centered cockpit that expanded the "crumple zone," the car was designed to protect drivers.

Although the CoT has its critics — they say the less aerodynamic vehicle makes for duller races — the new car has done its job. In early 2008, several drivers walked away from nasty wrecks, including a fiery, somersaulting crash in Texas that scared spectators but left rookie driver Michael McDowell with only a few lumps.

The 2007 NASCAR season saw other changes, none more attention-grabbing than Dale Earnhardt Jr.'s announcement in June that he was leaving Dale Earnhardt, Inc., the team his late father founded, to join Hendrick Motorsports, where Johnson and Gordon race. To make room for Junior, Kyle Busch moved to Joe Gibbs Racing, which announced a partnership with Toyota, a major newcomer to NASCAR's top circuit.

The "Chase for the Nextel Cup" (renamed the Sprint Cup at the end of 2007) also marked the debut of Formula One driver Juan Pablo Montoya, who kicked off his NASCAR career with a victory in Sonoma. And two recent IndyCar champions, Sam Hornish Jr., and Dario Franchitti, revealed their intentions to make the jump to NASCAR in 2008.

In such a topsy-turvy year, what more can change next season? With rising new stars and better competition all around in the racing world, the answer is: anything.

■ **Danica Patrick,** *b. March 25, 1982, Benoit, Wisconsin.* The 26-year-old IndyCar star has improved each year she's been driving, and 2007 was no exception. Patrick finished seventh overall with three podium appearances and arguably brought more attention to IndyCar than anyone since Mario Andretti. But Patrick has also been criticized for being more flash than talent. In April 2008, she silenced naysayers by winning in Japan, becoming the first woman to take an IndyCar race.

■ **Lewis Hamilton,** *b. January 7, 1985, Stevenage, England.* Forget for a moment that in 2007, Hamilton became the first black driver to compete in a Formula One race. Forget that he was just 23 going into his second F1 season. Instead, consider this: He's named after track star Carl Lewis. No wonder Hamilton's so fast. In his debut year, the young Briton came within a point of winning the F1 title, finishing second to Kimi Räikkönen after an improbable late-season collapse. But his four grand prix victories tied the rookie record set by Jacques Villeneuve in 1996.

Danica
Patrick

SIMON BRUTY

■ **Kyle Busch,** *b. May 2, 1985, Las Vegas, Nevada.* Busch was always precocious. He grew up racing in the Bullring at the Las Vegas Motor Speedway. By age 16, he was driving in the Craftsman Truck Series, prompting NASCAR to create a minimum age limit of 18 and boot Busch from competition. No matter. Two years later, the youngster was back to tear up the track. Nicknamed "Shrub" because he's the baby brother of fellow Sprint Cup driver Kurt, Busch has a rowdy racing style that wins him races, but annoys some of his competitors. In 2007, Busch finished fifth overall in the Nextel Cup Series.

Indy Racing League (IRL) Results

IRL CHAMPIONS	
YEAR	DRIVER
2007	Dario Franchitti
2006 (tie)	Dan Wheldon; Sam Hornish Jr.
2005	Dan Wheldon
2004	Tony Kanaan
2003	Scott Dixon
2002	Sam Hornish Jr.
2001	Sam Hornish Jr.
2000	Buddy Lazier
1999	Greg Ray
1998	Kenny Brack
1996–97	Tony Stewart
1996 (tie)	Buzz Calkins; Scott Sharp

IRL ROOKIES OF THE YEAR	
YEAR	DRIVER
2007	Ryan Hunter-Reay
2006	Marco Andretti
2005	Danica Patrick
2004	Kosuke Matsuura
2003	Dan Wheldon
2002	Laurent Redon
2001	Felipe Giaffone
2000	Airton Dare
1999	Scott Harrington
1998	Robby Unser
1996–97	Jim Guthrie
1996 (series' first year)	No award

Indianapolis 500 Winners

Dario Franchitti

YEAR	DRIVER	AVG MPH
2008	Scott Dixon	143.567
2007	Dario Franchitti (415*)	151.774
2006	Sam Hornish Jr.	157.085
2005	Dan Wheldon	157.603
2004	Buddy Rice (450*)	138.518
2003	Gil de Ferran	166.499
2001	Helio Castroneves	141.574
2000	Juan Montoya	167.607
1999	Kenny Brack	153.176
1998	Eddie Cheever Jr.	145.155
1997	Arie Luyendyk	145.827
1996	Buddy Lazier	147.956
1995	Jacques Villeneuve	153.616
1994	Al Unser Jr.	160.872
1993	Emerson Fittipaldi	157.207
1992	Al Unser Jr.	134.477
1991	Rick Mears	176.457
1990	Arie Luyendyk	185.981
1989	Emerson Fittipaldi	167.581
1988	Rick Mears	144.809
1987	Al Unser	162.175
1986	Bobby Rahal	170.722
1985	Danny Sullivan	152.982
1984	Rick Mears	163.612
1983	Tom Sneva	162.117
1982	Gordon Johncock	162.029
1981	Bobby Unser	139.084
1980	Johnny Rutherford	142.862
1979	Rick Mears	158.899
1978	Al Unser	161.363
1977	A.J. Foyt Jr.	161.331
1976	Johnny Rutherford (255*)	148.725
1975	Bobby Unser (435*)	149.213
1974	Johnny Rutherford	158.589
1973	Gordon Johncock (332.5*)	159.036
1972	Mark Donohue	162.962
1971	Al Unser	157.735
1970	Al Unser	155.749
1969	Mario Andretti	156.867
1960	Jim Rathmann	138.767
1959	Rodger Ward	135.857
1958	Jimmy Bryan	133.791
1957	Sam Hanks	135.601
1956	Pat Flaherty	128.490
1955	Bob Sweikert	128.213
1968	Bobby Unser	152.882
1967	A.J. Foyt Jr.	151.207
1966	Graham Hill	144.317
1965	Jim Clark	150.686
1964	A.J. Foyt Jr.	147.350
1963	Parnelli Jones	143.137

YEAR	DRIVER	AVG MPH
1962	Rodger Ward	140.293
1961	A.J. Foyt Jr.	139.130
1954	Bill Vukovich	130.840
1953	Bill Vukovich	128.740
1952	Troy Ruttman	128.922
1951	Lee Wallard	126.244
1950	Johnnie Parsons (345*)	124.002
1949	Bill Holland	121.327
1948	Mauri Rose	119.814
1947	Mauri Rose	116.338
1946	George Robson	114.820
1942–45	No races held during World War II	
1941	Floyd Davis; Mauri Rose	115.117
1940	Wilbur Shaw	114.277
1939	Wilbur Shaw	115.035
1938	Floyd Roberts	117.200
1937	Wilbur Shaw	113.580
1936	Louis Meyer	109.069
1935	Kelly Petillo	106.240
1934	Bill Cummings	104.863
1933	Louis Meyer	104.162
1932	Fred Fame	104.144
1931	Louis Schneider	96.629
1930	Billy Arnold	100.448
1929	Ray Keech	97.585
1928	Louis Meyer	99.482
1927	George Souders	97.545
1926	Frank Lockhart (400*)	95.904
1925	Peter DePaolo	101.127
1924	L.L. Corum; Joe Boyer	98.234
1923	Tommy Milton	90.954
1922	Jimmy Murphy	94.484
1921	Tommy Milton	89.621
1920	Gaston Chevrolet	88.618
1919	Howdy Wilcox	88.050
1917–18	No races held during World War I	
1916**	Dario Resta	84.001
1915	Ralph DePalma	89.840
1914	Rene Thomas	82.474
1913	Jules Goux	75.933
1912	Joe Dawson	78.719
1911	Ray Harroun	74.602

* Miles completed before race was called because of rain. ** Scheduled for 300 miles.

JOHN HARRELSON/NASCAR/GETTY

■ **Ayrton Senna,** *b. March 21, 1960, Sao Paolo, Brazil; d. May 1, 1994.* Introspective off the track and ferocious on it, Senna was a unique talent in motor sports. He often triumphed using inferior equipment and won three Formula One championships before his brilliant career ended in a deadly crash in 1994. Senna's legendary rivalry with Frenchman Alain Prost brought out the best — and worst — in both men. But in wet weather, no one could touch the Brazilian, whose most stunning performance came in a race he didn't win: the 1984 Monaco Grand Prix. Driving in torrential rain on hairpin streets, the rookie Senna blew by the field and had the leader, Prost, in his sights when the race was called for safety. But notice had been served. A driver of sublime skill and profound courage had arrived.

Ayrton Senna

SHUJI KAJIYAMA/AP

■ **Terry Labonte,** *b. November 16, 1956, Corpus Christi, Texas.* Not even a broken hand could stop Labonte from winning his second NASCAR Winston Cup championship in 1996. That's why he's called "the Iceman." In his 30-year career, Labonte's cool behind the wheel led him to 22 Winston/Nextel Cup victories and 17 top-10 overall finishes, a record that earned him the honor of being named one of NASCAR's 50 greatest drivers. With 851 starts, Labonte should also be considered an iron man. He logged more than 300,000 miles on the track.

NASCAR Races into Canada

In 2007, the Circuit Gilles Villeneuve hosted the first NASCAR Busch Series race in Canada. This road track sits on a man-made island in the St. Lawrence River. What is the name of the island?

To find out, begin at the letter that most resembles a pole. Then, make two counter-clockwise laps around the track, picking up every other letter (or symbol) to spell the answer.

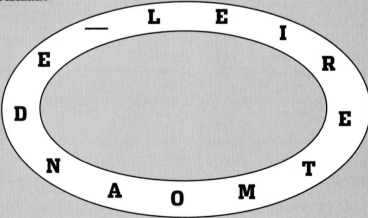

_ L E I R E T M O A N D E

_ _ _ _ _ _ _ _ _ _ _ _ _

ANSWERS ON PAGE 191

NASCAR Results

NASCAR CHAMPIONS

YEAR	DRIVER	YEAR	DRIVER	YEAR	DRIVER	YEAR	DRIVER
2007	Jimmie Johnson	1992	Alan Kulwicki	1977	Cale Yarborough	1962	Joe Weatherly
2006	Jimmie Johnson	1991	Dale Earnhardt	1976	Cale Yarborough	1961	Ned Jarrett
2005	Tony Stewart	1990	Dale Earnhardt	1975	Richard Petty	1960	Rex White
2004	Kurt Busch	1989	Rusty Wallace	1974	Richard Petty	1959	Lee Petty
2003	Matt Kenseth	1988	Bill Elliott	1973	Benny Parsons	1958	Lee Petty
2002	Tony Stewart	1987	Dale Earnhardt	1972	Richard Petty	1957	Buck Baker
2001	Jeff Gordon	1986	Dale Earnhardt	1971	Richard Petty	1956	Buck Baker
2000	Bobby Labonte	1985	Darrell Waltrip	1970	Bobby Isaac	1955	Tim Flock
1999	Dale Jarrett	1984	Terry Labonte	1969	David Pearson	1954	Lee Petty
1998	Jeff Gordon	1983	Bobby Allison	1968	David Pearson	1953	Herb Thomas
1997	Jeff Gordon	1982	Darrell Waltrip	1967	Richard Petty	1952	Tim Flock
1996	Terry Labonte	1981	Darrell Waltrip	1966	David Pearson	1951	Herb Thomas
1995	Jeff Gordon	1980	Dale Earnhardt	1965	Ned Jarrett	1950	Bill Rexford
1994	Dale Earnhardt	1979	Richard Petty	1964	Richard Petty	1949	Red Byron
1993	Dale Earnhardt	1978	Cale Yarborough	1963	Joe Weatherly		

WIN LEADERS

RANK	DRIVER
1	Richard Petty (200)
2	David Pearson (105)
3	Bobby Allison (84); Darrell Waltrip (84)
5	Cale Yarborough (83)
6	Jeff Gordon (78)
7	Dale Earnhardt (76)
8	Rusty Wallace (55)
9	Lee Petty (54)
10	Ned Jarrett (50); Junior Johnson (50)
12	Herb Thomas (48)
13	Buck Baker (46)
14	Bill Elliott (44)
15	Tim Flock (39)
16	Bobby Isaac (37)
17	Mark Martin (35)
18	Fireball Roberts (33)
19	Dale Jarrett (32)
20	Tony Stewart (29)
21	Rex White (28)

Note: Ranking is through June 2008.

ROOKIES OF THE YEAR

YEAR	DRIVER	YEAR	DRIVER	YEAR	DRIVER
2007	Juan Montoya	1982	Geoffrey Bodine	1969	Dick Brooks
2006	Denny Hamlin	1981	Ron Bouchard	1968	Pete Hamilton
2005	Kyle Busch	1980	Jody Ridley	1967	Donnie Allison
2004	Kasey Kahne	1979	Dale Earnhardt	1966	James Hylton
2003	Jamie McMurray	1978	Ronnie Thomas	1965	Sam McQuagg
2002	Ryan Newman	1977	Ricky Rudd	1964	Doug Cooper
2001	Kevin Harvick	1976	Skip Manning	1963	Billy Wade
2000	Matt Kenseth	1975	Bruce Hill	1962	Tom Cox
1999	Tony Stewart	1974	Earl Ross	1961	Woodie Wilson
1998	Kenny Irwin	1973	Lennie Pond	1960	David Pearson
1997	Mike Skinner	1972	Larry Smith	1959	Richard Petty
1996	Johnny Benson	1971	Walter Ballard	1958	Shorty Rollins
1995	Ricky Craven	1970	Bill Dennis		
1994	Jeff Burton				
1993	Jeff Gordon				
1992	Jimmy Hensley				
1991	Bobby Hamilton				
1990	Rob Moroso				
1989	Dick Trickle				
1988	Ken Bouchard				
1987	Davey Allison				
1986	Alan Kulwicki				
1985	Ken Schrader				
1984	Rusty Wallace				
1983	Sterling Marlin				

Ryan Newman and his #12 car

SIMON BRUTY

DAYTONA 500 WINNERS

YEAR	DRIVER	AVG MPH	YEAR	DRIVER	AVG MPH	YEAR	DRIVER	AVG MPH
2008	Ryan Newman	152.672	1991	Ernie Irvan	148.148	1974	Richard Petty	140.894
2007	Kevin Harvick	149.335	1990	Derrike Cope	165.761	1973	Richard Petty	157.205
2006	Jimmie Johnson	142.667	1989	Darrell Waltrip	148.466	1972	A.J. Foyt Jr.	161.550
2005	Jeff Gordon	135.173	1988	Bobby Allison	137.531	1971	Richard Petty	144.462
2004	Dale Earnhardt Jr.	156.345	1987	Bill Elliott	176.263	1970	Pete Hamilton	149.601
2003	Michael Waltrip	133.870	1986	Geoffrey Bodine	148.124	1969	Lee Roy Yarbrough	157.950
2002	Ward Burton	142.971	1985	Bill Elliott	172.265	1968	Cale Yarborough	143.251
2001	Michael Waltrip	161.783	1984	Cale Yarborough	150.994	1967	Mario Andretti	146.926
2000	Dale Jarrett	155.669	1983	Cale Yarborough	155.979	1966	Richard Petty	160.627
1999	Jeff Gordon	161.551	1982	Bobby Allison	153.991	1965	Fred Lorenzen	141.539
1998	Dale Earnhardt	172.712	1981	Richard Petty	169.651	1964	Richard Petty	154.334
1997	Jeff Gordon	148.295	1980	Buddy Baker	177.602	1963	Tiny Lund	151.566
1996	Dale Jarrett	154.308	1979	Richard Petty	143.977	1962	Fireball Roberts	152.529
1995	Sterling Marlin	141.710	1978	Bobby Allison	159.730	1961	Marvin Panch	149.601
1994	Sterling Marlin	156.931	1977	Cale Yarborough	153.218	1960	Junior Johnson	124.740
1993	Dale Jarrett	154.972	1976	David Pearson	152.181	1959	Lee Petty	135.521
1992	Davey Allison	168.256	1975	Benny Parsons	153.649			

NASCAR Results (cont.)

TALLADEGA 500 WINNERS

YEAR	DRIVER	AVG MPH	YEAR	DRIVER	AVG MPH	YEAR	DRIVER	AVG MPH
2008	Kyle Busch	157.167	1994	Jimmy Spencer	163.217	1980	Neil Bonnett	166.894
2007	Jeff Gordon	154.167	1993	Dale Earnhardt	153.858	1979	Darrell Waltrip	161.229
2006	Jimmie Johnson	142.880	1992	Ernie Irvan	176.309	1978	Lennie Pond	174.700
2005	Jeff Gordon	146.904	1991	Dale Earnhardt	147.383	1977	Donnie Allison	162.524
2004	Jeff Gordon	129.396	1990	Dale Earnhardt	174.430	1976	Dave Marcis	157.547
2003	Dale Earnhardt Jr.	144.625	1989	Terry Labonte	157.354	1975	Buddy Baker	130.892
2002	Dale Earnhardt Jr.	159.022	1988	Ken Schrader	154.505	1974	Richard Petty	148.637
2001	Bobby Hamilton	184.003	1987	Bill Elliott	171.293	1973	Dick Brooks	145.454
2000	Jeff Gordon	161.157	1986	Bobby Hillin	151.552	1972	James Hylton	148.728
1999	Dale Earnhardt	163.395	1985	Cale Yarborough	148.772	1971	Bobby Allison	145.945
1998	Bobby Labonte	163.439	1984	Dale Earnhardt	155.485	1970	Pete Hamilton	158.517
1997	Terry Labonte	156.601	1983	Dale Earnhardt	170.611	1969	Richard Brickhouse	153.778
1996	Jeff Gordon	133.387	1982	Darrell Waltrip	168.157			
1995	Sterling Marlin	173.188	1981	Ron Bouchard	156.737			

Note: From 1969 through 1988, the race was known as the Talladega 500. From 1989 through 2001, it was known as the Die Hard 500. In 2001, it was again called the Talladega 500. Since 2002, the race has been called the Aaron's 499.

COCA-COLA 600 WINNERS

YEAR	DRIVER	AVG MPH	YEAR	DRIVER	AVG MPH	YEAR	DRIVER	AVG MPH
2008	Kasey Kahne	135.772	1991	Davey Allison	138.951	1974	David Pearson	135.720
2007	Casey Mears	130.222	1990	Rusty Wallace	137.650	1973	Buddy Baker	134.890
2006	Kasey Kahne	128.840	1989	Darrell Waltrip	144.077	1972	Buddy Baker	142.255
2005	Jimmie Johnson	114.698	1988	Darrell Waltrip	124.460	1971	Bobby Allison	140.442
2004	Jimmie Johnson	142.763	1987	Kyle Petty	131.483	1970	Donnie Allison	129.680
2003	Jimmie Johnson	126.198	1986	Dale Earnhardt	140.406	1969	Lee Roy Yarbrough	134.361
2002	Mark Martin	137.729	1985	Darrell Waltrip	141.807	1968	Buddy Baker	104.207
2001	Jeff Burton	138.107	1984	Bobby Allison	129.233	1967	Jim Paschal	135.832
2000	Matt Kenseth	142.640	1983	Neil Bonnett	140.707	1966	Marvin Panch	135.042
1999	Jeff Burton	151.367	1982	Neil Bonnett	130.058	1965	Fred Lorenzen	121.772
1998	Jeff Gordon	136.424	1981	Bobby Allison	129.326	1964	Jim Paschal	125.772
1997	Jeff Gordon	136.745	1980	Benny Parsons	119.265	1963	Fred Lorenzen	132.418
1996	Dale Jarrett	147.581	1979	Darrell Waltrip	136.674	1962	Nelson Stacy	125.552
1995	Bobby Labonte	151.952	1978	Darrell Waltrip	138.355	1961	David Pearson	111.633
1994	Jeff Gordon	139.445	1977	Richard Petty	137.676	1960	Joe Lee Johnson	107.73
1993	Dale Earnhardt	145.504	1976	David Pearson	137.352			
1992	Dale Earnhardt	132.980	1975	Richard Petty	145.327			

BRICKYARD 400 WINNERS

YEAR	DRIVER	AVG MPH
2007	Tony Stewart	113.379
2006	Jimmie Johnson	137.182
2005	Tony Stewart	118.782
2004	Jeff Gordon	115.037
2003	Kevin Harvick	134.554
2002	Bill Elliott	125.033
2001	Jeff Gordon	130.790
2000	Bobby Labonte	155.912
1999	Dale Jarrett	148.194
1998	Jeff Gordon	126.772
1997	Ricky Rudd	130.814
1996	Dale Jarrett	139.508
1995	Dale Earnhardt	155.206
1994	Jeff Gordon	131.97

Note: The race is now known as the Allstate 400 at the Brickyard.

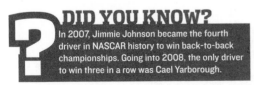

DID YOU KNOW?

In 2007, Jimmie Johnson became the fourth driver in NASCAR history to win back-to-back championships. Going into 2008, the only driver to win three in a row was Cael Yarborough.

Tony Stewart

NIGEL KINRADE

NASCAR Results (cont.)

YEAR	DRIVER	AVG MPH	YEAR	DRIVER	AVG MPH
\multicolumn{6}{c}{SOUTHERN 500 WINNERS}					
2008	Kyle Busch	140.350	1978	Cale Yarborough	116.828
2007	Jeff Gordon	124.372	1977	David Pearson	106.797
2006	Greg Biffle	135.127	1976	David Pearson	120.534
2005	Greg Biffle	123.031	1975	Bobby Allison	116.825
2004	Jimmie Johnson	125.044	1974	Cale Yarborough	111.075
2003	Terry Labonte	120.744	1973	Cale Yarborough	134.033
2002	Jeff Gordon	118.617	1972	Bobby Allison	128.124
2001	Ward Burton	122.773	1971	Bobby Allison	131.398
2000	Bobby Labonte	108.273	1970	Buddy Baker	128.817
1999	Jeff Burton	107.816	1969	Lee Roy Yarbrough	105.612
1998	Jeff Gordon	139.031	1968	Cale Yarborough	126.132
1997	Jeff Gordon	121.149	1967	Richard Petty	130.423
1996	Jeff Gordon	135.757	1966	Darel Dieringer	114.830
1995	Jeff Gordon	121.231	1965	Ned Jarrett	115.924
1994	Bill Elliott	127.952	1964	Buck Baker	117.757
1993	Mark Martin	137.932	1963	Fireball Roberts	129.784
1992	Darrell Waltrip	129.114	1962	Larry Frank	117.965
1991	Harry Gant	133.508	1961	Nelson Stacy	117.787
1990	Dale Earnhardt	123.141	1960	Buck Baker	105.901
1989	Dale Earnhardt	135.462	1959	Jim Reed	111.840
1988	Bill Elliott	128.297	1958	Fireball Roberts	102.590
1987	Dale Earnhardt	115.520	1957	Speedy Thompson	100.094
1986	Tim Richmond	121.068	1956	Curtis Turner	95.067
1985	Bill Elliott	121.254	1955	Herb Thomas	93.281
1984	Harry Gant	128.270	1954	Herb Thomas	94.930
1983	Bobby Allison	123.343	1953	Buck Baker	92.780
1982	Cale Yarborough	115.224	1952	Fonty Flock	74.510
1981	Neil Bonnett	126.410	1951	Herb Thomas	76.900
1980	Terry Labonte	115.210	1950	Johnny Mantz	76.260
1979	David Pearson	126.259			

Note: The race is now known as the Dodge Challenger 500.

Jeff Gordon and his #24 car

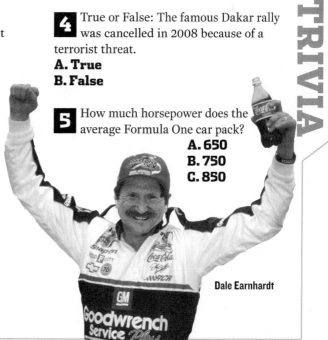

Dale Earnhardt

TRIVIA

1 Bill Elliot set the NASCAR speed record at Talladega in 1987. How fast did he go?
A. 188.203 mph
B. 205.762 mph
C. 212.809 mph

2 True or False: NASCAR is the number one spectator sport in the United States.
A. True
B. False

3 Dale Earnhardt won a record seven NASCAR Winston Cup titles. With whom does he share that record?
A. Junior Johnson
B. Richard Petty
C. Jeff Gordon

4 True or False: The famous Dakar rally was cancelled in 2008 because of a terrorist threat.
A. True
B. False

5 How much horsepower does the average Formula One car pack?
A. 650
B. 750
C. 850

1.C. 2.A 3.B. 4.A. 5.B

New Stars Take Center Court

Tennis produces a new star almost every year. In 2007, we found two of them, and from the same place: Serbia. Novak Djokovic used to be best known for his impersonations of other players. Not anymore. Djokovic was all business when he reached the finals of the U.S. Open and the semifinals of both the French Open and Wimbledon as a 20-year-old. In early 2008, the versatile Djokovic beat the world's top-ranked player, Roger Federer, to win the Australian Open and his first Grand Slam.

On the women's side, Ana Ivanovic burst onto the scene in 2007 by reaching the finals of the French Open and the semifinals of Wimbledon. Wielding a powerful forehand from the baseline, Ivanovic continued her outstanding play in 2008 — this time winning in Paris for her first Grand Slam title — and establishing herself as one of the top three players in the world.

Meanwhile Federer, the Swiss maestro, has seemingly mastered every shot and every angle of the game. In 2007, he broke the record for consecutive Grand Slam final appearances (10). He won the 2007 Australian Open, U.S. Open, and Wimbledon, making him the only man other than Bjorn Borg to take five straight titles at the All England Club. However, his mighty run at Wimbledon came to an end in 2008. After defeating Federer at the French Open in May, Rafael Nadal became the new king of grass in a thrilling five-set victory. The epic match has been called the greatest ever played.

Known for being a jokester, Novak Djokovic got serious and won the Australian Open in 2008.

Grand Slam Tournaments: Men's Champions

AUSTRALIAN CHAMPIONSHIPS

YEAR	WINNER	YEAR	WINNER	YEAR	WINNER
2008	Novak Djokovic	1976	Mark Edmondson	1939	John Bromwich
2007	Roger Federer	1975	John Newcombe	1938	Don Budge
2006	Roger Federer	1974	Jimmy Connors	1937	Vivian B. McGrath
2005	Marat Safin	1973	John Newcombe	1936	Adrian Quist
2004	Roger Federer	1972	Ken Rosewall	1935	Jack Crawford
2003	Andre Agassi	1971	Ken Rosewall	1934	Fred Perry
2002	Thomas Johansson	1970	Arthur Ashe	1933	Jack Crawford
2001	Andre Agassi	1969*	Rod Laver	1932	Jack Crawford
2000	Andre Agassi	1968	Bill Bowrey	1931	Jack Crawford
1999	Yevgeny Kafelnikov	1967	Roy Emerson	1930	Gar Moon
1998	Petr Korda	1966	Roy Emerson	1929	John C. Gregory
1997	Pete Sampras	1965	Roy Emerson	1928	Jean Borotra
1996	Boris Becker	1964	Roy Emerson	1927	Gerald Patterson
1995	Andre Agassi	1963	Roy Emerson	1926	John Hawkes
1994	Pete Sampras	1962	Rod Laver	1925	James Anderson
1993	Jim Courier	1961	Roy Emerson	1924	James Anderson
1992	Jim Courier	1960	Rod Laver	1923	Pat O'Hara Wood
1991	Boris Becker	1959	Alex Olmedo	1922	James Anderson
1990	Ivan Lendl	1958	Ashley Cooper	1921	Rhys H. Gemmell
1989	Ivan Lendl	1957	Ashley Cooper	1920	Pat O'Hara Wood
1988	Mats Wilander	1956	Lew Hoad	1919	A.R.F. Kingscote
1987	Stefan Edberg	1955	Ken Rosewall	1916–18	No tournament
1986	No tournament	1954	Mervyn Rose	1915	Francis G. Lowe
1985	Stefan Edberg	1953	Ken Rosewall	1914	Arthur Wood
1984	Mats Wilander	1952	Ken McGregor	1913	E. F. Parker
1983	Mats Wilander	1951	Richard Savitt	1912	J. Cecil Parke
1982	Johan Kriek	1950	Frank Sedgman	1911	Norman Brookes
1981	Johan Kriek	1949	Frank Sedgman	1910	Rodney Heath
1980	Brian Teacher	1948	Adrian Quist	1909	Tony Wilding
1979	Guillermo Vilas	1947	Dinny Pails	1908	Fred Alexander
1978	Guillermo Vilas	1946	John Bromwich	1907	Horace M. Rice
1977 (Dec.)	Vitas Gerulaitis	1941–45	No tournament	1906	Tony Wilding
1977 (Jan.)	Roscoe Tanner	1940	Adrian Quist	1905	Rodney Heath

FRENCH CHAMPIONSHIPS

YEAR	WINNER	YEAR	WINNER	YEAR	WINNER	YEAR	WINNER
2008	Rafael Nadal	1981	Bjorn Borg	1954	Tony Trabert	1936	Gottfried von Cramm
2007	Rafael Nadal	1980	Bjorn Borg	1953	Ken Rosewall	1935	Fred Perry
2006	Rafael Nadal	1979	Bjorn Borg	1952	Jaroslav Drobny	1934	Gottfried von Cramm
2005	Rafael Nadal	1978	Bjorn Borg	1951	Jaroslav Drobny	1933	Jack Crawford
2004	Gaston Gaudio	1977	Guillermo Vilas	1950	Budge Patty	1932	Henri Cochet
2003	Juan Carlos Ferrero	1976	Adriano Panatta	1949	Frank Parker	1931	Jean Borotra
2002	Albert Costa	1975	Bjorn Borg	1948	Frank Parker	1930	Henri Cochet
2001	Gustavo Kuerten	1974	Bjorn Borg	1947	Jozsef Asboth	1929	Rene Lacoste
2000	Gustavo Kuerten	1973	Ilie Nastase	1946	Marcel Bernard	1928	Henri Cochet
1999	Andre Agassi	1972	Andres Gimeno	1940–45	No tournament	1927	Rene Lacoste
1998	Carlos Moya	1971	Jan Kodes	1939	William McNeill	1926	Henri Cochet
1997	Gustavo Kuerten	1970	Jan Kodes	1938	Don Budge	1925**	Rene Lacoste
1996	Yevgeny Kafelnikov	1969	Rod Laver	1937	Henner Henkel		
1995	Thomas Muster	1968*	Ken Rosewall				
1994	Sergi Bruguera	1967	Roy Emerson				
1993	Sergi Bruguera	1966	Tony Roche				
1992	Jim Courier	1965	Fred Stolle				
1991	Jim Courier	1964	Manuel Santana				
1990	Andres Gomez	1963	Roy Emerson				
1989	Michael Chang	1962	Rod Laver				
1988	Mats Wilander	1961	Manuel Santana				
1987	Ivan Lendl	1960	Nicola Pietrangeli				
1986	Ivan Lendl	1959	Nicola Pietrangeli				
1985	Mats Wilander	1958	Mervyn Rose				
1984	Ivan Lendl	1957	Sven Davidson				
1983	Yannick Noah	1956	Lew Hoad				
1982	Mats Wilander	1955	Tony Trabert				

Rafael Nadal

* Became Open (amateur and professional).
** 1925 was the first year in which players from all countries were allowed to compete.

Grand Slam Tournaments: Men's Champions (cont.)

WIMBLEDON CHAMPIONSHIPS

YEAR	WINNER	YEAR	WINNER	YEAR	WINNER	YEAR	WINNER
2008	Rafael Nadal	1977	Bjorn Borg	1946	Yvon Petra	1907	Norman E. Brookes
2007	Roger Federer	1976	Bjorn Borg	1940–45	No tournament	1906	H. Laurie Doherty
2006	Roger Federer	1975	Arthur Ashe	1939	Bobby Riggs	1905	H. Laurie Doherty
2005	Roger Federer	1974	Jimmy Connors	1938	Don Budge	1904	H. Laurie Doherty
2004	Roger Federer	1973	Jan Kodes	1937	Don Budge	1903	H. Laurie Doherty
2003	Roger Federer	1972	Stan Smith	1936	Fred Perry	1902	H. Laurie Doherty
2002	Lleyton Hewitt	1971	John Newcombe	1935	Fred Perry	1901	Arthur W. Gore
2001	Goran Ivanisevic	1970	John Newcombe	1934	Fred Perry	1900	Reggie F. Doherty
2000	Pete Sampras	1969	Rod Laver	1933	Jack Crawford	1899	Reggie F. Doherty
1999	Pete Sampras	1968*	Rod Laver	1932	Ellsworth Vines	1898	Reggie F. Doherty
1998	Pete Sampras	1967	John Newcombe	1931	Sidney B. Wood Jr.	1897	Reggie F. Doherty
1997	Pete Sampras	1966	Manuel Santana	1930	Bill Tilden	1896	Harold S. Mahoney
1996	Richard Krajicek	1965	Roy Emerson	1929	Henri Cochet	1895	Wilfred Baddeley
1995	Pete Sampras	1964	Roy Emerson	1928	Rene Lacoste	1894	Joshua Pim
1994	Pete Sampras	1963	Chuck McKinley	1927	Henri Cochet	1893	Joshua Pim
1993	Pete Sampras	1962	Rod Laver	1926	Jean Borotra	1892	Wilfred Baddeley
1992	Andre Agassi	1961	Rod Laver	1925	Rene Lacoste	1891	Wilfred Baddeley
1991	Michael Stich	1960	Neale Fraser	1924	Jean Borotra	1890	William J. Hamilton
1990	Stefan Edberg	1959	Alex Olmedo	1923	Bill Johnston	1889	William Renshaw
1989	Boris Becker	1958	Ashley Cooper	1922	Gerald L. Patterson	1888	Ernest Renshaw
1988	Stefan Edberg	1957	Lew Hoad	1921	Bill Tilden	1887	Herbert F. Lawford
1987	Pat Cash	1956	Lew Hoad	1920	Bill Tilden	1886	William Renshaw
1986	Boris Becker	1955	Tony Trabert	1919	Gerald L. Patterson	1885	William Renshaw
1985	Boris Becker	1954	Jaroslav Drobny	1915–18	No tournament	1884	William Renshaw
1984	John McEnroe	1953	Vic Seixas	1914	Norman E. Brookes	1883	William Renshaw
1983	John McEnroe	1952	Frank Sedgman	1913	Anthony F. Wilding	1882	William Renshaw
1982	Jimmy Connors	1951	Dick Savitt	1912	Anthony F. Wilding	1881	William Renshaw
1981	John McEnroe	1950	Budge Patty	1911	Anthony F. Wilding	1880	John T. Hartley
1980	Bjorn Borg	1949	Fred Schroeder Jr.	1910	Anthony F. Wilding	1879	John T. Hartley
1979	Bjorn Borg	1948	Bob Falkenburg	1909	Arthur W. Gore	1878	P. Frank Hadow
1978	Bjorn Borg	1947	Jack Kramer	1908	Arthur W. Gore	1877	Spencer W. Gore

UNITED STATES CHAMPIONSHIPS

YEAR	WINNER	YEAR	WINNER
2007	Roger Federer	1980	John McEnroe
2006	Roger Federer	1979	John McEnroe
2005	Roger Federer	1978	Jimmy Connors
2004	Roger Federer	1977	Guillermo Vilas
2003	Andy Roddick	1976	Jimmy Connors
2002	Pete Sampras	1975	Manuel Orantes
2001	Lleyton Hewitt	1974	Jimmy Connors
2000	Marat Safin	1973	John Newcombe
1999	Andre Agassi	1972	Ilie Nastase
1998	Patrick Rafter	1971	Stan Smith
1997	Patrick Rafter	1970	Ken Rosewall
1996	Pete Sampras	1969	Stan Smith
1995	Pete Sampras	1969**	Rod Laver
1994	Andre Agassi	1968*	Arthur Ashe
1993	Pete Sampras	1968**	Arthur Ashe
1992	Stefan Edberg	1967	John Newcombe
1991	Stefan Edberg	1966	Fred Stolle
1990	Pete Sampras	1965	Manuel Santana
1989	Boris Becker	1964	Roy Emerson
1988	Mats Wilander	1963	Rafael Osuna
1987	Ivan Lendl	1962	Rod Laver
1986	Ivan Lendl	1961	Roy Emerson
1985	Ivan Lendl	1960	Neale Fraser
1984	John McEnroe	1959	Neale Fraser
1983	Jimmy Connors	1958	Ashley Cooper
1982	Jimmy Connors	1957	Mal Anderson
1981	John McEnroe	1956	Ken Rosewall

Roger Federer

BOB MARTIN

* Became Open (amateur and professional).

** Separate amateur event held.

Grand Slam Tournaments: Men's Champions (cont.)

UNITED STATES CHAMPIONSHIPS (cont.)

YEAR	WINNER	YEAR	WINNER	YEAR	WINNER	YEAR	WINNER
1955	Tony Trabert	1936	Fred Perry	1917	R.L. Murray	1898	Malcolm D. Whitman
1954	Vic Seixas	1935	Wilmer L. Allison	1916	Richard N. Williams	1897	Robert D. Wrenn
1953	Tony Trabert	1934	Fred Perry	1915	Bill Johnston	1896	Robert D. Wrenn
1952	Frank Sedgman	1933	Fred Perry	1914	Richard N. Williams	1895	Frederick H. Hovey
1951	Frank Sedgman	1932	Ellsworth Vines	1913	Maurice E. McLoughlin	1894	Robert D. Wrenn
1950	Arthur Larsen	1931	Ellsworth Vines	1912	Maurice E. McLoughlin	1893	Robert D. Wrenn
1949	Pancho Gonzales	1930	John H. Doeg	1911	William A. Larned	1892	Oliver S. Campbell
1948	Pancho Gonzales	1929	Bill Tilden	1910	William A. Larned	1891	Oliver S. Campbell
1947	Jack Kramer	1928	Henri Cochet	1909	William A. Larned	1890	Oliver S. Campbell
1946	Jack Kramer	1927	Rene Lacoste	1908	William A. Larned	1889	H.W. Slocum Jr.
1945	Frank Parker	1926	Rene Lacoste	1907	William A. Larned	1888	H.W. Slocum Jr.
1944	Frank Parker	1925	Bill Tilden	1906	William J. Clothier	1887	Richard D. Sears
1943	Joseph R. Hunt	1924	Bill Tilden	1905	Beals C. Wright	1886	Richard D. Sears
1942	Fred R. Schroeder Jr.	1923	Bill Tilden	1904	Holcombe Ward	1885	Richard D. Sears
1941	Bobby Riggs	1922	Bill Tilden	1903	H. Laurie Doherty	1884	Richard D. Sears
1940	Don McNeill	1921	Bill Tilden	1902	William A. Larned	1883	Richard D. Sears
1939	Bobby Riggs	1920	Bill Tilden	1901	William A. Larned	1882	Richard D. Sears
1938	Don Budge	1919	Bill Johnston	1900	Malcolm D. Whitman	1881	Richard D. Sears
1937	Don Budge	1918	R.L. Murray	1899	Malcolm D. Whitman		

James Blake

■ **James Blake,** *b. December 28, 1979, Yonkers, New York.* If tennis gave out trophies for toughness, Blake would have a full display case. As a teenager, he overcame severe curvature of the spine that required him to wear a back brace for years. In 2004, Blake fractured vertebrae in his neck. But returned the next year to reach the quarterfinals of the U.S. Open. By 2006, Blake was playing the best tennis of his career, winning five tournaments and cracking into the top 10 rankings for the first time. In 2007, he continued his success by helping the U.S. team win the Davis Cup for the first time in 12 years.

■ **Anna Chakvetadze,** *b. March 5, 1987, Moscow, Russia.* The young Russian had a breakthrough season in 2007, finishing in the top 10. In 2007, she made it to the quarterfinals of the Australian Open and the French Open and the semifinals of the U.S. Open, where she lost to Svetlana Kuznetsova, 3–6, 6–1, 6–1. Chakvetadze has a perfect 7–0 record in tournament finals.

■ **Rafael Nadal,** *b. June 3, 1986, Manacor, Spain.* Just 22 years old, Nadal is already considered the best clay court player of all time. He's undefeated at the French Open, having won the tournament four straight times. And no player in the modern era can boast a winning streak on any surface like Nadal's 81 consecutive victories on clay, a run that ended after two years with a loss to archrival Roger Federer in May 2007. With his deep shots, heavy topspin, and natural athleticism, Nadal's game is perfectly suited to clay. But he proved in 2008 that he's no one-trick pony. In June, Nadal defeated Federer to win Wimbledon. Nadal became the first player since Bjorn Borg in 1980 to win both the French Open and Wimbledon in the same year.

Grand Slam Tournaments: Women's Champions

AUSTRALIAN CHAMPIONSHIPS

YEAR	WINNER
2008	Maria Sharapova
2007	Serena Williams
2006	Amelie Mauresmo
2005	Serena Williams
2004	Justine Henin-Hardenne
2003	Serena Williams
2002	Jennifer Capriati
2001	Jennifer Capriati
2000	Lindsay Davenport
1999	Martina Hingis
1998	Martina Hingis
1997	Martina Hingis
1996	Monica Seles
1995	Mary Pierce
1994	Steffi Graf
1993	Monica Seles
1992	Monica Seles
1991	Monica Seles
1990	Steffi Graf
1989	Steffi Graf
1988	Steffi Graf
1987 (Jan.)	Hana Mandlikova
1986	No tournament
1985 (Dec.)	Martina Navratilova
1984	Chris Evert Lloyd
1983	Martina Navratilova
1982	Chris Evert Lloyd
1981	Martina Navratilova
1980	Hana Mandlikova
1979	Barbara Jordan
1978	Chris O'Neil
1977 (Dec.)	Evonne Goolagong Cawley
1977 (Jan.)	Kerry Melville Reid

Maria Sharapova

DAVID CALLOW

YEAR	WINNER
1975	Evonne Goolagong Cawley
1974	Evonne Goolagong Cawley
1973	Margaret Smith Court
1972	Virginia Wade
1971	Margaret Smith Court
1970	Margaret Smith Court
1969*	Margaret Smith Court
1968	Billie Jean King
1967	Nancy Richey
1966	Margaret Smith Court
1965	Margaret Smith Court
1964	Margaret Smith Court
1963	Margaret Smith Court
1962	Margaret Smith Court
1961	Margaret Smith Court
1960	Margaret Smith Court
1959	Mary Carter-Reitano

YEAR	WINNER
1958	Angela Mortimer
1957	Shirley Fry
1956	Mary Carter
1955	Beryl Penrose
1954	Thelma Long
1953	Maureen Connolly
1952	Thelma Long
1951	Nancye Wynne Bolton
1950	Louise Brough
1949	Doris Hart
1948	Nancye Wynne Bolton
1947	Nancye Wynne Bolton
1946	Nancye Wynne Bolton
1941–45	No tournament
1940	Nancye Wynne Bolton
1939	Emily Westacott
1938	Dorothy Bundy
1937	Nancye Wynne Bolton
1936	Joan Hartigan
1935	Dorothy Round
1934	Joan Hartigan
1933	Joan Hartigan
1932	Coral Buttsworth
1931	Coral Buttsworth
1930	Daphne Akhurst
1929	Daphne Akhurst
1928	Daphne Akhurst
1927	Esna Boyd
1926	Daphne Akhurst
1925	Daphne Akhurst
1924	Sylvia Lance
1923	Margaret Molesworth
1922	Margaret Molesworth

FRENCH CHAMPIONSHIPS

YEAR	WINNER
2008	Ana Ivanovic
2007	Justine Henin
2006	Justine Henin-Hardenne
2005	Justine Henin-Hardenne
2004	Anastasia Myskina
2003	Justine Henin-Hardenne
2002	Serena Williams
2001	Jennifer Capriati
2000	Mary Pierce
1999	Steffi Graf
1998	Arantxa Sánchez-Vicario
1997	Iva Majoli
1996	Steffi Graf
1995	Steffi Graf
1994	Arantxa Sánchez-Vicario
1993	Steffi Graf
1992	Monica Seles
1991	Monica Seles
1990	Monica Seles
1989	Arantxa Sánchez-Vicario
1988	Steffi Graf
1987	Steffi Graf
1986	Chris Evert Lloyd
1985	Chris Evert Lloyd
1984	Martina Navratilova
1983	Chris Evert Lloyd
1982	Martina Navratilova

YEAR	WINNER
1981	Hana Mandlikova
1980	Chris Evert Lloyd
1979	Chris Evert Lloyd
1978	Virginia Ruzici
1977	Mima Jausovec
1976	Sue Barker
1975	Chris Evert Lloyd
1974	Chris Evert Lloyd
1973	Margaret Smith Court
1972	Billie Jean King
1971	Evonne Goolagong Cawley
1970	Margaret Smith Court
1969	Margaret Smith Court
1968*	Nancy Richey
1967	Francoise Durr
1966	Ann Jones
1965	Lesley Turner
1964	Margaret Smith Court
1963	Lesley Turner
1962	Margaret Smith Court
1961	Ann Haydon
1960	Darlene Hard
1959	Christine Truman
1958	Zsuzsi Kormoczy
1957	Shirley Bloomer
1956	Althea Gibson
1955	Angela Mortimer

YEAR	WINNER
1954	Maureen Connolly
1953	Maureen Connolly
1952	Doris Hart
1951	Shirley Fry
1950	Doris Hart
1949	Margaret Osborne duPont
1948	Nelly Landry
1947	Patricia Todd
1946	Margaret Osborne
1940–45	No tournament
1939	Simone Mathieu
1938	Simone Mathieu
1937	Hilde Sperling
1936	Hilde Sperling
1935	Hilde Sperling
1934	Margaret Scriven
1933	Margaret Scriven
1932	Helen Wills Moody
1931	Cilly Aussem
1930	Helen Wills Moody
1929	Helen Wills Moody
1928	Helen Wills Moody
1927	Kea Bouman
1926	Suzanne Lenglen
1925**	Suzanne Lenglen

* Became Open (amateur and professional).
** 1925 was the first year in which players from all countries were allowed to compete.

Grand Slam Tournaments: Women's Champions (cont.)

WIMBLEDON CHAMPIONSHIPS

YEAR	WINNER	YEAR	WINNER	YEAR	WINNER
2008	Venus Williams	1982	Martina Navratilova	1956	Shirley Fry
2007	Venus Williams	1981	Chris Evert Lloyd	1955	Louise Brough
2006	Amelie Mauresmo	1980	Evonne Goolagong Cawley	1954	Maureen Connolly
2005	Venus Williams	1979	Martina Navratilova	1953	Maureen Connolly
2004	Maria Sharapova	1978	Martina Navratilova	1952	Maureen Connolly
2003	Serena Williams	1977	Virginia Wade	1951	Doris Hart
2002	Serena Williams	1976	Chris Evert Lloyd	1950	Louise Brough
2001	Venus Williams	1975	Billie Jean King	1949	Louise Brough
2000	Venus Williams	1974	Chris Evert Lloyd	1948	Louise Brough
1999	Lindsay Davenport	1973	Billie Jean King	1947	Margaret Osborne
1998	Jana Novotna	1972	Billie Jean King	1946	Pauline Betz
1997	Martina Hingis	1971	Evonne Goolagong Cawley	1940–45	No tournament
1996	Steffi Graf	1970	Margaret Smith Court	1939	Alice Marble
1995	Steffi Graf	1969	Ann Haydon Jones	1938	Helen Wills Moody
1994	Conchita Martinez	1968*	Billie Jean King	1937	Dorothy Round
1993	Steffi Graf	1967	Billie Jean King	1936	Helen Jacobs
1992	Steffi Graf	1966	Billie Jean King	1935	Helen Wills Moody
1991	Steffi Graf	1965	Margaret Smith Court	1934	Dorothy Round
1990	Martina Navratilova	1964	Maria Bueno	1933	Helen Wills Moody
1989	Steffi Graf	1963	Margaret Smith Court	1932	Helen Wills Moody
1988	Steffi Graf	1962	Karen Hantze Susman	1931	Cilly Aussem
1987	Martina Navratilova	1961	Angela Mortimer	1930	Helen Wills Moody
1986	Martina Navratilova	1960	Maria Bueno	1929	Helen Wills Moody
1985	Martina Navratilova	1959	Maria Bueno	1928	Helen Wills Moody
1984	Martina Navratilova	1958	Althea Gibson	1927	Helen Wills Moody
1983	Martina Navratilova	1957	Althea Gibson	1926	Kathleen McKane Godfree

* Became Open (amateur and professional).

TRIVIA

1 Which female star holds the record for fastest serve?
A. Jana Novotna
B. Brenda Schultz-McCarthy
C. Venus Williams

2 True or False: The term "love" in tennis scoring is thought to originate from the French "l'oeuf" for egg, which looks like a zero.
A. True
B. False

3 What was the first metal racket to gain widespread use?
A. Spalding Smasher
B. Prince Classic
C. Wilson T2000

4 What does Jimmy Connors hold the record for?
A. Career match wins in the Open Era
B. Career Grand Slam singles titles
C. Oldest player to win the U.S. Open

Jimmy Connors

1.B, 2.A, 3.C, 4.A

Grand Slam Tournaments: Women's Champions (cont.)

WIMBLEDON CHAMPIONSHIPS (cont.)

YEAR	WINNER	YEAR	WINNER	YEAR	WINNER
1925	Suzanne Lenglen	1909	Dora Boothby	1896	Charlotte Cooper
1924	Kathleen McKane	1908	Charlotte Cooper Sterry	1895	Charlotte Cooper
1923	Suzanne Lenglen	1907	May Sutton	1894	Blanche Bingley Hillyard
1922	Suzanne Lenglen	1906	Dorothea Douglass	1893	Charlotte Dod
1921	Suzanne Lenglen	1905	May Sutton	1892	Charlotte Dod
1920	Suzanne Lenglen	1904	Dorothea Douglass	1891	Charlotte Dod
1919	Suzanne Lenglen	1903	Dorothea Douglass	1890	Lena Rice
1915–18	No tournament	1902	Muriel Robb	1889	Blanche Bingley Hillyard
1914	Dorothea Lambert Chambers	1901	Charlotte Cooper Sterry	1888	Charlotte Dod
1913	Dorothea Lambert Chambers	1900	Blanche Bingley Hillyard	1887	Charlotte Dod
1912	Ethel Larcombe	1899	Blanche Bingley Hillyard	1886	Blanche Bingley
1911	Dorothea Lambert Chambers	1898	Charlotte Cooper	1885	Maud Watson
1910	Dorothea Lambert Chambers	1897	Blanche Bingley Hillyard	1884	Maud Watson

UNITED STATES CHAMPIONSHIPS

YEAR	WINNER	YEAR	WINNER	YEAR	WINNER
2007	Justine Henin	1961	Darlene Hard	1932	Helen Jacobs
2006	Maria Sharapova	1960	Darlene Hard	1931	Helen Wills Moody
2005	Kim Clijsters	1959	Maria Bueno	1930	Betty Nuthall
2004	Svetlana Kuznetsova	1958	Althea Gibson	1929	Helen Wills Moody
2003	Justine Henin-Hardenne	1957	Althea Gibson	1928	Helen Wills Moody
2002	Serena Williams	1956	Shirley Fry	1927	Helen Wills Moody
2001	Venus Williams	1955	Doris Hart	1926	Molla Bjurstedt Mallory
2000	Venus Williams	1954	Doris Hart	1925	Helen Wills Moody
1999	Serena Williams	1953	Maureen Connolly	1924	Helen Wills Moody
1998	Lindsay Davenport	1952	Maureen Connolly	1923	Helen Wills Moody
1997	Martina Hingis	1951	Maureen Connolly	1922	Molla Bjurstedt Mallory
1996	Steffi Graf	1950	Margaret Osborne duPont	1921	Molla Bjurstedt Mallory
1995	Steffi Graf	1949	Margaret Osborne duPont	1920	Molla Bjurstedt Mallory
1994	Arantxa Sánchez-Vicario	1948	Margaret Osborne duPont	1919	Hazel Hotchkiss Wightman
1993	Steffi Graf	1947	Louise Brough	1918	Molla Bjurstedt
1992	Monica Seles	1946	Pauline Betz	1917	Molla Bjurstedt
1991	Monica Seles	1945	Sarah Palfrey Cooke	1916	Molla Bjurstedt
1990	Gabriela Sabatini	1944	Pauline Betz	1915	Molla Bjurstedt
1989	Steffi Graf	1943	Pauline Betz	1914	Mary K. Browne
1988	Steffi Graf	1942	Pauline Betz	1913	Mary K. Browne
1987	Martina Navratilova	1941	Sarah Palfrey Cooke	1912	Mary K. Browne
1986	Martina Navratilova	1940	Alice Marble	1911	Hazel Hotchkiss
1985	Hana Mandlikova	1939	Alice Marble	1910	Hazel Hotchkiss
1984	Martina Navratilova	1938	Alice Marble	1909	Hazel Hotchkiss
1983	Martina Navratilova	1937	Anita Lizane	1908	Maud Barger-Wallach
1982	Chris Evert Lloyd	1936	Alice Marble	1907	Evelyn Sears
1981	Tracy Austin	1935	Helen Jacobs	1906	Helen Homans
1980	Chris Evert Lloyd	1934	Helen Jacobs	1905	Elisabeth Moore
1979	Tracy Austin	1933	Helen Jacobs	1904	May Sutton
1978	Chris Evert Lloyd			1903	Elisabeth Moore
1977	Chris Evert Lloyd			1902**	Marion Jones
1976	Chris Evert Lloyd			1901	Elisabeth Moore
1975	Chris Evert Lloyd			1900	Myrtle McAteer
1974	Billie Jean King			1899	Marion Jones
1973	Margaret Smith Court			1898	Juliette Atkinson
1972	Billie Jean King			1897	Juliette Atkinson
1971	Billie Jean King			1896	Elisabeth Moore
1970	Margaret Smith Court			1895	Juliette Atkinson
1969	Margaret Smith Court			1894	Helen Hellwig
1968*	Virginia Wade			1893	Aline Terry
1967	Billie Jean King			1892	Mabel Cahill
1966	Maria Bueno			1891	Mabel Cahill
1965	Margaret Smith			1890	Ellen C. Roosevelt
1964	Maria Bueno			1889	Bertha L. Townsend
1963	Maria Bueno			1888	Bertha L. Townsend
1962	Margaret Smith			1887	Ellen Hansell

Justine Henin

* Became Open (amateur and professional).
** Five-set final abolished.

Record Streaks

In March 2007, Guillermo Canas beat Roger Federer, ending Federer's 41-match winning streak. Federer's streak ties him for fourth place in the record books. Using the clues below, determine which retired players had 41-, 42-, 44-, and 46-match winning streaks and when.

1 Ivan Lendl had his streak in 1981–82, or he had a 42-game streak.

2 The Swedish player had the shortest streak or the earliest streak; the U.S. player had the longest streak or the most recent streak.

3 The 1979–80 streak (not Vilas's) was shorter than the 1983–84 streak, which was shorter than Lendl's.

4 Borg had his streak before Lendl, and Vilas had his streak before Borg.

5 The earliest record is the longest streak.

	41	43	44	46	1977	1979-80	1981-83	1983-84
Bjorn Borg								
Ivan Lendl								
John McEnroe								
Gullermo Viles								

ANSWERS ON PAGE 191

Billie Jean King, *b. November 22, 1943, Seattle, Washington.* No one did more for women's tennis — or women's sports — than King. Her resume puts her in select company: 39 Grand Slam titles, including 12 singles titles from 1966 to 1975. The speedy King won Wimbledon six times. However, it was her outspoken advocacy for women's rights that set her apart. King famously beat Bobby Riggs in the "Battle of the Sexes" in 1973.

Pete Sampras, *b. August 12, 1971, Washington, D.C.* A supremely athletic player, Sampras holds the record for Grand Slam singles titles (14). Sampras favored leaping overhead smashes, running forehands, and a serve-and-volley assault. His most potent weapon was his serve, which uncorked in a smooth, rocking motion and a wicked snap of the shoulder. His second serve was often better than most players' first offering.

Billie Jean King

Golden Boy

HEINZ KLUETMEIER

As a kid, Michael Phelps was so hyperactive that his mother took him to the swimming pool just to calm him down. Now, it's the world around him that can't seem to contain itself.

Phelps has been called "the best swimmer in the world" and "the greatest swimmer in history." One magazine went so far as to put him on the cover and call him "The Greatest Athlete of All Time." He is, at just 23 years old, the biggest fish in swimming's small pond.

The high praise is nothing new. Phelps, known as the "Baltimore Bullet," exploded on the scene at the 2000 Olympics in Sydney. He was the youngest U.S. male swimmer to compete in the Olympics since 1932 and the youngest male world record holder in modern history. He was just 15 years old.

Phelps became an international superstar after the 2004 Olympics in Athens, where he won six gold medals and two bronze. He fell just one gold short of Mark Spitz's record of seven golds, set in the 1972 Olympic Games, when he gave up his spot on the 400-meter medley relay team to Ian Crocker. The reason? Crocker, Phelps said, deserved "another shot to prove himself" after finishing second in the butterfly — to Phelps, of course. The relay team went on to win gold. At the 2007 world championships, Phelps won seven gold medals and broke five world records, and by April 2008, he had broken 23 world records.

Once again all eyes were on Phelps as he glided into the Olympics. Even his swimsuit attracted attention going into Beijing. Speedo's high-tech LZR Racer, four years in the making, debuted last February, looking like something out of a science fiction movie. Appropriately enough, NASA helped design the suit, which features seams that have been "ultrasonically bonded" instead of stitched. The idea is to keep water out and reduce the drag on a swimmer. The downside? It can

Considered the greatest swimmer in history, Michael Phelps holds six world records.

take up to 30 minutes to get into and costs a whopping $550.

After the introduction of the suit, records started falling like dominoes. By mid-April, 35 world records had been set in the suit. As U.S. swimmer Ryan Lochte said, "When I put it on, I feel like I'm some kind of action hero, ready to take on the world."

Not everyone was as enthusiastic about the suit. Purists cried foul and compared it to performance-enhancing drugs, calling the suit "technological doping" and "drugs on a hanger," even though it had been approved by FINA, swimming's governing body. This led to concerns that those wearing the LZR had an unfair advantage, leaving the swimming world with one frightening thought: Michael Phelps might actually be even faster now.

■ **Natalie Coughlin**, *b. August 23, 1982, Vallejo, California.* Coughlin finished with two golds, two silvers, and one bronze at the 2004 Games, tying the record for most medals by a U.S. female athlete in one Olympics. She grew up in a pool, swimming competitively from the age of six. Coughlin won 12 NCAA titles while at UC Berkeley, prompting SPORTS ILLUSTRATED to call her "The Future of U.S. Swimming." The three-time NCAA Swimmer of the Year was undefeated in dual meets over four years, going a remarkable 61–0. Coughlin set a world record in the 100-meter backstroke in 2007. She also took home five more medals, two of which were gold, at the world championships in Australia.

Natalie Coughlin

HEINZ KLUETMEIER

■ **Ryan Lochte**, *b. August 3, 1984, New York, New York.* Despite swimming in the shadow of teammate Michael Phelps, Lochte has been known to steal the spotlight on occasion. For example, there was the time he stood atop the podium at the 2007 world championships wearing a silver and diamond-encrusted "grill" over his teeth, like a rapper. Lochte has made a splash in the water as well, winning a gold in Athens as part of the 800-meter freestyle relay. And last April, he set four world records at the short-course world championships. One of his record-breaking swims came in the 200-meter individual medley, the same event in which he finished second to Phelps in Athens. The performance set up a huge showdown in Beijing between Lochte and Phelps in the 200-meter individual medley that placed Lochte squarely between Phelps and history.

Records: Men

FREESTYLE				
EVENT	**TIME**	**RECORD HOLDER**	**DATE**	**SITE**
50 meters	21.28	Eamon Sullivan, Australia (W)	3-28-08	Sydney, Australia
	21.59	Cullen Jones (A)	7-04-08	Omaha, Nebraska
100 meters	47.50	Alain Bernard, France (W)	3-22-08	Eindhoven, Netherlands
	47.78	Garrett Weber-Gale (A)	7-02-08	Omaha, Nebraska
200 meters	1:43.86	Michael Phelps (W, A)	3-27-07	Melbourne, Australia
400 meters	3:40.08	Ian Thorpe, Australia (W)	7-30-02	Manchester, England
	3:43.53	Larsen Jensen (A)	6-29-08	Omaha, Nebraska
800 meters	7:38.65	Grant Hackett, Australia (W)	7-27-05	Montreal, Canada
	7:45.63	Larsen Jensen (A)	7-27-05	Montreal, Canada
1,500 meters	14:34.56	Grant Hackett, Australia (W)	7-29-01	Fukuoka, Japan
	14:45.29	Larsen Jensen (A)	8-21-04	Athens, Greece

BACKSTROKE				
EVENT	**TIME**	**RECORD HOLDER**	**DATE**	**SITE**
50 meters	24.47	Liam Tancock, Great Britain (W)	4-02-08	Sheffield, Great Britain
	24.84	Randall Bal (A)	8-02-07	Paris, France
100 meters	52.89	Aaron Peirsol (W, A)	7-1-08	Omaha, Nebraska
200 meters	1:54.32	Ryan Lochte (W, A)	3-30-07	Melbourne, Australia
		Aaron Peirsol (W, A)	7-4-08	Omaha, Nebraska

KEY: W=World Record; A=American Record

Records: Men (Cont.)

EVENT	TIME	RECORD HOLDER	DATE	SITE
BREASTSTROKE				
50 meters	27.18	Oleg Lisogor, Ukraine (W)	8-02-02	Berlin, Germany
	27.39	Ed Moses (A)	3-31-01	Austin, Texas
100 meters	59.13	Brendan Hansen (W, A)	8-01-06	Irvine, California
200 meters	2:08.50	Brendan Hansen (W, A)	8-20-06	Victoria, Canada

EVENT	TIME	RECORD HOLDER	DATE	SITE
BUTTERFLY				
50 meters	22.96	Roland Schoeman, South Africa (W)	7-25-05	Montreal, Canada
	23.21	Ian Crocker (A)	7-25-05	Montreal, Canada
100 meters	50.40	Ian Crocker (W, A)	7-30-05	Montreal, Canada
200 meters	1:52.09	Michael Phelps (W, A)	3-28-07	Melbourne, Australia

EVENT	TIME	RECORD HOLDER	DATE	SITE
INDIVIDUAL MEDLEY				
200 meters	1:54.80	Michael Phelps (W, A)	7-04-08	Omaha, Nebraska
400 meters	4:05.25	Michael Phelps (W, A)	6-29-08	Omaha, Nebraska

EVENT	TIME	RECORD HOLDER	DATE	SITE
RELAYS				
400-meter medley	3:30.68	United States (W, A) (Aaron Peirsol, Brendan Hansen, Ian Crocker, Jason Lezak)	8-21-04	Athens, Greece
400-meter freestyle	3:12.46	United States (W, A) (Michael Phelps, Neil Walker, Cullen Jones, Jason Lezak)	8-19-06	Victoria, Canada
800-meter freestyle	7:03.24	United States (W, A) (Michael Phelps, Ryan Lochte, Klete Keller, Peter Vanderkaay)	3-30-07	Melbourne, Australia

KEY: W=World Record; A=American Record

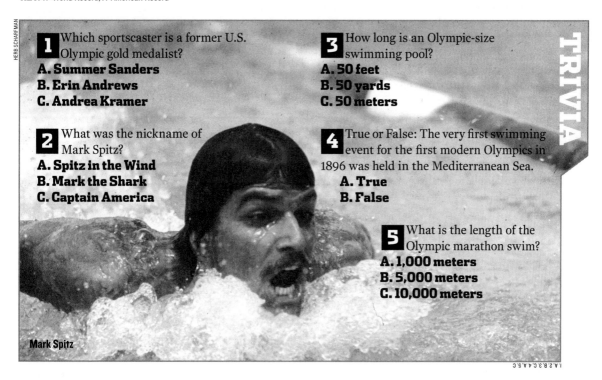

HERB SCHARFMAN

TRIVIA

1 Which sportscaster is a former U.S. Olympic gold medalist?
A. Summer Sanders
B. Erin Andrews
C. Andrea Kramer

2 What was the nickname of Mark Spitz?
A. Spitz in the Wind
B. Mark the Shark
C. Captain America

3 How long is an Olympic-size swimming pool?
A. 50 feet
B. 50 yards
C. 50 meters

4 True or False: The very first swimming event for the first modern Olympics in 1896 was held in the Mediterranean Sea.
A. True
B. False

5 What is the length of the Olympic marathon swim?
A. 1,000 meters
B. 5,000 meters
C. 10,000 meters

Mark Spitz

1.A, 2.B, 3.C, 4.A, 5.C

Records: Women

FREESTYLE				
EVENT	TIME	RECORD HOLDER	DATE	SITE
50 meters	23.97	Libby Trickett, Australia (W)	3-29-08	Sydney, Australia
	24.25	Dara Torres (A)	7-06-08	Omaha, Nebraska
100 meters	52.88	Libby Trickett, Australia (W)	3-27-08	Sydney, Australia
	53.40	Natalie Coughlin (A)	3-29-07	Melbourne, Australia
200 meters	1:55.52	Laure Manaudou, France (W)	3-28-07	Melbourne, Australia
	1:55.88	Katie Hoff (A)	7-08-08	Omaha, Nebraska
400 meters	4:01.53	Frederica Pellegrini, Italy (W)	3-24-08	Eindhoven, Netherlands
	4:02.20	Katie Hoff (A)	2-16-08	Columbia, Missouri
800 meters	8:16.22	Janet Evans (W, A)	8-20-89	Tokyo, Japan
1,500 meters	15:42.54	Kate Ziegler (W, A)	6-17-07	Mission Viejo, California

BACKSTROKE				
EVENT	TIME	RECORD HOLDER	DATE	SITE
50 meters	27.67	Sophie Edington, Australia (W)	3-23-08	Sydney, Australia
	28.00	Haley McGregory (A)	3-07-08	Austin, Texas
100 meters	58.97	Natalie Coughlin (W, A)	7-01-08	Omaha, Nebraska
200 meters	2:06.09	Margaret Hoelzer, (W, A)	7-05-08	Omaha, Nebraska

BREASTSTROKE				
EVENT	TIME	RECORD HOLDER	DATE	SITE
50 meters	30.31	Jade Edmistone, Australia (W)	1-30-06	Melbourne, Australia
	30.63	Jessica Hardy (A)	4-01-07	Melbourne, Australia
100 meters	1:05.09	Leisel Jones, Australia (W)	3-20-06	Melbourne, Australia
	1:06.20	Jessica Hardy (A)	7-25-05	Montreal, Canada
200 meters	2:20.54	Leisel Jones, Australia (W)	2-01-06	Melbourne, Australia
	2:22.44	Amanda Beard (A)	7-12-04	Long Beach, California

KEY: W=World Record; A=American Record

LEGENDS

Alexander Popov

■ **Alexander Popov**, *b. November 16, 1971, Volgograd, Russia.* Popov's nickname, the "Russian Rocket," said it all. Popov won the 50- and 100-meter freestyle at the 1992 Games in Barcelona, then repeated as champion of the 100-meter freestyle at the Atlanta Games. Popov became the first swimmer in nearly 80 years to secure back-to-back gold medals in the event. At the 2003 worlds, the 31-year-old captured the 50- and 100-meter events again to become the oldest champion in swimming history. He retired in 2005 at the age of 33, a dinosaur in swim years.

■ **Janet Evans**, *b. August 28, 1971, Fullerton, California.* Considered the greatest female distance swimmer in history, Evans made a huge splash at the 1988 Olympics in Seoul, South Korea. After claiming gold in the 400-meter individual medley, Evans also won the 400-meter and 800-meter freestyle. A year later, she captured seven national swimming titles. For her accomplishments, Evans was the recipient of the prestigious Sullivan Award in 1989, given to the nation's top amateur athlete. Evans defended her 800-meter title in the 1992 Games, further cementing her place in history.

Biggest Splash of 2008

Swimmers rewrote the record books this year, with Katie Hoff besting Janet Evans's 19-year-old American record in the 400 free with a 4:02.20 and claiming the U.S. open record in the 400 I.M. at the same meet.

Like Katie, the letters you write on the spaces are multi-talented: When joining the letters on the left, they end a word, and when joining the letters on the right, they begin a word. After filling all the spaces, transfer the letters to the boxes with the same numbers to reveal what made the biggest splash in swimming in 2008.

MEDA	___1	ANE
AREN	___2	NCHOR
LA	___3	ACE
SEE	___4	IVE
SPIT	___5	ONE
HER	___6	PEN
TAPE	___7	ELAY
MAGI	___8	LOSE
STAT	___9	VENT
SPLIT	___10	HAVE

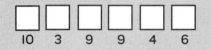
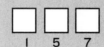

☐ ☐ ☐ ☐ ☐ ☐   ☐ ☐ ☐   ☐ ☐ ☐ ☐ ☐
10 3 9 9 4 6   1 5 7   7 2 8 9 7

ANSWERS ON PAGE 191

Records: Women (Cont.)

BUTTERFLY

EVENT	TIME	RECORD HOLDER	DATE	SITE
50 meters	25.46	Therese Alshammar, Sweden (W)	6-13-07	Barcelona, Spain
	26.00	Jenny Thompson (A)	7-26-03	Barcelona, Spain
100 meters	56.61	Inge de Bruijn, Netherlands (W)	9-17-00	Sydney, Australia
	57.34	Natalie Coughlin (A)	3-26-07	Melbourne, Australia
200 meters	2:05.40	Jessicah Schipper, Australia (W)	8-17-06	Victoria, Canada
	2:05.88	Misty Hyman (A)	9-20-00	Sydney, Australia

INDIVIDUAL MEDLEY

EVENT	TIME	RECORD HOLDER	DATE	SITE
200 meters	2:08.92	Stephanie Rice, Australia (W)	3-25-08	Sydney, Australia
	2:09.71	Katie Hoff (A)	7-02-08	Omaha, Nebraska
400 meters	4:31.12	Katie Hoff (W, A)	6-29-08	Omaha, Nebraska

RELAYS

EVENT	TIME	RECORD HOLDER	DATE	SITE
400-meter medley	3:55.74	Australia (W) (Emily Seebohm, Leisel Jones, Jessicah Schipper, Lisbeth Lenton)	3-31-07	Melbourne, Australia
	3:58.30	United States (A) (B.J. Bedford, Megan Quann, Jenny Thompson, Dara Torres)	9-23-00	Sydney, Australia
400-meter freestyle	3:33.62	Netherlands (W) (Inge Dekker, Ranomi Kromowidjojo, Femke Heemskerk, Marleen Veldhuis)	3-18-08	Eindhoven, Netherlands
	3:35.68	United States (A) (Natalie Coughlin, Lacey Nymeyer, Amanda Weir, Kara Lynn Joyce)	3-25-07	Melbourne, Australia
800-meter freestyle	7:50.09	United States (W, A) (Natalie Coughlin, Dana Vollmer, Lacey Nymeyer, Katie Hoff)	3-29-07	Melbourne, Australia

KEY: W=World Record; A=American Record

The Fastest Show on Earth

Tyson Gay was the best U.S. hope for gold in the 100-meter dash at the 2008 Beijing Olympics.

You might miss it in the blink of an eye. The 100-meter dash, the highlight of the Summer Games, lasts about only 10 seconds for runners who have trained years for this moment. The only event at the very first Olympics in ancient Greece in 776 B.C. was a "stade" — a race on flat ground. Almost 3,000 years later, the event remains unchanged and the core of the Games. The event is a measure of pure power and speed that has always awed sports fans. The winner is awarded the title of "Fastest Man in the World."

But many wonder if the age-old event has been tarnished.

Scandal is not new to the sport. Canadian sprinter Ben Johnson was stripped of his gold medal at the 1988 Games for the use of performance-enhancing drugs. He was later banned from racing for life after failing another drug test. But the track and field community has swirled with even more controversy about illegal drug use in recent years; it has particularly scarred this event.

U.S. sprinter Marion Jones, who won gold in the 100 meters at the 2000 Sydney Games, admitted to using steroids in 2008 and ended up in jail, in part due to denying her use to federal investigators. Tim Montgomery set a new world record for the event in 2002, with a time of 9.78. While he tested drug-free at the time, Montgomery was later found to be supplied with performance-enhancing drugs. He was stripped of his world record in December 2005. Justin Gatlin won the 100-meter dash at the 2004 Games and currently holds the title of Fastest Man in the World, but he did not defend his title in Beijing. He was banned from the sport in 2006 after testing positive for excessive testosterone.

Critics also complain that setting a world record in the 100-meter dash is not the same accomplishment it used to be. After all, the record has been tied or broken 18 times in the last 24 years.

And to be fair, they're right: Times can no longer be compared across decades. Equipment is constantly improved, athletes train much harder and longer than ever before, diets are better, and the track conditions are unique to each race.

But even with all its flaws, the whole world will still watch the 100-meter dash in Beijing and the anticipated showdown between countrymen Usain Bolt and Asafa Powell of Jamaica. In the end, there's still nothing more exciting than a great race.

Allyson Felix of the U.S. is a two-time world champion in the 200-meter dash.

■ **Gail Devers,** *b. November 19, 1966, Seattle, Washington.* Famous for her long fingernails, Devers won the 100 meters at the 1992 Games and was set to win the 100-meter hurdles before falling down on the last jump. In 1996, she repeated as 100-meter champion, only the second woman to win the event in back-to-back Games. She also won a gold in the 4 x 100 relay in Atlanta. A nine-time U.S. 100-meter hurdles champion, Devers competed in a remarkable four Olympic Games and is considered the greatest combination sprinter and hurdler ever.

Gail Devers

GEORGE TIEDEMANN

■ **Carl Lewis,** *b. July 1, 1961, Birmingham, Alabama.* It's hard to determine which of Lewis's many accomplishments is most impressive. In 1983, he won the 100 meters, 200 meters, and long jump at the U.S. national championships — the first person to do this in almost 100 years. He won 65 consecutive competitions in the long jump, a streak that lasted 10 years. Lewis has won nine Olympic gold medals, including four at the 1984 Games. And in 1996, his fifth Olympics, Lewis won his fourth gold in the long jump at the age of 35.

Coach Says

Do what the coach says (and only what the coach says) to reveal a fact about track and field great Jenn Stuczynski.

Jenn Stuczynski

MICHAEL ZITO/SPORTSCHROME

1 Coach says, "Cross off the words with fewer than four letters in row 6 and column B."

2 Coach says, "Cross off all the track and field events in row 3 and column E."

3 Cross off the pronouns in columns B and C.

4 Coach says, "Cross off all the synonyms of 'run.'"

5 Coach says, "Cross off all the multiples of 4 in row 5 and column F."

6 Coach says, "Read the remaining letters to solve the puzzle."

	A	B	C	D	E	F
1	RACE	IF	SHE	TROT	IS	FOUR
2	THE	BY	SPRINT	FIRST	100 METERS	AMERICAN
3	400 METERS	WOMAN	HAMMER	HURDLES	TO	CLEAR
4	SIXTEEN	HER	JOG	FEET	IN	DASH
5	THE	EIGHT	POLE	12	DISCUS	20
6	ON	VAULT	DART	FOR	LONG JUMP	DID

ANSWERS ON PAGE 191

World Records: Men

EVENT	MARK	RECORD HOLDER	DATE	SITE
100 meters	9.74	Usain Bolt, Jamaica	5-31-08	New York, New York
200 meters	19.32	Michael Johnson, United States	8-1-96	Atlanta, Georgia
400 meters	43.18	Michael Johnson, United States	8-26-99	Seville, Spain
800 meters	1:41.11	Wilson Kipketer, Denmark	8-24-97	Cologne, Germany
1,000 meters	2:11.96	Noah Ngeny, Kenya	9-5-99	Rieti, Italy
1,500 meters	3:26.00	Hicham El Guerrouj, Morocco	7-14-98	Rome, Italy
Mile	3:43.13	Hicham El Guerrouj, Morocco	7-7-99	Rome, Italy
2,000 meters	4:44.79	Hicham El Guerrouj, Morocco	9-7-99	Berlin, Germany
3,000 meters	7:20.67	Daniel Komen, Kenya	9-1-96	Rieti, Italy
Steeplechase	7:53.63	Saif Saaeed Shaheen, Qatar	9-3-04	Brussels, Belgium
5,000 meters	12:37.35	Kenenisa Bekele, Ethiopia	5-31-04	Hengelo, Netherlands
10,000 meters	26:17.53	Kenenisa Bekele, Ethiopia	8-26-05	Brussels, Belgium
20,000 meters	56:26.0	Haile Gebrselassie, Ethiopia	6-27-07	Ostrava, Czech Republic
Hour	21.285 kilometers	Haile Gebrselassie, Ethiopia	6-27-07	Ostrava, Czech Republic
25,000 meters	1:13:55.8	Toshihiko Seko, Japan	3-22-81	Christchurch, New Zealand
30,000 meters	1:29:18.8	Toshihiko Seko, Japan	3-22-81	Christchurch, New Zealand
Marathon	2:04:26.0	Haile Gebrselassie, Ethiopia	9-30-07	Berlin, Germany
110-meter Hurdles	12.87	Dayron Robles, Cuba	6-12-08	Ostrava, Czech Republic
400-meter Hurdles	46.78	Kevin Young, United States	8-6-92	Barcelona, Spain
10,000-meter Walk	38:46.4	Viktor Burayev, Russia	5-20-00	Moskva, Russia
20,000-meter Walk	1:17:25.6	Bernardo Segura, Mexico	5-7-94	Bergen, Norway
30,000-meter Walk	2:01:44.1	Maurizio Damilano, Italy	10-3-92	Cuneo, Italy
4 x 100-meter Relay	37.40*	United States (Mike Marsh, Leroy Burrell, Dennis Mitchell, Carl Lewis)	8-8-92	Barcelona, Spain
		United States (Jon Drummond, Andre Cason, Dennis Mitchell, Leroy Burrell)	8-21-93	Stuttgart, Germany
4 x 200-meter Relay	1:18.68	Santa Monica TC (Mike Marsh, Leroy Burrell, Dennis Mitchell, Carl Lewis)	4-17-94	Walnut, California
4 x 400-meter Relay	2:54.20	United States (Jerome Young, Antonio Pettigrew, Tyree Washington, Michael Johnson)	7-22-98	New York, New York
4 x 800-meter Relay	7:02.43	Kenya (Joseph Mutua, William Yiampoy, Ismael Kombich, Wilfred Bungei)	8-25-06	Brussels, Belgium
4 x 1,500-meter Relay	14:38.8	West Germany (Thomas Wessinghage, Harald Hudak, Michael Lederer, Karl Fleschen)	8-17-77	Cologne, Germany
High Jump	2.45 meters	Javier Sotomayor, Cuba	7-27-93	Salamanca, Spain
Pole Vault	6.14 meters	Sergei Bubka, Ukraine	7-31-94	Sestriere, Italy
Long Jump	8.95 meters	Mike Powell, United States	8-30-91	Tokyo, Japan
Triple Jump	18.29 meters	Jonathan Edwards, Great Britain	8-7-95	Goteborg, Sweden
Shot Put	23.12 meters	Randy Barnes, United States	5-20-90	Westwood, California
Discus Throw	74.08 meters	Jurgen Schult, East Germany	6-6-86	Neubrandenburg, Germany
Hammer Throw	86.74 meters	Yuri Syedikh, U.S.S.R.	8-30-86	Stuttgart, Germany
Javelin Throw	98.48 meters	Jan Zelezny, Czech Republic	5-25-96	Jena, Germany
Decathlon	9,026 points	Roman Sebrle, Czech Republic	5-27-01	Gotzis, Austria

* Pending expulsion

■ **Alan Webb,** *b. January 13, 1983, Ann Arbor, Michigan.* Webb became a celebrity in 2001 after setting the national high school record in the mile with a time of 3:53.43. It eclipsed the record set by Jim Ryun 36 years earlier. His key to success? Ice cream. Webb indulges in it before all big meets and his favorite is mint chocolate chip. He had an uncharacteristically poor performance at the 2004 Olympics and did not advance past the first round. But heading into the 2008 Games, Webb is back at the top of his game. In July 2007, Webb broke the U.S. record in the mile held by Steve Scott for 25 years. He was also the 2007 indoor mile champion and outdoor 1,500-meter champion.

Alan Webb

■ **Bryan Clay,** *b. January 3, 1980, Austin, Texas.* A decathlete, Clay attended the tiny university of Azusa Pacific in Los Angeles to train under coach Kevin Reid, still his coach to this day. There, Clay won the 2000 NAIA championship in the decathlon and emerged as one of the country's top athletes in the event. He came up just short of a gold medal in Athens, settling for silver instead. Clay has only gotten stronger since then. He finished the 2005 and 2006 seasons ranked No. 1 in the world in the decathlon. Clay was the first U.S. athlete in 10 years to finish first in back-to-back seasons. Riddled with injuries in 2007, Clay recovered to win the 2008 world indoor championship as he prepared for Beijing. His strongest events in the decathlon are the 100 meters, long jump, 110-meter hurdles, and discus.

PETER READ MILLER

World Records: Women

EVENT	MARK	RECORD HOLDER	DATE	SITE
100 meters	10.49	Florence Griffith Joyner, United States	7-16-88	Indianapolis, Indiana
200 meters	21.34	Florence Griffith Joyner, United States	9-29-88	Seoul, Korea
400 meters	47.60	Marita Koch, East Germany	10-6-85	Canberra, Australia
800 meters	1:53.28	Jarmila Kratochvílová, Czechoslovakia	7-26-83	Munich, Germany
1,000 meters	2:28.98	Svetlana Masterkova, Russia	8-23-96	Brussels, Belgium
1,500 meters	3:50.46	Qu Yunxia, China	9-11-93	Beijing, China
Mile	4:12.56	Svetlana Masterkova, Russia	8-14-96	Zurich, Switzerland
2,000 meters	5:25.36	Sonia O'Sullivan, Ireland	7-8-94	Edinburgh, Scotland
3,000 meters	8:06.11	Wang Junxia, China	9-13-93	Beijing, China
Steeplechase	9:01.59	Gulnara Samitova-Galkina, Russia	4-7-04	Iraklio, Greece
5,000 meters	14:11.15	Tirunesh Dibaba, Ethiopia	6-6-08	Oslo, Norway
10,000 meters	29:31.78	Wang Junxia, China	9-8-93	Beijing, China
20,000 meters	1:05:26.6	Tegla Loroupe, Kenya	9-3-00	Borgholzhausen, Germany
Hour	18.157 kilometers	Dire Tune, Ethiopia	6-12-08	Ostrava, Czech Republic
25,000 meters	1:27:05.9	Tegla Loroupe, Kenya	9-21-02	Mengerskirchen, Germany
30,000 meters	1:45:50.0	Tegla Loroupe, Kenya	6-6-03	Warstein, Germany
Marathon	2:15:25.0	Paula Radclifffe, Great Britain	4-13-03	London, England

World Records: Women (Cont.)

EVENT	MARK	RECORD HOLDER	DATE	SITE
100-meter Hurdles	12.21	Yordanka Donkova, Bulgaria	8-20-88	Stara Zgora, Bulgaria
400-meter Hurdles	52.34	Yuliya Pechenkina, Russia	8-8-03	Tula, Russia
10,000-meter Walk	41:56.23	Nadezhda Ryashkina, Russia	7-24-90	Seattle, Washington
20,000-meter Walk	1:26:52.3	Olimpiada Ivanova, Russia	9-6-01	Brisbane, Australia
4x100-meter Relay	41.37	East Germany (Silke Gladisch, Sabine Reiger, Ingrid Auerswald, Marlies Gohr)	10-6-85	Canberra, Australia
4 x 200-meter Relay	1:27.46	United States (LaTasha Jenkins, LaTasha Colander-Richardson, Nanceen Perry, Marion Jones)	4-29-00	Philadelphia, Pennsylvania
4 x 400-meter Relay	3:15.17	U.S.S.R. (Tatyana Ledovskaya, Olga Nazarova, Maria Pinigina, Olga Bryzgina)	10-1-88	Seoul, Korea
4 x 800-meter Relay	7:50.17	U.S.S.R. (Nadezhda Olizarenko, Lyubov Gurina, Lyudmila Borisova, Irina Podyalovskaya)	8-5-84	Moscow, Russia
High Jump	2.09 meters	Stefka Kostadinova, Bulgaria	8-30-87	Rome, Italy
Pole Vault	5.01 meters	Yelena Isinbayeva, Russia	8-12-05	Helsinki, Finland
Long Jump	7.52 meters	Galina Chistyakova, U.S.S.R.	6-11-88	Leningrad, Russia
Triple Jump	15.50 meters	Inessa Kravets, Ukraine	8-10-95	Goteborg, Sweden
Shot Put	22.63 meters	Natalya Lisovskaya, U.S.S.R.	6-7-87	Moscow, Russia
Discus Throw	76.80 meters	Gabriele Reinsch, East Germany	7-9-88	Neubrandenburg, Germany
Hammer Throw	77.80 meters	Tatyana Lysenko, Russia	8-15-06	Tallinn, Estonia
Javelin Throw	71.70 meters	Osleidys Menéndez, Cuba	8-14-05	Helsinki, Finland
Heptathlon	7,291 points	Jackie Joyner-Kersee, United States	9-24-88	Seoul, Korea
Decathlon	8,358 points	Austra Skujyte, Lithuania	4-15-05	Columbia, Missouri

TRIVIA

1 The 26-mile race known as a "marathon" is named after a city in which country?
A. Italy
B. Greece
C. Egypt

2 What happens if a runner drops the baton during a relay race?
A. Disqualified
B. Goes to back
C. Deducted 10 seconds

3 How many events are in a decathlon?
A. 5
B. 10
C. 15

4 Who is NOT a famous female Olympic athlete?
A. Jackie Joyner-Kersee
B. Florence Griffith Joyner
C. Joyner Florence-Griffith

5 Which of the following is an actual Olympic event?
A. Double Jump
B. Triple Jump
C. Quadruple Jump

6 What did Michael Johnson wear at the 1996 Olympics?
A. Gold belt
B. Gold shoes
C. Gold shorts

Michael Johnson

1.B, 2.A, 3.B, 4.C, 5.B, 6.B

Beijing's Moment

Ever since China won the bid to host the 2008 Olympic Games, the whole world has anticipated the massive coming-out party. With the Games in its capital of Beijing, China prepared to establish its place an as international power. But as Beijing built brand-new, state-of-the-art facilities in preparation for the Games, controversy also arose. Athletes spoke of the dangerous levels of pollution. For a time there was talk of the Olympics being boycotted by certain countries because of human rights issues. And then there was the torch, under heavy guard as it made its way around the world. An icon of the Olympic spirit became a symbol of protest against the Games' host country.

The Olympics have always been a global venue for the issues of the day. In 1920, the games were held in Antwerp, Belgium, to commemorate the suffering of the Belgian people in World War I. In 1936, the great African American sprinter Jesse Owens humiliated Adolf Hitler by winning four gold medals in Berlin, Germany. The 1952 Games in Helsinki, Finland, marked the start of the Cold War. In 1968, Tommie Smith *(see Legends, p. 176)* raised his fist and made the Black Power salute at the Mexico City Games. Palestinian terrorists murdered 11 Israeli athletes in Munich in 1972. And several countries boycotted the 1980 Moscow Games in communist Russia.

So it was no surprise that people were so upset over Beijing 2008. As China's economy has exploded over the last decade, the nation

of 1.3 billion people has turned into one of the world's great polluters. Worried about the smog that often chokes Beijing, the Chinese government relocated some power plants downwind and planned to shut off others during the Games. Of course, this led

CSPA/US PRESSWIRE

Beijing National Stadium — nicknamed the "Bird's Nest" — glows at night. The building is the site of the 2008 Olympic opening and closing ceremonies as well as the track and field events.

others during the Games. Of course, this led to complaints that many locals would have to go without electricity. The government also bulldozed historic neighborhoods to make room for new facilities.

Despite all the issues, the Games are scheduled to go on as planned and China is to have its moment in the sun. Let's hope the spirit of the Olympics, which are about bringing the world together in a peaceful, open celebration, will linger on in the Middle Kingdom.

TODAY'S STARS

■ **Shawn Johnson,** *b. January 19, 1992, Des Moines, Iowa.* Johnson started life with a high degree of difficulty. She was born cold and blue and without a pulse. But she showed a competitive spirit, even as an infant. Within nine months, Johnson was walking. Crib pull-ups soon followed. Gymnastics came later, at age three. Now 16, Johnson is one of the top gymnasts in the world. In the 2007 Pan American Games, she won four gold medals. In the world championships, she won the all-around competition and led the U.S. team to victory over China. She's also the two-time U.S. all-around champion.

Shawn Johnson

■ **Usain Bolt,** *b. August 21, 1986, Trelawny, Jamaica.* They call him "Lightning Bolt," and it's easy to see why: Bolt possesses supernatural speed. Running in just his fifth 100-meter race, Bolt smashed countryman Asafa Powell's world record, lowering the time to 9.72 seconds. With his tall, lean frame (6'5") and lanky gait, Bolt previously stood out in the 200 and 400 meters (he won silver in the 200 at the 2007 world championships). His running mechanics look unusual next to the compact, muscular strides of other 100-meter sprinters, but there's no arguing with the results.

GAME TIME

Olympic Anagrams

What is the only track and field event in which a men's world record has never been set at an Olympic Games?

Each of the phrases below is an anagram of an Olympic sport. Rearrange the letters of each phrase and write the sport in the boxes provided. If you identify the sports correctly, the letters in one of the columns (we're not telling which one) will spell the answer.

1. Tom in band
2. Sign my cast
3. Girls went
4. Flatkid dancer
5. Quiet snare
6. Blabs at elk
7. Elf in tight wig
8. Ran to hilt
9. A towel pro
10. In o ghost
11. Woken toad

ANSWERS ON PAGE 191

Past Summer Olympic Hosts

	YEAR	HOST	DATES	MEN	WOMEN	NATIONS
XXIX	2008	BEIJING, CHINA	August 8–24	5,775	4,725	205
XXVIII	2004	ATHENS, GREECE	August 13–29	6,452	4,412	202
XXVII	2000	SYDNEY, AUSTRALIA	September 15–October 1	6,582	4,069	199
XXVI	1996	ATLANTA, GEORGIA, USA	July 19–August 4	6,806	3,512	197
XXV	1992	BARCELONA, SPAIN	July 25–August 9	6,652	2,704	169
XXIV	1988	SEOUL, KOREA	September 17–October 2	6,197	2,194	159
XXIII	1984	LOS ANGELES, CALIFORNIA, USA	July 28–August 12	5,263	1,566	140
XXII	1980	MOSCOW, USSR	July 19–August 3	4,064	1,115	80
XXI	1976	MONTREAL, QUEBEC, CANADA	July 17–August 1	4,824	1,260	92
XX	1972	MUNICH, WEST GERMANY	August 26–September 11	6,075	1,059	121
XIX	1968	MEXICO CITY, MEXICO	October 12–27	4,735	781	112
XVIII	1964	TOKYO, JAPAN	October 10–24	4,473	678	93
XVII	1960	ROME, ITALY	August 25–September 11	4,727	611	83
XVI	1956	MELBOURNE, AUSTRALIA	November 22–December 8	2,938	376	72
XV	1952	HELSINKI, FINLAND	July 19–August 3	4,436	519	69
XIV	1948	LONDON, GREAT BRITAIN	July 29–August 14	3,714	390	59
XIII	1944	LONDON, GREAT BRITAIN	Canceled because of World War II			
XII	1940	TOKYO, JAPAN	Canceled because of World War II			
XI	1936	BERLIN, GERMANY	August 1–16	3,632	331	49
X	1932	LOS ANGELES, CALIFORNIA, USA	July 30–August 14	1,206	126	37
IX	1928	AMSTERDAM, THE NETHERLANDS	May 17–August 12	2,606	277	46
VIII	1924	PARIS, FRANCE	May 4–July 27	2,954	135	44
VII	1920	ANTWERP, BELGIUM	April 20–September 12	2,561	65	29
VI	1916	BERLIN, GERMANY	Canceled because of World War I			
V	1912	STOCKHOLM, SWEDEN	May 5–July 27	2,359	48	28
IV	1908	LONDON, GREAT BRITAIN	April 27–October 31	1,971	37	22
—	1906*	ATHENS, GREECE	April 22–May 2	877	7	20
III	1904	ST. LOUIS, MISSOURI, USA	July 1–November 23	645	6	12
II	1900	PARIS, FRANCE	May 14–October 28	975	22	24
I	1896	ATHENS, GREECE	April 6–15	241	0	14

* Medals won at these Games are not officially recognized by the IOC.

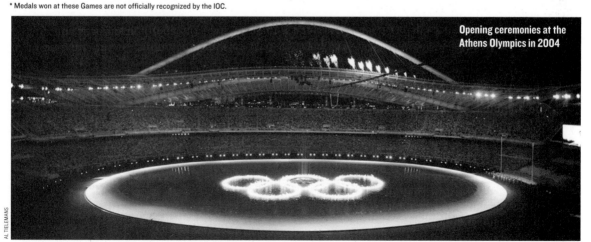

Opening ceremonies at the Athens Olympics in 2004

AL TIELEMANS

■ **Tommie Smith,** *b. June 6, 1944, Clarksville, Texas.* As is often the case in the Olympics, Smith's victory at the 1968 Games in Mexico City was about so much more than sports. Having just won gold and set a world record in the 200 meters, Smith and teammate John Carlos made history on the awards podium. While "The Star-Spangled Banner" played in Smith's honor, both he and Carlos raised a gloved fist in a Black Power salute. While controversial at the time, the gesture is now regarded as a crucial milestone in the civil rights movement. A statue of the moment now stands at their alma mater, San Jose State University. Smith also made history as the only man ever to hold 11 track and field world records at the same time.

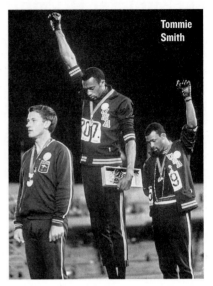

Tommie Smith

■ **Alexander Karelin,** *b. September 19, 1967, Novosibirsk, Russia.* Russia's real-life answer to Paul Bunyan, Karelin grew up in Siberia and became a standout Greco-Roman wrestler by running in thigh-deep snow, hauling logs through hinterland forests, and rowing on chilly lakes until his hands bled. Nicknamed the "Russian Bear," he grew to massive proportions (nearly 300 pounds, all muscle) and was a terror in Olympic competition. With his enormous strength, Karelin perfected a reverse body lock that he used to fling other behemoths through the air like toys. It was called the "Karelin Lift." The grappler won super heavyweight gold in 1988, 1992, and 1996. In 13 years of international competition, he lost only once — to U.S. wrestler Rulon Gardner in the 2000 Olympic finals.

All-Time Summer Olympic Medal Count: Nation

NATION	GOLD	SILVER	BRONZE	TOTAL
UNITED STATES	907	697	615	2,219
SOVIET UNION (1952–88)	395	319	296	1,010
GREAT BRITAIN	189	242	237	668
FRANCE	199	202	230	631
ITALY	189	154	168	511
GERMANY (1896–1936, 1992–PRESENT)	151	154	178	483
SWEDEN	140	157	179	476
HUNGARY	158	141	161	460
EAST GERMANY (1956–88)	159	150	136	445
AUSTRALIA	119	126	154	399
JAPAN	113	106	114	333
WEST GERMANY (1952–88)	77	104	120	301
FINLAND	101	83	114	298
CHINA	112	96	78	286
ROMANIA	82	88	114	284
POLAND	59	74	118	251
RUSSIA	85	79	84	248
CANADA	54	87	101	242
THE NETHERLANDS	65	76	94	235

Note: Medal count is through 2004 Olympics.

I-to-Eye

Find and circle the summer Olympics "I" words in the letter grid. Words can be up, down, left, right, or diagonal. Watch out! Wherever the letter "I" appears, there is a 👁 instead. ("TRIAL" would be TR👁AL.) When you've found all the words, start at the top and write the unused letters in order from left to right on the spaces to reveal where all the Is are.

BADMINTON
BEIBEI
BEIJING
BIKE
CHINA
DISCUS
DIVING
FIELD

FINISH
FOIL
INDIVIDUAL
NINI
OLYMPICS
POINT
RINGS

SAILING
SILVER
SWIM
TENNIS
TIME
WEIGHTLIFTING
WIN

Unused letters: __ __ __ __ __ __ __ __ __ __ __

__ __ __ __ __ __ __ __ __ __ __ __ __ __ __ __ __ __ __ __ __ __ __ __ __.

```
A D 👁 V 👁 N G L A L D O
E E Y E D S N N A R L W
E M B E 👁 J 👁 N G Y E 👁
F 👁 N 👁 S H T O M R 👁 N
N T S W C 👁 F P E M F M
      U E 👁 V
      S C L 👁
      S 👁 T N
      S R H D
      M L G 👁
      👁 👁 V
T N 👁 O P B E 👁 B E 👁 R
C H F A E N W D M K L 👁
T E N N 👁 S P U H 👁 E N
N O T N 👁 M D A B B W G
L P 👁 S S A 👁 L 👁 N G S
```

ANSWERS ON PAGE 191

1 En route to a gold medal in the 1992 Barcelona Olympics, Magic Johnson and the Dream Team beat their opponents by an average of how many points?
A. 44
B. 52
C. 32

Magic Johnson

2 True or False: The ceremonial shot put used in the first modern Olympics was a cannonball recovered from the battle for the Arkadi monastery during the Cretan revolution against the Ottoman Empire in 1866.
A. True
B. False

3 Dick Fosbury introduced the Fosbury Flop at the 1968 Games. What was it?
A. A stylish new hairstyle.
B. An improved way of jumping over the high bar backward.
C. A risky diving maneuver.

4 True or False: After winning five gold medals in swimming in the 1924 and 1928 Games, Johnny Weissmuller starred as the original Hollywood Tarzan.
A. True
B. False

5 At the first modern Olympic Games in Athens in 1896, which athlete won the first gold medal and in what event?
A. Carl Schumann (Germany), gymnastics
B. James Connolly (U.S.), triple jump
C. Spyridon Louis (Greece), marathon

1.A, 2.B, 3.B, 4.A, 5.B

Preparing for a Snow Show

The XXIX Summer Olympics in Beijing, China, took center stage in 2008, but half a world away, a different show was getting ready for the spotlight. The XXI Winter Olympics will take place February 12–28, 2010, in Vancouver, British Columbia, Canada. Thousands of athletes from across the world will compete in seven sports: skiing and snowboarding, bobsled, skating, luge, biathlon, ice hockey, and curling. In addition to the events included in the 2006 Olympics, the ski cross event will make its debut. The venues for the 2010 Games will include the mountain resort of Whistler, just north of Vancouver. Canada won 24 medals at the 2006 Games, good for third place in the final medal count. The home-slope advantage should help Canada challenge for the top spot in 2010.

The ski resort in Whistler, British Columbia, Canada, will host several of the ski and sliding events at the XXI Winter Olympic Games.

Winter Wonders

What former NFL star was also a member of the 1992 U.S. men's Olympic bobsled team in Albertville?

The NFL player didn't win a medal at the Olympics, but the nine athletes whose names are shown on the circles to the right did. At the end of each name is an extra letter. Find the name (they all read clockwise) in each circle and write the extra letter on the space provided. Transfer the letters from the spaces to the boxes with the same numbers to reveal the answer to the question.

2	8	5	4	9	2	8	3

1	7	3	6	8	5

ANSWERS ON PAGE 191

Turin 2006 Medal Count: Nation

NATION	GOLD	SILVER	BRONZE	TOTAL
GERMANY	11	12	6	29
UNITED STATES	9	9	7	25
CANADA	7	10	7	24
AUSTRIA	9	7	7	23
RUSSIA	8	6	8	22
NORWAY	2	8	9	19
SWEDEN	7	2	5	14
SWITZERLAND	5	4	5	14
SOUTH KOREA	6	3	2	11
ITALY	5	0	6	11
CHINA	2	4	5	11
FRANCE	3	2	4	9
NETHERLANDS	3	2	4	9

NATION	GOLD	SILVER	BRONZE	TOTAL
FINLAND	0	6	3	9
CZECH REPUBLIC	1	2	1	4
ESTONIA	3	0	0	3
CROATIA	1	2	0	3
AUSTRALIA	1	0	1	2
POLAND	0	1	1	2
UKRAINE	0	0	2	2
JAPAN	1	0	0	1
BELARUS	0	1	0	1
BULGARIA	0	1	0	1
GREAT BRITAIN	0	1	0	1
SLOVAKIA	0	1	0	1
LATVIA	0	0	1	1

■ **Bode Miller,** *alpine skier, b. December 10, 1977, Franconia, New Hampshire.* Miller won the overall alpine skiing World Cup title in 2005 and 2008. With 31 wins in World Cup events, Miller is the most successful U.S. alpine skier ever.

Bode Miller

FABRICE COFFRINI/AFP/GETTY IMAGES

■ **Maya Pedersen,** *skeleton racer, b. November 27, 1972, Thun, Switzerland.* After a fifth-place finish at the 2002 Salt Lake City Olympics, Pedersen took time off to start a family. She blasted back onto the scene in 2005, winning the world title and then the gold medal at the Turin Games in 2006. With her four world championship medals and six European championship medals, Pedersen is one of the most successful skeleton racers in the world.

■ **Pete Fenson,** *curler, b. February 29, 1968, Bemidji, Minnesota.* Fenson guided the U.S. curling team to its first-ever Olympic medal, winning the bronze in 2006. The son of curling parents, Fenson has led his team to five national championships and three appearances at the world championships.

Past Winter Olympic Hosts

	YEAR	HOST	DATES	MEN	WOMEN	NATIONS
XX	2006	TURIN, ITALY	February 10–16	1,611	996	84
XIX	2002	SALT LAKE CITY, UNITED STATES	February 8–24	1,513	886	77
XVIII	1998	NAGANO, JAPAN	February 7–22	1,389	787	72
XVI	1994	LILLEHAMMER, NORWAY	February 12–27	1,215	522	67
XVI	1992	ALBERTVILLE, FRANCE	February 8–23	1,313	488	64
XV	1988	CALGARY, CANADA	February 13–28	1,122	301	57
XIV	1984	SARAJEVO, YUGOSLAVIA	February 8–19	998	274	49
XIII	1980	LAKE PLACID, UNITED STATES	February 13–24	840	232	37
XII	1976	INNSBRUCK, AUSTRIA	February 4–15	892	231	37
XI	1972	SAPPORO, JAPAN	February 3–13	801	205	35
X	1968	GRENOBLE, FRANCE	February 6–18	947	211	37
IX	1964	INNSBRUCK, AUSTRIA	January 29–February 9	892	199	36
VIII	1960	SQUAW VALLEY, UNITED STATES	February 18–28	521	144	30
VII	1956	CORTINA D'AMPEZZO, ITALY	January 26–February 5	687	134	32
VI	1952	OSLO, NORWAY	February 14–25	585	109	30
V	1948	ST. MORITZ, SWITZERLAND	January 30–February 8	592	77	28
—	1944	CORTINA D'AMPEZZO, ITALY	Canceled because of World War II			
—	1940	GARMISCH-PARTENKIRCHEN, GERMANY	Canceled because of World War II			
IV	1936	GARMISCH-PARTENKIRCHEN, GERMANY	February 6–16	566	80	28
III	1932	LAKE PLACID, UNITED STATES	February 4–15	231	21	17
II	1928	ST. MORITZ, SWITZERLAND	February 11–19	438	26	25
I	1924	CHAMONIX, FRANCE	January 25–February 5	247	11	16

All-Time Winter Olympic Medal Count: Nation

NATION	GOLD	SILVER	BRONZE	TOTAL
NORWAY	98	98	84	280
UNITED STATES	79	79	58	216
SOVIET UNION (1956–88)	78	56	59	193
AUSTRIA	51	64	70	185
GERMANY	68	65	46	179
FINLAND	41	57	52	150
CANADA	38	38	43	119
SWEDEN	43	31	44	118
SWITZERLAND	37	37	43	117
EAST GERMANY (1956–88)	39	36	35	110

All-Time Winter Olympic Medal Count: Men

ATHLETE	SPORT	GOLD	SILVER	BRONZE	TOTAL
BJORN DAEHLIE, Norway	Nordic Skiing	8	4	0	12
OLE EINAR BJOERNDALEN, Norway	Biathlon	5	3	1	9
SIXTEN JERNBERG, Sweden	Nordic Skiing	4	3	2	9
RICCO GROSS, Germany	Biathlon	4	3	1	8
KJETIL ANDRE AAMODT, Norway	Alpine Skiing	4	2	2	8
A. CLAS THUNBERG, Finland	Speed Skating	5	1	1	7
IVAR BALLANGRUD, Norway	Speed Skating	4	2	1	7
VEIKKO HAKULINEN, Finland	Nordic Skiing	3	3	1	7
EERO MANTYRANTA, Finland	Nordic Skiing	3	2	2	7
BOGDAN MUSIOL, East Germany/Germany	Bobsled	1	5	1	7
THOMAS ALSGAARD, Norway	Nordic Skiing	4	2	0	6
GUNDE SVAN, Sweden	Nordic Skiing	4	1	1	6
VEGARD ULVANG, Norway	Nordic Skiing	3	2	1	6
JOHAN GROTTUMSBRATEN, Norway	Nordic Skiing	3	1	2	6
WOLFGANG HOPPE, East Germany/Germany	Bobsled	2	3	1	6
EUGENIO MONTI, Italy	Bobsled	2	2	2	6
VLADIMIR SMIRNOV, U.S.S.R./ United Team/Kazakhstan	Nordic Skiing	1	4	1	6
MIKA MYLLYLAE, Finland	Nordic Skiing	1	1	4	6
ROALD LARSEN, Norway	Speed Skating	0	2	4	6
HARRI KIRVESNIEMI, Finland	Nordic Skiing	0	0	6	6

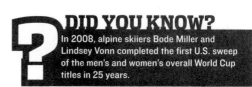

DID YOU KNOW?

In 2008, alpine skiers Bode Miller and Lindsey Vonn completed the first U.S. sweep of the men's and women's overall World Cup titles in 25 years.

All-Time Winter Olympic Medal Count: Women

ATHLETE	SPORT	GOLD	SILVER	BRONZE	TOTAL
RAISA SMETANINA, U.S.S.R./United Team	Nordic Skiing	4	5	1	10
LYUBOV EGOROVA, United Team/Russia	Nordic Skiing	6	3	0	9
LARISSA LAZUTINA, United Team/Russia	Nordic Skiing	5	3	1	9
STEFANIA BELMONDO, Italy	Nordic Skiing	2	3	4	9
CLAUDIA PECHSTEIN, Germany	Speed Skating	5	2	2	9
GALINA KULAKOVA, U.S.S.R.	Nordic Skiing	4	2	2	8
KARIN KANIA, East Germany	Speed Skating	3	4	1	8
GUNDA NEIMANN-STIRNEMANN, Germany	Speed Skating	3	4	1	8
URSULA DISL, Germany	Biathlon	2	4	2	8
MARJA-LIISA KIRVESNIEMI, Finland	Nordic Skiing	3	0	4	7
ELENA VALBE, United Team/Russia	Nordic Skiing	3	0	4	7
ANDREA EHRIG, East Germany	Speed Skating	1	5	1	7
LYDIA SKOBLIKOVA, U.S.S.R.	Speed Skating	6	0	0	6
BONNIE BLAIR, United States	Speed Skating	5	0	1	6
MANUELA DI CENTA, Italy	Nordic Skiing	2	2	2	6

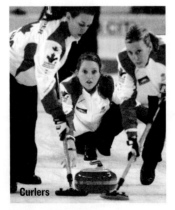

Athletes with Winter and Summer Medals

EDDIE EAGAN, United States — bobsled gold medal (1932); boxing gold medal (1920)

JACOB TULLIN THAMS, Norway — ski jumping gold medal (1924); yachting silver medal (1936)

CHRISTA LUDING-ROTHENBURGER, East Germany — speed skating gold medals (1984 and 1988), silver medal (1988), and bronze medal (1992); cycling silver medal (1988)

CLARA HUGHES, Canada — speed skating gold medal (2006), silver medal (2006), and bronze medal (2002); two cycling bronze medals (1996)

Clara Hughes

Bjorn Daehlie

■ **Bjorn Daehlie,** *cross country skier, b. June 19, 1967, Elverum, Norway.* Daehlie is the most successful Winter Olympics athlete the world has ever seen. During three Games (1992, 1994, and 1998), Daehlie racked up eight gold medals and four silvers, more than any other athlete in the history of the Winter Games. He was also wildly successful in World Championship competitions, winning nine times during the 1990s. Due to injury, he was forced to retire in 2001.

■ **Bonnie Blair,** *speed skater, b. March 18, 1964, Champaign, Illinois.* The most decorated U.S. woman in Winter Olympic history, Blair became the first American to win gold medals in three straight Games. Blair dominated the 500-meter race, winning gold in 1988, 1992, and 1994. In 1994, she became the first woman to skate the 500 meters in under 39 seconds. She has also won two gold medals in the 1,000 meters. She retired in 1995, after skating a personal best and a U.S. record of 1:18.05 in the 1,000 meters.

■ **Georg Hackl,** *luger, b. September 9, 1966, Berchtesgaden, Germany.* Considered the greatest luger of all time, Hackl was the first Olympic athlete to win medals at five Olympic Games in a row. He won gold medals in 1992, 1994, and 1998, and took home silver in 1988 and 2002. Known as the "Flying Sausage" for how he looks when he's soaring down the track, he has won a whopping 22 medals at the World Luge Championships and ten at the European Luge Championships. Hackl is one of only five Winter Olympians to ever win gold medals at three consecutive Olympic Games.

LEGENDS

BASEBALL

Major League Baseball
245 Park Avenue
New York, NY 10167
(212) 931-7800

Arizona Diamondbacks
Chase Field
401 East Jefferson Street
Phoenix, AZ 85001
(602) 462-6500

Atlanta Braves
Turner Field
755 Hank Aaron Drive
Atlanta, GA 30315
(404) 522-7630

Baltimore Orioles
Oriole Park at Camden Yards
333 W. Camden Street
Baltimore, MD 21201
(410) 685-9800

Boston Red Sox
Fenway Park
4 Yawkey Way
Boston, MA 02215
(617) 267-9440

Chicago Cubs
Wrigley Field
1060 West Addison Street
Chicago, IL 60613
(773) 404-2827

Chicago White Sox
U.S. Cellular Field
333 West 35th Street
Chicago, IL 60616
(312) 674-1000

Cincinnati Reds
Great American Ball Park
100 Main Street
Cincinnati, OH 45202
(513) 765-7000

Cleveland Indians
Progressive Field
2401 Ontario Street
Cleveland, OH 44115
(216) 420-4200

Colorado Rockies
Coors Field
2001 Blake Street
Denver, CO 80205
(303) 292-0200

Detroit Tigers
Comerica Park
2100 Woodward Avenue
Detroit, MI 48201
(313) 471-2000

Florida Marlins
Dolphin Stadium
2269 Dan Marino Boulevard
Miami Gardens, FL 33056
(305) 626-7400

Houston Astros
Minute Maid Park
501 Crawford Street
Houston, TX 77002
(713) 259-8000

Kansas City Royals
Kauffman Stadium
One Royal Way
Kansas City, MO 64129
(816) 921-8000

Los Angeles Angels of Anaheim
Angel Stadium of Anaheim
2000 Gene Autry Way
Anaheim, CA 92806
(714) 940-2000

Los Angeles Dodgers
Dodger Stadium
1000 Elysian Park Avenue
Los Angeles, CA 90012
(323) 224-1500

Milwaukee Brewers
Miller Park
One Brewers Way
Milwaukee, WI 53214
(414) 902-4400

Minnesota Twins
Metrodome
34 Kirby Puckett Place
Minneapolis, MN 55415
(612) 375-1366

New York Mets
Shea Stadium
123-01 Roosevelt Avenue
Flushing, NY 11368
(718) 507-6387

New York Yankees
Yankee Stadium
161st Street and River Avenue
Bronx, NY 10451
(718) 293-4300

Oakland Athletics
McAfee Coliseum
7000 Coliseum Way
Oakland, CA 94621
(510) 638-4900

Philadelphia Phillies
Citizens Bank Park
One Citizens Bank Way
Philadelphia, PA 19148
(215) 463-6000

Pittsburgh Pirates
PNC Park
115 Federal Street
Pittsburgh, PA 15212
(412) 323-5000

San Diego Padres
PETCO Park
100 Park Boulevard
San Diego, CA 92101
(619) 795-5000

San Francisco Giants
AT&T Park
24 Willie Mays Plaza
San Francisco, CA 94107
(415) 972-2000

Seattle Mariners
Safeco Field
P.O. Box 4100
Seattle, WA 98104
(206) 346-4000

St. Louis Cardinals
Busch Stadium
700 Clark Street
St. Louis, MO 63102
(314) 345-9600

Tampa Bay Rays
Tropicana Field
One Tropicana Drive
St. Petersburg, FL 33705
(727) 825-3137

Texas Rangers
Rangers Ballpark in Arlington
1000 Ballpark Way
Arlington, TX 76011
(817) 273-5222

Toronto Blue Jays
Rogers Centre
I Blue Jays Way
Suite 3200
Toronto, Ontario M5V IJI
Canada
(416) 341-1000

Washington Nationals
Nationals Park
1500 S. Capitol Street, S.E.
Washington, D.C. 20003
(202) 349-0400

PRO FOOTBALL

National Football League
280 Park Avenue
New York, NY 10017
(212) 450-2000

Arizona Cardinals
P.O. Box 888
Phoenix, AZ 85001
(602) 379-0101

Atlanta Falcons
4400 Falcon Parkway
Flowery Branch, GA 30542
(770) 965-3115

Baltimore Ravens
I Winning Drive
Owings Mills, MD 21117
(410) 701-4000

Buffalo Bills
One Bills Drive
Orchard Park, NY 14127
(716) 648-1800

Carolina Panthers
Ericsson Stadium
800 South Mint Street
Charlotte, NC 28202
(704) 358-7000

Chicago Bears
1000 Football Drive
Lake Forest, IL 60045
(847) 295-6600

Cincinnati Bengals
One Paul Brown Stadium
Cincinnati, OH 45202
(513) 621-3550

Cleveland Browns
76 Lou Groza Boulevard
Berea, OH 44017
(440) 891-5000

Dallas Cowboys
One Cowboys Parkway
Irving, TX 75063
(972) 556-9900

Denver Broncos
13655 Broncos Parkway
Englewood, CO 80112
(303) 649-9000

Detroit Lions
222 Republic Drive
Allen Park, MI 48101
(313) 216-4000

Green Bay Packers
Lambeau Field
1265 Lombardi Avenue
Green Bay, WI 54304
(920) 569-7500

Houston Texans
Two Reliant Park
Houston, TX 77054
(832) 667-2000

Indianapolis Colts
7001 W. 56th Street
Indianapolis, IN 46254
(317) 297-2658

Jacksonville Jaguars
One ALLTEL Stadium Place
Jacksonville, FL 32202
(904) 633-6000

Kansas City Chiefs
One Arrowhead Drive
Kansas City, MO 64129
(816) 920-9300

Miami Dolphins
2269 Dan Marino Boulevard
Miami Gardens, FL 33056
(305) 623-6100

Minnesota Vikings
9520 Viking Drive
Eden Prairie, MN 55344
(952) 828-6500

New England Patriots
Gillette Stadium
One Patriot Place
Foxboro, MA 02035
(508) 543-8200

New Orleans Saints
5800 Airline Drive
Metairie, LA 70003
(504) 733-0255

New York Giants
Giants Stadium
East Rutherford, NJ
07073
(201) 935-8111

New York Jets
1000 Fulton Avenue
Hempstead, NY 11550
(516) 560-8100

Oakland Raiders
1220 Harbor Bay Parkway
Alameda, CA 94502
(510) 864-5000

Philadelphia Eagles
NovaCare Complex
One NovaCare Way
Philadelphia, PA 19145
(215) 463-2500

Pittsburgh Steelers
3400 South Water Street
Pittsburgh, PA 15203
(412) 432-7800

San Diego Chargers
Qualcomm Stadium
4020 Murphy Canyon Road
San Diego, CA 92123
(858) 874-4500

San Francisco 49ers
4949 Centennial Boulevard
Santa Clara, CA 95054
(408) 562-4949

Seattle Seahawks
11220 N.E. 53rd Street
Kirkland, WA 98033
(425) 827-9777

St. Louis Rams
One Rams Way
St. Louis, MO 63045
(314) 982-7267

Tampa Bay Buccaneers
One Buccaneer Place
Tampa, FL 33607
(813) 870-2700

Tennessee Titans
460 Great Circle Road
Nashville, TN 37228
(615) 565-4000

Washington Redskins
21300 Redskin Park Drive
Ashburn, VA 20147
(703) 726-7000

OTHER LEAGUES
Canadian Football League
50 Wellington Street, East
3rd Floor
Toronto, Ontario M5E IC8
Canada
(416) 322-9650

NFL Europe
280 Park Avenue
New York, NY 10017
(212) 450-2000

PRO BASKETBALL

National Basketball Association
645 Fifth Avenue
New York, NY 10022
(212) 826-7000

Atlanta Hawks
Centennial Tower
101 Marietta Street, N.W.
Suite 1900
Atlanta, GA 30303
(404) 878-3800

Boston Celtics
226 Causeway Street, 4th Floor
Boston, MA 02114
(617) 854-8000

Charlotte Bobcats
333 East Trade Street
Charlotte, NC 28202
(704) 688-8600

Chicago Bulls
1901 W. Madison Street
Chicago, IL 60612
(312) 455-4000

Cleveland Cavaliers
One Center Court
Cleveland, OH 44115
(216) 420-2000

Dallas Mavericks
The Pavilion
2909 Taylor Street
Dallas, TX 75226
(214) 747-6287

Denver Nuggets
1000 Chopper Circle
Denver, CO 80204
(303) 405-1100

Detroit Pistons
Four Championship Drive
Auburn Hills, MI 48326
(248) 377-0100

Golden State Warriors
1011 Broadway
Oakland, CA 94607
(510) 986-2200

Houston Rockets
1510 Polk Street
Houston, TX 77002
(713) 758-7200

Indiana Pacers
125 South Pennsylvania Street
Indianapolis, IN 46204
(317) 917-2500

Los Angeles Clippers
1111 South Figueroa Street
Suite 1100
Los Angeles, CA 90015
(213) 742-7500

Los Angeles Lakers
555 North Nash Street
El Segundo, CA 90245
(310) 426-6000

Memphis Grizzlies
191 Beale Street
Memphis, TN 38103
(901) 888-4667

Miami Heat
601 Biscayne Boulevard
Miami, FL 33132
(786) 777-1000

Milwaukee Bucks
1001 North Fourth Street
Milwaukee, WI 53203
(414) 227-0500

Minnesota Timberwolves
600 First Avenue North
Minneapolis, MN 55403
(612) 673-1600

New Jersey Nets
390 Murray Hill Parkway
East Rutherford, NJ 07073
(201) 935-3900

New Orleans Hornets
1650 Poydras Street
Floor 19
New Orleans, LA 70113
(504) 593-4700

New York Knicks
Two Pennsylvania Plaza
New York, NY 10121
(212) 465-6471

Orlando Magic
8701 Maitland Summit Boulevard
Orlando, FL 32810
(407) 916-2400

Philadelphia 76ers
3601 South Broad Street
Philadelphia, PA 19148
(215) 339-7600

Phoenix Suns
201 East Jefferson Street
Phoenix, AZ 85004
(602) 379-7900

Portland Trail Blazers
One Center Court
Suite 200
Portland, OR 97227
(503) 797-9744

Sacramento Kings
One Sports Parkway
Sacramento, CA 95834
(916) 928-0000

San Antonio Spurs
One AT&T Center
San Antonio, TX 78219
(210) 444-5000

SPORTS DIRECTORY

Seattle SuperSonics
351 Elliott Avenue West
Suite 500
Seattle, WA 98119
(206) 281-5800

Toronto Raptors
40 Bay Street
Suite 400
Toronto, Ontario M5J 2X2
Canada
(416) 815-5600

Utah Jazz
301 West South Temple
Salt Lake City, UT 84101
(801) 325-2500

Washington Wizards
601 F Street, N.W.
Washington, DC 20004
(202) 661-5000

**Women's National
Basketball Association**
645 Fifth Avenue
New York, NY 10022
(212) 688-9622

Chicago Sky
20 West Kinzie Street
Suite 1000
Chicago, IL 60610
(312) 828-9550

Connecticut Sun
One Mohegan Sun Boulevard
Uncasville, CT 06382
(860) 862-4000

Detroit Shock
Five Championship Drive
Auburn Hills, MI 48326
(248) 377-0100

Houston Comets
Two Greenway Plaza
Suite 400
Houston, TX 77046
(713) 627-9622

Indiana Fever
125 S. Pennsylvania Street
Indianapolis, IN 46204
(317) 917-2500

Los Angeles Sparks
888 S. Figueroa Street
Suite 2010
Los Angeles, CA 90017
(213) 929-1300

Minnesota Lynx
600 First Avenue North
Minneapolis, MN 55403
(612) 673-1600

New York Liberty
Two Pennsylvania Plaza
New York, NY 10121
(212) 564-9622

Phoenix Mercury
201 East Jefferson Street
Phoenix, AZ 85004
(602) 514-8333

Sacramento Monarchs
One Sports Parkway
Sacramento, CA 95834
(916) 928-0000

San Antonio Silver Stars
One AT&T Center
San Antonio, TX 78219
(210) 444-5050

Seattle Storm
1201 Third Avenue
Suite 1000, 10th Floor
Seattle, WA 98101
(206) 217-9622

Washington Mystics
Verizon Center
3rd Floor
601 F Street, N.W.
Washington, DC 20004
(202) 527-7540

HOCKEY

National Hockey League
1251 Avenue of the Americas
47th Floor
New York, NY 10020
(212) 789-2000

Anaheim Ducks
Honda Center
2695 E. Katella Avenue
Anaheim, CA 92806
(714) 940-2900

Atlanta Thrashers
Centennial Tower
101 Marietta Street N.W.
Suite 1900
Atlanta, GA 30303
(404) 878-3800

Boston Bruins
TD Banknorth Garden
100 Legends Way
Boston, MA 02114
(617) 624-1900

Buffalo Sabres
HSBC Arena
One Seymour H. Knox III Plaza
Buffalo, NY 14203
(716) 855-4100

Calgary Flames
Pengrowth Saddledome
P.O. Box 1540
Station M
Calgary, Alberta T2P 3B9
Canada
(403) 777-4236

Carolina Hurricanes
RBC Center
1400 Edwards Mill Road
Raleigh, NC 27607
(919) 467-7825

Chicago Blackhawks
United Center
1901 W. Madison Street
Chicago, IL 60612
(312) 455-7000

Colorado Avalanche
Pepsi Center
1000 Chopper Circle
Denver, CO 80204
(303) 405-1100

Columbus Blue Jackets
Nationwide Arena
200 West Nationwide Boulevard
Columbus, OH 43215
(614) 246-4625

Dallas Stars
Dr Pepper StarCenter
2601 Avenue of the Stars
Frisco, TX 75034
(214) 387-5500

Detroit Red Wings
Joe Louis Arena
600 Civic Center Drive
Detroit, MI 48226
(313) 394-7000

Edmonton Oilers
11230-110th Street
Edmonton, Alberta T5G 3H7
Canada
(780) 414-4000

Florida Panthers
BankAtlantic Center
One Panther Parkway
Sunrise, FL 33323
(954) 835-7000

Los Angeles Kings
Toyota Sports Center
555 N. Nash Street
El Segundo, CA 90245
(310) 535-4500

Minnesota Wild
317 Washington Street
St. Paul, MN 55102
(651) 602-6000

Montreal Canadiens
Bell Centre
1260 de La Gauchtiere Street West
Montreal, Quebec H3B 5E8
Canada
(514) 932-2582

Nashville Predators
Sommet Center
501 Broadway
Nashville, TN 37203
(615) 770-2300

New Jersey Devils
Prudential Center
165 Mulberry Street
Newark, NJ 07102
(973) 757-6100

New York Islanders
1535 Old Country Road
Plainview, NY 11803
(516) 501-6700

New York Rangers
Madison Square Garden
Two Pennsylvania Plaza
14th Floor
New York, NY 10121
(212) 465-6486

Ottawa Senators
Scotiabank Place
1000 Palladium Drive
Ottawa, Ontario K2V 1A5
Canada
(613) 599-0250

Philadelphia Flyers
Wachovia Center
3601 South Broad Street
Philadelphia, PA 19148
(215) 465-4500

Phoenix Coyotes
6751 North White Out Way
Suite 200
Glendale, AZ 85305
(623) 772-3200

Pittsburgh Penguins
Mellon Arena
66 Mario Lemieux Place
Pittsburgh, PA 15219
(412) 642-1300

San Jose Sharks
HP Pavilion at San Jose
525 West Santa Clara Street
San Jose, CA 95113
(408) 287-7070

St. Louis Blues
Scottrade Center
1401 Clark Avenue
St. Louis, MO 63103
(314) 622-2500

Tampa Bay Lightning
St. Pete Times Forum
401 Channelside Drive
Tampa, FL 33602
(813) 301-6500

Toronto Maple Leafs
Air Canada Centre
40 Bay Street
Suite 400
Toronto, Ontario M5J 2X2
Canada
(416) 815-5700

Vancouver Canucks
General Motors Place
800 Griffiths Way
Vancouver, British Columbia V6B 6GI
Canada
(604) 899-4600

Washington Capitals
627 N. Glebe Road
Suite 850
Arlington, VA 22203
(202) 266-2200

COLLEGE SPORTS

**National Collegiate
Athletic Association**
(NCAA)
700 W. Washington Street
P.O. Box 6222
Indianapolis, IN 46206
(317) 917-6222

**Atlantic Coast
Conference**
P.O. Drawer ACC
Greensboro, NC 27417
(336) 854-8787

Big East Conference
222 Richmond Street
Suite 110
Providence, RI 02903
(401) 272-9108

Big Ten Conference
1500 West Higgins Road
Park Ridge, IL 60068
(847) 696-1010

Big 12 Conference
2201 Stemmons Freeway
28th Floor
Dallas, TX 75207
(214) 742-1212

Big West Conference
2 Corporate Park
Suite 206
Irvine, CA 92606
(949) 261-2525

Conference USA
5201 North O'Connor Boulevard
Suite 300
Irving, TX 75039
(214) 774-1300

Ivy League
228 Alexander Street
Princeton, NJ 08540
(609) 258-6426

Mid-American Conference
24 Public Square
15th Floor
Cleveland, OH 44113
(216) 566-4622

Pacific-10 Conference
800 South Broadway
Suite 400
Walnut Creek, CA 94596
(925) 932-4411

Southeastern Conference
2201 Richard Arrington
Boulevard North
Birmingham, AL 35203
(205) 458-3000

**Western Athletic
Conference**
9250 East Costilla Avenue
Suite 300
Englewood, CO 80112
(303) 799-9221

OTHER SPORTS

**Association of Tennis
Professionals Tour (ATP)**
201 ATP Boulevard
Ponte Vedra Beach, FL 32082
(904) 285-8000

**Championship Auto
Racing Teams (CART)**
5350 West Lakeview Parkway
South Drive
Indianapolis, IN 46268
(317) 715-4100

Indy Racing League
4565 West 16th Street
Indianapolis, IN 46222
(317) 492-6526

**Ladies Professional Golf
Association (LPGA)**
100 International Golf Drive
Daytona Beach, FL 32124
(386) 274-6200

Major League Soccer (MLS)
110 East 42nd Street
10th Floor
New York, NY 10017
(212) 450-1200

**National Association for
Stock Car Auto Racing
(NASCAR)**
1801 W. International
Speedway Boulevard
Daytona Beach, FL 32114
(386) 253-0611

PGA Tour
112 PGA Tour Boulevard
Ponte Vedra Beach, FL 32082
(904) 285-3700

United Soccer Leagues
14497 N. Dale Mabry Highway
Suite 201
Tampa, FL 33618
(813) 963-3807

**United States Olympic
Training Center**
One Olympic Plaza
Colorado Springs, CO 80909
(719) 632-5551

USA Basketball
5465 Mark Dabling Boulevard
Colorado Springs, CO 80918
(719) 590-4800

USA Cycling
One Olympic Plaza
Colorado Springs, CO 80909
(719) 866-4581

USA Hockey
1775 Bob Johnson Drive
Colorado Springs, CO 80906
(719) 576-8724

USA Luge
57 Church Street
Lake Placid, NY 12946
(518) 523-2071

USA Swimming
One Olympic Plaza
Colorado Springs, CO 80909
(719) 866-4578

USA Track & Field
One RCA Dome
Suite 140
Indianapolis, IN 46225
(317) 261-0500

USA Water Polo, Inc.
1631 Mesa Avenue
Suite A-1
Colorado Springs, CO 80906
(719) 634-0699

**U.S. Bobsled and Skeleton
Federation**
196 Old Military Road
P.O. Box 828
Lake Placid, NY 12946
(518) 523-1842

**U.S. Figure Skating
Association**
20 First Street
Colorado Springs, CO 80906
(719) 635-5200

**U.S. Ski and Snowboard
Association**
Box 100
1500 Kearns Boulevard
Park City, UT 84060
(435) 649-9090

U.S. Soccer Federation
1801 South Prairie Avenue
Chicago, IL 60616
(312) 808-1300

U.S. Speedskating
Utah Olympic Oval
5662 South Cougar Lane
Kearns, UT 84118
(801) 417-5360

**Women's Tennis
Association (WTA)**
One Progress Plaza
Suite 1500
St. Petersburg, FL 33701
(727) 895-5000

NFL

p. 6

I	V	L	N	S	E	T	G	H
N	E	H	G	V	T	L	S	I
T	G	S	I	H	L	E	V	N
L	S	I	H	T	G	V	N	E
H	N	G	E	I	V	S	T	L
E	T	V	L	N	S	H	I	G
G	L	T	V	E	N	I	H	S
V	H	N	S	L	I	G	E	T
S	I	E	T	G	H	N	L	V

p. 16

Brady bested Peyton Manning's record for most touchdown passes. (Brady had 50.)
Moss topped Jerry Rice's record for most touchdown receptions. (Moss had 23.)

BASEBALL

p. 22

```
      A V E R A G E
      R E L I E V E
    J O R G E
D O U B L E
      S E A S O N
    S T A N D S
    T H I R D
D E F E N S E
          R U N
```

p. 41

A B C D E F G H I J
3 2 7 0 1 9 5 8 6 4

NBA

p. 46

Wilt Chamberlain
Oscar Robertson
Kareem Abdul-Jabbar
Bob McAdoo
Dave Cowens
Moses Malone
Shaquille O'Neal
Allen Iverson

p. 54

Yao Ming

WNBA

p. 62

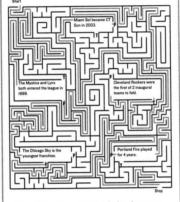

The Mystics entered the league in 1998; the Lynx in 1999.
The Orlando Miracle became the CT Sun in 2003.
The Portland Fire played for three years.

COLLEGE FOOTBALL

p. 70

Walter Camp Award > Player of the Year > Darren McFadden, Arkansas; Chuck Bednarik Award > Defensive Player of the Year > Dan Connor, Penn St.; Outland Trophy > Outstanding Interior Lineman > Glenn Dorsey, LSU; Fred Biletnikoff Award > Outstanding Wide Receiver > Michael Crabtree, Texas Tech

MEN'S COLLEGE BASKETBALL

p. 82

James Naismith, inventor of basketball.

WOMEN'S COLLEGE BASKETBALL

p. 94

California: S (Stanford)
Utah: C (Weber State)
Nebraska: O (Creighton)
Louisiana: R (Tulane)
Ohio: I (Xavier)
North Carolina: N (Wake Forest)
New Jersey: G (Seton Hall)

They were the leaders in SCORING.

NHL

p. 98

Jaromir Jagr had his fifteenth consecutive thirty-goal season in 2007, tying Mike Gartner's record.

p. 109

Brian — Three-time All-Star
Darryl — Best coaching career
Duane — Won Stanley Cup in first four seasons
Brent — Most goals (363)
Rich — Part of first twins to play in NHL (with Ron)
Ron — Highest draft pick (4th)

GAME ANSWERS

SOCCER

p. 114

WINS, TRAP, MATCH, DYNAMO, ASSIST, THROW-IN, OFFSIDE, SWEEPER, TURNOVER, FORMATION, YELLOW CARD

Dwayne De Rosario is the first two-time winner of the MLS Cup MVP award.

p. 119

Thirty-four were off her head.

ACTION SPORTS

p. 125

1. True
2. False — "Heel drag" happens when bindings are too close to the heel edge and the heels hang over the board edge.
3. False — "Corduroy" is a mechanically groomed surface good for carving.
4. False — The "fall line" is the path of least resistance down the hill.
5. True
6. True
7. False — "Grab" means to grab the board with a hand.
8. True

Torah Bright

p. 135

1 - Top tube
2 - Fork
3 - Hub
4 - Seat clamp
5 - Sprocket
6 - Rear brakes
7 - Grip
8 - Crank

Mike Spinner

GOLF

p. 140

```
    G R A N A D A
        K I M
      T U R N E R
I N K S T E R
            T U L L
          L E E
  L I N D L E Y
      A H N
```

MOTOR SPORTS

p. 148

Ile Notre-Dame

TENNIS

p. 159

Borg: 41 (1979–80)
Lendl: 44 (1981–82)
McEnroe: 42 (1983–84)
Vilas: 46 (1977)

SWIMMING

p. 165

Medal, Lane
Arena, Anchor
Lap, Pace
Seed, Dive
Spitz, Zone
Hero, Open
Taper, Relay
Magic, Close
State, Event
Splits, Shave

Speedo LZR racer (full-body racing suit)

TRACK & FIELD

p. 168

She is the first American woman to clear sixteen feet in the pole vault.

SUMMER OLYMPICS

p. 174

```
              B A D M I N T O N
G Y M N A S T I C S
              W R E S T L I N G
              T R A C K A N D F I E L D
              E Q U E S T R I A N
              B A S K E T B A L L
  W E I G H T L I F T I N G
  T R I A T H L O N
  W A T E R P O L O
    S H O O T I N G
    T A E K W O N D O
```

p. 177

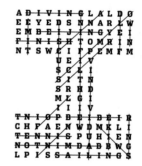

All eyes are on swimmer Michael Phelps.

WINTER OLYMPICS

p. 179

Julia Mancuso (W), Picabo Street (H), Apolo Anton Ohno (L), Hannah Teter (S), Shaun White (R), Shani Davis (K), Sasha Cohen (A), Chad Hedrick (E), Michelle Kwan (C)

Herschel Walker was a Heisman Trophy winner and running back for the Dallas Cowboys. He teamed with Brian Shimer for the 2-man bobsled.

GAME ANSWERS